LAW UNDER A DEMOCRATIC CONSTITUTION

Jeffrey Goldsworthy is a renowned constitutional scholar and legal theorist whose work on the powers of Parliament and the interpretation of constitutional and statute laws has helped shape debates on these topics across the English-speaking world. The importance of democratic constitutionalism is central to Professor Goldsworthy's work: it lies at the heart of his defence of Parliamentary supremacy and shapes his approach to both constitutional and statutory interpretation. In honour of Professor Goldsworthy's retirement, this collection provides new perspectives from a range of leading public law scholars and theorists on the legal and philosophical principles that govern the making and interpretation of laws in a constitutional democracy. It also addresses some of the challenges to democratic constitutionalism that have arisen in light of contemporary developments in Australia, Canada, New Zealand, the United Kingdom and the United States.

Law Under a Democratic Constitution

Essays in Honour of Jeffrey Goldsworthy

Edited by
Lisa Burton Crawford
Patrick Emerton
and
Dale Smith

•HART•
OXFORD • LONDON • NEW YORK • NEW DELHI • SYDNEY

HART PUBLISHING

Bloomsbury Publishing Plc

Kemp House, Chawley Park, Cumnor Hill, Oxford, OX2 9PH, UK

1385 Broadway, New York, NY 10018, USA

HART PUBLISHING, the Hart/Stag logo, BLOOMSBURY and the Diana logo are trademarks of Bloomsbury Publishing Plc

First published in Great Britain 2019

Reprinted 2020

A catalogue record for this book is available from the British Library.

Library of Congress Cataloging-in-Publication data

Names: Goldsworthy, Jeffrey Denys, honouree, contributor. | Burton Crawford, Lisa, editor. | Emerton, Patrick, editor. | Smith, Dale, 1973- editor.

Title: Law under a democratic constitution : essays in honour of Jeffrey Goldsworthy / edited by Lisa Burton Crawford, Patrick Emerton, Dale Smith.

Description: Oxford, UK ; Portland, Oregon : Hart Publishing, 2019. | Includes paper presented at "… the workshop commemorating Jeff's retirement, which was held at Monash University in July 2017. This workshop was generously supported by the Australian Research Council, the Centre for Comparative Constitutional Studies at the Melbourne Law School and the Monash University Faculty of Law."—ECIP introduction. | Includes List of Professor Jeffrey Goldsworthy's publications, bibliographical references and index.

Identifiers: LCCN 2018059535 (print) | LCCN 2018060297 (ebook) | ISBN 9781509920860 (EPub) | ISBN 9781509920853 (hardback)

Subjects: LCSH: Constitutional law—Congresses. | Law—Interpretation and construction—Congresses. | Constitutional law—Australia—Congresses. | Goldsworthy, Jeffrey Denys—Congresses. | BISAC: LAW / Public. | LCGFT: Festschriften.

Classification: LCC K3165.A6 (ebook) | LCC K3165.A6 .L39 2019 (print) | DDC 342—dc23

LC record available at https://lccn.loc.gov/2018059535

ISBN: HB: 978-1-50992-085-3
ePDF: 978-1-50992-087-7
ePub: 978-1-50992-086-0

Typeset by Compuscript Ltd, Shannon
Printed and bound in Great Britain by TJ International Ltd, Padstow, Cornwall

To find out more about our authors and books visit www.hartpublishing.co.uk. Here you will find extracts, author information, details of forthcoming events and the option to sign up for our newsletters.

TABLE OF CONTENTS

LIST OF CONTRIBUTORS

Larry Alexander is Warren Distinguished Professor of Law at the University of San Diego School of Law.

TRS Allan is Professor of Jurisprudence and Public Law at the University of Cambridge and Fellow of Pembroke College, Cambridge.

Nicholas Aroney is Professor of Constitutional Law at the University of Queensland.

Lisa Burton Crawford is Senior Lecturer at the University of New South Wales.

Richard Ekins is Associate Professor at the University of Oxford and Tutorial Fellow in Law at St John's College.

Patrick Emerton is Associate Professor at Monash University.

Jeffrey Goldsworthy is Emeritus Professor at Monash University, Professorial Fellow at the University of Melbourne and Adjunct Professor at the University of Adelaide.

Heidi M Hurd is Ross and Helen Workman Chair in Law and Professor of Philosophy at the University of Illinois.

Richard S Kay is Wallace Stevens Professor of Law Emeritus and Oliver Ellsworth Research Professor at the University of Connecticut School of Law.

Dale Smith is Associate Professor at the University of Melbourne.

Lawrence B Solum is Carmack Waterhouse Professor of Law at Georgetown University.

Kevin Toh is Senior Lecturer at the University College London.

Alison L Young is Sir David Williams Professor of Public Law at the University of Cambridge.

1

Introduction

This collection is published to mark the retirement of now Emeritus Professor Jeffrey Goldsworthy – one of the most distinguished constitutional theorists and legal philosophers that Australia has produced. Jeff's work traverses constitutional and administrative law doctrine, constitutional and statutory interpretation and legal philosophy, drawing insights from each field in order to illuminate the others. Few scholars could lay claim to such breadth and depth of expertise.

Jeff's contribution to legal scholarship is not easily captured in a small number of themes. Nevertheless, the title of this collection – *Law Under a Democratic Constitution* – was chosen to encapsulate one theme which we suggest is integral to Jeff's work. That is a deep commitment to what Jeff has described as the:

> democratic ideal of government by ordinary people, elected to represent the opinions and interests of ordinary people. According to this ideal, ordinary people have a right to participate on equal terms in the political decision-making that affects their lives as much as anyone else's, and should be presumed to possess the intelligence, knowledge and virtue needed to do so. Proponents of this ideal do not naively believe that such a method of government will never violate the rights of individuals or minority groups. But they do trust that, in appropriate political, social and cultural conditions, clear injustices will be relatively rare, and that in most cases, whether or not the law violates someone's rights will be open to reasonable disagreement. They also trust that over time, the proportion of clear rights violations will diminish, and 'that a people, in acting autonomously, will learn how to act rightly'.[1]

This commitment to democratic rule is central to Jeff's view that it is Parliament, not the courts, which should be chiefly responsible for resolving contentious political issues, including those concerning rights. It is also central to his accounts of both constitutional and statutory interpretation. Those accounts emphasise the centrality to the interpretive process of publicly available evidence of 'speaker's meaning' (very roughly, the meaning the lawmaker intended to communicate by enacting the legal text). They also emphasise the obligation on judges, typically, to give effect to that (publicly accessible) meaning, rather than giving effect to their own views about what law should have been made.

These ideas have not always proven to be fashionable. As Jeff has observed:

> The once popular idea of legislative sovereignty has been in decline throughout the world for some time. … A dwindling number of political and constitutional theorists continue to resist the 'rights revolution' that is sweeping the globe, by refusing to accept that judicial enforcement of a

[1] J Goldsworthy, *Parliamentary Sovereignty: Contemporary Debates* (Cambridge University Press, 2010) 9–10 (footnotes omitted). The internal quote is from R Dahl, *Democracy and Its Critics* (Yale University Press, 1989) 192.

> constitutionally entrenched Bill of Rights is necessarily desirable. To be one of them can feel like King Cnut trying to hold back the tide.[2]

But while he may have sometimes felt as if the tide were against him, Jeff never retreated from the fearless style of commentary which he perceived to be the defining role of a legal scholar. His philosophical commitments went hand in hand with commitments to intellectual integrity, and the rigorous and transparent analysis of the law. As the contributors to this volume observe, his work is 'measured',[3] 'careful'[4] and 'nuanced';[5] it is always meticulously researched and reasoned, and never hyperbolic.

It has also proven, over time, to be hugely influential. Jeff's writings on parliamentary sovereignty are widely regarded as seminal, particularly in the United Kingdom where it is now nearly mandatory to cite Jeff's work in any serious academic discussion of this topic.[6] His opposition to constitutionally entrenched bills of rights has also been influential across the common law world.[7] His 'pioneering' work on constitutional interpretation – and his particular account of how that should be done, which he calls 'moderate originalism' – is now recognised as having anticipated many of the more recent developments in originalist thought in the United States.[8] And, in recent years, Jeff has been an outspoken critic of sceptical approaches to the role of legislative intent in statutory interpretation, arguing for the indispensability of legislative intent as the central organising principle in the interpretive process.[9] His work on this topic has helped shape the views of current and former judges in the High Court of Australia, giving succour to those who are inclined to take the notion of legislative intent seriously,[10] and providing food for thought to some of those tempted by scepticism about legislative intent.[11]

This book is intended not only as a tribute to Jeff, but also to advance these important debates. The first three chapters – by Larry Alexander, Dale Smith, Patrick Emerton and Lisa Burton Crawford – examine the role of legislative intention in legal interpretation, an increasingly contentious topic. The chapters that follow – by Larry Solum, Nicholas Aroney, Heidi Hurd and Kevin Toh – suggest new ways of understanding Jeff's case for moderate originalism and, in some cases, new ways of resisting that argument. The final group of chapters – by Alison Young, Richard Kay, Richard Ekins and TRS Allan – discuss parliamentary sovereignty and some of the contemporary challenges it faces. We thank the authors for their valuable contributions. Jeff provides a response to each in chapter 13.

We also thank the authors and a larger group of academics for participating in the workshop commemorating Jeff's retirement, which was held at Monash University in July 2017. This workshop was generously supported by the Australian Research Council,

[2] Goldsworthy (n 1) 9.

[3] Richard Ekins, 'Models of (and Myths about) Rights Protection' in chapter 11 of this volume.

[4] TRS Allan, 'Political Obligation and Public Law' in chapter 12 of this volume.

[5] Heidi M Hurd, 'The Moral Motivations for Moderate Originalism' in chapter 7 of this volume.

[6] Alison L Young, 'Populism and Parliamentary Sovereignty: The Goldsworthy Solution' in chapter 9 of this volume; Richard S Kay, 'Democracy, Mixed Government and Judicial Review' in chapter 10 of this volume.

[7] Ekins (n 3).

[8] Lawrence B Solum, 'Goldsworthy on the Normative Justification for Originalism' in chapter 5 of this volume.

[9] Patrick Emerton and Lisa Burton Crawford, 'Statutory Meaning without Parliamentary Intention: Defending the High Court's "Alternative Approach" to Statutory Interpretation' in chapter 4 of this volume.

[10] See, eg, S Gageler, 'Legislative Intent' (2015) 41 *Monash University Law Review* 1, 10–11.

[11] See, eg, R French, 'The Courts and the Parliament' (2013) 87 *Australian Law Journal* 820, 825–26.

the Centre for Comparative Constitutional Studies at the Melbourne Law School and the Monash University Faculty of Law. We give special thanks to Farrah Ahmed, Jonathan Crowe, Julie Debeljak, Rosalind Dixon, Dan Meagher, Michael Moore, Scott Stephenson, Adrienne Stone and Lulu Weis for attending this workshop and providing detailed and insightful commentary on the papers that now form this volume. We also thank Grant Huscroft for taking part in this workshop. We are grateful to Roger Wu, Cate Read and Lachlan Peake for their assistance in copy-editing this volume, and to the Melbourne Law School Academic Research Service for its support. Finally, we thank the Australian Research Council for supporting this project under its *Discovery Projects* funding scheme (project number DP140102670) and Hart Publishing for the opportunity to publish this collection.

In conclusion, we suggest that one of the keenest insights into Jeff's career can be found in a footnote accompanying the above-quoted passage, in which Jeff defends the democratic ideal of government by ordinary people. In it, Jeff writes:

> I hope the term 'ordinary people' does not seem patronising. I cannot think of an alternative, and I regard myself as an 'ordinary person'.[12]

This statement speaks not only to Jeff's philosophical commitments, but also to his character. While he may describe himself as an 'ordinary person', Jeff is a true giant in his field. And yet, all those who have had the privilege of working with Jeff will tell a similar tale: that he is an exceptionally warm, generous and unpretentious person, who treats everyone he encounters with the same great kindness and respect. We have had the good fortune of working closely with Jeff for many years. He has been a doctoral supervisor to two of us, and a colleague and mentor to us all. We thank him for his guidance and support, and especially his friendship.

We hope that this collection makes a fitting tribute to this extraordinary scholar.

Lisa Burton Crawford, Patrick Emerton and Dale Smith

[12] Goldsworthy (n 1) 9.

2

Goldsworthy on Interpretation of Statutes and Constitutions: Public Meaning, Intended Meaning and the Bogey of Aggregation

LARRY ALEXANDER

I. Introduction

Jeffrey Goldsworthy has had a long and distinguished scholarly career. Much of his scholarship has been focused on legal interpretation. And it is that aspect of his scholarship that will be my focus here; for it is with respect to legal interpretation that Goldsworthy's views and mine intersect.

Rather than try to distill Goldsworthy's views from the many articles and book chapters in which they appear going back decades, I am going to examine their most recent iteration – a book chapter in which Goldsworthy contrasts his views on legal interpretation with my own. In doing so, I will try to demonstrate two points: (1) the superiority of my views as a theoretical matter; and (2) the irrelevancy of the differences between our views as a practical matter.

Before discussing Goldsworthy's views, however, I think it would be useful to give a summary of my views point by point, so that I can identify the precise point or points on which Goldsworthy and I part company.

II. Alexander on Interpretation in General and on Legal Interpretation in Particular[1]

A. On the Nature of Texts

1. A text, as I shall be using the term, is a set of symbols – of any kind – that is meant by its producer – the author(s) – to communicate a message to the intended audience. The symbols

[1] I just recently came across a forthcoming book chapter by the German legal philosopher Rolf Poscher, who quite elegantly makes the precise points that I adumbrate in what follows. See R Poscher, 'The Hermeneutics of Law' in MN Forster and K Gjesdal (eds), *The Cambridge Companion to Hermeneutics* (Cambridge University Press, 2019, forthcoming).

used can be marks, sounds, dots and dashes, smoke, flags, pictures – indeed, anything can be used as symbols capable of conveying messages. And although we are usually interested in the actual authors of a text, texts produced by one author can be appropriated by another author to convey the same or a different message. And one can meaningfully ask what message a text would convey if it had been produced, not by its actual author, but by some different author.

2. If there is no author – no person who produced the marks, sounds, etc in order to convey a message – then we do not have a text. The marks, sounds, etc may be a sign of something, much as smoke is a sign of fire, or geese flying south are a sign that winter is coming. Marks that might look like symbols, when we understand they are not – think of cloud formations that resemble the letters C-A-T – render certain questions nonsensical that would make sense were there an author. (Consider: Are the clouds speaking English or French? Are they referring to all felines or only to tabby cats?) Even when there is an author and a text, the text may be a sign of something other than the message conveyed. For example, the text may be a sign that the author has poor handwriting or can use word processing. Or its message may be a sign that the author was angry, or agitated, or in love.

3. Texts are individuated by the messages that their authors are intending to convey thereby. That is why the text of the US Constitution in Spanish can be the same as its text in English, or why its text in one font can be the same as its text in a different font. Even though those tokens of the text differ from one another, they are tokens of the same text if the message they convey is the same.

4. When our interest is in the actual authors of a text and the message that they intended to convey thereby, we are acting as 'originalists'. If we are unsure of the meaning of some word in the text, then, given that our interest is in the message that the actual authors intended to convey, we will consult dictionaries contemporaneous with their authoring, not later dictionaries. And when their words produce an ambiguity, to resolve it we will ask about the context in which they were authoring, not about contexts that post or pre-date their authoring.

5. The 'conventional meanings' of words – what meaning dictionaries would assign them – are merely the meanings most people at a particular time, and in a particular locale, would intend to convey by those words. These meanings are therefore time and place bound and can, and do, change over time and from place to place. But authors may and often do employ unconventional meanings. They may use codes, or idiolects, or malapropisms. If their intended audience understands the code or the idiolect that they are employing, or recognises the malapropism and its actual intended referent, then the authors can be successful in conveying their message to their intended audience. If one is interested in knowing what message the authors are intending to convey, one will want to know what code, idiolect, etc the author is employing.[2]

[2] Connie Rosati has quarreled with my assertion that texts do not by themselves declare the language in which they are written. She points out that a long sequence of symbols that look like a well-formed English sentence are quite unlikely to be in a language other than English, or to be markings made by natural forces. See CS Rosati, 'Alexander's "Simple-Minded Originalism"' in HM Hurd (ed), *Moral Puzzles and Legal Perplexities: Essays on the Influence of Larry Alexander* (Cambridge University Press, 2018). That is true; but what Rosati neglects is that when one infers that it is in English, one is inferring the existence of an English-speaking author who intentionally produced those symbols to convey a message. And even in such a case, without knowing more about the author

6. Authors rely on implicatures and implicitures in conveying their intended messages.[3] They often mean more, and sometimes less, than they actually say. 'John and Mary are married', uttered when they are observed walking together, usually conveys the message that they are married to each other. 'It is an aggravating circumstance to use a gun in the commission of a crime' usually conveys the message that it is aggravating when the gun is used as a weapon, but not as an item of barter for illegal drugs.[4]

B. On Interpreting Legal Texts

7. In whomever the authority to exact legal norms resides – in constitutional ratifiers, in legislatures, in administrators, in judges – then when they decide which norms to enact and attempt to communicate those norms through a written or oral text, the job of the intended audience is to figure out what norms the authors enacted and intended to communicate. If the audience chooses legal norms that differ from those which the authors chose to enact and communicate, the authority of the authors is undermined. Only originalism is authority preserving.

8. Any departure from originalism either transfers authority from the authors to someone else – for example, to judges – or to some mindless process, such as the process by which the meanings of words change over time, as would occur if contemporary dictionary meanings rather than the meanings contemporaneous with authorship were relied on in 'interpreting' legal texts.

9. Originalism is implicit in jurisprudential theories such as Scott Shapiro's planning theory of law.[5] When those with authority to make the plans, communicate the plans that they have decided upon, others must then follow the plans the planners intended – their originally intended plans. Shapiro denies that his theory implies originalism, but with respect, he is plainly mistaken. He thinks that if the planners trust others with a delegation of planning authority, that undermines originalism. But that is a confusion.[6] If the plan is to delegate, that *is* its original meaning. Shapiro is worried that if his theory is to be generally applicable, it must account for non-originalist interpretation, as that is common. But non-originalist interpretation really represents a transfer of authority – in Shapiro's case, planning authority – from one body or person to another, or to some mindless (non-planning) process. For Shapiro's theory, these transfers should be seen as problematic.

Another way of seeing this issue of trust is by reference to the distinction between norms that are rules and norms that are standards. When those with authority to enact legal norms

and her circumstances, one cannot tell whether the language is American English circa 2017 or American English circa 1789, or whether it is American English, South African English, Australian English, some other English-related idiolect, or even a Russian language code masquerading as English. We can only resolve these questions by reference to what we know about the author and her intended audience. We employ, as we always do in interpreting messages, circumstantial evidence: Was the text found in Australia or in America? Does it use words that are commonplace now but were not in 1789? And so on.

[3] An implicature is a thing implied by saying something else. An impliciture is an implicature that expands what is said.

[4] See, eg, *Smith v United States*, 508 US 223, 241 (1993) (Scalia J dissenting).

[5] SJ Shapiro, *Legality* (Cambridge, Massachusetts, Harvard University Press, 2011).

[6] See ibid 353–87.

enact standards, they are entrusting other actors – citizens, administrators, judges – to engage in first-order practical reasoning within the interstices of existing rules. That reasoning is not interpretation. Interpretation is at an end when the interpreters conclude that the authorities enacted a standard. That is the original intended meaning of the norm. Giving substance to that standard is not itself interpretation, however.

10. Interpretation of legal texts is an empirical, not a normative, endeavour. The interpreter wants to know what norm the authorities intended to communicate through their text. It is often quite difficult to answer the interpreter's question. The authorities may have expressed their intended norm poorly. Or the text may be old or ambiguous, and the context of its promulgation unclear or unknown. But however difficult interpretation may be, it is unavoidable if the norms that we are to be governed by are the norms intended by those with authority to govern us.

11. Finally, interpretation of legal texts must deal with the fact that some legal authorities are multi-member bodies and sometimes bicameral multi-member bodies, and can only enact legal norms with the concurrence of majorities or super-majorities. What is *the* intended meaning of a legal text when the members who voted to enact it did not intend to convey the same meanings and hence the same norms by it? This is the aggregation problem. On my view, it cannot be avoided. And when there is no shared meaning that the requisite number of norm enactors endorse, then the text they enact is legal gibberish. It is a composite of different intended norms that cannot be combined into a single norm. Perhaps that unfortunate result is rare. Perhaps it can be avoided by having those who vote for the text accept the meaning intended by some person or committee without having that meaning in mind themselves. I see no way, however, to make the aggregation problem disappear without at the same time undermining the authority of those who are supposed to possess it.

III. Goldsworthy on Interpretation in General and on Legal Interpretation in Particular, and the Alexander Response

Goldsworthy belongs to the majority wing of originalists, the original public meaning wing, whereas I belong to the author's intended meaning wing. Or, as he puts it, Goldsworthy is an 'objective intentionalist (OI)', and I am, by contrast, a 'subjective intentionalist (SI)'.[7]

Now although I characterised Goldsworthy's position as one that places him in the original public meaning camp – the OPM camp according to Goldsworthy's acronym for it – Goldsworthy himself wants to distinguish his OI from OPM as well as from SI. Indeed, Goldsworthy places himself in the intentionalist camp, so that any disagreement we have is even smaller and friendlier than I implied. Here is how Goldsworthy characterises the difference between his position and mine:

> SI maintains that judges should seek the lawmaker's actual subjective intentions, whereas OI holds that those intentions are relevant only insofar as they were publicly manifested, in that sufficient evidence of them was made readily available to the public or at least to legal advisers.[8]

[7] All references to Goldsworthy's views come from J Goldsworthy, 'Subjective versus Objective Intentionalism in Legal Interpretation' in Hurd (n 2).

[8] ibid 175.

Goldsworthy distinguishes general OI as an account of the meaning of any linguistic communication from legal OI, which he describes as 'a distinctively legal thesis about actual and/or desirable restrictions on what evidence of legislative intentions legal interpreters should take into account'.[9] Goldsworthy is a proponent of both general OI and legal OI, although he recognises that some, including our mutual friend Richard Ekins, can reject general OI in favour of general SI, but nonetheless accept legal OI.[10]

Goldsworthy's argument in favour of general OI seems to me to trade on a confusion between what is said and what is meant. Or, to put it in terms that I think are more apt, Goldsworthy's distinction is between what your audience is likely to take you to have meant by your statement, and what you intended them to take you to have meant by it. You may fail to convey your intended meaning for any number of reasons, many of which will be your fault. But I think that it is a mistake to say that the meaning of what you said is what the audience is likely to think is its meaning. Or at least it trades on an ambiguity about meaning.

For example, suppose I am using code to convey a message to my audience, a secret cell of insurgents. If I utter 'the red fish swims at dawn', and this is the code for 'blow up the dam', then my intended audience will likely understand me perfectly. The audience whom I am not intending to communicate with will not understand me. They will think that I meant to convey my thoughts about a colourful aquatic creature. That is precisely the point of my using a code. But if the security forces have broken my code, then they too, will understand my meaning.

Or consider malapropisms. If those with whom I am conversing know that I mean 'raises the question' when I say 'begs the question', then they will understand me perfectly. The fact that I do not use words in the way that they are conventionally used may cause others who are unaware of my particular idiolect to misunderstand me, but I may nevertheless convey my intended meaning to those who do understand my idiolect. And it will be quite accurate to say that what my statements mean is what the latter group, not the former, will take me to have meant.

I doubt that Goldsworthy disagrees with what I have said regarding codes, malapropisms, idiosyncratic idiolects, and so forth. Indeed, there are several passages that indicate his agreement. What causes him to dissent from SI appears to be that he equates the meaning of a statement with the uptake that the speaker's intended audience is likely to have, so that if one misuses a term, and one's audience does not have sufficient evidence that one is misusing it, then what it *means* is what the intended audience is likely to take it to mean – and not what the speaker intends to mean by it.[11]

Goldsworthy concludes his defence of general OI with a concession that I think shows that OI and SI are not opposed positions but are actually two different ways of characterising the same thing:

> But Alexander is right that 'objective' legislative intentions are conceptually dependent on subjective intentions. An 'objective' intention is what a reasonable audience would conclude was the author's 'subjective' intention, given all the publicly available evidence of it. Indeed, the existence

[9] ibid.

[10] ibid 176. Ekins's views are most felicitously set forth in R Ekins, *The Nature of Legislative Intent* (Oxford, Oxford University Press, 2016).

[11] Goldsworthy (n 7) 178.

> of a subjective intention is a crucial presupposition of an attribution of an objective intention to the author of a text. If we knew that the creators of a text had no relevant subjective intention (for example, they were monkeys pounding randomly on keyboards), we would have no rational basis for attributing any objective intention to the text either.[12]

In other words, an audience is always seeking the intended meaning of the author even if, quite possibly due to the fault of the author, the audience's reasonable uptake is not what the author intended it to be.

Goldsworthy, after defending general OI, turns to legal OI. For even if one accepts general SI, as Richard Ekins does, one can still advocate legal OI, as Ekins himself does. According to legal OI, legislative intended meaning may be inferred only from publicly available evidence.[13]

At this point, I want to advert to my statement at the outset of my reply to Goldsworthy – that Goldsworthy is a member of the OPM wing of originalism, even though Goldsworthy himself distinguishes between his legal OI position and OPM. For as he later says, OPM is a version of OI, and his quote from Larry Solum reveals that OPM – and Solum is perhaps its leading proponent – is pretty much identical to OI as Goldsworthy elaborates it.[14]

Let me also put aside the possibility that a legal system might have rules limiting legal interpreters to only certain types of evidence. As I said, such rules, if they existed, would have to be legally superior to the authority of the legislators, as the rules would legally constrain how they could communicate their intended norms.

With that possibility put aside, is there more than a dime's worth of difference between (legal) OI and (legal) SI? Hardly. Rational lawmakers take cognisance of the evidence of their intended meaning that their target audience is likely to possess. The aforementioned Richard Ekins, quoted approvingly by Goldsworthy, asserts that 'the secret diary or private correspondence of the … lawmaker is irrelevant (even if discovered and published) to the legal meaning and effect of his enactments'.[15] But why would a rational lawmaker expect that his *secret* intended meaning would be the uptake of an audience not in on the secret? Remember that the author's intended meaning is just the uptake that she wants to produce in her audience. So if the author intends her audience to think 'cat', then 'cat' is her intended meaning, even if she claims in her secret diary to mean 'dog'. Secret intended meanings are incoherent. At most, one can speak in a code understandable by an audience of one with whose uptake the speaker is solely concerned.

The real nub of the disagreement between the legal OI and legal SI camps has to do with what happens when the publicly available evidence points to meaning A, but the lawmakers intended meaning B, and mistakenly believed that meaning B would be the uptake of their target audience. It is on this point that legal OI and legal SI might diverge.

So suppose the lawmakers intended meaning B but, given what their audience could be expected to know, expressed meaning B sufficiently inaptly to warrant the reasonable member of the target audience to believe the lawmakers meant A. And suppose that at some time subsequent to when the lawmakers promulgated their text, publicly available

[12] Goldsworthy (n 7) 179.
[13] Goldsworthy (n 7) 180.
[14] See Goldsworthy (n 7) 182.
[15] See Ekins (n 10) 247.

evidence comes into our possession and shows that the lawmakers intended meaning B. Legal SI – my view – would dictate that we now say that the legal norm which the text communicates is B, not A. That is so even though it is perfectly understandable why, before the evidence we now possess had become publicly available, interpreters would conclude that the text communicated A. And that 'misinterpretation' may be laid at the feet of the lawmakers, who mistakenly believed that the evidence which we now possess was publicly available at the time of promulgation. The point is, we (faultlessly) misunderstood them then, but we do understand them now.

That is the position legal SI takes. Does legal OI differ? Does it take the position that the promulgated norm is A, despite the existence of publicly available evidence that B was intended? It bears emphasis that both positions rely only on evidence which is publicly available. For no rational communicator can be said to have intended an uptake while aware that her target audience lacked the evidence necessary to infer that intended uptake. Nor could we ever discover that the intended uptake was B rather than A without evidence that the lawmakers could have assumed, albeit erroneously, its audience possessed. Without such evidence, the mistake about what was intended would remain unknown.

My conclusion on the basis of the analysis above is that Goldsworthy is wrong to think there is a dime's worth of difference between legal SI and legal OI.[16] Legal OI and its equivalent, OPM, will produce the same interpretations as legal SI. Nor will or should they differ on what to do about any period during which the texts are misinterpreted: No one should suffer because of reasonable reliance on an interpretation later shown to have been mistaken. And neither legal OI nor legal SI can avoid the aggregation problem, as that problem can be revealed by publicly available evidence. If my legal SI is in a stew, Goldsworthy's legal OI is in it with me.

[16] Goldsworthy's view, that legal SI and legal OI will produce different results in some cases, is expressed at the end of his chapter. See Goldsworthy (n 7) 188.

3

What is Statutory Purpose?

DALE SMITH*

I. Introduction

Over the past few decades, an impressive body of work has developed exploring theoretical issues relating to statutory interpretation. Philosophically-informed accounts of the meaning (or, as I shall say, the *linguistic content*) of statutory provisions have been proposed. Theories of legislative intent have become more sophisticated, and the sceptical challenge to the existence or utility of legislative intent has been refined in important respects. Increasingly rigorous accounts of textualism and intentionalism have been offered, as well as some robust challenges to the distinction between these two schools of thought.

Jeff Goldsworthy has been in the vanguard of these developments. Since the early 1990s, he has offered a sophisticated, neo-Gricean account of the linguistic content of constitutional and statutory texts.[1] He has also played an important role in the debate about whether intentions can be ascribed to the legislature and, if so, on what basis.[2]

At the same time, less effort has been made to better understand the concept of statutory purpose, or to explore the role that purpose does or should play in statutory interpretation. This is, of course, a broad generalisation. For example, while it is not the central theme in Goldsworthy's writings about statutory interpretation, we will see that he offers an interesting and suggestive account of statutory purpose. Nevertheless, when one considers the amount of work that has been done to better understand the linguistic content of statutory provisions and on legislative intent, and to develop interesting and plausible versions of textualism and intentionalism, it is fair to say that comparatively little attention has been paid to statutory purpose.

* Earlier versions of this paper were presented at a workshop at Monash University to commemorate the retirement of Professor Jeff Goldsworthy, and at a workshop at Sydney Law School to commemorate the retirement of Professor Tom Campbell. I am very grateful to audience members at both events. I am especially grateful to Farrah Ahmed for extremely helpful comments on an earlier draft, and to Jeff Goldsworthy for his very helpful advice about this paper and about much else over the past 17 years. This research was supported under the Australian Research Council's *Discovery Projects* funding scheme (project number DP140102670).

[1] See, eg, J Goldsworthy, 'Implications in Language, Law and the Constitution' in G Lindell (ed), *Future Directions in Australian Constitutional Law: Essays in Honour of Professor Leslie Zines* (Sydney, Federation Press, 1994) 150; J Goldsworthy, 'Moderate Versus Strong Intentionalism: Knapps and Michaels Revisited' (2005) 42 *San Diego Law Review* 669; J Goldsworthy, 'Constitutional Implications Revisited' (2011) 30 *University of Queensland Law Journal* 9.

[2] See, eg, J Goldsworthy, *Parliamentary Sovereignty: Contemporary Debates* (Cambridge, Cambridge University Press, 2010) 232–51; R Ekins and J Goldsworthy, 'The Reality and Indispensability of Legislative Intentions' (2014) 36 *Sydney Law Review* 39; J Goldsworthy, 'Legislative Intention Vindicated?' (2013) 33 *OJLS* 821.

Indeed, there is no consensus – among theorists or practitioners – about what statutory purpose *is*. It is common for judges to appeal to statutory purpose, and for commentators to discuss the appropriate role of statutory purpose, without explaining what they mean by the term. Even where an explicit characterisation is provided, we shall see that there are at least three schools of thought regarding how statutory purpose is to be understood, and there has been minimal dialogue between those schools of thought.

This should be of concern. Appeals to purpose appear to play a prominent role in judicial reasoning about statutes, and in judges' characterisation of their interpretive practices.[3] Legislatures, too, appear to take the concept seriously. In many jurisdictions, it is common for a statute to contain an express statement of (what the legislature takes to be) its purpose, whether in a preamble or an objects clause. And, in some jurisdictions, there is a statutory requirement that courts interpret legislation in a way that promotes the statutory purpose.[4]

It seems important, therefore, that we have a clear understanding of what statutory purpose is, and of what role it does and should play in statutory interpretation. Perhaps we should be sceptical about judicial and legislative invocations of statutory purpose. Objects clauses are often notoriously unhelpful, and courts sometimes read down statutory requirements to privilege the interpretation that (best) promotes the statutory purpose.[5] Moreover, there are well-known objections to judicial reliance on statutory purpose, some of which are discussed below. Nevertheless, whether or not we ultimately arrive at a sceptical conclusion, we should first ensure that we understand the concept whose utility is being questioned.

The aim of this paper is to advance our understanding of what statutory purpose is, as a precursor to considering what role (if any) it does and should play in statutory interpretation. I begin, in section II, by identifying three approaches to understanding the concept of statutory purpose. Statutory purpose has variously been equated with the intentions of certain legislators (or the legislature as a whole), with the intentions that a *reasonable* legislator would have had if he or she had enacted the statute, and with some 'objective' purpose that may depart from any intentions that (actual or reasonable) legislators may have had. I shall suggest that there appear to be significant problems with each of these approaches.

In section III, I suggest a way of understanding the first approach – which equates statutory purpose with the intentions of the legislature, or of certain legislators – that avoids many of the objections to that approach. I start by distinguishing between the legislature's communicative intentions and its legal intentions, before suggesting that statutory purpose is concerned with the latter. I then consider whether legal intentions should be understood as directed toward the norm that the statutory provision is to contribute to the content of the law ('norm-intentions') or toward the state of affairs that the provision is to bring about ('application-intentions'). While the former suggestion may appear attractive, I argue

[3] In the UK, see, eg, *Attorney-General's Reference (No 5 of 2002)* [2004] 4 All ER 901 at [31]; in Australia, see, eg, *Project Blue Sky Inc v Australian Broadcasting Authority* (1998) 194 CLR 355 at 384. In the US, even Justice Scalia has acknowledged that statutory purpose has an important – though limited – role to play: see nn 69–71 below.

[4] These statutory requirements come in differing strengths. In some jurisdictions, the interpretation that best promotes the statutory purpose must be preferred: see, eg, *Acts Interpretation Act 1901* (Cth), s 15AA. In other jurisdictions, the requirement is merely that an interpretation that promotes the statutory purpose be preferred to one that does not: see, eg, *Interpretation of Legislation Act 1984* (Vic), s 35(a). In the latter case, the statutory requirement says nothing about a situation in which two interpretations each promote the statutory purpose, but to different extents. See *Chugg v Pacific Dunlop Ltd* (1990) 170 CLR 249 at 262.

[5] See, eg, *Thiess v Collector of Customs* (2014) 250 CLR 664 at 672.

that we should understand legal intentions in terms of application-intentions. However, the legislature may have multiple application-intentions with regard to a single statute, only some of which should count as part of the statutory purpose. Thus, I go on to suggest some constraints on which of the legislature's application-intentions count. I finish by addressing the possibility that different legislators will have different application-intentions.

II. Three Understandings of Statutory Purpose

There are at least three broad understandings of statutory purpose reflected in the literature. Some writers treat statutory purpose as equivalent to certain intentions of the legislature (or of a certain set of legislators).[6] Others understand it in terms of the intentions that a reasonable legislator would have had, had they enacted the statute in question. Finally, statutory purpose is sometimes understood as some sort of 'objective' purpose, separate from any intention of the legislature. I shall suggest that, if it is not to collapse into the second approach, this third approach is best understood as concerned with the functional role that the statute plays within the legal system.

In this section, I explore these understandings of statutory purpose in greater depth, and contend that each appears to face substantial obstacles. This will set the scene for section III, where I offer a version of the first approach – which understands statutory purpose in terms of certain intentions of the legislature – that avoids many of those obstacles.

Before commencing, three caveats are called for. First, the three approaches I discuss are not exhaustive: not everyone who writes about statutory purpose endorses, or presupposes, one of these accounts.[7] However, each of the three approaches has been suggested by influential writers on the topic, and at least the first two are widely held. As will emerge, all three approaches also raise theoretically important issues.

Second, the three understandings of statutory purpose I discuss may not be mutually exclusive. Indeed, we shall see that some writers appear to endorse two of the three approaches. In doing so, they are not necessarily being inconsistent. It is possible that we use the phrase 'statutory purpose' to pick out more than one factor relevant to the interpretation of legislation. Or it may be that there are multiple purposes in play (eg a specific and a broader purpose), each of which is to be understood in a different way.

Third, I should say something about the type of problem with which I shall be concerned in this section. There are well-known objections to all but the most limited use of statutory purpose.[8] For example, it is argued that more extensive uses of purpose undermine

[6] For ease of exposition, I shall talk of the intentions of 'the legislature', understanding this to cover both the possibility that the relevant intentions are held by the legislature in its own right and the possibility that the relevant intentions are those shared by certain legislators (which are then attributed to the legislature as a whole). Of course, many people are sceptical about whether legislatures can have intentions in either sense. I discuss this sort of scepticism below.

[7] In particular, I leave to one side morally-laden conceptions of statutory purpose that take their place within a broader, anti-positivist theory of law. Such conceptions include the view that statutory purpose is an interpretive concept (see R Dworkin, *Law's Empire* (Oxford, Hart Publishing, 1998) 346 for hints of this view), and Michael Moore's claim that a statute's purpose is 'the *function* [the] statute serves in an ideally just and well-ordered society' (MS Moore, 'A Natural Law Theory of Interpretation' (1985) 58 *Southern California Law Review* 277, 354).

[8] I say more about *which* uses of statutory purpose are relatively uncontroversial in the text accompanying nn 69–71 below.

the carefully crafted compromises that are made in the legislative process and reflected in the statutory text.[9] It is also objected that permitting judges to interpret a statute in light of its purpose confers on the judiciary enormous discretion (eg in deciding which of several possible purposes to privilege) and/or runs the risk that judges will abuse their position by attributing to the statute the purpose they believe it *should* have.[10] However, my primary focus is not on these sorts of objections. Rather, it is on objections that are specific to the particular understandings of statutory purpose I consider. That is, my main concern is with objections to understanding statutory purpose in a certain way, not with objections to certain uses of statutory purpose. (Admittedly, the two sets of objections may be related. For example, it may be an objection to a particular understanding of statutory purpose that it exacerbates the concerns about the use of purpose in statutory interpretation.)

A. Statutory Purpose and Legislative Intent

A common way of understanding the concept of statutory purpose is in terms of certain intentions of the legislature. For example, Goldsworthy claims that 'A purpose is a kind of intention: an intention to achieve something.'[11] He infers from this that, strictly speaking, legal texts such as statutes cannot have purposes (because they cannot have intentions). Rather, a reference to the purpose of a legal text should be understood as a reference to the purpose (ie the intention) of the people who designed or used that text.[12] In the case of statutes, the purpose is naturally understood in terms of the intentions of the lawmaker – that is, the legislature.[13]

One appealing feature of this approach is that it fits with linguistic usage in other contexts, where we often use 'purpose' and 'intention' interchangeably. For example, we might say that both my intention and my purpose in walking quickly to the station is to arrive in time to catch the next train. However, there appear to be significant problems with treating 'purpose' and 'intention' as interchangeable in the context of statutory interpretation. For one thing, it is controversial whether the legislature can have intentions, given that it consists of a multitude of members who may have conflicting (or no) intentions with regard to a particular statute.[14] If statutory purpose is understood in terms of the legislature's intentions but the legislature cannot have intentions, then there is no such thing as statutory purpose.

[9] See, eg, JF Manning, 'What Divides Textualists from Purposivists?' (2006) 106 *Columbia Law Review* 70, 92, 96, 99–109.

[10] See, eg, A Scalia and BA Garner, *Reading Law: The Interpretation of Legal Texts* (St Paul, Thomson/West, 2012) 18–19; A Scalia, *A Matter of Interpretation* (Princeton, Princeton University Press, 1997) 17–18.

[11] J Goldsworthy, 'Functions, Purposes and Values in Constitutional Interpretation' in R Dixon (ed), *Australian Constitutional Values* (Oxford, Hart Publishing, 2018) 45. See also Goldsworthy, *Parliamentary Sovereignty* (n 2) 233.

[12] Goldsworthy, 'Functions, Purposes and Values' (n 11) 45; Goldsworthy, *Parliamentary Sovereignty* (n 2) 233.

[13] While Goldsworthy sometimes leaves open the question of whether it is the designer's or the user's intentions that count, in the case of statutes he generally focuses on the legislature's intentions: see, eg, Goldsworthy, *Parliamentary Sovereignty* (n 2) 233. Other commentators have also understood statutory purpose in terms of certain intentions of the lawmaker: see, eg, N Duxbury, *Elements of Legislation* (Cambridge, Cambridge University Press, 2012) 176.

[14] Compare R Dworkin, *A Matter of Principle* (Cambridge MA, Harvard University Press, 1985) 38–57 with Ekins and Goldsworthy (n 2).

I shall not seek to resolve the debate about legislative intent in this paper. I do, however, want to suggest that this debate does not pose a *distinct* problem for writers such as Goldsworthy, who understand statutory purpose in terms of certain intentions of the legislature. If legislatures cannot have intentions, then the implications go far beyond issues of statutory purpose. Obviously, it would follow that references to legislative intent – and hence any version of intentionalism – are also problematic. And it would be doubtful that any linguistic content could be attributed to statutes beyond the semantic meaning of the words in the statute, since mainstream philosophy of language treats pragmatic content as a function of the speaker's intentions.[15] This would render questionable any attempt to (say) fill ellipses in, or draw implications from, the statutory text, at least if this is meant to involve identifying the statute's linguistic content.[16] And scepticism about legislative intent seems to entail a more general scepticism about ascribing mental states – any mental state, not just intentions – to any multi-member body whose members may have conflicting beliefs, desires, intentions, etc. This would extend to many corporations and associations, and to appellate courts.[17]

None of this shows that sceptics about legislative intent are mistaken, or provides any insight into how intentions are to be ascribed to legislatures. However, it does suggest that, if scepticism about legislative intent is a problem for advocates of the present understanding of statutory purpose, they have plenty of company.

There is a more troubling objection to the present understanding of statutory purpose. Legislative intent and statutory purpose are usually thought of as discrete concepts. The relationship between the two is disputed. Some people think of statutory purpose as contributing to, or shedding light on, legislative intent. Others regard statutory purpose and legislative intent as separate constituents of a statute's legal effect.[18] However, if it is to play any of these roles, statutory purpose must be conceptually distinct from legislative intent. Yet, if statutory purpose is understood in terms of the legislature's intentions, the distinction between legislative intent and statutory purpose seems to vanish.

The standard response to this problem is to treat statutory purpose as a particularly broad or general intention. For example, Lawrence Solan suggests that legislative intent refers to the more specific goals the legislature had in enacting the statute, whereas statutory purpose refers to the legislature's more abstract goals.[19] Similarly, Neil Duxbury suggests

[15] See generally D Smith, 'Is the High Court Mistaken about the Aim of Statutory Interpretation?' (2016) 44 *Federal Law Review* 227, 237; Ekins and Goldsworthy (n 2) 56–57. Concerning the distinction between semantic and pragmatic content, see D Smith, 'The Practice-Based Objection to the Standard Picture' (unpublished manuscript) 3.

[16] Goldsworthy, *Parliamentary Sovereignty* (n 2) 236–38. There is room for disagreement about how big a problem this is. For example, Andrei Marmor claims that pragmatic enrichment is often (but not always) precluded in the legislative context anyway, independent of any general scepticism about legislative intent: A Marmor, 'The Pragmatics of Legal Language' (2008) 21 *Ratio Juris* 423.

[17] In *Zheng v Cai* (2009) 239 CLR 446, the High Court of Australia treated as unproblematic the suggestion that a church (an incorporated association) has intentions, while expressing scepticism about the possibility that a legislature could have intentions. The Court did not explain how these positions could be reconciled, beyond asserting that the context is different. (I am grateful to Lisa Burton Crawford and Patrick Emerton for drawing the discussion in *Zheng* to my attention.)

[18] I understand a statute's legal effect in terms of the contribution the statute makes to the content of the law. For a more detailed discussion, see Smith, 'The Practice-Based Objection' (n 15) 2–3.

[19] LM Solan, *The Language of Statutes: Laws and Their Interpretation* (Chicago, University of Chicago Press, 2010) 142.

that we can distinguish between legislative intent and statutory purpose on the basis that references to the latter are often references to '*general* legislative intent'.[20] This might explain why statutory purpose is sometimes used as evidence of legislative intent (since the legislature's general intention may shed light on its more specific intention), and also why they are sometimes treated as separate contributors to legal effect (if we think that a statute's legal effect is shaped both by the specific intention the legislature had and by its more general aim).

However, to assess whether this response is satisfactory, we need to know more about the distinction between specific and general intentions. When is an intention sufficiently specific to count as the legislative intent, and when is an intention sufficiently general to count as the statutory purpose? We might appeal to the metaphor of a chain or ladder of intentions. The idea behind this metaphor is that, with regard to any statute, the legislature has a number of intentions of varying degrees of specificity, and the more specific intentions are (seen as) ways of achieving the more general intentions. Goldsworthy gives an example in a constitutional context:

> [C]onstitution-makers may enact a set of words in order to establish a particular constitutional norm, that judicial salaries be fixed, in order to secure judicial independence, in order to secure the impartiality of judicial decision-making, in order to secure justice and the rule of law, in order to promote human dignity (and the chain may or may not end there).[21]

Transposed to the statutory context, the thought might be that we can distinguish between specific and general intentions by reference to where the intention is located on this ladder of intentions. However, all this tells us is that statutory purpose is higher up the ladder than legislative intent. It does not tell us where to locate either concept on the ladder.[22] In Goldsworthy's example, is the legislative intent that judicial salaries be fixed or that judicial independence be secured? Is the statutory purpose to secure judicial independence or to secure the impartiality of judicial decision-making (or perhaps even to promote justice and the rule of law)? The distinction between specific and general intentions does not provide a basis on which to answer these questions.

A similar problem confronts the related proposal to understand statutory purpose in terms of the end that the legislature sought to achieve by enacting the statute and legislative intent in terms of the means that the legislature chose to pursue that end. The ladder of intentions metaphor can be understood in terms of a series of intermediate ends, each of which is, in turn, instrumental to achieving the more general ends further up the ladder. We therefore face the same difficulty in deciding where on the ladder to locate legislative intent and statutory purpose.

In addition, there may be reason to characterise statutory purpose in a way that is sensitive, not only to the end the legislature sought to achieve, but also the means it chose to

[20] Duxbury (n 13) 176 (fn omitted).

[21] Goldsworthy, 'Functions, Purposes and Values' (n 11) 44.

[22] The metaphor of a chain of intentions or purposes dates back to M Radin, 'Statutory Interpretation' (1930) 43 *Harvard Law Review* 863, 876–78. It is normally invoked as part of a sceptical argument about the utility of statutory purpose. For example, Radin contends that almost any end is itself a means to a further end (which is how the chain is generated), and so judges have a *choice* about the level of generality at which to describe the statutory purpose. Goldsworthy's discussion of the metaphor is more neutral, but he does not suggest that it can be used to resolve the problem discussed in the text.

achieve that end. This may result in a more precise characterisation of the statutory purpose, and may help to alleviate an important concern about appeals to purpose – namely, that they overlook the significance of the legislature's choice of the means by which the desired end is to be achieved.[23]

B. Statutory Purpose and Standards of Reasonableness

We will return to the idea that statutory purpose is to be understood in terms of certain intentions of the legislature in section III. For now, let us consider an alternative approach that has been particularly influential in the United States. On this approach, statutory purpose is concerned, not with the intentions of the actual legislature, but rather with the intentions (or aims, or goals) that a reasonable legislator would have had if he or she had enacted the statute (on the assumption that he or she was familiar with the statutory text, with other statutes *in pari materia* and with relevant principles of statutory interpretation).[24]

This view is often traced back to the legal process materials of Hart and Sacks.[25] They argue that, when identifying the statutory purpose, a court 'should assume, unless the contrary unmistakably appears, that the legislature was made up of reasonable persons pursuing reasonable purposes reasonably'.[26] This, they suggest, involves comparing the new law (ie the law that applies after the enactment of the statute) with the old law (ie the law that applied before the statute was enacted), and asking why reasonable legislators would have enacted the new law to replace the old law.

However, there may be an important difference between Hart and Sacks' view and the approach I want to consider in this section. Arguably, Hart and Sacks offer advice about how to identify a statute's purpose, rather than making a claim about what statutory purpose *is*. By contrast, the view I am interested in makes a metaphysical claim about what constitutes statutory purpose, not an epistemic claim about how to identify that purpose.

This understanding of statutory purpose has the virtue of suggesting a clear distinction between legislative intent and statutory purpose. Legislative intent is concerned with the intentions of the actual legislature; statutory purpose is concerned with the intentions (or aims, or goals) that a reasonable legislator would have had, had he or she enacted the statute.

Prima facie, this understanding of statutory purpose has another advantage over the understanding considered in the previous section. Because it equates statutory purpose with the intentions of a reasonable legislator, not those of the actual legislature, it appears that the present view is unaffected by sceptical arguments about legislative intent. Those arguments pertain to whether intentions can be attributed to the actual legislature, and so might be thought to have no bite against the view that statutory purpose is fixed by reference to the intentions of a hypothetical, reasonable legislator.[27]

[23] For an expression of this concern, see R Ekins, *The Nature of Legislative Intent* (Oxford, Oxford University Press, 2012) 250–51.

[24] See Manning (n 9) 90–91 (suggesting that this is the way in which purposivists understand statutory purpose).

[25] HM Hart and AM Sacks, *The Legal Process: Basic Problems in the Making and Application of Law* (Cambridge Massachusetts, Foundation Press, 1994).

[26] ibid 1415.

[27] Manning (n 9) appears to attach great weight to this purported advantage of the present understanding of statutory purpose.

In the previous section, I argued that scepticism about legislative intent does not pose a distinctive problem for the suggestion that we should understand statutory purpose in terms of the legislature's intentions. However, to the extent that scepticism about legislative intent does pose a problem for that understanding of statutory purpose, I doubt that the present approach is any better off. A reasonable legislator can have intentions, but so can an actual legislator. The problems arise when we seek to identify *which* of the legislator's intentions are relevant, and when we seek to move from the intentions of individual legislators to those of the legislature as a whole.[28] It is not clear that focusing on reasonable, rather than actual, legislators helps here. Even a reasonable legislator may have multiple intentions with regard to a statute, and those intentions may conflict in unforeseen circumstances. (The reasonable legislator is familiar with the statutory text, other statutes *in pari materia* and relevant principles of statutory interpretation, but is not omniscient.) Similarly, even reasonable people can disagree about controversial legal and political issues, raising doubts about whether we can treat the intentions of any *one* reasonable legislator as representative. Put differently, on the present proposal, with *which* reasonable legislator should we be concerned?

There are further problems with the suggestion that statutory purpose should be understood in terms of the intentions that a reasonable legislator would have had. First, it is unclear why the intentions of a hypothetical legislator are of legal significance. They may be of evidential relevance: if we have reason to believe that the actual legislators were reasonable, we might consider what a reasonable legislator would have intended as a way of obtaining insight into the intentions of the actual legislators. However, why should we accept the claim that the intentions of a reasonable legislator help constitute a statute's legal effect? To the extent that the authority of a statute flows from the authority of the lawmaker, it is the actual legislature's intentions, not those of a hypothetical reasonable legislator, that matter.[29] It follows that, on the present understanding, it is unclear why we should treat *statutory purpose* as legally relevant.

We may ultimately conclude that statutory purpose does *not* help constitute a statute's legal effect, but merely plays an evidential role. However, it is a disadvantage of the present understanding of statutory purpose that it makes that conclusion appear inescapable, without any need to engage with the critiques of the use of statutory purpose (based, for example, on the need to respect legislative compromise) that are usually offered in support of that conclusion.

Second, there are some statutes that no reasonable legislator would have enacted. Of course, judgements of reasonableness vary, and so we are unlikely to agree about which statutes this is true of. Nevertheless, it is likely that most readers will accept that there are some such statutes. It is unclear how we can apply the current suggestion – which requires a consideration of the intentions that a reasonable legislator would have had if he or she had enacted the statute – to statutes that a reasonable legislator would *not* have enacted. Perhaps the current suggestion supports the conclusion that there is no statutory purpose in such cases. Yet this seems the wrong conclusion to draw. There may be reasons why purpose

[28] See, eg, Dworkin, *A Matter of Principle* (n 14) 38–57.

[29] For the argument that, to the extent that the authority of a legal text flows from the authority of the lawmaker, we must attach weight to the (actual) lawmaker's intentions, see J Raz, *Between Authority and Interpretation: On the Theory of Law and Practical Reason* (Oxford, Oxford University Press, 2009) 235.

should not play a role in interpreting a statute that a reasonable legislator would not have enacted, but it is implausible to suggest that the statute has no purpose at all (*cf* an unreasonable or immoral purpose).

C. Statutory Purpose and Functional Role

It is sometimes suggested that statutory purpose consists, at least in part, of some sort of 'objective' purpose.[30] It is tempting to understand this suggestion as referring to the intentions of a reasonable legislator, rather than those of the actual legislature, in which case it collapses into the approach discussed in the previous section.[31] However, there is another way of understanding this suggestion that directs attention away from intentions (whether actual or reasonable). We might think of statutory purpose as constituted by the role the statute plays within the broader legal system, given the other laws that exist within that legal system. On this view, a statute's purpose cannot be understood solely by reference to facts about the statute itself (including facts about the intentions with which the statute was enacted). Rather, it must be understood by reference to the way in which the statute interacts with other relevant legal materials, and this may be at least partly independent of the lawmaker's *intentions* as to how it will interact with those materials.

This suggestion may enjoy some support in the literature. While Hart and Sacks are more commonly associated with the previous understanding of statutory purpose, they may also endorse the present understanding. They suggest that a statute has both a particular purpose and a general purpose. While identifying the particular purpose requires a consideration of the intentions that a reasonable legislator would have had if he or she had enacted the statute, they suggest that the general purpose concerns how the statute 'is to be fitted into the legal system as a whole'.[32]

It is possible that Hart and Sacks understand *both* purposes in terms of the intentions of a reasonable legislator. On this reading, they suggest that a reasonable legislator would have intentions concerning both what the statute will achieve and how it will fit with the rest of the legal system. However, recall that the reasonable legislator's intentions are shaped by his or her awareness of the surrounding legal materials and relevant principles of statutory interpretation. Thus, it might be thought that asking how a reasonable legislator would intend that the statute fit with the rest of the legal system is simply a heuristic for identifying the role that the statute in fact plays within the broader legal system.[33] In any case, it is this understanding of statutory purpose that I shall consider in this section.

Goldsworthy denies that statutes (or other legal texts) can have purposes that are independent of the lawmaker in this way. He argues that laws are deliberately created by people,

[30] For example, Aharon Barak understands statutory purpose in terms of a combination of a 'subjective' purpose (dependent, in part, on the lawmaker's intentions) and an 'objective' purpose: A Barak, *Purposive Interpretation in Law* (Princeton, Princeton University Press, 2005) Ch 3.

[31] Barak's account of a statute's objective purpose is complex, incorporating both elements of the 'reasonable legislator' approach and an appeal to 'the fundamental values of the legal system' (ibid 90).

[32] Hart and Sacks (n 25) 1414.

[33] This fits with the suggestion in the previous section that Hart and Sacks may be offering epistemic guidance as to how we identify statutory purpose, rather than a metaphysical thesis about what constitutes statutory purpose.

and so the purposes of those laws must be the purposes of the people who created them.[34] This appears to tie purposes back to intentions (arguably, the intentions of actual people, rather than those of a hypothetical, reasonable person).

In the present context, Goldsworthy treats 'purpose' and 'function' as synonyms.[35] Thus, his argument appears to be based on a broader claim about the function of artifacts[36] – namely, that their function is fixed by reference to the intentions of the people who create them (or, perhaps, the people who use them). This is a popular view in philosophical writings about artifacts.[37] However, it is not the only possible view. On another view, an artifact's function is fixed by reference to the role the artifact plays in the world, not the role someone intends it to play.[38] This suggests that – even if we regard a statute as an artifact and treat its purpose as equivalent to its function – statutory purpose could be understood independently of anyone's intentions, but rather in terms of the role the statute plays in the legal system. Since any statute must take its place within a vast network of other laws, it does not seem implausible to claim that the role the statute plays within the legal system is influenced by those other laws, in ways that may diverge from the intentions the lawmaker had when enacting the statute.

So the present proposal for understanding statutory purpose is more plausible than it might appear. Nevertheless, it suffers from a major problem. Perhaps a statute's legal effect is equivalent to its purpose. However, this is a conclusion that requires substantive argument; it should not be treated as an a priori conceptual truth. To adopt an understanding of the concept of statutory purpose from which it follows that a statute's legal effect is equivalent to its purpose would be to stack the deck against those who argue (on substantive grounds) either that statutory purpose does *not* contribute to legal effect or that it is only *one* factor that helps constitute a statute's legal effect. Thus, just as we need to distinguish between the concepts of legislative intent and statutory purpose, we also need a conceptual distinction between a statute's legal effect and its purpose.

The problem with the present proposal for understanding statutory purpose is that it threatens to collapse this distinction. I have suggested that we should understand a statute's legal effect in terms of the contribution the statute makes to the content of the law. Yet it is not clear how this differs from the role the statute plays within the broader legal system. In other words, it is unclear how – on the present proposal – the concept of statutory purpose differs from that of a statute's legal effect.

[34] Goldsworthy, 'Functions, Purposes and Values' (n 11) 48.

[35] Goldsworthy, 'Functions, Purposes and Values' (n 11) 44.

[36] Following Hilpinen, we can think of an artifact as 'an object that has been intentionally made or produced for a certain purpose' (R Hilpinen, 'Artifact' in EN Zalta (ed), *The Stanford Encyclopedia of Philosophy*, Winter 2011 edn, available at plato.stanford.edu/archives/win2011/entries/artifact). A statute might be thought to be an artifact in this sense.

[37] See generally AL Thomasson, 'Public Artifacts, Intentions and Norms' in M Franssen, P Kroes, TAC Reydon and PE Vermaas (eds), *Artefact Kinds: Ontology and the Human-Made World* (Cham, Springer, 2014) 45–46. For an endorsement of this view in the legal context, see KM Ehrenberg, *The Functions of Law* (Oxford, Oxford University Press, 2016) Ch 2.

[38] See, eg, CL Elder, 'Artifacts and Mind-Independence' in Franssen et al, ibid (though Elder's way of cashing out this thought – by treating the function of an artifact-type as fixed by reference to whatever caused past tokens of that type to be reproduced – is not particularly congenial to the present understanding of statutory purpose). I am grateful to Jan Mihal for drawing Elder's work to my attention.

III. Statutory Purpose as Application-Intentions

A. The Distinction between Communicative and Legal Intentions

One might conclude from this brief survey that the prospects for developing a satisfactory account of statutory purpose are bleak. Each of the approaches I have considered seems to face considerable difficulties. However, in this section, I shall suggest a way of developing the first approach – which links statutory purpose with the legislature's intentions – which avoids at least some of the problems identified in section II.A. While it remains hostage to the debate about whether legislatures can have intentions, it leads to a sharper distinction between statutory purpose and legislative intent than is achieved by appealing to the distinction between general and specific intentions. As we shall see, it also possesses several other advantages.

The starting point for developing this proposal is Mark Greenberg's distinction between two types of intention that a legislature may have.[39] On the one hand, there is the legislature's *communicative intention*, which we might understand as its intention to convey certain information to its audience via the words used in the statute (in part, by having its audience recognise its intention to convey this information). On the other hand, there is the legislature's *legal intention*, which Greenberg defines as its intention 'with respect to the legal impact of the enactment'.[40]

I propose that legislative intent be understood in terms of the legislature's communicative intentions, whereas statutory purpose be understood in terms of its legal intentions.[41] This suggestion will require refinement as we proceed. In particular, more needs to be said about what is meant by a 'legal intention'. However, the initial attraction of this suggestion is that it shows that statutory purpose can be understood as an intention of the legislature, and yet as distinct from legislative intent. Moreover, it treats legislative intent and statutory purpose as different *types* of intention (the former being an intention to communicate certain information; the latter being an intention to produce a certain legal impact), rather than relying on a vague distinction between general and specific intentions.

A similar distinction can be found in some existing discussions of statutory interpretation. For example, Tom Campbell distinguishes between how legislators 'intended the words of the statute to be understood'[42] and their 'further' intentions in enacting the statute

[39] M Greenberg, 'Legislation as Communication? Legal Interpretation and the Study of Linguistic Communication' in A Marmor and S Soames (eds), *Philosophical Foundations of Language in the Law* (Oxford, Oxford University Press, 2011) 241–42.

[40] ibid 241.

[41] I appeal to Greenberg for the limited purpose of distinguishing between communicative and legal intentions. Despite suggesting the distinction, Greenberg is sceptical about whether legislatures can have intentions, and I do not want to endorse that scepticism. More generally, I put the distinction to a different use than Greenberg. He distinguishes between communicative and legal intentions to illustrate the limits to the assistance that philosophy of language and linguistics can provide in the context of statutory interpretation (since these disciplines cannot supply an argument for focusing on communicative, rather than legal, intentions). By contrast, I propose that statutory purpose be understood in terms of the legislature's legal intentions (characterised in a particular way). Thanks to George Pavlakos for pressing me to be clearer about these matters.

[42] T Campbell, *The Legal Theory of Ethical Positivism* (Aldershot, Dartmouth Publishing Co, 1996) 141.

(such as the policy goal they sought to achieve), and he describes the latter as the legislators' 'purpose'.[43] The former set of intentions are (roughly) what I am calling communicative intentions; the latter resemble what I am calling legal intentions.

Similarly, Scott Soames distinguishes between 'what was said' in enacting a statute (which, he claims, depends on the communicative intentions that can reasonably be ascribed to the speaker) and the 'further legislative goals [that] were intended by legislators'.[44] The latter look like legal intentions, to be contrasted with the legislature's communicative intentions (or, for Soames, the communicative intentions that can reasonably be ascribed to the legislature).[45]

My proposal for distinguishing between legislative intent and statutory purpose may also fit with some general tendencies in our thinking about these concepts. Legislative intent is often thought to bear on the statute's linguistic content, or to be limited to those intentions that the legislature conveyed via the words used in the statute.[46] Understanding legislative intent in terms of communicative intentions vindicates such thoughts (on the plausible assumption that communicative intentions contribute to linguistic content). By contrast, statutory purpose is often understood in terms of the legislature's intention to make a change to the law, or to the world more generally (eg by remedying a mischief that the existing law does not address).[47] This may fit with understanding statutory purpose in terms of the legislature's legal intentions (depending on precisely how we understand the notion of a legal intention).

B. A Closer Look at Legal Intentions

To properly assess my proposed way of understanding statutory purpose, we need a better grasp of what is meant by a 'legal intention'. As we have seen, Greenberg defines a legal intention as an intention 'with respect to the legal impact of the enactment'. However, the reference to 'legal impact' is ambiguous. It could be a reference to the type of impact (a *legal* type, as opposed to some other type) or to what is being impacted (an impact *on the law*). Greenberg understands legal impact in the latter way – he goes on to describe a legal intention as 'an intention, by enacting a given statute, in order to change the law in a particular way'.[48] However, I shall argue that, if we are to understand statutory purpose in terms of legal intentions, we should adopt something like the former view – roughly, that a legal intention is an intention to make a change in the world by legal means.

Let us approach this issue by considering an observation of Goldsworthy's. He points out that the lawmaker may have various aims when introducing a legal text – eg to establish a particular legal norm, to achieve certain beneficial consequences for the community or to

[43] ibid.

[44] S Soames, 'Toward a Theory of Legal Interpretation' (2011) 6 *New York University Journal of Law and Liberty* 231, 240.

[45] Soames insists that communicative intentions should generally have priority over legal intentions (ibid 241). I shall not express a view about this issue: my aim is to suggest a certain understanding of statutory purpose, not to defend a particular role for purpose to play in statutory interpretation.

[46] See, eg, Ekins and Goldsworthy (n 2).

[47] See, eg, O Jones, *Bennion on Statutory Interpretation*, 6th edn (London, LexisNexis, 2013) 846.

[48] Greenberg, 'Legislation as Communication?' (n 39) 242.

acquire or retain political power.[49] Any of these could potentially be understood as a 'legal intention', and hence as being the statutory purpose.

There is a broad consensus that 'ulterior' purposes, such as the acquisition or retention of political power, do not count.[50] However, if we set ulterior purposes to one side, this still leaves open whether legal intentions are what we might call *norm-intentions* (the intention to contribute a particular norm to the content of the law) or what are often called *application-intentions* (the intention that the statute produce certain outcomes or achieve certain consequences).[51] Either might plausibly be said to be intentions as to what legal impact the statute will have: the norm-intention view corresponds with an understanding of legal impact as impact on the law; the application-intention view corresponds with an understanding of legal impact as impact on the world by legal means. In the rest of this section, I shall consider which is the better way of understanding the concept of a legal intention, given the characterisation of statutory purpose in terms of legal intentions.[52]

i. Norm-Intentions

It is tempting to understand legal intentions (and hence statutory purpose) in terms of norm-intentions.[53] First, the legislature might be thought of as a norm-generating institution. If so, it seems natural to understand legal intentions in terms of the norms the legislature intended to generate. Second, understanding legal intentions as norm-intentions precludes treating very general intentions (eg to promote public safety) as the statutory purpose, and hence ameliorates some of the concerns about the use of purpose in statutory interpretation.[54] It is unlikely that the legislature would intend that the norm a provision contributes to the law is that public safety is to be promoted (as opposed to intending to contribute a more specific norm, with the hope or even expectation that that norm will promote public safety). For one thing, this would leave it to the law-applier to decide *how* public safety is to be promoted. For another thing, a great many statutes aim to promote public safety; if this was also the norm that each of those statutes contributed to the law, then they would all have an identical legal effect.

[49] Goldsworthy, 'Functions, Purposes and Values' (n 11) 44.

[50] See, eg, Goldsworthy, 'Functions, Purposes and Values' (n 11) 44; Campbell (n 42) 143; Soames (n 44) 250.

[51] Greenberg draws a similar distinction in the course of endorsing the norm-intention understanding of legal intentions: M Greenberg, 'What Makes a Method of Legal Interpretation Correct? Legal Standards vs. Fundamental Determinants' (2017) 130 *Harvard Law Review Forum* 105, 111 fn 19.

[52] One might say that statutory purpose includes *both* types of intention. Indeed, this may be Goldsworthy's view. He suggests that the lawmaker's intention to establish a particular norm and its desire to achieve certain beneficial consequences may both be relevant, at least when interpreting constitutions: Goldsworthy, 'Functions, Purposes and Values' (n 11) 44. However, for the reasons that follow, a consideration of the legislature's norm-intentions is unlikely to add anything to a consideration of legislative intent.

[53] Whether we understand legal intentions as norm-intentions or application-intentions, different provisions (or sets of related provisions) within the same Act will often be the subject of different legal intentions, and hence have different purposes. However, for convenience, I will often talk about the purpose of a statute, rather than the purpose of a statutory provision or set of provisions.

[54] These concerns include that appeals to statutory purpose allow courts to ride roughshod over careful legislative decisions about the extent to which a particular purpose should be pursued, or about how to balance that purpose against other legislative aims: see, eg, Manning (n 9); Ekins (n 23) 250–51. The more abstract the purpose being invoked, the more pressing these concerns might be thought to be.

There may appear to be a third reason to focus on norm-intentions, rather than application-intentions. We might think that, for both rule of law and separation of powers reasons, the legislature has the power only to lay down general rules, not to dictate the particular instances to which those rules apply. If so, its intention to introduce a particular norm into the law may be legally relevant, but its intention to achieve a certain consequence (where this is understood in terms of the norm applying to certain individual cases) is not.

However, there is a major obstacle to understanding legal intentions in terms of norm-intentions. While it is controversial what role statutory purpose plays in the interpretation of legislation, any proposed understanding of the concept of statutory purpose should leave open the possibility that it plays a distinct, non-trivial role. This requires that our understanding of statutory purpose differ from our understanding of other concepts relevant to statutory interpretation (such as legislative intent). Indeed, not only must there be a conceptual distinction, but the distinction should be drawn in such a way that we can imagine statutory purpose adding something that these other factors do not. Otherwise, we prejudge what should be substantive debates about the appropriate role of statutory purpose by adopting a certain understanding of that concept.

If we understand legislative intent as the legislature's communicative intention and statutory purpose as its norm-intention, then there is a conceptual distinction between the two. The norm that the legislature intended to convey by enacting the statutory provision could conceivably differ from the norm it intended the provision to contribute to the content of the law. However, while the two *could* come apart, they are unlikely to do so. The legislature has an obvious incentive to ensure that its norm-intentions are reflected in its communicative intentions. If it wants a particular norm to be added to the law, would it not want to convey that fact? The legislature can surely be expected to understand that part of the point of enacting a statutory provision is to *convey* (to the norm-applier and/or the norm-subjects) which norm it intends the provision to contribute to the content of the law.

Thus, the problem with understanding statutory purpose in terms of norm-intentions is that it is unlikely that the legislature's norm-intentions will differ from its communicative intentions, and hence it is unlikely that a consideration of statutory purpose will add anything to a consideration of legislative intent. While we might ultimately conclude that statutory purpose should not play a significant role in interpretation, this should turn on substantive issues (such as whether considering a statute's purpose rides roughshod over carefully crafted legislative compromises). We should try to avoid understanding the concept of statutory purpose in a way that leads to that conclusion without any need to consider those substantive issues.

We can imagine cases where the legislature's norm-intention does depart from its communicative intention. For example, the legislature may seek to introduce a secret law, and so may not want to *convey* the norm it intends to contribute to the content of the law. Or the legislature may mis-speak, and hence fail in its attempt to convey which norm it intends to contribute to the content of the law. Again, however, we should seek to avoid an account of statutory purpose from which it follows – on conceptual, not substantive, grounds – that purpose could only ever play a role with regard to secret laws or instances of legislative mis-speaking.[55]

[55] Even critics of purposivism typically allow that the role of statutory purpose extends beyond correcting instances of legislative mis-speaking: see text accompanying nn 69–71 below.

After drawing the distinction between communicative and legal intentions, Greenberg suggests that they often come apart. His main argument for this conclusion is that

> lawmakers can be wrong about which specific linguistic contents will achieve their legal intentions. Legislators frequently do not consider the statutory language with care. In addition, it is difficult to anticipate all the legal and practical consequences of specific rules.[56]

The claim that the legislature's communicative intentions may produce undesired consequences, due to a careless use of language or a failure to anticipate certain eventualities, is plausible. This is especially so given that a statute may remain part of the law for a considerable period of time, and hence may apply to circumstances quite different from those in which it was made.

However, Greenberg's argument does not show that the legislature's communicative intentions often come apart from its norm-intentions. Norm-intentions are intentions to contribute a particular norm to the content of the law, not to bring about certain consequences. While giving effect to the legislature's communicative intentions might often fail to bring about the consequences the legislature desired, doing so *is* likely to give effect to the legislature's norm-intentions (since, for the reasons already given, it is likely that the legislature will *convey* what norm it intends to contribute to the content of the law).[57]

What Greenberg's argument does establish is that the legislature's communicative intentions may often come apart from its application-intentions. The latter concern the consequences that the legislature wanted to bring about by enacting the statute. For the reasons Greenberg gives, these consequences may not be brought about by giving effect to the legislature's communicative intentions.

This is borne out by Greenberg's example of a case where the legislature's communicative and legal intentions came apart. In *Saadeh v Farouki*,[58] Congress amended a statute with the aim of restricting diversity jurisdiction (ie the scope for an action to be brought in a federal court where the parties are citizens of different states, or one party is a citizen of a state and the other is a foreign citizen). The amendment specified that a permanent resident of the United States is to be regarded as a citizen of the state in which he or she resides. This addressed the scenario where a permanent resident living in a state sues a citizen of that state (or vice versa). However, Congress appears not to have considered an alternative scenario, where a permanent resident living in a state sues a foreign citizen who is not a permanent resident of that state. In this second scenario, upholding Congress' communicative intentions would have the effect of *expanding* diversity jurisdiction.

The important point for our purposes is that Congress' norm-intentions did not come apart from its communicative intentions. To the contrary, Congress successfully communicated the norm it intended to contribute to the law. The problem was that it did not anticipate the second scenario, and so was mistaken in its belief that this norm would produce the desired consequences.

[56] Greenberg, 'Legislation as Communication?' (n 39) 243–44.

[57] Even if the legislature's communicative intentions and norm-intentions did come apart, Greenberg's point would apply equally to the latter. The norm that the legislature intended to contribute to the content of the law could also bring about undesired consequences, either because it was carelessly conceived or due to a failure to anticipate certain eventualities. In circumstances the legislature did not anticipate, the norm it intended to contribute to the content of the law would be no more likely to produce the desired result than the norm it intended to communicate by enacting the statute.

[58] *Saadeh v Farouki*, 107 F.3d 52 (DC Cir 1997) (discussed in Greenberg, 'Legislation as Communication?' (n 39) 242–43).

Things are different if we consider Congress' application-intentions. There *is* a conflict between the norm that Congress intended to communicate (and which it intended to add to the content of the law) and the consequences it intended to bring about by amending the statute. This appears to be Greenberg's point when he notes that Congress' communicative intentions would, in the second scenario, produce the opposite result to the one it was seeking.[59]

ii. Application-Intentions

In the previous section, I argued that – while understanding statutory purpose in terms of norm-intentions may appear attractive – it would mean that statutory purpose rarely departs from legislative intent. Thus, understanding statutory purpose in this way precludes the possibility that purpose could play a substantial role in statutory interpretation. Is there an alternative understanding of legal intentions, and hence of statutory purpose, that avoids this result?

I suggested that the main alternative to understanding legal intentions in terms of norm-intentions is to understand them in terms of application-intentions. As the discussion in the previous section indicates, understanding legal intentions in terms of application-intentions does provide support for the claim that legal and communicative intentions often come apart. It therefore renders it conceivable that statutory purpose could play a significant role in the interpretation of legislation.

However, if we are to understand statutory purpose in terms of application-intentions, we need a firmer grasp of what is meant by an application-intention. I have characterised an application-intention as an intention that the statute produce a certain outcome or achieve a certain consequence. Somewhat more formally, we can understand this in terms of an intention, on the part of the legislature, to bring about a certain *state of affairs* by enacting the statute.[60]

This characterisation of application-intentions may need further fine-tuning. For example, it may be that an application-intention is to be specified not only in terms of the state of affairs that the legislature intended to bring about by enacting the statute, but also

[59] This does, however, raise a puzzle, since – as noted above – Greenberg characterises legal intentions in terms of norm-intentions, not application-intentions.

[60] As I use the phrase, a state of affairs takes the form: *X's being Y* (eg the state of affairs of *Socrates' being wise*): see M Textor, 'States of Affairs' in EN Zalta (ed), *The Stanford Encyclopedia of Philosophy*, Winter 2016 edn, available at plato.stanford.edu/archives/win2016/entries/states-of-affairs/. This involves attributing a property (eg being wise) to an object (eg Socrates). In the case of statutory purposes, the property and the object may both be very complex, which can lead to a certain clunkiness when expressing the state of affairs in the form: X's being Y. I shall therefore typically express intended states of affairs more informally. However, my claim is that, in each case, the statutory purpose can be expressed in terms of an intention to bring about a state of affairs of X's being Y. (I am grateful to Larry Solum for a very helpful discussion of these issues.)

Soames suggests that we should understand statutory purpose in terms of the reasons that are publicly offered to justify enacting the statute: Soames (n 44) 250. (Goldsworthy also endorses this view: Goldsworthy, 'Functions, Purposes and Values' (n 11) 44.) While those reasons could be understood as referring to the need to introduce a particular norm into the law, they are more naturally understood as referring to the goals or policy objectives the statute is said to promote. Understood in this way, Soames' view bears some similarity to the view presented in the text. However, focusing on the state of affairs the legislature intended to bring about, rather than on its policy objectives, may facilitate precision in the specification of the statutory purpose. Legislators may also be more likely to agree about what state of affairs should be brought about than on the reasons *why* it should be brought about. If so, my approach may make it easier to ascribe intentions to the legislature as a whole. See further section III.B.iv.

in terms of the *means* by which the legislature intended to bring about that state of affairs.[61] However, sticking with the more straightforward characterisation of application-intentions for now, we can see that application-intentions differ from both norm-intentions and communicative intentions (ie legislative intent) in two respects. First, the subject-matter of the intentions is different. Legislative intent and norm-intentions concern the statute's effect on the law, whereas application-intentions focus on effects in the world (ie the state of affairs the legislature intends to bring about). Second, legislative intent must, and norm-intentions typically will, be communicated by enacting the statute, whereas application-intentions need not be. The legislature may intend to bring about a certain state of affairs without intending to *communicate* what state of affairs it intends to bring about. It may choose simply to communicate the norm it expects will bring about the desired state of affairs.[62] Alternatively, the legislature may indicate what state of affairs it intends to bring about, not in the statute itself, but in the extrinsic materials.

In many cases, there will be more than one state of affairs that the legislature intends to bring about by enacting the statute. That is, the legislature may have multiple application-intentions, with each application-intention being an intention to bring about a discrete state of affairs. For example, in enacting a particular tax statute, the legislature may have at least the following four application-intentions:

1. to bring about a state of affairs in which the common good is promoted;
2. to bring about a state of affairs in which a fair rate of corporate tax is paid;
3. to bring about a state of affairs in which a particular tax rebate (Y) is available to a certain type of corporation in particular circumstances (Z); and
4. to bring about a state of affairs in which company X claims tax rebate Y in circumstances Z.

It is tempting to say that one of these four application-intentions must count as the *real* statutory purpose. However, this is defensible only if there is a principled basis on which to make this selection. One might doubt whether such a basis is available.

One noticeable feature of these four application-intentions is that they differ in their degree of generality. Bringing about the state of affairs in #3 is intended to contribute to bringing about the more general state of affairs in #2, which in turn is intended to contribute to bringing about the even more general state of affairs in #1. Similarly, the state of affairs in #4 is (intended to be) a particular instantiation of the obtaining of the general state of affairs in #3.

Thus, any attempt to specify one of #1–4 as *the* statutory purpose appears to face a similar difficulty to the one that led us, in section II.A., to reject the suggestion that we should distinguish between legislative intent and statutory purpose by reference to how general the intentions are. There is no principled basis on which to specify the level of generality at which the statutory purpose should be stated. As a result, there seems to be no principled way of selecting one of the four application-intentions and treating it as *the* statutory purpose.

[61] See text to n 23 for some possible motivations for endorsing this position.

[62] Ekins makes an analogous point when he argues that the legislature may communicate an intention to enact a plan without intending to convey its *reasons* for adopting that plan: Ekins (n 23) 250.

Even if there *was* a principled basis on which to specify the requisite level of generality, there are occasions on which the legislature has multiple application-intentions that do *not* differ in terms of their degree of generality.[63] For example, the legislature may have two distinct goals when enacting a statute, reflected in two discrete states of affairs that it seeks to bring about, and neither of those states of affairs may be subsumed within the other. We cannot select one of these application-intentions as the 'real' statutory purpose based on their differing degrees of generality, because they do not differ in this way.

Or consider a case where the legislature intends to bring about a state of affairs, X, by bringing about another state of affairs, Y. For example, the legislature may be concerned about children dropping out of school to traffick drugs, and might conclude that the best way to address this problem is to decriminalise the drugs in question and arrange for their distribution by the State. It therefore enacts legislation to that effect. The statute may make no reference to the issue of school dropout rates. Nevertheless, it is plausible that the legislature has both a direct application-intention (to bring about a state of affairs in which drugs are distributed by the State) and an indirect application-intention (to thereby bring about a state of affairs in which more children stay at school, rather than dealing drugs).[64]

We might well think that both the direct and indirect application-intentions contribute to the statutory purpose. In any case, we cannot choose between them by reference to their degree of generality, since they do not differ in this way. This can be seen from the fact that the legislature could have approached the problem from the opposite direction – it might have sought to strengthen school attendance requirements, in the hope that this would disrupt the drug trade (by ensuring that children attend school, rather than trafficking drugs during school hours). By contrast, in the example of the tax rebate, the chain of means-ends reasoning cannot be reversed in this way. It makes sense to say that the legislature intended to provide a tax rebate as a means of promoting the common good; it does not make sense to say that the legislature intended to promote the common good as a means of providing a tax rebate.

(The existence of indirect application-intentions suggests that, in some cases, specifying the statutory purpose is not simply a matter of specifying the legislature's application-intentions. It also involves specifying the relationship between those application-intentions. In our example, the legislature not only intends (1) to bring about a state of affairs in which drugs are distributed by the State and (2) to bring about a state of affairs in which more children stay at school, rather than dealing drugs, but also intends (3) to bring about the latter state of affairs by bringing about the former state of affairs.)

For these reasons, we should abandon the attempt to find, in every case, a single application-intention that constitutes the statutory purpose. In many cases, the legislature will have multiple application-intentions when enacting a statute, and we will not be able to identify one of these intentions as the 'real' statutory purpose. This is not, in itself, a problem. That the legislature often – perhaps always – has more than one purpose in

[63] This may raise a further problem for the suggestion, discussed in section II.A., that we can distinguish between statutory purpose and legislative intent by reference to the degree of generality of the legislature's various intentions.

[64] I am grateful to Farrah Ahmed for pointing out the existence of indirect intentions, and for the example used in the text.

enacting a statutory provision is relatively uncontroversial.[65] On the present proposal, this is understood in terms of the legislature having multiple application-intentions, each of which corresponds to one of the states of affairs the legislature sought to bring about by enacting the provision. More than one of these application-intentions may be legally relevant (because each contributes to, or sheds light on, the provision's legal effect), and our understanding of statutory purpose should be broad enough to encompass this multiplicity of legally relevant application-intentions.

However, not every application-intention the legislature has when enacting a statute should be regarded as part of the statutory purpose. In the next section, I shall discuss some of the constraints on which application-intentions count; for now, I shall mention two reasons why we should *want* such constraints. First, treating all of the legislature's application-intentions as relevant would risk producing an account of statutory purpose so capacious as to be robbed of utility. If a statute's purpose consisted of an indefinitely long list of application-intentions, then appeals to purpose would be unlikely to assist in ascertaining its legal effect.

Second, once we allow that more than one of the legislature's application-intentions may be legally relevant, we must acknowledge the possibility that those application-intentions will come into conflict. Returning to the earlier example of the tax statute, it may turn out that providing the tax rebate to the relevant type of corporation does *not* help bring about a state of affairs in which a fair rate of corporate tax is paid, producing a conflict between application-intentions #2 and #3. The possibility of such conflicts is inherent in the approach I am proposing. However, if there are constraints on which application-intentions are part of the statutory purpose, this will at least ameliorate the problem (since we need only worry about conflicts between those application-intentions that are legally relevant).

For these reasons, we should look for some constraints on which application-intentions count as part of the statutory purpose. Those constraints should be sufficiently stringent that the concept of statutory purpose is not too capacious. However, we should not expect those constraints to be so stringent that – for any given statutory provision – there is only a single application-intention that satisfies them. We can understand a statutory provision's purpose as consisting of the sub-set of the legislature's application-intentions that satisfy those constraints.

In the next section, I offer some suggestions as to what these constraints are. The list of constraints I discuss may not be exhaustive. Moreover, many of them depend on normative considerations regarding what role purpose should play when interpreting legislation. However, this does not mean that my account breaches the methodological stricture I insisted on in earlier sections – namely, that an account of what statutory purpose is should not prejudge substantive debates about the role purpose should play. The constraints I identify should be acceptable to any plausible account of the role that purpose should play in interpreting legislation. Therefore, they can be endorsed without taking sides in substantive debates about the proper role of statutory purpose.

[65] See the oft-quoted passage from *Rodriguez v United States*, 480 US 522 (1987) at 525–26: 'no legislation pursues its purposes at all costs. Deciding what competing values will or will not be sacrificed to the achievement of a particular objective is the very essence of legislative choice – and it frustrates rather than effectuates legislative intent simplistically to assume that whatever furthers the statute's primary objective must be the law.'

iii. Which Application-Intentions Count?

Earlier, I mentioned the possibility that ulterior purposes (such as an intention that the ruling party be re-elected) could count as legal intentions, and hence as part of the statutory purpose. It might be thought that understanding statutory purpose in terms of application-intentions commits one to treating ulterior purposes as relevant in this way. This is because an ulterior purpose can be understood as an intention to bring about a certain state of affairs (eg the ruling party's re-election) by enacting the statute, and hence as an application-intention.

However, any plausible account of the role that purpose should play in statutory interpretation will treat ulterior purposes as irrelevant. Thus, on the present proposal, they do not fall within the sub-set of application-intentions that constitute the statutory purpose.

That ulterior purposes should not be considered when interpreting statutes is relatively uncontentious.[66] *Why* this is so is more controversial. Soames suggests that ulterior purposes vary between legislators, and so cannot be ascribed to the legislature as a whole.[67] This may often be true, and – where it is true – it precludes ulterior purposes from counting as application-intentions *of the legislature*. However, it may be that some ulterior purposes *can* be ascribed to the legislature. For example, members of the majority party might support a statute with the intention that doing so will increase the chances of their party winning the next election. Depending on one's theory of legislative intent, this intention may be ascribable to the legislature as a whole, since it is shared by a majority of legislators.[68]

An alternative basis for excluding ulterior purposes is that they cannot play the roles that it has been suggested that statutory purpose might play. For example, there is broad agreement that appeals to statutory purpose are permissible to help identify a statute's linguistic content.[69] Yet ulterior purposes do not provide reliable evidence of a statute's linguistic content. Those purposes are meant to be *hidden*, and so considering them is unlikely to shed light on what information the legislature intended to communicate to its audience by enacting the statute (information that it intended its audience to acquire, in part, by *recognising* its intention to communicate that information).

It is also relatively uncontroversial to suggest that appeals to statutory purpose are permissible to help fill gaps in the law where a statute's linguistic content is ambiguous or vague.[70] Yet it would not be appropriate to draw on ulterior purposes in this way. For example, a court cannot appeal to the Government's intention to get re-elected to help resolve indeterminacies in a statute, without the court becoming an agent in the Government's re-election campaign.

[66] See n 50 above and accompanying text.

[67] Soames (n 44) 250. He adds that, in any case, such purposes are irrelevant, but he offers no further argument for this claim.

[68] Soames may have in mind a different account of legislative intent, which does *not* support ascribing this intention to the legislature as a whole. If so, his argument for excluding ulterior purposes depends on that account of legislative intent being vindicated.

[69] This is accepted even by textualists such as Scalia: see Scalia and Garner (n 10) 20, 56. The relevance of a statute's purpose to identifying its linguistic content is often explained on the basis that the words of the statute must be understood in context, and the statute's purpose forms part of the context: see, eg, Scalia and Garner (n 10) 20; *Thiess* (n 5) at 672.

[70] Scalia and Garner (n 10) 56. Goldsworthy offers an interesting (but qualified) challenge to this consensus: Goldsworthy, 'Functions, Purposes and Values' (n 11) 52–54.

Finally, and more controversially, it has been suggested that statutory purpose can, in certain circumstances, provide a legitimate basis for departing from a statute's linguistic content.[71] Again, it would be inappropriate to appeal to ulterior purposes in this context. Whatever reasons there may be for departing from a statute's linguistic content, the fact that doing so would assist the Government to get re-elected cannot plausibly be said to be one of them.

Let us turn to a second constraint on which application-intentions count as part of the statutory purpose. An application-intention that is so narrow that it singles out a particular individual for favourable or unfavourable treatment is also precluded from being part of the statutory purpose. In the example of the tax statute in the previous section, this rules out application-intention #4 – namely, an intention to bring about a state of affairs in which company X obtains rebate Y.

Again, multiple arguments could be offered in support of this constraint. One might appeal to an understanding of the rule of law, according to which the value of legality requires governance via general rules, rather than particular orders (or, at least, requires that particular orders be made by reference to general rules).[72] Or one might appeal to a conception of the separation of powers, according to which the legislature has the power only to lay down general rules, not to dictate the particular instances to which those rules apply. Either of these views might be taken to support the conclusion that the legislature's intentions as to how its statutes will impact particular individuals are legally irrelevant.

A third constraint follows from the fact that we need a characterisation of statutory purpose according to which purpose could assist in resolving disputes about how to interpret statutory provisions. This, after all, is the point of appealing to statutory purpose, and so we want an understanding of the concept that is compatible with purpose playing this role.[73] This rules out certain very broad application-intentions. Appealing again to the example of the tax statute, application-intention #1 falls foul of this requirement. Knowing that the legislature intended to produce a state of affairs in which the common good is promoted is unlikely to assist in resolving interpretive disputes, given the abstractness of the concept of the common good and the many ways in which the common good can be promoted.[74]

[71] In fact, there is broad agreement on this point. The disagreement is about *when* purpose should play this role. Scalia and Garner suggest that it should do so only 'in the rare case of an obvious scrivener's error' (Scalia and Garner (n 10) 57). Goldsworthy is more permissive, while still maintaining that cases where it is permissible to depart from the statute's linguistic content represent the exception, rather than the rule: Goldsworthy, *Parliamentary Sovereignty* (n 2) 231, 243–47. (See also Ekins (n 23) 249–50; Soames (n 44) 252–53.) For a more liberal approach, see LL Fuller, 'Positivism and Fidelity to Law – A Reply to Professor Hart' (1958) 71 *Harvard Law Review* 630, 661–69 (though Fuller's position is complicated: he clearly believes that the role of statutory purpose often justifies departing from what Hart would regard as the core meaning of a term, but he appears to believe – I think mistakenly – that there is a tenable account of linguistic content according to which the role he ascribes to purpose can be understood as contributing to, rather than departing from, a statute's linguistic content).

[72] See, eg, LL Fuller, *The Morality of Law*, revised edn (New Haven, Yale University Press, 1964) 46–49; J Raz, 'The Rule of Law and Its Virtue' in *The Authority of Law*, 2nd edn (Oxford, Oxford University Press, 2009) 215–16.

[73] The requirement is not that the application-intention assists in resolving *every* interpretive dispute. That would be asking too much. Rather, it is that the application-intention assists in resolving *some* interpretive disputes. Those disputes must be ones that have actually arisen or could plausibly arise. That an application-intention assists in resolving some far-fetched interpretive dispute that is unlikely ever to arise is not enough to show that it can play the role(s) we might expect statutory purpose to play.

[74] This also suggests a response to an objection to my understanding of statutory purpose offered by Patrick Emerton. My approach involves distinguishing between communicative intentions (which constitute legislative intent) and application-intentions (a sub-set of which constitutes statutory purpose). Yet, the objection goes, that

(Recall that ulterior purposes have already been excluded from consideration. Thus, it cannot be argued that application-intention #1 is useful because it excludes such purposes.)

By contrast, application-intention #2 may not breach this constraint. Knowing that the aim of the statute is to promote a fair rate of corporate tax might assist in resolving some interpretive disputes, because it suggests a standard of fairness, rather than (say) economic efficiency.

This third constraint not only excludes application-intentions that are too broad, such as the intention to promote the common good, but also any application-intention whose content mirrors that of the legislature's communicative intention. Treating that application-intention as part of the statutory purpose would be redundant, since it will already have been taken into account when considering legislative intent.[75]

This may rule out application-intention #3, in the example of the tax statute discussed above. If, as seems likely, the legislature's communicative intention is to convey that companies of type X are eligible to claim tax rebate Y in circumstances Z, considering an application-intention to bring about a state of affairs in which companies of type X claim tax rebate Y in circumstances Z may not add anything to a consideration of the legislature's communicative intention.[76]

Earlier, I suggested four application-intentions the legislature might have with regard to the tax statute. We have now seen that #1 and #4, and quite possibly #3, breach the constraints on which application-intentions form part of the statutory purpose. Does it follow that the (only) purpose of the tax statute is application-intention #2 (ie to bring about a state of affairs in which a fair rate of corporate tax is paid)? Not necessarily. Application-intentions #1–4 can all be identified without knowing much about the context in which the tax statute was introduced or the goal(s) the legislature thought would be promoted by providing the rebate. Once we learn more about the context, we may discover that the legislature had further application-intentions that satisfy the constraints discussed above. For example, we might find that the legislature intended to bring about a state of affairs in which local manufacturers of certain goods are better placed to compete with overseas manufacturers.[77]

distinction is blurred if we characterise application-intentions as intentions to bring about a certain state of affairs. For example, one component of any communicative intention is an intention to bring about a state of affairs in which the intended audience has uptake of one's communicative intentions. However, even if this intention counts as an application-intention, it breaches the constraint discussed in the text, and so is not part of the statutory purpose. The intention to bring about a state of affairs in which the intended audience has uptake of one's communicative intentions is not the sort of intention that can assist in resolving real-life interpretive disputes.

More specific components of a communicative intention (eg the intention to communicate a specific content, X, by enacting the statute) will not fall foul of this constraint, and could also be characterised as application-intentions (eg the intention to bring about a state of affairs in which X is communicated). However, treating these intentions as part of the statutory purpose would be redundant, since they have already been taken into account when considering legislative intent.

[75] This constraint guarantees that statutory purpose will differ from legislative intent. Not only are they different types of intention (as discussed above), but any application-intention whose content mirrors that of the legislature's communicative intention is excluded from forming part of the statutory purpose.

[76] I put the point tentatively, because there is a subtle difference in the content of the two intentions. The communicative intention is to convey that a permission is granted (companies of type X are *permitted* to claim the rebate), whereas the application-intention is that companies of type X in fact claim the rebate. Perhaps the additional information conveyed by application-intention #3 means that it is not redundant.

[77] It may be that the state of affairs can be stated more specifically still (eg as one in which local manufacturers are better able to compete with overseas manufacturers *by offsetting certain costs that local manufacturers incur but overseas manufacturers do not*).

This further application-intention is neither so broad nor so narrow as to fall foul of the constraints discussed above, and differs sufficiently from the legislature's communicative intention that consideration of the application-intention could assist in resolving some of the interpretive disputes that are likely to arise with regard to the statute. It may therefore represent another aspect of the statutory purpose, alongside application-intention #2.

I have identified three relatively uncontroversial constraints on which application-intentions count as part of the statutory purpose. There may be more. Nevertheless, as the discussion in the previous paragraph suggests, sometimes more than one application-intention will satisfy these constraints. Again, this should not come as a surprise – it is a commonplace that a statute may have more than one purpose; that legislatures sometimes intend to achieve multiple things by enacting a statute (or a provision). However, it does mean that – once we turn to consider what role statutory purpose should play in the interpretation of legislation – we will need to say something about how this multiplicity of purposes is to be managed, especially in circumstances where the various application-intentions conflict.

While the existence of multiple application-intentions does raise problems, it also represents an opportunity. The multiplicity of legally relevant application-intentions potentially gives the concept of statutory purpose the flexibility necessary for it to assist in resolving a broad range of interpretive disputes.

iv. Disagreement about Application-Intentions

I shall finish by considering an important objection to my proposal that we should understand statutory purpose as a sub-set of the legislature's application-intentions. The objection is that there will often be widespread disagreement among legislators about what state of affairs the statute is meant to bring about, and hence we will not be able to attribute any application-intention to the legislature as a whole (or, at least, no application-intention that is not so abstract as to breach the third set of constraints discussed in the previous section).[78]

This objection should be distinguished from a more general scepticism about whether legislatures can have intentions. As I argued in section II.A., this general scepticism raises issues that extend well beyond our concern with understanding statutory purpose. Rather, the present objector argues that – while it may be possible for a legislature to have intentions – it is unlikely to have any *application-intentions*. Legislators may agree on the statutory text – perhaps they even share certain communicative intentions about that text and/or agree on what norms they intend the statute to contribute to the content of the law – but there is unlikely to be agreement about what change in the world they want the statute to bring about. Very often, the objector suggests, different legislators support a statute for different reasons, and this divergence in their reasons correlates to a divergence in the state of affairs they intend the statute to produce.[79] If this is right, understanding statutory purpose in terms of the legislature's application-intentions would be problematic, because it would follow that, very often, there is no statutory purpose.

[78] In a sense, this worry is the opposite of the one considered in section III.B.ii. – not that the legislature has too many application-intentions, but rather that it has too few.

[79] This is to be contrasted with cases where legislators intend the statute to bring about the same state of affairs, but desire that state of affairs for different reasons: see n 60 above.

One way of responding to this objection is to endorse a 'non-aggregative' account of legislative intent, according to which the legislature's intentions are not fixed by aggregating the intentions of some or all of the legislators.[80] On such an account, we may be able to ascribe an application-intention to the legislature even if there is widespread disagreement among legislators about what state of affairs the statute is meant to bring about.[81] Indeed, it may be that the legislature can have an application-intention that no individual legislator shares.

However, I do not want to rely on this response, because I wish to remain neutral about how intentions are to be ascribed to the legislature. Rather, I begin by pointing to two features of my account of statutory purpose that provide grounds for optimism that the existence of disagreement among legislators does not undermine that account (on any plausible theory of how intentions are to be ascribed to the legislature).

First, I need not maintain that every statute has a purpose. It may be that there are cases in which the objector is right – the disagreement among legislators is such that there is no state of affairs that the legislature as a whole intends to bring about. Provided this is not true in too many cases, I can allow that my account of statutory purpose entails that some statutes lack a purpose, while maintaining that it is compatible with purpose playing an important role in the interpretation of many other statutes.

Second, recall that there can be many different states of affairs that a statute is intended to bring about. All we need is sufficient agreement on *one* of these application-intentions in order to ascribe a purpose to the statute (provided that application-intention satisfies the constraints discussed in the previous section). Conversely, the objector needs to show that, for *each* of those intentions, there is too much disagreement among legislators for the legislature as a whole to hold the intention.

For example, where there is widespread disagreement among legislators about the specific state of affairs the statute is meant to bring about, it may be open to us to ascend the ladder of generality described in section III.B.ii. to find a purpose on which there *is* sufficient agreement. Admittedly, there may be some cases in which this purpose is too abstract to be useful. Indeed, in extreme cases, it may be that all the legislators agree on is that the statute should bring about a state of affairs in which the common good is promoted. However, on other occasions, there may be a more general characterisation of the statute's purpose that both attracts sufficient support from legislators and can assist in resolving some interpretive disputes.

Finally, it is worth challenging the suggestion that disagreement about application-intentions is typically rampant among legislators. While attention often focuses on controversial statutes, in most jurisdictions there are many statutes that are relatively uncontentious, at least among legislators.[82] If every statute was the subject of disagreement, horse-trading and ultimately compromise, it would be hard to see how modern legislatures could produce the enormous volume of legislation that most of them in fact produce. Where a statute

[80] For one such account, see Ekins (n 23).

[81] This will, however, depend on what conditions the account requires to be met for an intention to be ascribed to the legislature.

[82] Perhaps the United States is an exception; I leave that as an open question.

is relatively uncontentious, we might expect legislators to share quite specific application-intentions, which can then be attributed to the legislature as a whole.[83]

This suggests that we should be cautious in generalising about disagreement regarding application-intentions. In some cases, the statute may be uncontroversial, such that legislators share application-intentions with regard to it. In these cases, ascribing a purpose to the statute may be unproblematic. In other cases, legislators may diverge with regard to some application-intentions while sharing others. For example, they may differ in terms of the specific state of affairs they intend the statute to bring about, but share an intention to bring about a more general state of affairs. Or they may agree that the statute has a direct purpose, while disagreeing about whether it also has a further, indirect purpose. In these cases, there is still a statutory purpose, but it may be limited to the application-intention(s) on which legislators agree. Finally, there may be some cases in which disagreement is so rampant that we cannot ascribe any (useful) purpose to the statute at all.

IV. Conclusion

I have argued for a particular understanding of statutory purpose, according to which a statute's purpose consists of a sub-set of the legislature's application-intentions. An application-intention, in turn, is to be understood as an intention to bring about a certain state of affairs by enacting the statute. Understanding statutory purpose in this way avoids many of the problems that confront other understandings of the concept. I have also identified some of the constraints that determine *which* of the legislature's application-intentions constitute the statutory purpose.

My focus has been on what statutory purpose is. I have not sought to ascertain what role it does or should play in statutory interpretation. Unlike some other understandings of statutory purpose, the account I have offered is compatible with purpose playing a range of different roles. Whether it does or should play any or all of those roles is a matter for further enquiry. However, my hope is that obtaining a better understanding of the concept of statutory purpose leaves us better placed to undertake that enquiry.

[83] Alternatively, many legislators may be indifferent to the enactment of the statute, and hence not stand in the way of those legislators who seek to bring about its enactment. I do not believe that indifference of this sort precludes an intention being ascribed to the legislature as a whole, but I shall not argue for that claim here.

4

Statutory Meaning without Parliamentary Intention: Defending the High Court's 'Alternative Approach' to Statutory Interpretation

PATRICK EMERTON AND LISA BURTON CRAWFORD

In *Zheng v Cai*, a unanimous High Court of Australia said that:

> judicial findings as to legislative intention are an expression of the constitutional relationship between the arms of government with respect to the making, interpretation and application of laws. … the preferred construction by the court of the statute in question is reached by the application of rules of interpretation accepted by all arms of government in the system of representative democracy.[1]

In saying this, the Court endorsed an earlier explanation by French J, while a judge of the Federal Court, that 'legislative intention' does not:

> describe some antecedent mental state of the parliament, but … an attributed intention based on inferences drawn from the statute itself. … It operates as a persuasive declaration or an acceptance that the interpretation adopted is legitimate in a representative democracy characterised by parliamentary supremacy and the rule of law. … Where the words expressed by Parliament are interpreted by the Court according to commonly understood rules of interpretation a court is entitled to make the normative statement that it has interpreted them in accordance with the legislative intention.[2]

Subsequently in *Plaintiff S10/2011 v Minister for Immigration*, the plurality stated:

> The principles and presumptions of statutory construction which are applied by Australian courts, to the extent to which they are not qualified or displaced by an applicable interpretation Act, are part of the common law. In Australia, they are the product of what in *Zheng v Cai* was identified as the interaction between the three branches of government established by the *Constitution*.

[1] *Zheng v Cai* (2009) 239 CLR 446, 445–46 [28] (French CJ, Gummow, Crennan, Kiefel and Bell JJ).

[2] *NAAV v Minister for Immigration and Multicultural and Indigenous Affairs* ('*NAAV*') (2002) 123 FCR 298, 411–12 (French J). Other instances where this passage has been endorsed by the High Court include: *Certain Lloyd's Underwriters v Cross* (2012) 248 CLR 378, 389–90 [25]; *Momcilovic v The Queen* (2011) 245 CLR 1, 44–45 [38] (French CJ), 85 [146] (Gummow J); *Lacey v Attorney-General (Qld)* (2011) 242 CLR 573, 592 [43]–[44].

> These principles and presumptions do not have the rigidity of constitutionally prescribed norms, as is indicated by the operation of interpretation statutes, but they do reflect the operation of the constitutional structure in the sense described above.[3]

These judicial pronouncements set out an approach to statutory interpretation – what we call the *alternative approach* – that appears to contradict the long-held view, in the United Kingdom and Australia, that statutes should be interpreted in such a way as to give effect to the intentions of the Parliament that enacted them.[4] As Ekins and Goldsworthy explain:

> For at least six centuries, common law courts have maintained that the primary object of statutory interpretation 'is to determine what intention is conveyed either expressly or by implication by the language used', or in other words, 'to give effect to the intention of the [lawmaker] as that intention is to be gathered from the language employed having regard to the context in connection with which it is employed'. This has often been described as 'the only rule', 'the paramount rule', 'the cardinal rule' or 'the fundamental rule of interpretation, to which all others are subordinate'. In the leading case of *Cooper Brookes*, Mason and Wilson JJ said: '[t]he fundamental object of statutory construction in every case is to ascertain the legislative intention … The rules [of interpretation] … are no more than rules of common sense, designed to achieve this object'. Likewise, Gleeson CJ has said that 'the object of a court is to ascertain and give effect to, the will of Parliament'. It follows that '[j]udicial exposition of the meaning of a statutory text is legitimate so long as it is an exercise … in discovering the will of Parliament: it is illegitimate when it is an exercise in imposing the will of the judge'. The proposition that the will or intention of Parliament is the object of interpretation has been affirmed in leading cases and textbooks on statutory interpretation in England, Australia, Canada and the United States for ages (literally).[5]

Ekins and Goldsworthy insist that the alternative approach to statutory interpretation advocated by many members of the High Court is flawed, because parliamentary intention is both *real* and *indispensable* to the process of statutory interpretation, and because the contrary view is illogical, undemocratic, and strains the constitutional distribution of powers between the legislative and judicial branch.[6]

In this chapter, we examine whether legislative intention is indispensable to the interpretive process, as Ekins and Goldsworthy argue. We then turn to consider the merits of the alternative approach, and in particular the suggestion that the principles of statutory interpretation somehow reflect the constitutional distribution of powers, especially as between Parliament and the courts. We argue that the meaning of a statute can be ascertained without having to ascertain the sort of intention, on the part of the Parliament that enacted it, that Ekins and Goldsworthy argue for. While much about the alternative approach itself remains uncertain, we indicate some tenable bases on which it might be said that the principles of statutory interpretation are grounded in the constitutional structure. Our argument draws upon general considerations from the philosophy of language, together with distinctive

[3] *Plaintiff S10/2011 v Minister for Immigration and Citizenship* (2012) 246 CLR 636, 666 [97] (Gummow, Hayne, Crennan and Bell JJ).

[4] Though see J Blaker, who argues that Australia's courts have never embraced intentionalism: 'Is Intentionalist Theory Indispensable to Statutory Interpretation?' (2017) 43(1) *Monash University Law Review* 238.

[5] R Ekins and J Goldsworthy, 'The Reality and Indispensability of Legislative Intentions' (2014) 36 *Sydney Law Review* 39, 39–40 (citations omitted).

[6] See especially Ekins and Goldsworthy, ibid; Richard Ekins, *The Nature of Legislative Intent* (Oxford, Oxford University Press, 2013).

features of the Australian constitutional order. The chapter thereby provides a theoretically-grounded reconstruction and a partial defence of the alternative approach, which to date remains under-theorised.[7]

I. Dispensing with Legislative Intention

The origins and evolution of the alternative approach are charted in detail by Blaker,[8] who describes it as a form of 'textualism'.[9] We prefer to call it 'legalism', for it is broadly similar to the favoured approach for construing Australia's written *Constitution*.[10] It obviously emphasises the text of the statute itself, but also a set of interpretative principles said to be grounded in the constitutional structure.

The alternative approach appears to involve three, interrelated claims. This section considers its approach to legislative intention; the following section considers its connection to the *Constitution*.

A. Legislative Intention is Not Real

The first and perhaps most striking claim of the alternative approach is that legislative intention is a 'fiction'.[11] At its strongest, this is the claim that it is impossible for a group, such as Parliament, to form a mental state. As Gageler J has said (extra-curially):

> The legislature, of course, is a legislative body following a legislative process. The legislature has no psychological state of mind. The intention of the legislature is not the psychological state of mind of any one or more legislators. The intention of the legislature is an objective construct – an attributed or imputed characteristic.[12]

[7] In this chapter we do not consider the extent to which the process of statutory interpretation might depart from that of ascertaining the meaning of a statute. For a critical discussion of this issue in the Australian context, see Dale Smith, 'Is the High Court Mistaken about the Aim of Statutory Interpretation?' (2016) 44(2) *Federal Law Review* 227.

[8] Blaker (n 4). Note also Gageler J's (extra-curial) suggestion that the reappraisal of the nature of parliamentary intention and the object of statutory interpretation was prompted by the enactment of laws that permitted courts to consider extrinsic materials such as second reading speeches: S Gageler, 'Legislative Intention' (2015) 41(1) *Monash University Law Review* 1, 7.

[9] Blaker (n 4) 239–40.

[10] J Goldsworthy, 'Devotion to Legalism' in J Goldsworthy (ed), *Interpreting Constitutions: A Comparative Study* (Oxford, Oxford University Press, 2007) 106.

[11] *Mills v Meeking* (1990) 169 CLR 214, 234 (Dawson J); *Corporate Affairs Commission (NSW) v Yuill* (1991) 172 CLR 319, 339 (Gaudron J), 345–46 (McHugh J); *R v Hughes* (2000) 202 CLR 535, 563 [60] (Kirby J). As Ekins and Goldsworthy explain, '[t]his judicial skepticism was preceded by, and is elaborated at length in, the jurisprudential literature': above n 5, 63. For examples, some of which are cited by Ekins and Goldsworthy, see M Radin, 'Statutory Interpretation' (1930) 43 *Harvard Law Review* 863, 869–72; CR Sunstein, 'Interpreting Statutes in the Regulatory State' (1989) 103(2) *Harvard Law Review* 405, 433; WN Eskridge, Jr, 'The New Textualism' (1990) 37 *UCLA Law Review* 621, 641–45, 666–67; JF Manning, 'Textualism and Legislative Intent' (2005) 91 *Virginia Law Review* 419, 428–34, 450; JF Manning, 'Without The Pretense Of Legislative Intent' (2017) 130 *Harvard Law Review* 2397, 2399–400; R Dworkin, *Law's Empire* (Oxford, Hart Publishing, 1998); J Waldron, *Law and Disagreement* (New York, Oxford University Press, 1999).

[12] Gageler (n 8) 7.

Hayne J has made (extra-curially) a similar but more nuanced claim:

> If a legislature had thoughts, it could utter words with the intention of expressing those thoughts. If an utterance of the legislature were ambiguous, one could look to facts bearing on the legislature's intention to express a thought in order to resolve that ambiguity. *But legislatures do not have thoughts.* If they have intentions, they are seldom intentions of sufficient granularity to disambiguate words in a provision. They might be intentions as to goal, or means, or purpose, but they will not be intentions of the kind a speaker has when uttering a sentence (namely, an intention to utter a thought).[13]

Speaking specifically of Parliament, Gummow J has said:

> The difficulty has been in ascertaining the intention of Parliament rather than in giving effect to it when it is known. Indeed, as everyone knows, the intention of Parliament is somewhat of a fiction. Individual members of Parliament, or even the government, do not necessarily mean the same thing by voting on a Bill or, in some cases, anything at all.[14]

And similarly, that 'statute law may be the result of a compromise between contending factions and interest groups and of accommodations between and within political organisations which are not made public and cannot readily be made apparent to a court'.[15]

There is a lack of clarity in Gummow J's remarks, as to whether the problem is metaphysical (as Hayne and Gageler JJ present it) or rather epistemological: is it that Parliament *has no* intentions, or that the court cannot reliably ascertain them? A further complication in making sense of the High Court's scepticism about legislative intention is that the Court has been less dismissive of other legally-relevant collective intentions. For instance, the Court has expressly contrasted 'the intention of the legislature', which is concerned with 'examination by the judicial branch of government of the subject, scope and purpose of the text enacted by the legislature', with the intention of a private collective actor.[16] When asking whether such an actor – in the case at hand, a church incorporated as a not-for-profit association[17] – had made a payment to a person intending to benefit the recipient of the payment, or rather a tortfeasor who was liable to her, the Court did not express any doubts about the reality of the intention in question.[18] The High Court's particular scepticism towards the possibility of *Parliament* forming a relevant and ascertainable intention that would inform the process of statutory interpretation suggests, therefore, that the alternative approach is driven to a significant extent by constitutional considerations.

Ekins has defended the reality of legislative intentions at length, and in their joint article Ekins and Goldsworthy reiterate the main points of this defence. Ekins argues that 'legislative intent is what is proposed for legislative action', which is 'the plan that the statute as enacted is to set out for the community'.[19] Ekins and Goldsworthy are well aware of the problems surrounding attributions of intentions to collectives, both in general and as an aspect of the theory of statutory interpretation,[20] but respond to them by showing that

[13] K Hayne, 'Statutes, Intentions and the Courts: What Place Does the Notion of Intention (Legislative or Parliamentary) Have in Statutory Construction?' (2013) 13(2) *Oxford Commonwealth Law Journal* 271, 277.

[14] *Mills v Meeking* (n 11), 234.

[15] *Wik Peoples v Queensland* (1996) 187 CLR 1, 168–69.

[16] *Zheng v Cai* (n 1) 455 [27].

[17] *Zheng v Cai* (n 1) 451 [5].

[18] *Zheng v Cai* (n 1) 453–55 [18]–[27].

[19] Ekins (n 6) 230–31.

[20] See the discussion in Ekins and Goldsworthy (n 5) 62–64.

'the legislature is a complex purposive group – an institution – that forms and acts on intentions, which arise from but are not reducible to the intentions of the members of the group (the individual legislators)'[21] and which therefore is able 'to choose to change the law in some reasoned way'.[22]

The difficulty this argument faces is that its account of the intentions of legislatures, as group agents, is far too thin to do the work that a theory of interpretation requires. Ekins and Goldsworthy point to the legislature's intention (constituted by the common intentions of its members) to make law and change the law by following certain institutional procedures.[23] However, when it comes to identifying the intention with which a particular piece of legislation is enacted, Ekins and Goldsworthy have relatively little to say:

> The Bill is a proposal for legislative action because it is a plan to change the law. It is a detailed text, setting out how the law will change if it is enacted. One finds the legislative intention in the plan that coordinates legislators, which explains their joint action. The detail of the proposal is the focal point for argument and action. …
>
> In enacting a statute, the legislature promulgates (utters) a statutory text that makes clear to the community at large how it – the legislature – has chosen to change the law. … [T]he text embodies the legislature's primary plans, or intentions. It need not matter if a plan embodies some compromise between contending policies: legislators must have believed there were good reasons to compromise, and the nature of their compromise may be discernible from the text and publicly available contextual and purposive evidence. …
>
> This plan is what the legislature as a whole is reasonably taken to have intended, due to the supporting structure of interlocking individual intentions that constitute the legislature's secondary or standing intentions.[24]

This tells us that the legislators have common intentions to enact statutory text embodying a plan. Because the legislators have these common intentions, it furthermore tells us that the legislature, as a group agent, has such intentions. It tells us, further, that the legislators may have, on occasion at least, a common intention to give effect to a compromise in doing so; and that this may be knowable. But to point out that the legislators have, and in virtue of their institutional location are capable of exercising, a collective intention to legislate, and that on such-and-such an occasion did so, does not, in itself, vindicate a role for legislative intention in ascertaining the meaning of a statute. We may know that the legislature intended to produce a statutory text embodying a plan – ie that the legislature intended to legislate – but knowledge that the legislature intended to do this does not tell us what their promulgated text means nor what the plan is that it embodies.

Ekins and Goldsworthy make the following further remarks about the place of intention in interpretation:

> When interpreters read that statutory text, in the rich context of enactment, it makes good sense for them to strive to infer, from the publicly available evidence, the plan that the legislature has

[21] Ekins and Goldsworthy (n 5) 64.

[22] Ekins and Goldsworthy (n 5) 63.

[23] Ekins and Goldsworthy (n 5) 65–66. Their further claim that the legislature of necessity stands ready to do this 'for good reasons' and 'for the common good' (at 65) is unargued and implausible. For instance, the capture of a legislature by a particular class or caste determined to act in its own self-interest – whether or not it *purports* to act for the common good – would not render the legislature some other sort of institution. See also below n 26.

[24] Ekins and Goldsworthy (n 5) 65–67.

> chosen to enact. … Communication through the medium of a natural language generally and necessarily relies on the ability of its intended audience to infer the speaker's intended meaning from contextual as well as textual clues. …
>
> Hence, when reasonable legislators vote for or against a Bill, they understand what is before them not to be a text with a sparse literal meaning, but a complex and reasoned plan to pursue particular means to achieve certain ends.[25]

But this does not take things any further. Intentions to *enact a text with meaning going beyond the sparsely literal on the basis of contextual clues*, perhaps also *on the basis of a compromise*, do not amount to intentions to enact any particular meaning. And Ekins and Goldsworthy have nothing more to say about the particularity of meaning than that it is to be inferred by reference to context and purpose.[26] Indeed, on their account *even the legislators* who constitute the group agent cannot ascertain what it is that their collectively enacted text meant except by undertaking the same reasoning process as an interpreter:

> when they [ie individual legislators] vote for or against it, they vote for or against not only the text, but the plan that the text has been designed by their colleagues to communicate. The plan is 'open' to them, in that they could learn more about it if they wanted to, by using much the same methods as subsequent interpreters, who infer the plan from its text and publicly available contextual evidence of its purpose.[27]

So far from being an account of an actual group intention – 'the interlocking intentions of individuals' constituting 'a plan of action that [the group's] members adopt'[28] – when it comes to the details of legislative content we are given nothing but an inferential posit. Ekins and Goldsworthy characterise the alternative approach in the following terms:

> legislative intention is not something that exists before judicial interpretation, but instead, is a product or construct of interpretation; or in other words, that it is not the object that the process of statutory interpretation aims to discover, but rather is whatever that process produces.[29]

For the reasons just given, their account of the legislative intentions *that might yield the meaning of a particular statute* – as opposed to those intentions that constitute the legislative process – seem no different. Indeed, even Goldsworthy has noted that an account of the sort he and Ekins advocate may not satisfactorily explain why the content of a bill – then Act – is 'richer than the text that embodies it'.[30]

At this point we set aside the question of whether legislative intentions are real and turn to the question of whether or not they are (as Ekins and Goldsworthy claim) indispensable.

[25] Ekins and Goldsworthy (n 5) 65–67. Footnotes, referring to Ekins (n 6), have been omitted.

[26] We disregard the reference to *reasonable* legislators. No explanation is given of the relationship between what reasonable legislators would do and the intentions of any actual legislators; and earlier in their paper Ekins and Goldsworthy eschew interpretive appeals to *reasonable legislatures* on the ground that this is equivalent to what the interpreter 'think[s] the legislature *ought* to have intended': above n 5, 49.

[27] Ekins and Goldsworthy (n 5) 67.

[28] Ekins and Goldsworthy (n 5) 64.

[29] Ekins and Goldsworthy (n 5) 41.

[30] J Goldsworthy, 'Legislative Intention Vindicated?' (2013) 33 *Oxford Journal of Legal Studies* 821, 828.

B. Legislative Intention is Dispensable

In the preceding discussion we distinguished two classes of legislative intention: intentions to legislate, and intentions to enact a particular statutory text having a particular meaning. If we consider the first such class of intentions, it is worth noting that the adherent of the alternative approach need not concede the sort of connection between intention and legislative process that Ekins and Goldsworthy argue for. Consider the following passage from Radin:

> What gives the intention of the legislature obligating force? In theology or in literature, that question answers itself; but in law, the specific individuals who make up the legislature are men to whom a specialized function has been temporarily assigned. That function is not to impose their will even within limits on their fellow-citizens, but to 'pass statutes,' which is a fairly precise operation. That is, they make statements in general terms of undesirable and desirable situations, from which flow certain results. As a rule, the statements must be made in the words of a specified language. A statute made in Latin at the present time is no statute, although the intention of the legislature can be as well or as ill made out from Latin as from English. A statute which presented a photograph of two automobiles and printed the legend beneath it that drivers who get into the situation pictured above would be prosecuted would not be a statute, although intention would be no less easily, and perhaps more easily, discoverable in this way than in set words. When the legislature has uttered the words of a statute, it is *functus officio*, not because of the Montesquieuan separation of powers, but because that is what legislating means.[31]

Although Radin eschews reliance upon one (Montesquieuan) set of constitutional notions, he relies upon another, namely, *what is involved in legislating*. We will return in more detail below to the place of constitutional considerations in the alternative approach, but at this point – and consistently with the suggestion in the preceding discussion that the alternative approach's scepticism about legislative intention is grounded in constitutional as much as metaphysical considerations – we can see that in order to understand that the texts enacted by parliaments are *laws*, or, in Ekins and Goldsworthy's terms, *plans* of a certain sort, we do not need to rely upon the actual intention of the Parliament, nor the actual intentions of its members. In virtue of the constitutional role of the Parliament as an institution, its enactments are necessarily to be taken as such – at least by an interpreting court, which has no standing to go behind this constitutional prescription.[32]

[31] Radin (n 11) 871.

[32] In this context, therefore, it is in fact not necessary, if we are to treat legislative text *as* text, that anyone has had the intention of producing it as a meaning-bearing text: *cf* L Alexander and S Prakash, '"Is That English You're Speaking?" Why Intention Free Interpretation is an Impossibility' (2004) 41 *San Diego Law Review* 967, 976–77. That is not to say that some very minimal collective intentions may not be necessary to constitute an assemblage of persons as a meeting of the legislature, but those intentions would be notably thinner than the ones that Ekins and Goldsworthy and Alexander and Prakash point to. It is also worth noting that, while it may be the case that legislatures in Australia have a (collective) intention to legislate in English, this could equally be regarded as an intention-independent constitutional principle, such that Australian legislation will be *taken* to be enacted in English whatever the intention (collective or otherwise) of legislators: *cf* Alexander and Prakash, ibid, 974–75. This also answers their remarks about scrivener's errors (at 979–81; see also similar doubts expressed by Manning (n 11) 425 fn 22), which can be corrected not by reference to subjective intentions, but by reference to an institutionally-mandated requirement that the statute be treated as a coherent whole.

But what about the meaning of an individual statute? The second key claim of the alternative approach is that the meaning of a statute can be ascertained without ascertaining the intention of the Parliament that enacted it. As Hayne J wrote (extra-curially):

> a speaker's or author's intentions may bear on – but not necessarily determine – the meaning of the utterance. It by no means follows, however, that a text or utterance has no meaning, or cannot be understood, if it is not interpreted according to someone's actual intention. That is, it does not follow that statutes must be construed by reference to, let alone in accordance with, an understanding of an author's intention or the 'intention' of a group (whether designated as authors or not). Expressions in a language have a conventional significance – that is, a significance independent of what the speaker or author means by the expression. To claim that, absent an identifiable intention, an utterance or text is meaningless is to misunderstand the conventional nature of language.[33]

Goldsworthy is not ignorant of the fact that linguistic items convey conventional meanings. But he argues that, if there is really no such thing as legislative intention, 'then parliaments could only enact bare texts, with very sparse literal meanings, prone to ambiguity, vagueness and gaps, and shorn of presuppositions and other implications.'[34]

But as we all know, statutes are not treated as 'bare texts'. They are construed having regard to context and purpose, and in light of a rich set of interpretive principles, most of which have been established for some time. Ekins and Goldsworthy appeal to the role these considerations play in the process of statutory interpretation to advance their claim of indispensability.[35]

Turning first to the principles of statutory interpretation, Ekins and Goldsworthy argue that these principles simply do not make sense if they are untethered from parliamentary intention, because these canons have always been understood as heuristics for ascertaining that intention.[36] On this view, if regard is not had to parliamentary intention, there is nothing to explain why these principles exist, to anchor their content, or to prevent their unfettered evolution in a way that thwarts the exercise of legislative power, for:

> without any conviction that the interpretive process is anchored by actual legislative intentions, the courts would constantly be tempted to change the principles, and even if change were a gradual

[33] Hayne (n 13) 277–78.

[34] J Goldsworthy, 'Is Legislative Supremacy under Threat?' (2016) 60(11) *Quadrant* 56, 60. The concept of 'literal meaning' is itself ambiguous. Thus, Goldsworthy sometimes writes as if idiomatic phrases do not carry their literal meaning (see, eg, the discussion of 'peace, order and good government' in J Goldsworthy, 'Interpreting the Constitution in Its Second Century' (2000) 24 *Melbourne University Law Review* 677, 681) but clearly these idioms are conventionally-established and are no more dependent upon speaker intentions to convey their meaning than are any other words and phrases.

[35] Ekins and Goldsworthy (n 5) offer a further reason in favour of the indispensability of legislative intention (reason C at 53), but it can very quickly be put aside: they point to the familiar phenomenon of statutes themselves referring to their *intended* effects (eg a Commonwealth statute that states of itself that it is not intended to limit the operation of any consistent or complementary State law), and say that such statutory language places a sceptic about legislative intentions 'in the same predicament as someone attempting to make sense of a statutory reference to unicorns'. In fact it puts the sceptic about intentions in the same predicament as the atheist who nevertheless says 'Bless you' when someone sneezes: one can use a figure of speech without being committed to a literal understanding of it. For instance, 'is not intended to limit' can easily be treated as a figure of speech for *is not to be taken as limiting*, and similarly for other such statutory occurrences of references to legislative intentions.

[36] Ekins and Goldsworthy (n 5) 54. Although they also allow for the operation of principles of rectification, they suggest that these may also be attributed to 'a more general, standing intention that the courts should intervene in this way to save [the legislature] from its errors' (at 61). Gageler charts the case law that explained the principles as interpretive heuristics in 'Legislative Intention', above n 8, especially at 3–4.

> process, the end result might be a new set of principles that departed more or less drastically from what Parliament has obviously chosen or decided.[37]

They cite the principle of legality – which has ostensibly evolved from a heuristic for ascertaining Parliament's intention to a kind of 'manner and form requirement' for limiting statutory encroachment upon common law rights and privileges – as a possible example.[38]

We accept, as Goldsworthy and Ekins state,[39] that the act of legislating is in some sense a communicative act, and we accept that it employs natural, human language. However, we argue that the act of legislating is a very different communicative act from that of writing a letter, or speaking to a friend, or even making a private legal instrument (like a contract). Rather, our account emphasises that the act of legislating, unlike other communicative acts, is an exercise of public power conferred (in Australia) by the *Australian Constitution*. Hence, the act of interpreting legislation is not governed by the same principles that would apply to other forms of communication. The meaning of the texts that Parliament enacts is informed by the nature of Parliament as an institution, established by a constitution that distributes power between legislative, executive and judicial branches of government. We take up this issue in section II below, where we argue, consistently with the High Court in its articulation of the alternative approach, that – at least within the Australian constitutional context – the principles of interpretation must be understood as grounded in the *Constitution* itself.[40]

Secondly, Ekins and Goldsworthy emphasise the importance of *purpose* to statutory interpretation,[41] particularly in circumstances where legislative purpose is used to justify a non-literal or non-pedantic application of a statutory rule.[42] An example that they give is of a statute that 'prohibited the sale of "any food intended for, but unfit for, human consumption"'. This was applied to the sale of caustic soda to children who had asked for lemonade, even though caustic soda is not, literally, food.[43] And purpose, they say, 'is surely a kind of intention'.[44] They make a similar appeal to intention as being the basis for resolving ambiguities and correcting drafting errors in statutory language,[45] and they say that *context* as a source of interpretative guidance only makes sense 'because information about the circumstances in which a statement was made illuminates the intentions or purposes of the speaker or writer'.[46] Indeed, they argue that inexplicit content, such as ellipses, tacit assumptions and deliberate implications, cannot be explained – as a matter of linguistic theory – except by appeal to intentions.[47]

[37] Ekins and Goldsworthy (n 5) 44. We put to one side the seemingly question-begging nature of this objection (ie in assuming that Parliament is able to choose or decide upon principles to guide the interpretation of its enactments).

[38] Ekins and Goldsworthy (n 5) 44.

[39] Ekins and Goldsworthy (n 5) 44–45, 47, 51–54, 58, 66–67.

[40] As this suggests, our focus is on federal legislation in the Australian context, and we do not seek to show that this approach would be legitimate in other jurisdictions, though we have made some comment on its potential application in other legal systems elsewhere: P Emerton and L Burton Crawford, 'Parliament, the People and Interpreting the Law: *Miller v Secretary of State for the European Union*' (2017) 35(2) *University of Queensland Law Journal* 331.

[41] Ekins and Goldsworthy (n 5) 57–58.

[42] Ekins and Goldsworthy (n 5) 51–53.

[43] Ekins and Goldsworthy (n 5) 52.

[44] Ekins and Goldsworthy (n 5) 57.

[45] Ekins and Goldsworthy (n 5) 53–54.

[46] Ekins and Goldsworthy (n 5) 58.

[47] Ekins and Goldsworthy (n 5) 54–57.

We do not dispute that purpose and context are important to interpretation in the ways that Ekins and Goldsworthy point to. However, the claim that one cannot make sense of statutory purpose or statutory context except by reference to the subjective mental states of authors is not correct.[48] In the remainder of this sub-section we explain why that claim need not be true *in general*. Then, in section II, we explain why it is not true as far as the interpretation of statutes within the Australian constitutional context is concerned.

Ekins and Goldsworthy say that 'statutes – like other inanimate objects – do not have purposes; only the people who make or use them do'.[49] They further claim that:

> if a statute was 'designed to serve or achieve' some purpose or object, then some person or people designed it to do this, and they could have had such a design only by having certain subjective intentions … It therefore cannot be a purpose or object that is merely 'imputed' to the statute by operation of law.[50]

But this is wrong, both in general and in the context of linguistic productions. Inanimate objects can have purposes – for instance, a knife, everything else being equal, has the purpose (or function) of cutting. It may be that the knife's function is itself a consequence of its being built by someone having an appropriate intention – this paper will not discuss the metaphysics of artefacts, nor complexities that might arise when (say) the knife is built within a fully automated factory, or when someone tricks someone else into building something. Nevertheless, the knife has a purpose.

Gageler J has expressed doubt (extra-curially) about the attribution of purposes to artefacts:

> The same razor can have the objective purpose of shaving a beard, sharpening a pencil or slitting a throat. The same nylon rope might have the objective purpose of tying down a load or serving as a line for the hanging of washing. Does it also have the objective purpose of bungee jumping? To find out, it might be prudent to check the manufacturer's specifications. The information contained in those specifications is unlikely to be thought unreliable merely because the manufacturer is an organisation and merely because the specifications were written by a group of individuals within that organisation.[51]

The manufacturer's specifications, however, do not tell us what anyone's subjective mental state was. Rather, they tell us more about the properties of the artefact – for example,

[48] Although Ekins and Goldsworthy emphasise what they call *objective* legislative intentions, they contend that 'objective intentions are necessarily dependent on subjective intentions': Ekins and Goldsworthy (n 5) 46. There is some ambiguity, which we do not pursue further, over whether they treat objective intentions as an epistemic guide or constraint in relation to the ascertainment of subjective intentions, or whether they treat objective intentions – which of course are not *actual* mental states at all – as constitutive of legislative intentions, with the idea of subjective intentions then playing a type of regulative role in the construction of objective intentions out of the available evidence. See also below, text to n 61 and the paragraphs that follow.

[49] Ekins and Goldsworthy (n 5) 57.

[50] Ekins and Goldsworthy (n 5) 58. The quoted phrase is from the judgment of Deane J in *Richardson v Forestry Commission* (1988) 164 CLR 261, 311. Interestingly, Deane J referred to 'the purpose or object … which [the law] *can be seen* to be designed to serve or achieve' (emphasis added). The contrast between actual intentions and inferences to intentions that may or may not really exist, which Deane J appears to be aware of but which is elided by Ekins and Goldsworthy will be discussed in the next section.

[51] Gageler (n 8) 11.

what is the load-bearing capacity of the nylon rope? This additional information may help clarify the artefact's purpose(s). Its availability does not show that the artefact lacks a purpose.

Texts, too, can have purposes that are independent of the mental states of those who created them. Consider, for instance, a sign on the inside of an Australian hotel room door that contains, as its first words, the large, bolded phrase 'IN THE EVENT OF FIRE'. The position of the sign, and its typography, suggest something like a warning, but concerning what? After all, stripped of context, the words – taken as words of English – are ambiguous: they might be a warning about what to do in the event of coming under artillery, missile or small arms fire. But, when encountered in the context of a hotel room, one does not need to read on to the smaller print that begins 'If you think a fire has broken out …' in order to recognise that the sign contains instructions about what to do in the event of a fire breaking out in the hotel. It seems quite uncontentious to say that the purpose of the sign is to tell the room occupant, by way of English language instructions, what to do in the event of a fire. But need any person have the purpose of telling the occupant this? The maker of the sign need not have – for all we know the sign might have been produced in a sign factory staffed by illiterates, or by people who cannot read or write English. And the designer of the sign may not have had any intention to tell anyone of anything – it would make no difference to the purpose of the sign, for instance, if the original designer had thought that the whole thing was for use as a demonstration model to explain to graphic design students how to design evacuation instruction signs for hotel rooms. The person who fixed the sign to the door may not, and need not, have known what the sign was for. That person may have acted under instructions, but no single instructor need have had the salient purpose either: for instance, one person may have ordered a host of warning signs with the purpose of satisfying a regulatory requirement, while another person directed that they be placed in the room without having any regard to what they actually said. (We might even think that part of what characterises a well-functioning organisation, such as the hotel administration in our example, is that it is capable of ensuring that signs having the purpose of instructing occupants on what to do if a fire breaks out can be appropriately placed in the rooms, even if no person has the purpose of providing any such warning or instruction.)

The sign serves its purpose not because of the subjective intentions of anyone involved in its design, manufacture or placement, but because the occupant of the room in which it is found is entitled – given the context – to impute certain intentions to the (purely notional) author of its words, namely, the intention to use the phrase *in the event of* in its ordinary English sense, and the intention to use the word *fire* to refer to a *building fire* (as opposed to *artillery, missile or small arms fire*). Imputing those intentions is part and parcel of recognising the sign's purpose, and is licensed by familiarity not with anyone's mental states, but with the world, and the things in the world the words (so interpreted) refer to: in particular, by the knowledge that buildings are vulnerable to fire, and that when they catch fire the people inside them can die, particularly if they are in a multi-floor building with which they are not very familiar, and hence that the topic is something worth giving instructions about. That same knowledge lets the occupant know that the warning sign has no relevance to (say) the lighting of a match in the hotel room, because this does not pose the salient danger; and likewise lets the occupant know that the phrase 'if you think a fire has broken out' should not be treated literally, or, at least, not pedantically exhaustively. Thus, the instructions would be equally applicable if the occupant thought that a fire had not so much *broken out* as *been lit*.[52]

To see another way in which meaning arises independently of subjective mental states, consider section 92 of the *Australian Constitution*, which provides that 'trade, commerce, and intercourse among the States … shall be absolutely free'. *From what* does this provision establish the *absolute freedom* of interstate trade, commerce and intercourse?[53] This is a question about the reference of the phrase *absolutely free*. And that question cannot be answered simply by inspecting the subjective mental states of the *Constitution*'s authors: they were not coining new language and new usages, after all, but using language with a long prior tradition of use, including in relation to trade policy; and in any event their mental states may simply have been incomplete – for instance, they may have been advocates of free trade without having any very strong technical grasp of what sorts of burdens free trade is free from. Ekins and Goldsworthy implicitly concede this latter point in their discussion of the following example:

> [I]f I order a hamburger in a restaurant, and carefully list all the ingredients I want, I do not think it necessary to specify that they should be fresh and edible, the meat cooked, and so on. If I thought about this at all, I would expect it to be taken for granted.[54]

The tell-tale phrase is 'if I thought about this at all'. That is to say, my request for a hamburger in the circumstances described would be a request for one that is edible and so on regardless of my individual subjective intentions. It is not the presence or absence of a certain mental state that determines the reference of the words that I use to make the order (ie that 'meat'

[52] Larry Alexander and Saikrishna Prakash argue that 'even the most ardent textualists make assumptions about context' and hence 'are closet intentionalists because they make certain assumptions about the text that are not based solely on the text': 'Mother May I? Imposing Mandatory Prospective Rules of Statutory Interpretation' (2003) 20 *Constitutional Commentary* 97, 101 fn 9; and see also Alexander and Prakash (n 32) 979, where they argue that 'context is universally regarded as relevant only because it is evidence of authorial intent'. As the discussion in the text shows, there is no need to appeal to subjective authorial intentions in order to ground interpretive assumptions relying upon context. William N Eskridge, Jr and Philip P Frickey point to the need to have regard to context in interpreting statutes as an objection to textualism: 'Statutory Interpretation as Practical Reasoning' (1990) 42 *Stanford Law Review* 321, 341–43. The need to have regard to context is unarguable; our point is simply that having regard to context does not mean seeking out subjective intentions of authors. Manning, 'Textualism and Legislative Intent' (n 11) makes a similar point (at 434):

> Legislative intent, to the extent textualists invoke it, is a framework of analysis designed to satisfy the minimum conditions for meaningful communication by a multi-member body without actual intentions to judges, administrators, and the public, who all form a community of shared conventions for decoding language in context.

However, Manning then goes on to emphasise shared assumptions, understandings and practices in the use of words (at 434–38), whereas we emphasise understanding of the reference of the statutory text. A recent plurality High Court judgment seems to make a point similar to ours:

> [C]ommon law principles which inform the construction of statutes conferring decision-making authority … are not derived by logic alone and cannot be treated as abstractions disconnected from the subject matter to which they are to be applied. They are not so delicate or refined in their operation that sight is lost of the fact that 'decision-making is a function of the real world'.

Hossain v Minister for Immigration and Border Protection [2018] HCA 34 [28] (citation omitted). We would emphasise that, on the alternative approach to interpretation, these 'common law' principles must be understood to have their foundation ultimately in the *Constitution*, as was suggested in *Plaintiff S10/2011* (n 3).

[53] This example of ellipsis in a legal text is introduced and discussed in Ekins and Goldsworthy (n 5) 55.

[54] Ekins and Goldsworthy (n 5) 55–56.

refers to *cooked meat*, etc) but rather the fact that there is an established and mutually understood human practice of eating hamburgers, of ordering them in restaurants, etc. We can see this if we imagine that the customer who orders the hamburger in fact wished it to be delivered uncooked or inedible: when the waiter brings the hamburger ready to eat, can the customer send it back, complaining that 'I didn't order a *cooked and edible* hamburger!'? No – the waiter, in virtue of the received practice around the use of the word *hamburger* in the context of ordering in restaurants, was entitled to have taken the customer (regardless of subjective mental states) to have referred to a cooked and edible hamburger.

What this example shows is that, at least in some circumstances, we are able to resolve interpretive ambiguities, and establish non-literal or non-pedantic meanings, because of our familiarity with the things that language – including statutory language – refers to; and these things, of course, include such common human vulnerabilities as building fires, and such common human activities as trading goods across borders, and selling stuff – 'food', 'hamburgers' – for consumption. In such circumstances, it is not our knowledge of *words*, nor our knowledge of *others' minds*, but our knowledge of the world in general, that generates interpretive consequences from purpose and context.[55] Of course, many everyday conversations are all about learning the contents of another's mind. In these sorts of situations, we do not rely just on received understandings of particular words or phrases, or upon contextual inferences to salience. We also ask people to clarify and elaborate, or whether they misspoke in their use of a word, etc. But for reasons that will be explained in the next section the circumstance of statutory enactments are not like this.

This chapter will not give an account of how the phenomena described above work in a technical sense – for instance, of how, as a matter of technical semantic theory, the reference of 'food' becomes expanded on some occasion of production to include *caustic soda or other non-food sold as if it were food to be consumed*; or how the reference of 'fire' becomes disambiguated as *building fire* rather than *artillery, missile or small arms fire*; or how speakers are able to generate linguistic meaning by using words or phrases (such as the *absolute freedom* of trade across borders) in accordance with established traditions of use.[56] But the foregoing discussion has shown that there are circumstances in which these processes do not, and indeed cannot, depend in any simple fashion on the intentions or purposes of those who actually produce the linguistic items in question.

None of this is to deny that sometimes it can be unclear *what* exactly the purpose or context is that will help us make sense of a piece of text. For instance, suppose the sign on the hotel door was instead on the door of a military barracks. Do the instructions apply if a fire breaks out in the building, if the building comes under fire, or both? Or, to return to the example from the *Constitution*, if there were differing models of free trade being discussed among political economists in the late nineteenth century, which one did the authors of the *Constitution* refer to with their words *absolutely free*? These are difficult questions that can go to the heart of statutory interpretation. In the preceding sub-section we argued that Ekins and Goldsworthy's account of legislative intentions lacks the resources to answer them.

[55] For an example of this point in the context of health regulations, see Sunstein (n 11) 497.

[56] For a technical analysis of some of these matters, see P Emerton, 'Political Freedoms and Entitlements in the Australian Constitution – An Example of Referential Intentions Yielding Unexpected Legal Consequences' (2010) 38 *Federal Law Review* 169.

Our answer is that one must do the best one can by application of the principles of interpretation having regard to context and evident purpose.

II. How the Constitution Informs Statutory Interpretation

The third claim of the alternative approach, namely that statutory interpretation is an expression of constitutional structure, is the most inchoate, but potentially the most important, and it is the focus of the rest of this chapter.

A. The Alternative Approach is Grounded in the Constitutional Structure

The alternative approach appears to be premised on the view that there is no constitutional imperative for a court to interpret legislation in accordance with the intentions of the Parliament that enacted it; to the contrary, courts are duty bound to interpret the statutory text in accordance with the established canons of construction, which are not heuristics for ascertaining what Parliament intended. Arguably, the refutation of this claim is the core of Ekins and Goldsworthy's attack upon the alternative approach: they argue that the alternative approach will inevitably lead courts to overstep the legitimate boundaries of judicial power, and usurp or at least frustrate the exercise of the legislative power that has been vested in the federal Parliament.

This is presented as a constitutional concern in the strict sense, for in the Australian legal system it is established that federal courts can only exercise judicial (and not legislative) power.[57] The High Court has elsewhere stated that it is no part of the judicial power of the Commonwealth to make or change statute law; that (at least, federal) courts cannot choose the content of the law.[58] Ekins and Goldsworthy argue that the alternative approach 'is not consistent with the constitutional grant of legislative power to Parliament'.[59] More broadly, they claim that the alternative approach is '[not] conducive to the health of a democracy'.[60] Elsewhere, Goldsworthy argues that parliamentary intention 'is the anchor that prevents the judges from drifting too far from Parliament's communication of its intentions through the text of the statute understood in the light of the context of its enactment'.[61]

Yet, as we have seen, the judicial advocates of the alternative approach have suggested that it – and the more specific principles of statutory interpretation – are grounded in the *Constitution*.[62] The constitutional distribution of powers, and the interaction between the

[57] *R v Kirby; Ex parte Boilermakers' Society of Australia* (1956) 94 CLR 254.

[58] Note Ekins and Goldsworthy's critique of this claim, above n 5 at 62, in setting out their account of the judicial powers of rectification and of selecting between alternatives when statutory meaning is truly indeterminate.

[59] Ekins and Goldsworthy (n 5) 45.

[60] Ekins and Goldsworthy (n 5) 45.

[61] Goldsworthy, 'Is Legislative Supremacy under Threat?' (n 34) 57.

[62] The idea that some interpretive principles might be grounded in the *Constitution* seems relatively uncontentious: see, eg, Sunstein (n 11) 468–73. The claim that *all* can be is obviously more ambitious. However, it does answer an objection raised by Alexander and Prakash, 'Mother May I?' (n 52) 102 that the courts lack 'the power to dictate interpretive rules to Congress'. If the interpretive principles are constitutionally grounded then the courts are obliged to declare and apply them. See further below, n 97 and text thereto.

branches of government, is said to guide and constrain the interpretive process, and ensure its legitimacy.

The Court has also emphasised that these principles are known to and accepted by all branches of government, which is apparently linked to their legitimacy.[63] This, together with the retention of the label of 'parliamentary intention' as a disciplining device, ensures that the courts do not radically alter the process of statutory interpretation, or otherwise overreach the limits of judicial power. As French J put it:

> 'legislative intention', as a legitimising and normative term, has real work to do and cannot be dismissed as mere fiction. Its use in the process of statutory interpretation is of fundamental importance because it directs courts to objective criteria of construction which are recognised as legitimate. … [The rules of construction] are rules whose application is reasonably predictable and being understood and predictable attract acceptance as criteria of the legitimacy of their product. Where the words expressed by Parliament are interpreted by the Court according to commonly understood rules of interpretation a court is entitled to make the normative statement that it has interpreted them in accordance with the legislative intention. This function has not been viewed with universal approval (A C Hutchison, 'The Rise and Ruse of Administrative Law and Scholarship' (1985) 48 *Modern Law Review* 293 at p 305): 'It is the court's construction of legislative words and not the words themselves that is law.' However the meaning of a legislative word is not like a rock lying on the ground waiting to be found. It is a product of interpretation which is legitimate if and only if the interpretation process invokes criteria which, whether developed by courts or decreed by statute, or both, are broadly understood by the Legislature, the Executive and the judiciary.[64]

Or, as Gageler J wrote (extra-curially):

> Whether or not legislative intention is appropriate to describe an objective attribute of the legislature, the quest objectively to find legislative intention is not inappropriate to describe the self-restraint which courts have traditionally brought to their role as the ultimate interpreters of legislated texts. Legislative intention, if it is nothing more, is 'a message *for judges about judging*'; even if conceived as a fiction, it is:
>
> a fiction with a purpose: to help judges better serve the separation of powers … remind[ing] judges that it is not *their* decisions, but the *people's* decisions, that count in a democracy … the point [being] not to supplant text … but to constrain judges' ideological and cognitive biases.[65]

Whether the judicially-articulated suggestion that the term *legislative intention* is able to serve as a disciplining device, and the extent to which that would differ from Goldsworthy's notion of an 'anchor', is a matter that we put to one side, as this at least in part is an empirical question about processes of judicial reasoning. In the next sub-section, we explain how the structure and operation of the *Constitution*, and in particular its distribution of powers, informs the approach to statutory interpretation, before then considering how it might underpin and inform the more specific principles of statutory interpretation. While we argue that these may well be 'an expression of the constitutional relationship between the arms of government with respect to the making, interpretation and application of laws', we reject the claim that the *acceptance* of these principles by the other branches of government provides them with some constitutional foundation.

[63] See, eg, *Zheng v Cai* (n 1) 445 [28] (French CJ, Gummow, Crennan, Kiefel and Bell JJ).

[64] *NAAV* (n 2) 412 [432].

[65] Gageler (n 8) 14, citing VF Nourse, 'A Decision Theory of Statutory Interpretation: Legislative History by the Rules' (2012) 122 *Yale Law Journal* 70, 85. Emphasis in original.

B. The Australian Constitutional Framework

The *Australian Constitution* brought the Australian legal system into being. The Australian legislature – the Parliament – is, like the other branches of the federal Government, a creature of the *Australian Constitution*. Section 1 of the *Constitution* vests the 'legislative power of the Commonwealth' in the Parliament;[66] this is the only lawmaking power the Parliament enjoys.

What is legislative power under the *Constitution*? Other, interlocking provisions of the *Constitution* reveal that the legislative power of the Commonwealth is a 'power to make laws for the peace, order and good government of the Commonwealth', subject to the *Constitution*. The words and phrases used here are not free-standing, but have their own inherited meaning. We know that the words 'peace, order and good government' do not impose justiciable constraints on legislative power; rather, they are an imperial idiom for the conferral, on a colonial legislature, of plenary legislative power akin to that of the Parliament in Westminster.[67] They are words of exhortation, reflecting the framers' view that the democratically elected Parliament could be entrusted to act in the best interests of the Commonwealth.

Although the legal meaning of this phrase is well-understood, it has sometimes been suggested that the use of the word 'law' in the *Constitution* itself limits the legislative power of the Commonwealth, in that it imports constraints or requirements as to what counts as a valid example of that kind.[68] One of us has previously argued that this is not correct.[69] The position at the federal level is similar to that of the States, as stated by Dawson J in *Kable v Director of Public Prosecutions*, and reiterated in *Duncan v New South Wales*: 'The word "laws" is synonymous with the word "statutes"'.[70] This is significant for present purposes, because it shows that the only legal tool that Parliament has at its disposal, for lawmaking purposes, is the enactment of statute law. This is consistent with Dicey's description of the situation in the United Kingdom:

> the commands of Parliament (consisting as it does of the Crown, the House of Lords, and the House of Commons) can be uttered only through the combined action of its three constituent parts, and must, therefore, always take the shape of formal and deliberate legislation. The will of Parliament can be expressed only through an Act of Parliament.[71]

Parliament, and the laws it makes, interact with and generate legal consequences for the other branches of government, and the people, in several constitutionally-mandated ways. This reveals further facts about Parliament as an institution, and hence about the laws that it enacts. The Parliament itself consists of members who must be directly chosen by the

[66] Although it is common to refer to ss 51 and 52 of the *Constitution* as the source of legislative power, it seems more accurate to describe those provisions as delineating the scope of the power conferred by s 1. The Houses of Parliament also have certain non-legislative powers, such as the power to punish for contempt. These derive from s 49 of the *Constitution* and the *Parliamentary Privileges Act 1987* (Cth).

[67] J Goldsworthy, 'Implications in Language, Law and the Constitution' in G Lindell (ed), *Future Directions in Australian Constitutional Law: Essays in Honour of Professor Leslie Zines* (Sydney, Federation Press, 1994) 175.

[68] See, eg, *Plaintiff S157/2002 v Commonwealth* (2003) 211 CLR 476, 513 [102].

[69] L Burton Crawford, 'The Entrenched Minimum Provision of Judicial Review and the Limits of "Law"' (2017) 45 *Federal Law Review* 569.

[70] *Kable v Director of Public Prosecutions (NSW)* (1996) 189 CLR 51, 76 (Dawson J).

[71] AV Dicey, *Introduction to the Study of the Law of the Constitution* (London, McMillan, 1915) 403.

people of the Commonwealth and of the several States.[72] And 'all laws made by the Parliament of the Commonwealth under the Constitution, shall be binding on the courts, judges, and people of every State and of every part of the Commonwealth'.[73] Commonwealth law will cause inconsistent State law to become inoperative,[74] and in certain circumstances may displace the operation of constitutionally-mandated rules that would otherwise apply.[75] Parliament is, thus, the supreme representative and lawmaking body of what the preamble to the *Constitution* describes as an 'indissoluble Federal Commonwealth'.[76]

Section 61 of the *Constitution* gives the executive power to, inter alia, execute and maintain the laws of the Commonwealth. Chapter III of the *Constitution* establishes the judicature, vested with the judicial power of the Commonwealth. The High Court is given certain jurisdiction, including original jurisdiction to, in certain circumstances, review the actions of 'officers of the Commonwealth' and to hear matters arising under any laws made by the Parliament.[77] Thus, the laws enacted by the Parliament are to be executed and adjudicated by the other branches of government in certain constitutionally-mandated ways, even as they are binding upon them, the people and the States.

Goldsworthy has emphasised that the power to legislate belongs to Parliament and cannot be usurped by the courts, for both constitutional and normative reasons. He is critical of those that argue that the production of statutory meaning is 'the joint responsibility of Parliament and the courts',[78] acting in a 'collaborative enterprise'.[79] At least within the Australian constitutional context, we wholeheartedly agree. The preceding outline of that context shows how and why this is so: the Parliament makes laws, which are *binding* upon judges; and the judicial power encompasses the adjudication of matters arising under statute, but not the authoring (or co-authoring) of statutes. But this does not settle the question of *how* statutes obtain their meaning, and the role (if any) that Parliament's intention plays in this matter.

Dicey articulates one conception of the method whereby this takes place. The fact that Parliament can only express its lawmaking will by enacting legislation, he said,

> is no mere matter of form; it has most important practical effects. It prevents those inroads upon the law of the land which a despotic monarch … might effect by ordinances or decrees … The principle that Parliament speaks only through an Act of Parliament greatly increases the authority of the judges. A Bill which has passed into statute immediately becomes subject to judicial interpretation, and the English Bench have always refused, in principle at least, to interpret an Act of Parliament otherwise than by reference to the words of the enactment. An English judge will take no notice of the resolutions of either House, of anything which may have passed in debate

[72] Sections 7, 24.

[73] Covering clause 5.

[74] Section 109.

[75] See, eg, s 49, which provides that '[t]he powers, privileges, and immunities of the Senate and of the House of Representatives, and of the members and the committees of each House, *shall be such as are declared by the Parliament, and until declared shall be* those of the Commons House of Parliament of the United Kingdom, and of its members and committees, at the establishment of the Commonwealth' (emphasis added); and see also the *Parliamentary Privileges Act 1987* (Cth), s 5.

[76] Preamble to the *Commonwealth of Australia Constitution Act 1900* (63 & 64 Victoria, Ch 12).

[77] Sections 75, 76. Sections 71 and 77 together permit Parliament to confer similar jurisdiction on other courts.

[78] TRS Allan, 'Legislative Supremacy and Legislative Intention: Interpretation, Meaning and Authority' (2004) 63(3) *Cambridge Law Journal* 685, 689.

[79] P Joseph, 'Parliament, the Courts and the Collaborative Enterprise' (2004) 15 *King's College Law Journal* 321.

> (a matter of which officially he has no cognisance), or even of the changes which a Bill may have undergone between the moment of its first introduction to Parliament and of its receiving the Royal assent. … [This] contributes greatly both … to the authority of judges and to the fixity of the law.[80]

Dicey's remarks about the authority of judges must be treated with care. At least transposed to the Australian context, this cannot be understood as authority to *contribute* to the content of statute law. Rather, in the Australian legal system, only the courts may authoritatively ascertain and declare the meaning of the statutes that Parliament enacts.[81] That authority derives from the conferral of judicial power by the *Constitution*, which is a superior law to those enacted by Parliament.

Dicey's remarks also capture the significance of the fact that, when Parliament enacts a statute, it engages in a legally prescribed manner of communication that is very unlike the communication that an ordinary person might engage in when writing or speaking. To borrow the words of Gageler J, '[t]he legislature … is a legislative body following a legislative process'.[82] It is *Parliament* alone – not its members, nor its subordinate organs – which has been vested with the legislative power, and this power extends only to the power to enact legislative texts. Hence legislative texts are free-standing relative to the body that enacted them. This is so for two reasons: when Parliament enacts a statute it is establishing *law*, with all the consequences for other branches of government, and the people, that we have outlined above; and *all the Parliament can do* to contribute to the content of the law is to enact statutes. It cannot explain or clarify in the ways that an ordinary person can. To return to Radin's observation, once the statute is enacted, Parliament is *functus officio*. If a court interprets legislation in a way that thwarts what Parliament, or (some or all of) its members, hoped to achieve, the only response lawfully available to Parliament is to make more statutes, which will again fall to the courts to be interpreted.[83]

This free-standing character of legislative texts means that when interpreting statutory texts within the Australian constitutional context the approach must be radically different from that taken to construing ordinary conversations, or letters, or even private legal instruments. It is exactly the sort of circumstance described in sub-section I.B., in which those who encounter the text to be interpreted are entitled to impute intentions to use words in accordance with certain established referential practices, without needing to look behind the context and salient purpose to the actual intentions of the authors of the text. This includes the courts, which – in performing their constitutional function as authoritative interpreters of legislation – are not required to look behind the statutory text to other doings or properties (including mental states or motivations) of the Parliament and its members.[84]

[80] Dicey (n 71) 403–404. Sunstein (n 11) at 431 makes a similar remark in the American context, that Congress enacts statutes rather than its own views about what those statutes mean; those views, while relevant, are not controlling unless they are in the statute. The words, not the 'intent,' represent the law. The enactment, not the legislature's unenacted views, binds the public and the judges.

[81] See further L Burton Crawford, 'Who Decides the Validity of Executive Action? No-Invalidity Clauses and the Separation of Powers' (2017) 24 *Australian Journal of Administrative Law* 81.

[82] Gageler (n 8) 7.

[83] Gageler J (n 8) at 16 attributes to Justice Nye Perram the description of it as 'A relationship in which one party is only ever allowed to speak and in which another party is only ever allowed to interpret'.

[84] This explains the importance of *definitions* in statutes. In ordinary conversational contexts, it is possible and indeed common to use words and phrases in new or idiosyncratic ways without formally explaining that this is being done, because the audience can be expected to guess at the mental state that lies behind the usage, to ask for

The courts are not duty-bound to strive to give effect *in that fashion* to the enactments produced by Parliament; they are not obliged to come to the text merely as a guide or a pointer to the will that lies behind it, as government actors in a rather different constitutional order might be obliged to give effect to the 'ordinances or decrees' of a despot.

An example of statutory interpretation undertaken by the High Court in the manner just described is provided by the judgment of French CJ and Hayne J in *Certain Lloyd's Underwriters v Cross*.[85] This case concerned the interpretation of a statute that defined the phrase 'personal injury damages' as having the same meaning as in a second statute. That second statute, which defined the phrase, went on to establish both a regime in respect of liability for personal injury damages, and to exclude certain sorts of personal injuries from the operation of that regime. The question was whether those exclusions also informed the meaning of the phrase in the first statute. Their Honours held that they did not. Their reasoning for this conclusion was, in part, purely textual: the first statute 'did not refer to the operation or application of' the second act; nor did it 'direct attention to whatever was identified as being the legal effect or consequence which the [second statute] produced by using that defined expression in its various provisions'.[86] But they also noted that

> Each Act used the defined expression 'personal injury damages' as part of a larger composite phrase: '*award* of personal injury damages' in the [second] Act and '*claim* for personal injury damages' in the [first] Act … The hinge on which the relevant operation of each Act turned was the larger composite phrase and not the defined expression 'personal injury damages'. … There is no textual reason to limit the expression 'personal injury damages' in the [first statute] to those *claims* for personal injury damages the award of which was regulated by the [second statute].[87]

That is to say, when one identifies the actual subject matter regulated by each statute – *claims* for personal injury damages in one, *awards* of personal injury damages in the other – one sees that they are different things, and that there is no shared property of those different things – that is to say, nothing about the context or salient purpose – that suggests that limitations that apply in respect of the regulation of the latter should be understood as applying in respect of the regulation of the former.

The two pieces of legislation had been enacted concurrently, and this was argued to be a reason for taking the contrary view as to the proper interpretation of the first statute.[88] In response to this, however, their Honours stated that

> The purpose of legislation must be derived from what the legislation says, and not from any assumption about the desired or desirable reach or operation of the relevant provisions. … It is

clarification if unsure, etc. But in a context in which the audience is entitled to impute intentions in accordance with established practices and on the basis of context and salient purpose, clarification of meaning must be undertaken expressly if there is no established practice that will make it clear, or the author of the text wishes to depart from or modify or precisify the usage that otherwise would be conveyed. (We saw this point borne out in section I.B. above, in the non-statutory context of ordering a hamburger from a waiter: a customer who wishes to have the hamburger delivered uncooked or inedible must explain that the word *hamburger* is not being used in accordance with the established practice of ordering meals in restaurants.)

[85] *Certain Lloyd's Underwriters* (n 2).

[86] *Certain Lloyd's Underwriters* (n 2) 392–93 [33].

[87] *Certain Lloyd's Underwriters* (n 2) 393 [35]. Emphasis original.

[88] *Certain Lloyd's Underwriters* (n 2) 386–87, 394–95 [17], [38]–[40]. The alternative approach clearly de-emphasises extrinsic materials such as second reading speeches and explanatory memoranda, but as the quote illustrates does not exclude reference to such material. Two recent statutory interpretation cases are illustrative in

> not legitimate to identify a legislative purpose not apparent from the text of the relevant provisions (or in this case even expressed in some extrinsic material), to examine extrinsic material and notice that there is nothing positively inconsistent with the identified purpose, and then to answer the question of construction by reference to the purpose that was initially assumed.[89]

This is a clear judicial statement both of an approach to interpretation that treats the legislative text as free-standing, and of the grounding of that approach in a conception of the legitimate role of the courts.

C. How the Constitution Informs and Underpins the Principles of Statutory Interpretation

Imputing intentions in the way that we have described will not resolve all interpretive uncertainties. The 'canons of construction' also play a role here. However, in order to avoid the objectionable understanding of Dicey's reference to judicial authority, it is necessary to show that the constitutional structure gives rise to and informs the more specific principles or 'canons' that are brought to bear in order to ascertain the meaning of a statutory text.[90] In other words, it is imperative to show that the principles of statutory construction, once untethered from parliamentary intention, reflect something more than judges' view as to what the law should be.

In the previous sub-section we noted that the power vested in Parliament to make laws is simply a power to enact statutes, which imposes no general constraints as to the content or quality of that law. But this conclusion about the lawful scope of the legislative power of the Commonwealth does not foreclose inquiry into the broader characteristics of Parliament as a lawmaking institution given the basic features of the Australian constitutional structure.

this respect. The plurality judgment in the recent statutory interpretation case *Probuild Constructions (Aust) Pty Ltd v Shade Systems Pty Ltd* [2018] HCA 4 drew upon Hansard (at [36], [39], [40], [43]) to confirm that the arbitration regime established by the statute in question, which operated without prejudice to common law contractual rights, was intended to operate summarily and speedily and hence ought not to be subject to judicial review for error of law on the face of the record (at [48] (Kiefel CJ, Bell, Keane, Nettle and Gordon JJ):

> To permit potentially costly and time-consuming judicial review proceedings to be brought on the basis of error of law on the face of the record, regardless of whether an adjudicator had exceeded the limits of their statutory functions and powers, would frustrate the operation and evident purposes of the statutory scheme.

In *Probuild*, Gageler J did not refer to Hansard and decided the matter purely by reference to considerations of coherence (both of interpretive principles and of the statutory scheme): [78], [81]–[82]. However, in *SZTAL v Minister For Immigration And Border Protection* [2017] HCA 34, His Honour, agreeing with the plurality about the centrality of context to the interpretive task ([14] (Kiefel CJ, Nettle and Gordon JJ, [36]–[37] (Gageler J)), went on to refer to Hansard in order to confirm the statutory purpose ([43]–[44]) whereas the plurality resolved the question of context solely by reference to features of the statute itself unconcerned with purpose ([17]).

The use of extrinsic materials by American textualists to establish 'a background understanding of the problems Congress was trying to address' is noted in JT Molot, 'The Rise and Fall of Textualism' (2006) 106(1) *Columbia Law Review* 1, 3, 39.

[89] *Certain Lloyd's Underwriters* (n 2) 390 [26], 395 [41].

[90] In its recent decision in *R (Miller) v Secretary of State for Exiting the European Union* [2016] EWHC 2768 (Admin), the High Court of England and Wales appears to ground the canons of construction in exactly the sort of judicial authority that we have ruled out in the Australian context, suggesting significant differences between the two jurisdictions' understandings of the nature and process of statutory interpretation: see the discussion in Emerton and Burton Crawford (n 40) 335–37.

We therefore draw an important distinction between, on the one hand, what Parliament can validly do, and, on the other hand, the considerations that inform the intentions which, all things being equal, we are entitled to impute to Parliament as the author of legislative texts.[91] The principles of statutory interpretation thus represent starting points for identifying the intentions that can be imputed to Parliament as an author of statutory texts, having regard to the nature of that institution understood in its constitutional context.[92]

In discussions of interpretive principles, it is common to refer to things that one can *presume* or *expect* Parliament to have or to have not intended. We regard this as a way of referring to intentions that an interpreter is entitled to impute to the Parliament in the manner that we have described above. And when Parliament enacts a statute that departs from the meaning one would otherwise take the text to bear, given its context and salient purpose, it is common to describe an interpretive presumption as having been 'rebutted'; but this is not strictly accurate. In these circumstances, rather, some element of the text (eg a definition, or some other feature of wording or structure) precludes an interpreter being entitled to impute the intention which otherwise, in light of the constitutional context and salient statutory purpose, would be imputed. Indeed, when we refer to 'principles of statutory interpretation' or the 'canons of construction', it is more accurate to think of these as shorthand phrases for the contribution that the constitutional context makes to interpretive considerations.

How might the text and structure of the *Constitution* inform what it is, and is not, legitimate for a court to impute to Parliament? The constitutional text does not provide specific, detailed guidance. But there are aspects of that text which, we argue, make it legitimate for the courts to impute certain intentions to Parliament. In this modest sense, it might be argued that certain principles and presumptions of interpretation presently applied by the courts reflect the constitutional structure. However, we do not comment on the strength or weakness with which these interpretive principles are presently applied.

Consider, for example, the presumption of perspectivity. When Parliament enacts a statute that changes the law, the courts presume that change was intended to have only prospective effect. It is not implausible to say that this presumption reflects the constitutional structure; the nature of the legislative power vested in the Parliament vis-à-vis the judicial power given to the courts. This is because, as the *Constitution* makes clear, the constitutional effect of an exercise of legislative power is to make law which binds all people and the other branches of government, as well as triggering other constitutionally mandated effects (sub-section II.B. above). In these circumstances, a judicial interpreter may legitimately impute an intention that the legislation has only prospective effect; the difficulty and

[91] The drawing of a similar distinction can be seen in WMC Gummow, 'The Constitution: Ultimate Foundation of Australian Law?' (2005) 79 *Australian Law Journal* 167, 177 ('[T]here is a contrast between the approach taken by the High Court to the construction of statutes, and the disfavour with which it has come to regard the use of common law principles or values to restrain the reach of heads of legislative power under the *Constitution*. It is one thing to deny legislative power and another to encourage clear statements of legislative intent.'). We would emphasise that, on the approach we are developing, 'common law' interpretive principles are to be grounded ultimately in the *Constitution* rather than the common law. See also above n 52.

[92] See also Gageler, who describes the 'grounds of review' as the default position: 'The Legitimate Scope of Judicial Review' (2001) 21 *Australian Bar Review* 279, 287. See further L Burton Crawford, *The Rule of Law and the Australian Constitution* (Sydney, Federation Press, 2017) Ch 7. We discuss the interpretation of statutory conferrals of executive power in sub-section II.D. below.

unfairness of binding people to laws that are unknown – and more importantly, *unknowable* – is well-established. This does not mean that the Parliament cannot validly enact retrospective law: it can. But if a statute gives no positive indication that it is intended to have retrospective effect, interpreters are entitled to impute the contrary intention to the legislature, that is, that Parliament did not retrospectively subject the people and other branches of government to new legal norms.

Consider, for another example, the presumption that statutory executive powers have legal limits. This too could be said to reflect the constitutional structure. In the Australian constitutional context, all federal executive power ultimately derives from s 61 of the *Constitution*. Though its scope remains, in some respects, uncertain, it includes the power to execute and maintain the laws of the Commonwealth – and hence the executive may exercise those powers conferred on it by ordinary legislation. Parts of the *Constitution* (namely, Chapter III) ensure that the exercise of executive power is reviewable by the courts, at least in certain circumstances. This element of context might be said to permit imputation of an intention that the powers conferred by a statute upon an executive officer are not at large, but rather are subject to legal limitations, which can be enforced by the courts.

This may ground the basic proposition that executive powers conferred by statute are not at large. It does not necessarily tell us much about how broad or narrow they should be: about the more *specific* ways in which executive power should be limited. But here too, guidance may be found. First, statutory executive power is, considered in light of s 61 of the *Constitution*, the power to execute the laws of the Commonwealth. It is not unreasonable to impute an intention to Parliament that the content of the power conferred is informed by that statute: by its subject matter, its purpose, its scope. Thus, if a power is conferred by a statute concerned with the prevention of terrorist acts, an intention may be imputed that the power is confined by reference to that subject matter, and cannot be exercised, for example, for the purpose of protecting the environment or stimulating the economy.[93]

Further, the exercise of executive power (like the exercise of legislative power) is necessarily an expression of constitutional power. The executive officer is a public official, not a private citizen; executive power can only be exercised in a legal or public capacity. Hence, when interpreting a statutory conferral of executive power, an intention may be imputed that the power is confined in this sort of way, and so does not authorise the executive officer to do certain things that are incongruent with their constitutional role. Thus we might interpret statutory conferrals of executive power on the presumption that Parliament has not authorised bad faith, or fraud.[94]

D. The Evolution of Interpretive Principles

The preceding sub-section argued that it is not implausible to argue that certain principles and presumptions presently applied by the High Court reflect the constitutional text and structure. This sub-section addresses one aspect of the alternative approach which, we

[93] This idea is far from radical: Dicey (n 71) at 409 noted that '[executive] [p]owers, however extraordinary, are never really unlimited, for they are confined by the words of the Act itself'.

[94] See, eg, *Commissioner of Taxation v Futuris Corporation* (2008) 237 CLR 146.

argue, is implausible: that is, that the principles of statutory interpretation derive their legitimacy from the fact they are known to and accepted by the other branches of government.

The High Court has said that the principles of interpretation reflect not only the constitutional structure, but also its 'operation', and 'the interaction between the three branches of government'.[95] This suggests that the principles may develop, not merely because constitutional interpretation reveals that change is required, but because the branches of government come to accept that legislation will be interpreted in certain ways. As Blaker has observed, this raises interesting and difficult questions: first and foremost, why should acceptance by the other branches of government contribute to the legitimacy of an interpretive principle?[96] There is a degree of contradiction here. If Parliament is incapable of holding a mental state (such as an intention), then it cannot 'know' or 'accept' a principle of statutory interpretation, either. It is also unclear what evidence could lead the Court to conclude that certain principles were known and accepted. Perhaps it is best to think of acceptance as itself a kind of construct: Parliament is deemed to know and accept a principle if it has been regularly applied by the courts in the past.

Even so, the fact that a principle has been regularly applied by courts in the past does not mean it is legitimate, unless there is some further justification available. In other words, there must be some basis on which it could have been said that the principle was legitimate when it was first applied. Otherwise, every principle of statutory interpretation applied by the courts would have been illegitimate at some prior point in time.[97]

More importantly, if interpretive principles do and must reflect the constitutional structure, then the fact that an interpretive principle has been accepted by the branches of government cannot demand its continued application if the courts subsequently discover that its constitutional foundation was flawed. And conversely, it must be possible for new interpretive constraints to be discovered, as our understanding of the *Constitution* increases, and as new forms of legislation are enacted and the distribution of powers between the legislative, executive and judiciary plays out in the context of these.[98]

There are clear examples in which the courts have revised long-standing interpretive principles, or created new ones. An example of constitutionally-grounded *correction* of interpretive principle is found in *Plaintiff S157/2002*, in which the High Court significantly altered its approach to construing privative clauses. This change in approach was motivated by (a) a greater awareness of the 'entrenched minimum provision of judicial review' established by s 75 of the *Constitution* and (b) an appreciation that jurisdictional error – by and large, the gateway to the High Court's judicial review jurisdiction – was a broader and different concept than previously understood.[99]

An example of constitutionally-grounded recognition of a new principle is found in *Plaintiff M79/2012 v Commonwealth*.[100] This is one in a large body of cases that consider

[95] *Plaintiff S10/2011* (n 3) 666 [97].

[96] Blaker suggests that the court is, in this regard, moving towards a theory of interpretation advocated by Raz: J Raz, *Between Authority and Interpretation* (Oxford, Oxford University Press, 2009) 120–21, 284.

[97] As noted above, n 62, a version of this concern is expressed by Alexander and Prakash, 'Mother May I?' (n 52) 102.

[98] See also *Probuild Constructions (Aust) Pty Ltd v Shade Systems Pty Ltd* (n 88) [58] (Gageler J).

[99] For a different view on this matter, see J Waller, 'Gone but Not Forgotten: In Defence of *Hickman*' (2018) 46(2) *Federal Law Review* 259.

[100] *Plaintiff M79/2012 v Commonwealth* (2013) 252 CLR 336.

the scope of the Minister for Immigration's power to issue certain kinds of visa under the *Migration Act 1958* (Cth). At issue was a provision that empowers the Minister to grant a certain kind of visa 'if the Minister thinks that it is in the public interest to do so' and that states that, in exercising that power, the Minister is not bound by certain other parts of the Act, nor by the regulations made under the Act. Hayne J concluded (in dissent) that, properly construed, the legislation does not confer a power confined only by the public interest criterion; the statute established other applicable limitations, not expressly excluded by the provision in question. Though His Honour thought that in this case the meaning of the statutes was clear, he went on to suggest that if a provision of this sort, purporting to excuse executive decision makers from generally applicable legal requirements, was ambiguous, then it should be read narrowly. As he put it, interpreting such a provision would require

> close consideration of fundamental questions about the relationship between the Parliament and the Executive. And it may be that consideration of those questions would have to begin by examining the present significance of the protest recorded in The Bill of Rights (1 Will & Mar Sess 2 c 2) against the assumed 'Power of Dispensing with and Suspending of Lawes and the Execution of Lawes without Consent of Parlyament' and the provisions of that Act declaring 'That the pretended Power of Suspending of Laws or the Execution of Laws by Regall Authority without Consent of Parlyament is illegall' and 'That the pretended Power of Dispensing with Laws or the Execution of Laws by Regall Authoritie as it hath beene assumed and exercised of late is illegall'.[101]

Thus the Court should err on the side of caution, lest the executive be permitted to dispense with statute law. The imputation of such an intention to Parliament is ultimately grounded in the principle of parliamentary supremacy, itself historically grounded in *The Bill of Rights*.[102]

Hence we do not agree with the claim, made by several members of the High Court, that the principles of statutory interpretation derive their legitimacy from the fact they are known and accepted by the other branches of government, or simply long-standing. The process of examining the text and structure of the *Constitution* and identifying how it might justify the imputation of various intentions to Parliament appears to be a far more fruitful inquiry.

III. Conclusion

This chapter has provided a partial defence of the alternative approach to statutory interpretation advocated by the Australian High Court, especially as against the criticisms made by Ekins and Goldsworthy. It has begun to develop and defend a theoretically-grounded reconstruction of the alternative approach, drawing upon general considerations from the philosophy of language, but also upon distinctive features of the Australian constitutional order.

The act of legislating, we argue, is an exercise of public power conferred by the *Australian Constitution*, very different from other communicative acts. The meaning of the texts that

[101] ibid 366–67 [85]–[87].

[102] *A v Hayden* (1984) 156 CLR 532, 540 (Gibbs CJ), 550 (Mason J), 562 (Murphy J), 580 (Brennan J); *Plaintiff M79/2012* (n 100) 366–67 [85]–[87] (Hayne J); *Plaintiff M68/2015 v Minister for Immigration and Border Protection* (2016) 257 CLR 42 (specifically the judgment of Gageler J).

Parliament enacts is informed by the nature of Parliament as an institution, established by a constitution that distributes power between legislative, executive and judicial branches of government. We have argued that the constitutional structure, and distribution of powers between those branches of government, is able to provide a tenable foundation for the principles of statutory interpretation presently recognised by the High Court, without the need to resort to the concept of legislative intention. A full defence of the alternative approach would show how this can be done for the full range of interpretive principles, but we leave that task for another occasion.

5

Goldsworthy on the Normative Justification for Originalism

LAWRENCE B SOLUM

I. Introduction

In *The Case for Originalism*, Jeffrey Goldsworthy made an elegant and sophisticated argument for originalism as a theory of constitutional practice.[1] This chapter will investigate one important component of Goldsworthy's argument, which I shall call 'the normative component' of the case for originalism. The best way to begin is by laying out the whole argument using Goldsworthy's own concise statement, with some omissions indicated by ellipses, and some minor changes in terminology indicated by square brackets:

> 1. A constitution, like any other law, necessarily has a meaning that pre-exists judicial interpretation of it.
> 2. The meaning of a law is part (perhaps all) of what it is; therefore, to change the meaning of a law is to change the law.
> 3. The original meaning of a constitution is … 'its utterance meaning' ….
>
> …
>
> 4. When a constitution itself requires that it be changed only by some special democratic procedure, this binds judges as well as other officials.
>
> …
>
> 5. Any judge who violated that requirement would flout the constitution itself, the rule of law, the principle of democracy, and (in many federal systems) the principle of federalism.
> 6. When interpreting such a constitution, the judges' primary duty is to reveal and clarify its pre-existing meaning. When that meaning is [underdeterminate], their secondary duty is to … supplement it. …[2]

Goldsworthy refers to each of these numbered statements as propositions, adding two additional steps that anticipate objections,[3] but the six propositions quoted above are the core of his affirmative justification for originalism.

In this chapter, I will undertake a sympathetic examination of the normative component of Goldsworthy's case for originalism – as expressed in Propositions 4, 5 and 6.[4]

[1] J Goldsworthy, 'The Case for Originalism' in G Huscroft and BW Miller (eds), *The Challenge of Originalism: Theories of Constitutional Interpretation* (Cambridge, Cambridge University Press, 2011) 42.

[2] ibid 42–43.

[3] ibid 43.

[4] When I refer to Goldsworthy's numbered propositions, I will capitalise the word Proposition for the sake of clarity of reference.

The examination is sympathetic, because I largely agree with Goldsworthy's argument. I will attempt to probe Goldsworthy's arguments for possible weaknesses and unstated assumptions, and to make some suggestions for how his argument might be repaired, strengthened or elaborated.

This chapter focuses on the normative component of the case for originalism, because I believe that the moral and legal components of the case for originalism raise the most controversial issues – the issues where critics of originalism will take their 'last stand,' so to speak. But this focus on the normative elements of Goldsworthy's case for originalism should not obscure the originality and importance of Goldsworthy's treatment of the linguistic issues. Propositions 1, 2 and 3 reflect Goldsworthy's pioneering work on these issues. That work anticipated developments in the United States and elsewhere. That work has been profoundly influential and remains the most sophisticated body of work on issues at the intersection of the philosophy of language and constitutional theory.

Here is the roadmap. Section II. situates Goldsworthy's argument in the landscape of contemporary constitutional theory – understood parochially from the viewpoint of constitutional theory in the United States. Section III. evaluates the case for originalism from the inside by offering an internal assessment of Goldsworthy's normative arguments. Section IV. looks at the argument from the outside, offering some concerns that originate from outside of Goldsworthy's theoretical framework. The conclusion in section V. makes some comments on the significance of Goldsworthy's argument.

II. Situating the Case for Originalism

Before digging into the substance of Goldsworthy's case for originalism, I will offer some terminological and conceptual observations and clarifications, beginning with the obvious question, 'What is originalism?'

A. What is Originalism?

Goldsworthy is making the case for 'originalism', but there is no consensus among constitutional theorists or practitioners about what 'originalism' is. The word 'originalism' is a neologism introduced by Professor Paul Brest in the following passage: 'By "originalism" I mean the familiar approach to constitutional adjudication that accords binding authority to the text of the Constitution or the intentions of its adopters'.[5] Brest was a critic of the textualist and intentionalist positions for which he coined a label, but the name stuck and was adopted by theorists who came to call themselves 'originalists'. The subsequent history of originalism is too complex to summarise in a few sentences,[6] but it includes the defence

[5] P Brest, 'The Misconceived Quest for the Original Understanding' (1980) 60 *Boston University Law Review* 204.

[6] The story can be told from various perspectives, but a comprehensive history of the originalist constitutional theory – as opposed to the role of originalism in politics and judicial practice – is yet to be told. Among the historical accounts of originalism, are the following. See, eg, J O'Neill, *Originalism in American Law and Politics: A Constitutional History* (Baltimore, MD, Johns Hopkins University Press, 2005); LE Sawyer, 'Principle and Politics in the New History of Originalism' (2017) 57 *American Journal of Legal History* 198; V Kesavan and MS Paulsen, 'The Interpretive Force of the Constitution's Secret Drafting History' (2003) 91 *Georgetown Law Journal* 1113.

of what has come to be called 'original intentions originalism' by Richard Kay,[7] the emergence of 'public meaning originalism' – prompted by Justice Antonin Scalia's suggestion that originalists 'change the label from the Doctrine of Original Intent to the Doctrine of Original Meaning'[8] – and the subsequent emergence of what has sometimes been called 'the New Originalism' in the work of Randy Barnett[9] and Keith Whittington.[10]

Whittington and then Barnett introduced the interpretation–construction distinction, which marks the difference between the discovery of the linguistic meaning of the constitutional text ('interpretation') and the determination of the legal effect associated with the text ('construction').[11] Subsequent theorists have introduced additional forms of originalism, including 'original methods originalism' (associated with Michael Rappaport and John McGinnis)[12] and 'original law originalism' (developed by William Baude[13] and Stephen Sachs).[14] Much of the American development of originalist theory was anticipated by Jeffrey Goldsworthy in a series of articles developing originalist theory in the Australian context, but with a sophisticated awareness of developments in the United States.[15]

The theoretical diversity of contemporary originalist theory in the academy led Thomas Colby and Peter Smith to contend that 'originalism is not a single, coherent, unified theory of constitutional interpretation, but is rather a disparate collection of distinct constitutional theories that share little more than a misleading reliance on a common label'.[16] While Colby and Smith are correct to observe that there are significant differences among originalists, they are wrong to deny that originalism has a unifying core. That core is specified by two theoretical ideas upon which almost all originalists agree. We can call these ideas the Fixation Thesis and the Constraint Principle.[17] In simplified form, these ideas can be articulated as follows:

> *The Fixation Thesis*: The original meaning of the constitutional text is fixed at the time each provision is framed and/or ratified.[18]

[7] RS Kay, 'Adherence to the Original Intentions in Constitutional Adjudication: Three Objections and Responses' (1988) 82 *Northwestern University Law Review* 226.

[8] 'Address by Justice Antonin Scalia before the Attorney General's Conference on Economic Liberties in Washington, DC (June 14, 1986)' in *Original Meaning Jurisprudence: A Sourcebook* (Washington, DC, United States Department of Justice, 1987) 101, 106. Scalia's suggestion was taken up by Gary Lawson, Steven Calabresi, and Saikrishna Prakash. G Lawson, 'Proving the Law' (1992) 86 *Northwestern University Law Review* 859, 875; SG Calabresi and SB Prakash, 'The President's Power to Execute the Laws' (1994) 104 *Yale Law Journal* 541, 553.

[9] R Barnett, 'An Originalism for Nonoriginalists' (1999) 45 *Loyola Law Review* 611.

[10] KE Whittington, *Constitutional Interpretation: Textual Meaning, Original Intent, and Judicial Review* (Lawrence, University Press of Kansas, 1999); KE Whittington, *Constitutional Construction: Divided Powers and Constitutional Meaning* (Cambridge, Massachusetts, Harvard University Press, 1999).

[11] For an overview of the interpretation–construction distinction and the role that it plays in contemporary originalism, see LB Solum, 'Originalism and Constitutional Construction' (2013) 82 *Fordham Law Review* 453; see also LB Solum, 'The Interpretation–Construction Distinction' (2010) 27 *Constitutional Commentary* 95; RE Barnett, 'Interpretation and Construction' (2011) 34 *Harvard Journal of Law & Public Policy* 65.

[12] JO McGinnis and MB Rappaport, 'Original Methods Originalism: A New Theory of Interpretation and the Case against Construction' (2009) 103 *Northwestern University Law Review* 751, 769.

[13] See W Baude, 'Is Originalism Our Law?' (2015) 115 *Columbia Law Review* 2349.

[14] See SE Sachs, 'Originalism as a Theory of Legal Change' (2015) 38 *Harvard Journal of Law & Public Policy* 817, 875.

[15] J Goldsworthy, 'Originalism in Constitutional Interpretation' (1997) 25 *Federal Law Review* 1, 21; J Goldsworthy, 'Interpreting the Constitution in Its Second Century' (2000) 24 *Melbourne University Law Review* 677, 683.

[16] TB Colby and PJ Smith, 'Living Originalism' (2009) 59 *Duke Law Journal* 239.

[17] 'Fixation Thesis' and 'Constraint Principle' are capitalised to indicate that these are proper names of theoretical constructs as articulated in the manner specified here.

[18] For a more precise explication of the Fixation Thesis, see LB Solum, 'The Fixation Thesis: The Role of Historical Fact in Original Meaning' (2015) 91 *Notre Dame Law Review* 1.

> *The Constraint Principle*: Constitutional practice, including the elaboration of constitutional doctrine and the decision of constitutional cases, should be constrained by the original meaning of the constitutional text. At a minimum, constraint requires that constitutional practice be consistent with original meaning (as specified below).[19]

For the purposes of this chapter, 'originalism' is a family of constitutional theories that almost all affirm fixation and constraint in some form. Nonoriginalist constitutional theories deny either fixation or constraint: for example, some living constitutionalists believe that judges should have the power to change constitutional doctrine so that it reflects contemporary circumstances and values, even if that requires the adoption of constructions that are inconsistent with the original meaning of the constitutional text.

Goldsworthy does not use the language of 'fixation' and 'constraint', but his case for originalism includes claims that are best understood as affirming both ideas. Thus, Propositions 1, 2 and 4 imply the Fixation Thesis or something very close to it. In his elaboration of Proposition 4, Goldsworthy explicitly affirms that conceptual content of fixation in slightly different words. For example, he writes:

> The conventional meaning of many words that appear in Shakespeare's plays have shifted over the last four centuries, but it does not follow that their meanings within his plays have shifted. The words as used in his plays continue to mean what they meant when he first used them.[20]

Goldsworthy does not use the term 'constraint', but it is clear that his Propositions 4, 5, 6 express approximately the same idea as the Constraint Principle.

Goldsworthy also puts forth a view about the nature of original meaning. He rejects intentionalism and instead affirms the view that the original meaning of the constitutional text is its 'utterance meaning'. It seems clear that Goldsworthy's notion of the utterance meaning of a constitutional text is closely related to 'public meaning'. Whether his view is distinguishable from the views of public meaning advanced by Gary Lawson or myself is an interesting and subtle question, but it will not be pursued in this chapter.[21]

B. The Interpretation–Construction Distinction

One of the most fundamental distinctions in legal theory marks the difference between 'legal content' and 'communicative content'.[22] Constitutional texts (and other legal texts such as statutes and contracts) have both communicative content (roughly linguistic meaning) and legal content (such as doctrines of constitutional law). Thus, the First Amendment to the *United States Constitution* includes the Free-Speech Clause with relatively sparse communicative content, but that clause has given rise to a complex body of free-speech doctrine that is far richer in content than the linguistic meaning of the words 'freedom', 'of'

[19] This version of the two ideas is from LB Solum, 'The Constraint Principle: Original Meaning and Constitutional Practice' (Unpublished, 13 April 2018) https://ssrn.com/abstract=2940215 (last accessed 7 November 2018) (on file with author).

[20] Goldsworthy, 'The Case for Originalism' (n 1) 52.

[21] Lawson's view is expressed in Lawson (n 8). A full statement of my view will be set forth in 'The Public Meaning Thesis' (unpublished manuscript on file with the author).

[22] LB Solum, 'Communicative Content and Legal Content' (2013) 89 *Notre Dame Law Review* 479.

and 'speech'. We can think of the communicative content of a constitutional provision as the set of propositions that are communicated by the text. The legal content associated with a provision consists of a set of propositions of law. In some cases, legal content may be a direct translation of communicated propositions into legal propositions, but this is not necessarily the case. Consider the Constitution of the Confederate States of America: this text has communicative content, but it no longer gives rise to any operative legal content.

The distinction between communicative content and legal content gives rise to the interpretation-construction distinction. The distinction was introduced into contemporary constitutional theory by Keith Whittington initially, and later by Randy Barnett. The distinction has a long history,[23] but for the purposes of this chapter, I will use the words 'interpretation' and 'construction' in stipulated technical senses, as follows:

> *Constitutional Interpretation*: The phrase 'constitutional interpretation' is stipulated to refer to the activity that discerns the communicative content (roughly, linguistic meaning) of the constitutional text.
>
> *Constitutional Construction*: The phrase 'constitutional construction' is stipulated to refer to the activity that determines the content of constitutional doctrine and the legal effect of the constitutional text (including the decision of constitutional cases by the courts).[24]

Goldsworthy does not explicitly adopt the terminology of the interpretation-construction distinction, but his work employs the basic idea using different terminology. Thus, in a portion of Proposition 6 omitted above, Goldsworthy distinguishes between the meaning of a constitutional provision and supplementation of that meaning.[25] So far as I can discern, there is nothing in *The Case for Originalism* that is inconsistent with the interpretation-construction distinction.

C. Disentangling the Normative and Factual Elements of the Case for Originalism

In general, the justification for originalism includes both normative and factual claims.[26] The Fixation Thesis is not a normative claim; the idea that meaning is fixed follows from

[23] See generally G Klass, 'Interpretation and Construction 1: Francis Lieber' (*New Private Law: Project on the Foundations of Private Law*, 19 November 2015) http://blogs.harvard.edu/nplblog/2015/11/19/interpretation-and-construction-1-francis-lieber-greg-klass/ (last accessed 7 November 2018); G Klass, 'Interpretation and Construction 2: Samuel Williston' (*New Private Law: Project on the Foundations of Private Law*, 23 November 2015) https://blogs.harvard.edu/nplblog/2015/11/23/interpretation-and-construction-2-samuel-williston-greg-klass/ (last accessed 7 November 2018); G Klass, 'Interpretation and Construction 3: Arthur Linton Corbin' (*New Private Law: Project on the Foundations of Private Law*, 25 November 2015) http://blogs.harvard.edu/nplblog/2015/11/25/interpretation-and-construction-3-arthur-linton-corbin-greg-klass/ (last accessed 7 November 2018); see also R Poscher, 'The Hermeneutic Character of Legal Construction' in S Glanert and F Girard (eds), *Law's Hermeneutics: Other Investigations* (London, Routledge, 2017) 207.

[24] These definitions were presented in Solum, 'Originalism and Constitutional Construction' (n 11) 457.

[25] Goldsworthy, 'The Case for Originalism' (n 1) 42–43.

[26] I do not mean to take a strong stand on the fact–value distinction and, in particular, I am not assuming that there are no 'moral facts' and I certainly do not believe there are no legal facts. It might be more precise to distinguish between 'normative and non-normative claims', or 'normative facts versus facts that are not normative in nature'.

facts about the way that language works. The fact that the communicative content of the constitutional text is fixed at the time that each provision is framed, and ratified, does not entail the conclusion that the fixed communicative content should constrain constitutional practice. It is at the very least possible that judges and officials would accept the Fixation Thesis but deny the Constraint Principle. The Fixation Thesis is a factual claim about the communicative content of the constitutional text. The Constraint Principle is a normative claim about constitutional practice.

The Constraint Principle is normative because it is a claim about how legal practice ought to go; if the Constraint Principle is true or correct, then it follows that constitutional actors ought to do certain things and refrain from doing others. In the sense that I am using the word 'normative', this is simply what it means to be a normative claim.

In debates about constitutional theory, we can distinguish two types of normative claims: moral and legal. As I am using the term 'normative', a normative claim provides a reason for action or evaluation. Moral claims are obviously normative. If an action is morally right, this provides a reason for performing the action. Legal claims are normative as well. If an action is legally required, that provides a reason for performing the action. Of course, there are deep questions about the nature of legal normativity and its relationship to morality. For the purposes of this chapter, I will assume that all-things-considered moral claims override legal claims.

But even if all-things-considered moral obligations trump legal duties, it may nonetheless be the case that legal duties can alter our moral obligations. We may have *pro tanto* moral reasons to act or refrain from acting, and these *pro tanto* moral reasons might be overridden, once legal obligations and permissions are taken into account. For example, one might have a *pro tanto* moral reason to take food from its owner and provide it to a hungry person, but once the legal rights of the owner are considered, the moral reason might be overridden and one would then have an all-things-considered moral reason not to perform the action. In the constitutional sphere, the executive might have a *pro tanto* reason of political morality to adopt a policy that would alleviate some social evil, but that *pro tanto* reason might be overridden if the action would constitute an exercise of lawmaking power that is reserved to the legislature.

There are many further complications. It is not clear whether there is a general obligation to obey the law; and if there is such an obligation, questions arise as to whether it is defeasible and, if so, under what conditions. Philosophical anarchists take the position that there is no general obligation to obey the law, but arguments for such an obligation have been made. Moreover, whether or not there is a general obligation to obey the law, there may be such an obligation with respect to a particular legal system that is reasonably just – even if particular laws are themselves not morally optimal. These issues are further complicated by the divide in general moral philosophy between consequentialist, deontological and aretaic theories. These questions are deep and, on this occasion, we shall have to finesse them by making certain reasonable (but contestable) assumptions.

For the purposes of this chapter, I will assume that the full case for originalism must provide a moral justification. Let me call this the 'Requirement of Moral Justification' (or RMJ). Even if there is an obligation to obey the law, and even if the Constraint Principle (or something like it) is part of the law, a critic of originalism can argue that the law should be changed on the ground that the Constraint Principle lacks normative justification, and that there are all-things-considered reasons to change that law so as to legally authorise departure from constraint. This is not to say that RMJ renders the legal case for the Constraint Principle (or something like it) irrelevant. If constraint is legally required, then many constitutional actors may view themselves as obligated to act in accord with original meaning – unless and until the constitution is changed. Of course, a fully-developed argument for RMJ would require a much fuller discussion than that provided in this short paragraph. Here, RMJ is simply an assumption, accompanied by an explanation of the assumption's plausibility.

In *The Case for Originalism*, Goldsworthy's argument includes both normative and factual elements. Propositions 1, 2 and 3 make factual claims about communicative content (linguistic meaning). Propositions 4, 5 and 6 make normative arguments. Some of these arguments are moral, some are legal, and some are either ambiguous or make both moral and legal claims.

Recall Proposition 4: '[w]hen a constitution itself requires that it be changed only by some special democratic procedure, this binds judges as well as other officials'. This claim is best understood as legal in nature: the claim that judges and officials are 'bound' by constitutional provisions that limit amendments to those that are approved by a specific procedure is a claim about what is legally required of judges and officials.

Proposition 5 makes both moral and legal claims. Recall that Proposition 5 claims that any judge who violated the requirement that some constitution be changed only by a special democratic procedure would 'flout' (act contrary to): (1) 'the constitution itself', (2) 'the rule of law', (3) 'the principle of democracy' and (4) 'the principle of federalism' (if the constitution establishes a federal system).

The first of these claims ('the constitution itself') might appear, on its surface, to be purely legal in nature. Acting contrary to the constitution is acting contrary to law. However, in his explication of the constitution-itself argument, Goldsworthy does explicitly make moral claims. Here is the relevant passage:

> A working constitution that is generally accepted as morally authoritative is indeed morally authoritative because it is essential to decent, civilized life – provided that it does not include moral flaws so egregious that they outweigh that benefit. This is because it provides the community with incalculable benefits of an established and accepted set of procedures for making collective decisions binding on all its members; in other words, because the only realistic alternative is usually some form of grievous civil strife, such as anarchy or civil war.[27]

This aspect of the constitution-itself argument is clearly moral in nature. In the discussion that follows in section III., I will consider both the legal and moral dimensions of Goldsworthy's constitution-itself argument.

The second claim is ambiguous: the 'rule of law' could be understood as either a legal or moral claim. It might be that Goldsworthy's rule of law argument is that violations of the Constraint Principle are violations of the law: this interpretation is suggested by this statement: 'Originalism is motivated by respect for the requirements of the constitution itself, and therefore of the rule of law'.[28] Again, the argument has two dimensions – each considered separately below.

[27] Goldsworthy, 'The Case for Originalism' (n 1) 59.
[28] Goldsworthy, 'The Case for Originalism' (n 1) 57.

The third claim refers to the principle of democracy. Goldsworthy's explication of the fourth argument makes it clear that he rejects the argument that originalism is justified by a principle of popular sovereignty.[29] Although his explanation does not directly refer to the idea of democratic legitimacy, he does invoke the idea of 'democratic control over constitutional change'.[30] That claim sounds in political morality, and I will classify it as a purely moral claim.

The fourth and final claim ('the principle of federalism') is not amplified in any explicit way in Goldsworthy's explication of Proposition 5. My understanding of the claim is that it is legal in nature. Goldsworthy does not attempt to make an argument of political morality for the principle of federalism, but it seems obvious that circumventing the federalism component of a constitutional amendment procedure would run afoul of the legal principle of federalism that is contained in many constitutions. Although we cannot be sure, I believe that the best understanding of Goldsworthy's claim is that his federalism argument sounds in law and not morality.

III. Internal Assessment of Goldsworthy's Normative Arguments

I will begin with the legal components of Goldsworthy's case for originalism and then move to the moral elements. Before proceeding further, I want to emphasise my admiration for Goldsworthy's statement of the normative case for originalism. No effort prior to Goldsworthy's is as sophisticated, rich and well-argued. My own work on these issues, the current version of which is developed in an unpublished manuscript entitled *The Constraint Principle*, stands (I hope squarely) on Goldsworthy's shoulders. Moreover, although I am sceptical about the legal component of Goldsworthy's case for originalism, I am largely in agreement with the underlying thrust of the moral component. If I probe for weaknesses and unstated assumptions, it is because I believe that Goldsworthy's arguments are important and, for that reason, should be developed in their best possible form.

A. The Legal Component of the Case for Originalism

The legal component of Goldsworthy's case for originalism includes four distinct elements: (1) the amendment procedures argument, (2) the constitution-itself argument, (3) the rule of law argument, and (4) the principle of federalism argument. The first of these elements is from Proposition 4 and the remaining three elements are drawn from Proposition 5. These arguments contain both moral and legal dimensions, but the discussion that follows is focused solely on the legal dimension of these four arguments; the moral arguments are discussed in the section that immediately follows.

It goes without saying that the argument that originalism is already the law can only be made in the context of a particular legal system. Thus, originalism might be the law

[29] Goldsworthy, 'The Case for Originalism' (n 1) 58.
[30] Goldsworthy, 'The Case for Originalism' (n 1) 59.

in Australia but not in the United States. In this chapter, I am not assessing the claim that originalism is the law in Australia; my focus will be on the United States. Nonetheless, there are parallels between the two cases, and some of the argumentative moves that I make in the American case may also be relevant to the Australian case.

The question at hand is whether compliance with the Constraint Principle (or something like it) is legally required in the United States. Some theorists have thought the answer to this question is obviously 'yes', because the legal content produced by a legal text must, as a matter of logic, be the 'meaning' of the text. The idea is that originalism provides the correct theory of constitutional 'interpretation' and that it is obvious that judges and officials are obligated to follow the Constitution (as made explicit by the Constraint Principle). But this seemingly simple argument is based on a conflation between interpretation (understood as the activity that discerns the meaning of the constitutional text) and construction (understood as the activity that determines the legal effects of the text, including the content of constitutional doctrine). From the fact that a constitutional text has communicative content (CC), it does not follow that officials and judges must give the constitution corresponding legal content (LC). The assumption that it does has been dubbed 'the standard picture' by Mark Greenberg, and whatever the merits of the standard picture, it is not a necessary truth that the legal content associated with a constitutional text is simply a translation of the communicative content into legal rules.[31] It is at least possible that the propositions of law associated with a constitution would be inconsistent with the communicative content.

Some theorists believe that the answer to the question whether the Constraint Principle is legally required is clearly 'no'. This belief is usually grounded on the observation that the legal content of constitutional doctrine frequently contradicts the communicative content of the text of the United States' Constitution. These contradictions are not limited to a few isolated cases; instead, the tension between original meaning and constitutional doctrine exists across a wide variety of constitutional contexts, ranging from separation of powers and federalism to the freedom of speech and the unenumerated constitutional right to privacy. For example, the First Amendment of the *United States Constitution* begins with the phrase, 'Congress shall make no law', but the Supreme Court has applied the First Amendment to the judiciary and the executive in many cases; for example, *New York Times v Sullivan*.[32] These Supreme Court cases are clearly part of American constitutional law, and therefore, some theorists believe that it is obviously true that originalism is not the law – in other words, the Constraint Principle is not itself a rule of constitutional law.[33]

[31] M Greenberg, 'The Standard Picture and Its Discontents' in L Green and B Leiter (eds), *Oxford Studies in Philosophy of Law* (Oxford, Oxford University Press, 2011) Vol 1, 39; M Greenberg, 'The Moral Impact Theory of Law' (2014) 123 *Yale Law Journal* 1288, 1296–99; M Greenberg, 'Legislation as Communication? Legal Interpretation and the Study of Linguistic Communication' in A Marmor and S Soames (eds), *Philosophical Foundations of Language in The Law* (Oxford, Oxford University Press, 2011) 217, 223–24; M Greenberg, 'What Makes A Method of Legal Interpretation Correct? Legal Standards vs Fundamental Determinants' (2017) 130 *Harvard Law Review Forum* 105, 107.

[32] *New York Times v Sullivan*, 376 US 254 (1964).

[33] A more nuanced version of this position appears in RH Fallon, 'How to Choose a Constitutional Theory' (1999) 87 *California Law Review* 535, 547:

> If the Constitution's status as ultimate law depends on practices of acceptance, then the claim that the written Constitution is the only valid source of constitutional norms loses all pretense of self-evident validity. As originalists candidly admit, originalist principles cannot explain or justify much of contemporary

But once again, things are not simple. Some court decisions are mistaken as a matter of law: from the fact that a decision has been made by the Supreme Court and is therefore binding on the lower courts and officials, it does not follow that the decision is correct. One way to make this clear is to distinguish between the deep structure and the surface structure of constitutional law.[34] It is at least possible that the deep structure of constitutional law in a particular jurisdiction is originalist and that some features of the surface structure are mistakes.[35] William Baude has pursued a similar line in his magisterial: 'Is Originalism Our Law?'[36]

Goldsworthy distributes his version of the positivist argument among several closely related claims, including the amendment-argument in Proposition 4 and the constitution-itself, rule-of-law and federalism arguments in Proposition 5. On my understanding of Goldsworthy, all of these arguments express the same basic idea: the law requires originalism – at least in some jurisdictions. This can be seen from the fact that the constitution specifies the procedure for change by formal amendment, from the nature of the constitution, from the notion of the rule of law and from the principle of federalism (in some constitutions). For this reason, I will treat all of these arguments as one argument: the positive law requires originalism (or more specifically, the Constraint Principle) in legal system L (where L could be Australia, the United States, or some other national or subnational legal system with a written constitution).

Goldsworthy acknowledges the existence of judicial decisions in the United States that are inconsistent with originalism, quoting Justice Scalia's statement that 'it would be foolish to pretend that … [originalism] has become … the dominant mode of interpretation in the courts.'[37] I believe that the crucial argument made by Goldsworthy is contained in the following passage:

> Even when judges purport to enforce unenumerated, supposedly implied principles, they invariably claim to have discovered those principles in the constitution, not added them to it. This surely indicates that they know that they lack lawful authority deliberately to change the constitution. If there is a discrepancy between what they say they do and what on occasions they actually do, the former is better evidence of the scope of their lawful authority than the latter. Any claim about the lawful scope of judicial authority must be able to pass the test of public candor: If that claim is not and cannot be candidly asserted in public by the judges themselves, it is almost certainly false.[38]

constitutional law. Important lines of precedent diverge from original understandings. Judges frequently take other considerations into account. Moreover, the public generally accepts the courts' nonoriginalist pronouncements as legitimate – not merely as final, but as properly rendered.

[34] The terminology is borrowed from Noam Chomsky. See N Chomsky, *Aspects of the Theory of Syntax* (Cambridge, Massachusetts, MIT Press, 1965). For application to constitutional law, see BF Havel, 'The Constitution in an Era of Supranational Adjudication' (2000) 78 *North Carolina Law Review* 257, 280.

[35] For my own statement of the positivist argument in tentative form in a working paper, see LB Solum, 'Semantic Originalism' (Unpublished, 22 November 2008) https://papers.ssrn.com/sol3/papers.cfm?abstract_id=1120244 (last accessed 7 November 2018) (on file with author).

[36] See Baude (n 13).

[37] See A Scalia, 'Foreword' (2008) 31 *Harvard Journal of Law & Public Policy* 871, 871, quoted in Goldsworthy, 'The Case for Originalism' (n 1) 56.

[38] Goldsworthy, 'The Case for Originalism' (n 1) 56–57. Goldsworthy makes an additional claim that I believe is not sufficient to rebut the positivist argument that originalism is not the law. His additional argument focuses on the cases in which judges act 'creatively' by 'supplementing' the constitutional text when it is underdeterminate (at 56), but my judgement is that there are at least some important Supreme Court cases in the United States that cannot be explained in this way. A full evaluation of this claim would require us to examine many Supreme Court cases and determine whether the Court is supplementing or amending the Constitution: such an evaluation is beyond the scope of this chapter.

Goldsworthy's argument runs together ideas that can be teased apart. One portion of the argument is a normative argument that seems to be about the values of publicity and transparency; I believe that Goldsworthy is referring to these values when he introduces 'the test of public candor'. Transparency and publicity are important values of political morality, but I do not believe that it is plausible to argue that the test of public candor is a legal principle that renders living constitutionalist opinions invalid if they fail to pass the test. Hence, this portion of the argument is best understood as sounding in political morality and not law.

The other aspect of Goldsworthy's argument does make a legal claim – that judicial practice is best understood as committing to originalism as a matter of principle and hence that the deep structure of constitutional law is originalist. The difficulty with this argument is that when nonoriginalist judges justify their decisions, they are not employing originalism as the standard of constitutional fidelity. Instead, they invoke the function, purpose, ideals, principles, or spirit of the constitution. But as we all know, adherence to the purpose of a legal text can be invoked as a justification for acting contrary to the communicative content (or linguistic meaning) of the text. References to constitutional function (and similar ideas) might superficially resemble a commitment to the constitutional text (and hence originalism) but, in fact, the opposite may be true. Reference to the function of the constitutional text may well signal commitment to the idea that the constitutional text is not legally binding on judges. Of course, the failure to be explicit about the invocation of a power to override the communicative content of the constitutional text may be contrary to the values of transparency and publicity, but those are best understood as moral values and not as legal rules.

Moreover, it seems likely that, in many cases, judges do not attempt to justify their decisions by reference to the constitutional text at all. An unusually candid example is found in Justice Richard Posner's concurring opinion in *Hively*,[39] which contains the following remarkable statement:

> [I]nterpretation can mean giving a fresh meaning to a statement (which can be a statement found in a constitutional or statutory text) – a meaning that infuses the statement with vitality and significance today. An example of this last form of interpretation – the form that in my mind is most clearly applicable to the present case – is the Sherman Antitrust Act, enacted in 1890, long before there was a sophisticated understanding of the economics of monopoly and competition. Times have changed; and for more than thirty years the Act has been interpreted in conformity to the modern, not the nineteenth-century, understanding of the relevant economics. The Act has thus been updated by, or in the name of, judicial interpretation – the form of interpretation that consists of making old law satisfy modern needs and understandings. And a common form of interpretation it is, despite its flouting 'original meaning'.[40]

Justice Stephen Breyer of the United States Supreme Court is not quite as clear as Judge Posner, but his monograph *Active Liberty* is transparently anti-originalist.[41] This is not the occasion to rehearse the evidence but, in my opinion, many opinions of the United States Supreme Court cannot be construed as affirming originalism in principle but departing from originalism in practice.

[39] *Hively v Ivy Tech Community College of Indiana*, 853 F.3d 339, 352 (7th Cir 2017).

[40] ibid 352–53.

[41] S Breyer, *Active Liberty: Interpreting a Democratic Constitution*, revised edn (New York, Oxford University Press, 2008); I Somin, '"Active Liberty" and Judicial Power: What Should Courts Do to Promote Democracy?' (2006) 100 *Northwestern University Law Review* 1827, 1850 (describing Breyer's critique of originalism in *Active Liberty*).

I have not formed any ultimate judgement about the thesis that originalism or the Constraint Principle is part of the deep structure of constitutional law in the United States. I am not fully convinced by Goldsworthy's version of the argument; nor am I convinced by the more extensive version of the argument advanced by William Baude. But even if the argument were successful, it would not make a complete case for originalism. Many originalists conceive of originalism as a project of law reform: originalism is not yet the law, but it should be. Living constitutionalists can advance their project in the same way. If Goldsworthy and Baude are correct, then living constitutionalists can – and some surely will – argue that living constitutionalism should be adopted as a programme of law reform.

B. The Moral Component of the Case for Originalism

As I understand the moral components of Goldsworthy's case for originalism, it has two primary components: one based on the ideal of the rule of law, and the other based on the idea of democratic legitimacy. The rule-of-law argument is found in the moral understanding of Goldsworthy's amendment argument in Proposition 4, and the constitution-itself and rule-of law arguments in Proposition 5. The democratic legitimacy argument is found in the principle-of-democracy argument in Proposition 5.

i. The Rule of Law Argument

The moral version of the rule-of-law argument is based on the idea that the rule of law is an ideal of political morality. The idea is that originalism complies with the rule-of-law principle, but that living constitutionalism (nonoriginalism) does not.

I have already quoted one of the key passages above. Goldsworthy argues that adherence to a constitution is required for the rule of law. He might be understood as arguing that an originalist constitutional practice 'provides the community with incalculable benefits of an established and accepted set of procedures for making collective decisions binding on all its members', and that 'the only realistic alternative is usually some form of grievous civil strife, such as anarchy or civil war'.[42] But this understanding of Goldsworthy's position is unsatisfactory. His own statement of the argument does not claim that originalism is the only alternative to civil strife, but instead identifies a 'working constitution' as the institution that confers the benefits of the rule of law.

The real work is done by a subsequent argument, which I shall dub the 'restrictions argument'. Goldsworthy states the argument as follows:

> The constitution protects and empowers, as well as restricts, subsequent generations, and these benefits are inseparable from the restrictions: They are two sides of the same coin. If some attempt to evade the restrictions by acting unconstitutionally, others may be tempted to follow suit, putting the constitution itself at risk along with the protection and empowerment it provides. The procedures that a constitution prescribes for its own amendment exemplify this coincidence of empowerment and restriction. … If judges, for example, were openly to change the constitution

[42] Goldsworthy, 'The Case for Originalism' (n 1) 59.

> contrary to the prescribed amendment procedure, other legal officials might be tempted to follow suit (which is why, when judges occasionally do so, they pretend not to).[43]

Notice that Goldsworthy is making an empirical claim about a causal mechanism. The argument is that nonoriginalist constitutional practice by judges would encourage other officials to violate the constitution, eventually undermining the rule of law, leading to civil strife.

If this causal claim is true, one might ask why the rule of law has not given way in the United States? The United States Supreme Court has engaged in substantial nonoriginalist constitutional practice for many decades – arguably since the New Deal Court in the late thirties and early forties, and certainly since the Warren Court of the fifties and sixties. If the causal claim were true, then sufficient time has passed for the causal processes to play out. If the rule of law still holds in the United States, then it might be argued that this fact disproves the efficacy of the causal mechanism that Goldsworthy postulates.

One line of rejoinder to the American counterexample to the causal claim is suggested by Goldsworthy's qualification of his claim: he has suggested that the damage to the rule of law occurs in cases in which judges 'openly … change the constitution' without amendment. Goldsworthy's claim that the United States Supreme Court has not openly claimed that it has the power to amend the Constitution is correct, but it is not so clear that the Court has not been open about adopting a nonoriginalist approach to constitutional interpretation. The relevant political actors – eg, members of Congress and their staff – are sophisticated actors with an institutional capacity to understand the difference between abstract professions of fidelity to the Constitution that are self-understood as consistent with living constitutionalism, and the more rigorous demands of originalism and the Constraint Principle. It seems very unlikely that Congress fails to understand that the current Supreme Court is not an originalist court, and that many of the important decisions of the past several decades are inconsistent with the communicative content of the constitutional text.

Nonetheless, it might be argued that the United States is at risk of serious damage to the rule of law – eventually, if not in the very near future. It might be argued that constitutional practice in the United States is subject to what might be called a downward spiral of politicisation. As political actors come to recognise that nonoriginalist judging can allow the ideological and political preferences of the Justices to determine the outcome of politically salient issues, there may be strong incentives to politicise the judicial selection process. Presidents will have incentives to select their ideological allies as Supreme Court Justices and the Senate will have incentives to use the confirmation process to affect the ideological composition of the Court. For example, one might interpret the Senate's failure to act on Merrick Garland's nomination to replace Antonin Scalia on the Supreme Court as motivated by the hope that a Republican President would be elected who would then appoint a more conservative Justice. This action by Republicans might provoke Democrats to retaliate; for example, if control of the Senate returns to Democrats in 2018, the Senate might refuse to act on any Supreme Court nominations by a Republican President. Heightened awareness of the politicisation of the process might lead to the delegitimation of the Supreme Court's authority to decide constitutional cases which bind the lower courts, legislatures and executive officials – at both the national and state levels. Thus, Goldsworthy's claim about damage

[43] Goldsworthy, 'The Case for Originalism' (n 1) 59.

to the rule of law could be correct in the long run, even if the process of politicisation has not yet reached the stage where the rule of law is in imminent danger.

ii. The Democratic Legitimacy Argument

Goldsworthy's principle-of-democracy argument is not developed in depth. Goldsworthy seems to assume that his readers accept the claim that the democratic legitimacy of the institution of judicial review is seriously damaged by violations of the Constraint Principle. I agree with the gist of Goldsworthy's argument, but there are many complications that must be taken into account.

The principle-of-democracy argument (like the legal argument) is context dependent. It might hold in Australia, but fail in the United States. As Goldsworthy himself recognises, the democratic pedigree of many constitutions is dubious. The unamended *United States Constitution*, as well as the first 12 amendments, were adopted by an electorate that excluded the vast majority of the population: women, slaves, Native Americans and non-property qualified white males were all excluded from direct participation in the ratification process. The *Canadian Constitution* was even less democratic, tracing its origins to action by the Parliament of the United Kingdom. The Constitution of the United States does have a process for amendment in Article V, but that process requires two-thirds of both houses of Congress to propose an amendment (or call a convention) and ratification by three-fourths of the state legislatures.

Moreover, it is not clear that the United States Supreme Court actually acts undemocratically when it violates the Constraint Principle; Corinna Lain, for example, has argued that many of the Supreme Court's most controversial decisions moved the law in a direction favoured by democratic majorities.[44] Thus, many opponents of originalism believe that the democratic legitimacy argument cuts against originalism and not for it. For these reasons, a fully developed version of the democratic legitimacy argument requires more depth than provided in Goldsworthy's brief statement.

These difficulties with the democratic legitimacy argument might be overcome in various ways. Democratic legitimacy is best understood as a scalar and not a binary: that is, the democratic legitimacy of a given institution is not an all or nothing affair, but is instead a matter of degrees. The democratic legitimacy of a constitutional system that adheres to the Constraint Principle must be compared to the alternative – and a strong case can be made that an imperfectly legitimate originalist constitutional practice is, nonetheless, more legitimate than a constitutional practice that allows a simple majority of the highest court the power to adopt amending constitutional constructions – even if their decisions are endorsed by the public in the opinion polls. In the case of the United States, five members of the Supreme Court can effectively change the Constitution. Supreme Court Justices are not elected, and they serve for life terms. The only mechanism for removing the Justices, impeachment, is difficult and conviction requires a supermajority (two-thirds) vote by the Senate. Much more would need to be said, but the brief summary in this paragraph is sufficient to demonstrate that the full case for originalism on democratic legitimacy grounds would require a lengthy and complex argument.

[44] C Barrett Lain, 'Upside-Down Judicial Review' (2012) 101 *Georgetown Law Journal* 113.

IV. Some External Reflections on Goldsworthy's Case for Originalism

Goldsworthy's *The Case for Originalism* is compact, spanning some 28 pages. It would be unreasonable to expect an in-depth examination of the foundational issues in constitutional theory in a short, programmatic statement of the arguments for originalism. Nonetheless, future work on this topic by Goldsworthy and others could be improved by reflection on questions about the structure of the debate over originalism, and the appropriate methods for justifying normative constitutional theories. In this section, I will raise two such issues. The first raises the question whether originalism can be justified without consideration of the alternatives. The second issue involves the question as to what methods of justification are appropriate when normative constitutional theories are assessed from the moral point of view.

A. The Need for Pairwise Comparison

Goldsworthy's *The Case for Originalism* does not have much to say about the alternatives to originalism, but surely the normative case for originalism must take the alternatives into account.[45] This complicates the task of justifying originalism, because there is no single alternative. Instead, there are many different forms of nonoriginalism, including the following:

Constitutional Pluralism: This is the view that law is a complex argumentative practice with plural forms of constitutional argument.[46]

Constructive Interpretation: This is Ronald Dworkin's theory, also called 'law as integrity' or the 'moral readings' theory.[47]

Common Law Constitutionalism: This is the view that the content of constitutional law should be determined by a common-law process.[48]

Popular Constitutionalism: This is the view that 'We the People' (the polity) can legitimately change the constitution through processes such as transformative appointments that do not formally amend the text.[49]

Multiple Meanings: This is the view that the constitutional text has multiple linguistic meanings and that constitutional practice should choose between these meanings on a case by case basis.[50]

[45] The legal case is different. If originalism is legally required, then the existence of alternatives is irrelevant from the legal point of view.

[46] See P Bobbitt, *Constitutional Interpretation* (Oxford, Blackwell Publishers, 1991) 12–13.

[47] See RM Dworkin, *Freedom's Law: The Moral Reading of the American Constitution* (Cambridge, Massachusetts, Harvard University Press, 1996) 2–3. The moral readings view is now strongly associated with James Fleming. See, eg, JE Fleming, 'Fidelity, Change, and the Good Constitution' (2014) 62 *American Journal of Comparative Law* 515, 515.

[48] DA Strauss, *The Living Constitution* (Oxford, Oxford University Press, 2010).

[49] For a description of popular constitutionalism, see L Alexander and LB Solum, 'Popular? Constitutionalism?' (2005) 118 *Harvard Law Review* 1594.

[50] See CR Sunstein, 'Formalism in Constitutional Theory' (2017) 32 *Constitutional Commentary* 27; RH Fallon, 'The Meaning of Legal "Meaning" and Its Implications for Theories of Legal Interpretation' (2015) 82 *University of Chicago Law Review* 1235.

Superlegislature: This is the view that the Supreme Court (or Constitutional Court) should act as an ongoing committee of constitutional revision, with the power to adopt amending constructions of the constitutional text on the basis of the same kinds of reasons that would be admissible in a constitutional convention.[51]

Thayerianism: This is a family of views that require courts to defer to the legislature, with three variants:

Constrained Thayerianism is the view that courts should defer to the legislature, but that Congress itself should be constrained by the original meaning of the constitutional text.

Unconstrained Thayerianism is the view that courts should defer to the legislature and that the legislature should have the constitutional power to revise the constitutional text, either by adopting amending legislation, or by creating implicit amendments through ordinary statutes.[52]

Representation Reinforcement Thayerianism is the view that courts should defer to the legislature except when judicial review is necessary to preserve democracy, including protection of discreet and insular minorities and protection of democratic processes.[53]

Constitutional Antitheory: There are four views that are 'antitheoretical' in the sense that they deny that constitutional practice should be guided by any normative theory, whether that theory be originalist or nonoriginalist:

Particularism is the view that constitutional practice should be guided by salient situation-specific normative considerations in particular constitutional situations.[54]

Pragmatism is the similar view, associated with Judge Richard Posner that constitutional decisions should be made pragmatically on the basis of various normative considerations.[55]

Eclecticism is the view that different judges should embrace different approaches to constitutional interpretation and construction, and that even a single judge should adopt different approaches on different occasions.[56]

Opportunism is the view that theoretical stances should be deployed strategically to achieve ideological or partisan goals.[57]

[51] B Leiter, 'Constitutional Law, Moral Judgment, and the Supreme Court as Super-Legislature' (2015) 66 *Hastings Law Journal* 1601.

[52] Both constrained and unconstrained Thayerianism are inspired by the work of James Thayer. See JB Thayer, 'The Origin and Scope of the American Doctrine of Constitutional Law' (1893) 7 *Harvard Law Review* 129.

[53] This view is strongly associated with John Hart Ely. JH Ely, *Democracy and Distrust: A Theory of Judicial Review* (Cambridge, Harvard University Press, 1980).

[54] Constitutional particularism would draw on moral particularism. J Dancy, 'Moral Particularism' (*Stanford Encyclopedia of Philosophy*, revised 22 September 2017) http://plato.stanford.edu/entries/moral-particularism/ (last accessed 7 November 2018).

[55] RA Posner, 'Legal Pragmatism Defended' (2004) 71 *University of Chicago Law Review* 683 ('The ultimate criterion of pragmatic adjudication is reasonableness'.).

[56] Although eclecticism seems implicit in the discourse of constitutional theory, no theorist of whom I am aware has explicitly articulated this position.

[57] For obvious reasons, adherents of constitutional opportunism will not publicly announce their position.

Constitutional Rejectionism: These views reject the constitution as an authoritative source of law.

> Anticonstitutionalism is the view that the communicative content of constitutions, in general, should play no role in constitutional practice.[58]
>
> Constitutional Replacement theories would allow the text of a normatively attractive replacement constitution to play a role in constitutional practice, but reject any constraining role for the current constitution of a particular jurisdiction; eg, the Constitution of the United States.[59]

Ideally, the case for originalism would be made by a process of pairwise comparison, with each of the major rivals considered. But once we begin to go down this road, it becomes apparent that the issues are more complex than acknowledged by Goldsworthy. For example, the democratic legitimacy argument is implicitly based on a comparison of originalism with a rival view that grants the highest court the power to invalidate legislation or executive action on the basis of the policy preferences of the members of the court. But many of the rivals to originalism do not have this feature. For example, the Thayerian family of nonoriginalist theories severely constrains the power of the highest court to invalidate legislation; the representation-reinforcement variant of Thayerianism limits judicial invalidation of legislation to cases where judicial action actually increases the democratic legitimacy of the system. But other rivals seem to suffer from severe problems of democratic legitimacy – the 'superlegislature' view is a prime example.

B. Procedures of Justification

Goldsworthy recognises that originalism may lead to 'grave injustice' in a particular case and, by extension, could produce systematic injustice.[60] Much of the resistance to originalism in the United States is focused on this objection, but the problem of injustice for originalism is most serious when there is a lack of social consensus on the question regarding whether a given law, executive action, or judicial decision is truly unjust. In cases where there is social consensus, the ordinary democratic politics will usually be able to correct the injustice. In the much rarer cases, where injustice is required (as opposed to merely permitted) by the constitutional text, constitutional amendments will be possible – given a supermajoritarian consensus in favour of the amendment. The difficulties arise in cases where there is substantial disagreement about whether a given practice is unjust. In the United States, the paradigm case of such disagreement is abortion and the Supreme Court's decision in *Roe v Wade*. Many citizens believe that a right to reproductive autonomy is essential to the equal citizenship and personhood of women – and that a society that does not provide such a right is fundamentally unjust to a degree that undermines legitimacy.

[58] LM Seidman, *On Constitutional Disobedience* (New York, Oxford University Press, 2013).

[59] S Levinson, *Our Undemocratic Constitution: Where the Constitution Goes Wrong (And How We the People Can Correct It)* (Oxford, Oxford University Press, 2006).

[60] Goldsworthy's Proposition 8 deals with this objection. Goldsworthy, 'The Case for Originalism' (n 1) 43.

Other citizens believe that the right to life of the unborn is morally equivalent to the right to life of human persons, and hence that a constitutional right to abortion is fundamentally unjust – again, to a degree, that undermines legitimacy. Given the fact of pluralism which characterises modern democratic societies, fundamental disagreements of this sort are likely to exist – although the specific issues may change over time. Citizens affirm a wide variety of views about morality and religion, and given freedom of conscience, expression and religion, this pluralism is not likely to go away.

What general method is appropriate for the justification of a normative constitutional theory? Should a constitutional theorist aim to develop a constitutional theory that fits the theorist's own normative beliefs? Or does the context of constitutional theory require that theorists consider normative disagreement and aim, instead, at a theory that could receive broad support from reasonable citizens with a wide range of moral, political, and ideological beliefs?

One possible strategy for the justification of normative constitutional theories would take the form of deductive arguments that begin with value premises upon which all or almost all reasonable citizens can agree. This strategy might work in a society with a strong consensus on a single moral or religious doctrine – or an overlapping consensus among various doctrines that converge to support a normative constitutional theory.

We can begin our investigation of these questions with the idea of reflective equilibrium. The notion of 'reflective equilibrium', familiar from the work of John Rawls,[61] has been invoked as providing an appropriate method for resolving theoretical debates in normative constitutional theory.[62] How would this method apply to the question concerning whether to affirm the Constraint Principle in particular and originalism in general? We can begin to answer this question by explicating the idea of reflective equilibrium.

Given the nature of the problems of constitutional theory, we should not expect that the claims made about constitutional meaning will usually be justified by deductive proof. Of course, deductive proof is likely to play a role at the level of supporting detail. Some positions in constitutional theory may involve contradictions, and these positions are demonstrably false. But in other cases, our starting points will be our pre-reflective beliefs about various matters, ranging from the very particular and concrete to the general and abstract. Such starting points will include relatively particular beliefs like '*Brown v Board* was rightly decided', and relatively abstract beliefs like 'The rule of law values of predictability, certainty, consistency, and publicity are an important component of political morality'. In this picture, the method of constitutional theory starts with an examination of our pre-reflective beliefs and their relationships. Some beliefs may be inconsistent. In that case, one or more of the beliefs may need to be reexamined and revised. Gradually, our pre-reflective beliefs will become more refined and coherent. At some stage, the theorist will begin to regard some of these beliefs as considered judgements. A wholly successful constitutional theory will bring

[61] J Rawls, *A Theory of Justice* (Cambridge, Massachusetts, Harvard University Press, 1971).

[62] See RH Fallon, 'Arguing in Good Faith about the Constitution: Ideology, Methodology, and Reflective Equilibrium' (2017) 84 *University of Chicago Law Review* 123; MN Berman, 'Reflective Equilibrium and Constitutional Method: Lessons from John McCain and the Natural-Born Citizenship Clause' in G Huscroft and BW Miller (eds), *The Challenge of Originalism: Theories of Constitutional Interpretation* (New York, Cambridge University Press, 2011) 246.

all of our considered judgements into reflective equilibrium – a relationship of consistency and mutual support.

So far, the description of the method of reflective equilibrium has treated constitutional theory as operating within the discourse of constitutional practice. But it is not the case that our beliefs about constitutional theory fall or stand independently of our beliefs about other matters. Consider an analogy to tort law. Normative tort theory may require recourse to general normative legal theory which, in turn, must be reconciled with moral philosophy and political theory. Given a consequentialist approach to tort theory, the normative evaluation of particular tort rules may best be accomplished by utilisation of the tools of economics, which themselves may involve formal techniques. Likewise, originalist constitutional theory uses tools drawn from the philosophy of language and theoretical linguistics as the basis for claims about meaning (eg, the Fixation Thesis and the Public Meaning Thesis). The Constraint Principle is a thesis in normative constitutional theory, but its validity may depend in part on our beliefs about nonconstitutional matters within law, and a variety of other matters outside of law.

The method of reflective equilibrium may begin with our pre-reflective beliefs about various matters. Let us call these initial beliefs 'intuitions' and, in the case of constitutional matters, 'constitutional intuitions'.[63] We have beliefs about various matters (eg, about facts, physics, and aesthetics), but let us stipulate for present purposes that our constitutional intuitions are normative beliefs which are constitutionally salient. Thus, our constitutional intuitions include beliefs about the rightness or wrongness of particular cases (both real and hypothetical), about the moral soundness of constitutional doctrines and principles and about more general normative matters, such as the normative attractiveness of democratic self-government, the importance of the rule of law and so forth.

The method of reflective equilibrium assumes that there is a contrast between our intuitions (before reflection) and our 'considered judgements'. Let us use this latter phrase to designate beliefs that have been subject to reflection and evaluation. The method of reflective equilibrium assumes that our intuitions are subject to revision for various reasons. Thus, one might have an intuitive belief that *Griswold v Connecticut*[64] was correctly decided (as a matter of normative constitutional theory), but after reflection one might conclude that this intuition was incorrect and that *Griswold* was an error. The initial belief might be based on a first-order normative judgement that the decision of married couples to use contraception should not be regulated by the state, and the revision might be motivated by the second-order consideration that the courts should not have the power to create constitutional rights absent authorisation to do so by the constitutional text. Given the complexity of constitutional law and theory, it would be quite surprising if all of our pre-reflective beliefs were already in a state of perfect consistency and mutual support. Some of our beliefs will have to give way to others; other sets of beliefs may need to be modified systematically to bring them into reflective equilibrium.

[63] By using the term 'intuition', I do not mean to imply anything deep about the nature or epistemic basis of these beliefs. For example, I do not mean to imply that our moral beliefs are produced by a faculty of moral intuition, much less that there is a special faculty of constitutional intuition.

[64] *Griswold v Connecticut*, 381 US 479 (1965).

Our normative beliefs about constitutional matters exist at a variety of levels of generality, ranging from beliefs about particular cases (actual and hypothetical), to midlevel principles and constitutional doctrines, and highly abstract beliefs about political morality. Thus, we may have a belief that *Brown v Board*[65] was decided correctly, that the Equal Protection Clause forbids discrimination on the basis of race and that a principle of equal citizenship should govern the basic structure of society. To reach reflective equilibrium, we seek to make our beliefs at all of these levels of generality consistent and mutually supportive. Reflective equilibrium does not assume that beliefs at one point on the continuum, between specific considered judgements about particular matters and general considered judgements about abstract matters, have priority.[66] We might begin with a high level of confidence in our intuitions about a particular case and a lower level of confidence in our intuition about an abstract principle, or vice versa.

Rawls distinguished between wide and narrow reflective equilibrium, and this distinction is particularly important with respect to constitutional matters in a pluralist society. Because the exegesis of Rawls's theory is not important for the purpose of the matters at hand, I will introduce a third idea, 'broad reflective equilibrium', which is the specific notion that is deployed in the argument that follows.

The distinction between narrow, wide and broad reflective equilibrium can be articulated in various ways, but for present purposes, let us stipulate to the following definitions that are tailored to the constitutional context:

Narrow Reflective Equilibrium: The considered judgements of an *individual* on constitutional theory are in narrow reflective equilibrium when they are consistent and mutually supportive with each other.

Wide Reflective Equilibrium: The considered judgements of an *individual* on constitutional theory are in wide reflective equilibrium if they consider the 'conditions under which it would be fair for reasonable people to choose among competing principles [of constitutional theory], as well as evidence that the resulting principles constitute a feasible or stable conception of justice, that is, that people could sustain their commitment to such principles'.[67]

Broad Reflective Equilibrium: The considered judgements of a *political community* are in broad reflective equilibrium when a broad group of citizens are each in wide reflective equilibrium, such that there is an overlapping consensus on constitutional principles that are sufficiently similar to provide adequate guidance for constitutional practice.

There can be narrow reflective equilibrium at the individual level, but widespread disagreement about constitutional theory. And it is possible, and perhaps likely, that there

[65] *Brown v Board of Education of Topeka*, 347 US 483 (1954).

[66] Thus, the version of reflective equilibrium that I am articulating here does not assume the priority of the particular. One can imagine a particularist form of reflective equilibrium that did assume particular beliefs have priority over more general beliefs.

[67] N Daniels, 'Reflective Equilibrium' (*Stanford Encyclopedia of Philosophy*, revised 14 October 2016) http://plato.stanford.edu/entries/reflective-equilibrium/ (last accessed 7 November 2018). Daniels' definition is not specific to constitutional theory.

can be wide reflective equilibrium at the individual level, but that different individuals reach different conclusions about which constitutional principles can be the focus of a stable agreement. The emergence of broad reflective equilibrium requires that such disagreements be addressed with the aim of reaching an overlapping consensus on a set of constitutional principles that enable a stable and consistent constitutional practice. There can be broad reflective equilibrium, even though there is disagreement on a variety of issues in constitutional theory. For example, if there were overlapping consensus on several different originalist theories that affirmed the Fixation Thesis and the Constraint Principle, the remaining disagreements (eg, between public meaning theories and original methods theories) would not be so serious as to prevent the emergence of a reasonably consistent and stable constitutional jurisprudence. Broad reflective equilibrium does not require full constitutional consensus (where almost all constitutional actors affirm the same constitutional theory).[68]

Should constitutional theory aim at narrow, wide or broad reflective equilibrium? And what difference does this distinction make to the justification of the Constraint Principle? These questions are important and deep. The aim of the discussion that follows is to provide reasons for believing that constitutional theory ought to employ the method of broad reflective equilibrium (or wide reflective equilibrium in the alternative), but that the method of narrow reflective equilibrium is not appropriate.

Let us begin by examining the contrary position – that narrow reflective equilibrium provides the correct method of justification for normative constitutional theory. From the point of view of an individual (a judge or a constitutional theorist), narrow reflective equilibrium will result in a constitutional theory that is coherent. The individual theorist's views will be consistent and mutually supporting. Narrow reflective equilibrium will ensure that the individual's constitutional views are consistent with that individual's general views about political morality. Narrow reflective equilibrium begins with individual intuitions and ends with reflective equilibrium among considered judgements – from the point of view of the individual.

But it is clear that narrow reflective equilibrium does not provide the kind of justification that is appropriate to a constitutional theory for a pluralist society in which there is disagreement about deep matters – what Rawls called comprehensive religious and philosophical conceptions of the good. Our discussion of deep and shallow justifications shows why this is the case. If each individual seeks *internal consistency*, then different individuals will reach reflective equilibrium on different constitutional theories. But the primary role of a normative constitutional theory is not to provide *internal consistency*, but instead to provide a shared basis for agreement on a framework for the decision of constitutional cases. Narrow reflective equilibrium for each individual will produce a plurality of inconsistent views corresponding to the plurality of views about deep matters.

[68] The degree of consensus that is required is best understood as a function of principled constitutional stability. Disagreement that is consistent with a stable constitutional order, affirmed on the basis of principle (and not a result of the exercise of raw power), is consistent with broad reflective equilibrium.

This point can be illustrated (albeit simplistically) by considering five hypothetical justices, each of whom seeks narrow reflective equilibrium for their own constitutional theory:

Justice Immanuel holds a comprehensive deontological theory of the good and the right. His constitutional theory requires that the plain meaning of the Constitution be observed strictly and without exception by all officials and citizens.

Justice Jeremy holds a comprehensive welfarist theory of the good and the right. His constitutional theory requires that each constitutional case be decided in the way that produces the greatest sum of preference-satisfaction.

Justice Rosalind holds a comprehensive virtue-centred theory of the good and the right. Her constitutional theory requires that each constitutional case be decided in accord with the virtue of practical wisdom, so as to promote human flourishing.

Justice Francis holds a comprehensive religious conception of the good and the right. His constitutional theory emphasises the promotion of the true faith as the central aim of constitutional decisionmaking and, in particular, requires that the Constitution be interpreted to acknowledge the privileged role of the true faith in matters such as state support for religion.

Justice Gerald holds a theory of political morality in which equality of income and resources is the highest political value. His constitutional theory emphasises the promotion of economic equality as the central aim of constitutional decisionmaking.

The justices are each in narrow reflective equilibrium with respect to their own deep views, but none of the justices can affirm the method of any of the others. Moreover, members of the public who affirm a different comprehensive conception than any of the justices would have good reason to view those justices' constitutional theories as both wrong and illegitimate: internal consistency is not a sufficient basis for a shared agreement among citizens given the fact of reasonable pluralism.

Now consider the contrasting case of broad reflective equilibrium. Broad reflective equilibrium aims for consistency and mutual support among considered judgements that can be stated as public reasons. Each Justice would consider the fact of pluralism and seek agreement on constitutional principles that can be affirmed on the basis of considered judgements that can be shared by an overlapping consensus of reasonable citizens. Narrow reflective equilibrium is structured so as to produce constitutional dissensus – with different individuals and groups affirming different constitutional theories. Broad reflective equilibrium aims at constitutional consensus; more precisely, broad reflective equilibrium should aim at the greatest convergence among constitutional views that is practicable. Practicability could be theorised in various ways; for example, we might define the practicable by reference to Rawls's notion of the burdens of judgement.[69]

To reach broad reflective equilibrium, each of the hypothetical justices will need to avoid direct reliance on their own comprehensive views and instead seek public reasons or midlevel agreements. Given the fact of pluralism, constitutional theory requires principled

[69] J Rawls, *Political Liberalism* (New York, Columbia University Press, 2005) 36–37, 55–57.

compromise (broad reflective equilibrium) and not internal consistency (narrow reflective equilibrium). Because broad reflective equilibrium aims at an overlapping consensus among reasonable citizens, its achievement requires engagement among constitutional theorists, and between constitutional theorists and the wider political culture.

V. Conclusion

Goldsworthy's *The Case for Originalism* is, in my opinion, the single best version of what its title promises – a comprehensive justification for originalism, both as a theory of constitutional interpretation (and hence as a theory of the meaning of a constitutional text) and as an account of constitutional construction (and hence as a theory of constitutional practice). Although Goldsworthy's chapter is both relatively recent and admirably compact, it does more to illuminate debates about constitutional theory from an originalist perspective than anything (of which I am aware) that preceded it. The aim of this chapter has been to raise some questions about Goldsworthy's argument, to suggest ways in which it might be improved, and to make some suggestions regarding methods of argument about constitutional theory. None of what I have sought to accomplish in this chapter would have been possible without Goldsworthy's pioneering efforts.

More broadly, Goldsworthy has laid the foundations for a compelling case for originalism. Goldsworthy is surely correct that the communicative content of the constitutional text, fixed at the time of framing and ratification, is the actual 'meaning' of the text – if meaning is understood in its linguistic sense. And Goldsworthy has given us the foundational ideas for building the case that adherence to the original meaning will advance the rule of law and transparency – when originalism is compared to most of the forms of nonoriginalist living constitutionalism advocated by contemporary constitutional theorists. The opponents of originalism have yet to answer Goldsworthy's case, much less build the normative case for particular forms of nonoriginalist living constitutionalism. Despite the fact that originalism has occupied the centre stage in constitutional theory for much of the past four decades, it seems clear that much work needs to be done – both by the advocates of originalism and its opponents.

6

Originalism and Explanatory Power: Text, Structure and the Interpretation of Constitutions

NICHOLAS ARONEY*

I. Introduction

Jeffrey Goldsworthy's approach to constitutional interpretation consists of two important components. The first component is his general theory of interpretation. Drawing on contemporary philosophy of language, Goldsworthy proposes that the implications of an utterance are determined by inferences concerning the intentions of its speaker or author.[1] The second important component of his approach concerns the application of his general theory to the interpretation of particular aspects of constitutions. Throughout the course of his distinguished career, Goldsworthy has addressed an array of significant constitutional questions, ranging from the interpretation of key words, phrases and sentences in constitutions, to the interpretation of entire paragraphs and chapters and of the structural relationships between them.

Goldsworthy's general theory offers a sophisticated and compelling basis upon which to engage with specific questions of constitutional interpretation. However, there is also something of an explanatory gap, I venture to suggest, between his general theory and the interpretation of constitutions, particularly as it relates to the scale on which interpretation occurs. This is because, as I will seek to explain, Goldsworthy's general theory is especially geared to the interpretation of particular words, phrases and sentences in constitutions, rather than wider linguistic structures on the scale of entire paragraphs, divisions and chapters. This is not to say that Goldsworthy's theory is not able to be adapted to the

* It is an honour to contribute a chapter to a festschrift for Jeffrey Goldsworthy. Jeff's scholarship needs no commendation from me. Many legal scholars endeavour to combine legal theory and jurisprudence with the study of substantive areas of law, but very few have done so with as much distinction and insight as Jeff. The thesis I wrote under Jeff's supervision was deeply indebted to his work and benefited significantly from his incisive analysis and evaluation of its arguments. This chapter is an attempt to develop some themes that emerged out of that study: N Aroney, *The Constitution of a Federal Commonwealth: The Making and Meaning of the Australian Constitution* (Cambridge, Cambridge University Press, 2009).

[1] J Goldsworthy, 'Implications in Language, Law and the Constitution' in G Lindell (ed), *Future Directions in Australian Constitutional Law: Essays in Honour of Professor Leslie Zines* (Sydney, Federation Press, 1994) 150. See also J Goldsworthy, 'The Case for Originalism' in G Huscroft and BW Miller (eds), *The Challenge of Originalism: Theories of Constitutional Interpretation* (Cambridge, Cambridge University Press, 2011) 42.

resolution of questions of interpretation that arise on this larger scale. Indeed, much of Goldsworthy's work has involved the scrutiny and criticism of structural implications that are said to arise when entire paragraphs, chapters or parts of a constitution are interpreted, or when parts of a constitution are considered in relation to one another. Goldsworthy's approach is to argue that structural implications of this kind are only justified when they are genuinely necessary, in the sense that the available evidence makes the implication inescapable, that it cannot reasonably be denied that the implication was intended by the relevant lawmakers. Goldsworthy shows compellingly that many putative structural implications fail this test of necessity. However, because his general theory of linguistic interpretation focusses on how individual phrases and sentences are to be interpreted, it does not offer a full account of how, in general terms, meaning is generated on this larger scale. In particular, his general theory does not offer a full account of how we combine consideration of the specific texts of constitutions with consideration of their wider structural features, in order to arrive at an interpretation that makes sense of them both. To grapple with such interpretive questions – not only of text, but also of structure – requires a mediating theory, broadly consistent with Goldsworthy's basic approach to interpretation. In this chapter, I seek to offer the outlines of such a theory.

The chapter is organised as follows. Section II offers a summary of Goldsworthy's general interpretative theory. Section III discusses how Goldsworthy's theory applies to particular questions of constitutional interpretation, both textual (at the scale of individual words, phrases and sentences) and structural (at the scale of entire paragraphs, chapters and constitutions considered as integrated wholes). Section IV then turns to an exposition of the mediating theory I propose in this chapter – one that offers an account of how we combine considerations of text with considerations of structure, in order to arrive at an interpretation that makes sense of them both. This account considers the role of several distinguishable methods or modes of constitutional argumentation routinely used by courts, all of which are implicated in some way or other in Goldsworthy's theory. Borrowing terminology made famous by Philip Bobbitt (but without adopting Bobbitt's particular approach),[2] I call these methods 'textual', 'structural', 'historical', 'ethical', 'prudential' and 'doctrinal',[3] to which I would also add, in a carefully qualified way, modes of constitutional argument that might be called 'comparative' and 'international'. Others have proposed different lists.[4] Some argue that one particular method of reasoning is to be preferred.[5] Others, like Bobbitt, argue that all such methods are legitimately used by judges from time to time, and that there is no master principle that determines when and how each method ought to be used.

In this chapter I argue that, consistently with Goldsworthy's moderately originalist approach, while constitutional interpretation certainly proceeds on the basis of all of the modes or methods of constitutional reasoning, this should occur in a manner in which each method is illuminated and disciplined by the others. On this approach, I propose that

[2] For criticism of Bobbitt's use of the term 'modality', see LB Solum, 'Originalism and Constitutional Construction' (2013) 82 *Fordham Law Review* 453, 480 fn 96.

[3] P Bobbitt, *Constitutional Interpretation* (Oxford, Blackwell Publishers, 1991) 12–13.

[4] See, eg, RH Fallon, 'A Constructivist Coherence Theory of Constitutional Interpretation' (1987) 100 *Harvard Law Review* 1189; JM Balkin, 'Arguing About the Constitution: The Topics in Constitutional Interpretation' (2018) 33 *Constitutional Commentary* 145.

[5] Some examples are given in nn 36–41 below.

the goal of interpretation is to arrive at an account that offers the best explanation of the constitution – in a sense analogous to, although not identical with, the way in which the idea of 'explanatory power' is understood and used within the physical and social sciences.[6] My suggestion is that it is in the mutual illuminating and disciplining work of each of the modalities – textual, structural, historical, ethical, prudential, doctrinal and comparative – that one is enabled to arrive at the best explanation of the constitution. The interpretation of the constitution that possesses the most explanatory power, I argue, is the one that can account most convincingly for the constitution's finest textual details and its most general organising structures and relationships. However, I argue that this is made possible only when the constitution is understood in the light of the historical processes by which it came into being and the historically determined ethical principles and prudential judgements that demonstrably shaped its drafting; for it is these historically-conditioned processes, principles and judgements that help us to make sense of the textual details of constitutions and the structural relationships between them.[7] Moreover, the history of the constitution may also show that some other constitution, or some principle of international law, demonstrably influenced the drafting of the constitution. To the extent that this is the case, comparative constitutional law and international law can also illuminate our understanding of the constitution, but only as this is illuminated and disciplined by the other modalities. An approach to interpretation that elevates any one of the modalities to pre-eminence over the others tends to produce results that lack explanatory power. My argument is that it is by virtue of the mutually illuminating and disciplining role of the modalities that one is enabled to arrive at the most powerful explanation, and therefore the best interpretation, of the constitution.

While in this chapter I propose an approach that is meant to address an explanatory gap in Goldsworthy's work, I believe it is an approach that is broadly consistent with his general theory and is in several ways implied by it. Goldsworthy's general theory proposes an approach to constitutional interpretation disciplined by the best available evidence of the intentions of the framers of the constitution. This is its essential historical element. But it is also a theory disciplined by the task of identifying the meaning of the particular words, sentences, paragraphs and larger structural features of the constitution. This is its textual and structural element. While Goldsworthy does not appear to take sides between inclusive and exclusive legal positivism, he affirms that constitutions, like the law generally, can include moral principles. However, for Goldsworthy, it is always a question of whether and, if so, to what extent lawmakers have intentionally incorporated them.[8] In this respect – although in this respect only – Goldsworthy's theory incorporates an important

[6] I discuss the crucial role of explanatory power in the natural and social sciences, as well as the similarities and the differences between constitutional interpretation and scientific explanation, in N Aroney, 'Explanatory Power, Theory Formation and Constitutional Interpretation: Some Preliminaries' (2013) 38 *Australian Journal of Legal Philosophy* 1.

[7] In this respect, as in others, I understand the role of ethical and prudential considerations in a manner that is sharply different from Philip Bobbitt, who focusses on the ethical and prudential judgements that are made by the courts, rather than the ethical and prudential judgements made by the framers when they drafted the constitution. This is also the reason why I do not engage here with Larry Solum's argument that while text, structure and history are relevant to the 'interpretation' of constitutions, ethics, prudence and doctrine are relevant to the 'construction' of its legal effect. See Solum (n 2) 479–83.

[8] J Goldsworthy, *The Sovereignty of Parliament: History and Philosophy* (Oxford, Clarendon Press, 1999) 256–59.

ethical element. The same applies to the prudential compromises that may be embodied in a constitution's text and structure, or the influence of other constitutions or principles of international law. Goldsworthy's theory offers a reason why these too ought to be taken into consideration in interpretation, but only to the extent that, on the best available evidence, the framers of the constitution deliberately gave effect to such compromises, or were influenced by those models, in the drafting of the constitution.

II. Goldsworthy on Interpretation

As I understand it, Goldsworthy's general theory of constitutional interpretation is based on two fundamental propositions. The first is that constitutions are authoritative legal documents that ought to be interpreted in a manner that respects their authority.[9] The second is that the authoritative meaning of a constitution is best understood in light of contemporary philosophy of language, which proposes that 'what is implied by any use of language is determined by inferences concerning the intentions of the speaker or author'.[10]

Goldsworthy's account of contemporary language philosophy is as follows. First, he distinguishes between sentence meaning, speaker's meaning and utterance meaning. Sentence meaning is the meaning of a sentence abstracted from its context. It is the meaning a hearer (or reader) will discern in the sentence, if he or she were to rely only on the semantic meaning of its words and on the rules of syntax for the construction of its meaning. Sentence meaning thus depends solely on semantics and syntax. It does not consider the pragmatics of communication, such as the conventional norms governing communication generally, the factual context of a communication, and pre-existing beliefs and values shared by a speaker and his or her audience.[11] Speaker's meaning, by contrast, is the meaning a speaker intends to convey. It is subjective to the speaker,[12] and therefore cannot be known directly by others. However, it can be grasped by the speaker's audience on the basis of the semantics, syntax and pragmatics of the communication. Lastly, the meaning graspable by the speaker's audience is the utterance meaning of the communication. Utterance meaning is sentence meaning supplemented by persuasive evidence of speaker's meaning.[13]

[9] J Goldsworthy, 'The Constitution and Its Common Law Background' (2014) 25 *Public Law Review* 265, 268. Goldsworthy argues that '[a] working constitution that is generally accepted as morally authoritative is indeed morally authoritative because it is essential to a decent, civilised life – provided that it does not include moral flaws so egregious that they outweigh that benefit': Goldsworthy, 'The Case for Originalism' (n 1) 59. Goldsworthy also appeals to principles such as democracy, federalism and the rule of law to justify originalism. In the case of Australia, because the people alone have the authority to change the Constitution, it is therefore illegitimate for judges to change it by 'interpretation': J Goldsworthy, 'Interpreting the Constitution in Its Second Century' (2000) 24 *Melbourne University Law Review* 677, 683–84.

[10] Goldsworthy, 'Implications' (n 1) 150.

[11] According to HP Grice, there are four maxims of communication: quantity (make your contribution as informative as required; do not make your contribution more informative than is required); quality (try to make your contribution truthful: do not say what you believe to be false, do not make claims for which you lack adequate evidence); relation (be relevant); and manner (be perspicuous: avoid obscurity of expression, avoid ambiguity, be brief, be orderly). See HP Grice, *Studies in the Way of Words* (Cambridge, Massachusetts, Harvard University Press, 1989) Ch 2.

[12] I pass over the potentially significant distinction here, between speech and writing, speaker and hearer, writer and reader.

[13] Goldsworthy, 'Implications' (n 1) 150–52.

Persuasive evidence of the speaker's meaning is derived from the factual context, from conventional norms of communication, and from shared beliefs and values. Because it is assisted by pragmatics, utterance meaning both confines and expands the sentence meaning of a communication: it can confine literal overstatements, expand literal understatements and supply words, concepts and understandings that are literally unstated but deliberately implied. As such, pragmatics enables us to grasp the import of linguistic devices such as metaphor, irony and sarcasm. It also helps us to understand how a legal document, such as a constitution or statute, might contain implications that are not expressly stated in the document.

Goldsworthy considers that courts ought to direct their interpretive efforts to the discernment of the utterance meaning of legal texts. He also considers that this is what, on the whole, they in fact do.[14] Courts should not, therefore, limit themselves to sentence meaning (as if this were possible).[15] Utterance meaning is the goal. It is what courts generally aim for, and it is what they should aim for, because legal texts should be treated as authoritative. Moreover, because utterance meaning is the goal, evidence of speaker's meaning is relevant and important.[16] When applied to constitutional interpretation, this suggests that courts ought to consider the available evidence of the intentions of the framers of the constitution, as expressed in the language they used, understood in the context in which they used it.

Goldsworthy's next step is to explain the relation between sentence meaning, utterance meaning and speaker's meaning on the one hand, and express meaning and implicit meaning on the other. It may be tempting to associate express meaning with sentence meaning, and implied meaning with speaker's meaning, but there is no simple equivalence between them. While the exact distinction between express and implied meaning is difficult to identify, both types of meaning are aspects of utterance meaning.

Express meaning is more than sentence meaning because the express meaning of a sentence includes communication of the specific things to which the statement refers, but the tools of semantics and syntax do not enable us to discern what these specific things are. It is only our shared knowledge of the context of a sentence that enables us to do this. Goldsworthy suggests we consider the sentence, 'I'll see you at the bank'. Without knowledge of the context of this sentence, we have no basis upon which to discern the identity of the two persons referred to in the sentence (the subject 'I' and the object 'you'), and we have no basis upon which to decide which kind of 'bank' is being referred to, and what particular bank of that kind is intended (is it a financial bank or a river bank, and if the former, is it the Commonwealth Bank on campus or the Westpac Bank in town?). Only the pragmatics of the sentence – the factual context, conventional norms and shared beliefs and values – enable us to discern the particular things that are expressly referred to in the sentence. For this reason, our understanding of the express meaning of a sentence must depend on the best evidence we have of the particular things to which the speaker is referring. Semantically, a term can have more than one meaning, and it will often be necessary to rely on

[14] This coheres with the proposition that philosophy of language is simultaneously an account of how communication actually works, and of the norms that have to be followed for it to work.

[15] Goldsworthy, 'Implications' (n 1) 163.

[16] Goldsworthy, 'Implications' (n 1) 166.

the pragmatics of the sentence to discern, as best we can, the speaker's intended express meaning.[17] That is why express meaning is an aspect of utterance meaning.

Implicit meaning is also an aspect of utterance meaning. Consider the sentence, 'I enjoyed the concert last night'. At the level of sentence meaning, we would ordinarily interpret this to mean that the speaker genuinely enjoyed the concert. But what if the speaker is being deliberately ironic or sarcastic? The ordinary semantic meaning of the word, 'enjoyed', is positive, but the speaker may deliberately intend quite the opposite, and be entirely confident that you, the hearer, will understand the speaker's ironic intent due to the context of the statement, and certain understandings that you both have – the raised eyebrows, the rolling of the eyes, the tone of voice used, and your knowledge that the speaker had told you earlier that he did not want to attend the concert. These external cues enable you to understand the speaker's implied meaning.

That said, it is not only the pragmatics of a sentence that enable us to discern implied meaning. Sometimes implications can be discerned through logical inferences derived on the basis of semantics and syntax alone. For this is how logical syllogisms work. If I tell you that 'all men are rational' and that 'Socrates is a man', you will understand, as a logical implication of my two statements, that 'Socrates is rational'. You may also infer that I deliberately intended you to draw that inference, but the logical inference itself depends on the sentence meaning of the words, not the utterance meaning.

For Goldsworthy, implicit meaning includes logical implications, implications from deficient expression, deliberate implications and implicit assumptions. Each of these kinds of implicit meaning, except deliberate implications,[18] arises in the interpretation of legal texts.[19] Implicit assumptions are especially necessary because virtually all words, and sentences, are ambiguous in terms of their sentence meaning. At this level of meaning, the only way to eliminate ambiguity is to provide definitions of terms and specifications of referents, but such is the nature of sentence meaning, these definitions and specifications would then require similar determinations of their ambiguous terms, and so on *ad infinitum*. Interpretation clauses in statutes offer definitions of key terms, but these clauses never attempt to define all the terms used (including the terms used to provide the definitions in the interpretation clauses), because otherwise there would be an infinite regress of definitions. The way we get around this is by recourse to implicit assumptions about the meanings and referents of words.[20] Communication is facilitated by the frequent use of implicit assumptions, which enable us to communicate concisely and relevantly, without the need for pedantic and verbose qualifications in order to explicitly exclude all manner of bizarre interpretations that might otherwise be made at a sentence meaning level.

[17] Goldsworthy, 'Implications' (n 1)152–53.

[18] A deliberate implication arises when a speaker intentionally flouts a maxim of communication to convey an implied meaning. For example, to the question, 'is he bright?', the response might be, 'he has good handwriting'. In this example, Grice's maxim of 'relation' is flouted, because whether someone has good handwriting is irrelevant to whether the person is bright. Answering in this way implies that the speaker does not wish to say anything about whether the fellow is bright, because he is not. Lawmakers do not intentionally make deliberate implications of this kind: Goldsworthy, 'Implications' (n 1) 164.

[19] A deficient expression occurs when a speaker accidentally contravenes a maxim of communication, rather than deliberately. It is certainly possible, although not desirable, that a lawmaker may make this kind of mistake: Goldsworthy, 'Implications' (n 1) 164–65.

[20] Goldsworthy, 'Implications' (n 1) 158.

Because implicit assumptions usually operate unconsciously, it can be difficult to distinguish between genuine implications and matters which a speaker has neglected to address, and does not intend to imply. Goldsworthy suggests that the process of uncovering implicit assumptions is not a mechanical undertaking, but rather occurs on the basis of common sense. For example, common law courts have historically implied terms in contracts by asking whether both parties, when asked by an officious bystander if a particular term was part of the contract, would have responded, 'yes, of course'.[21] According to Goldsworthy, an interpreter should recognise an implicit assumption as being part of the speaker's meaning only when such a conclusion is necessary, in the sense of a kind of psychological necessity, where the evidence compels the interpreter to acknowledge the implication: the implication is inescapable and cannot reasonably be denied; it is obvious. This is to suggest that such implications must be necessary in a rigorous sense. They are not merely convenient or desirable; they must be so obvious that they go without saying.[22] This is because implicit assumptions, as an aspect of utterance meaning, turn on the best evidence of the speaker's meaning. The goal is to draw inferences as to what the speaker actually meant. Goldsworthy argues that psychological necessity is the touchstone because implications in language are not absolutely fixed by conventions of semantics and syntax; they turn on all the available evidence of the speaker's meaning, and that evidence, by its nature, is not demonstrative, but only probabilistic.[23]

Goldsworthy notes that, for these reasons, two extreme views about the nature of legal interpretation are implausible and overstated: legal formalism, which proposes that the law is discovered by a passive and receptive interpreter; and legal realism, which proposes that the law is constructed by an active and creative interpreter. Rather, according to Goldsworthy, legal interpretation is a specialised form of general linguistic interpretation. It therefore seeks to identify the utterance meaning of a legal text. This task is neither entirely passive nor entirely active, for it involves a good faith effort to identify the sentence meaning of the text, supplemented by a good faith effort to discern the speaker's meaning, based on all the available evidence. This task is not merely passive and receptive because the speaker's meaning can never be known directly, and must be reconstructed on the basis of the semantics, syntax and pragmatics of the text, understood in its context. The task is not entirely active and creative, however, because it is disciplined by our shared knowledge of the text and its context, and our shared adherence to the rules of semantics, syntax and pragmatics.

Goldsworthy is therefore critical of both textual literalism and creative realism as modes of constitutional interpretation. Textual literalism is deficient because it relies solely on semantics and syntax to construct sentence meaning. Limiting interpretation to semantics and syntax leaves us with a high level of vagueness, ambiguity, and unresolved gaps in meaning. To resolve the problem, the interpreter is given a very wide latitude of creative or constructive 'interpretation'. For, on this approach, judges can only 'consult their own best theory of ideal rationality, which amounts to their own best theory of morality'.[24]

[21] Goldsworthy, 'Implications' (n 1) 158–61.

[22] I discuss the distinction between 'necessary' and 'desirable' implications in N Aroney, 'A Seductive Plausibility: Freedom of Speech in the Constitution' (1995) 18(2) *University of Queensland Law Journal* 249.

[23] Goldsworthy, 'Implications' (n 1) 168–70.

[24] Goldsworthy, 'Implications' (n 1) 167.

As a consequence, if the best evidence we have of the speaker's meaning is abandoned as a touchstone of interpretation, judges can make a legal text 'mean' almost anything. This may sound extreme, but any response that 'of course the courts can't or won't do this' depends on the pragmatics of interpretation.

Goldsworthy considers that the well-known touchstone of 'practical necessity' – the idea that an implication is required to enable a legal text to operate effectively – is not a sufficient basis upon which to establish an implication. It is not sufficient because the legislator may simply have overlooked the question as to whether a specific state of affairs was necessary for a particular rule of law to be given practical effect. When such a matter is overlooked, the speaker has not actually formed the view, and has not actually intended to imply, that the matter in question is to be taken for granted. The mere fact (if such can be established) that a specific state of affairs is practically necessary to enable a legal text to operate effectively does not, of itself, make that state of affairs something that the legislator actually intended. In such cases, the legislation may be deficient because it has failed to recognise the need to establish the state of affairs necessary to achieve its objective in an effective manner. But when a court encounters such a situation – where the evidence suggests that the legislator never even considered the question, rather than the situation where the legislator deliberately meant to imply that such a state of affairs must obtain – the judges are not discerning an implication of the law, they are remedying its deficient expression. Goldsworthy argues that in such cases, if the court does intervene, it should frankly acknowledge that it is rectifying the statute, rather than discovering an implicit assumption.[25]

Goldsworthy's theory suggests, although I do not think he anywhere elaborates, that we might refer to a fourth kind of meaning, which we could call 'hearer's meaning' or 'reader's meaning': the meaning that a hearer or reader will attribute to an oral or written communication. Reader's meaning is distinct from the other three kinds of meaning because it is possible that a reader may interpret a communication to have a meaning that is different from not only its speaker's meaning and sentence meaning, but also from its utterance meaning. While a proficient reader will interpret a communication competently in terms of the semantic meaning of the words, the syntax of the sentence, and the full pragmatics of the situation, a less competent reader will sometimes make mistakes – semantically, syntactically or pragmatically. Reader's meaning is the meaning a reader attributes to a communication, whether competently or not.[26]

Viewed in this way, utterance meaning is a decisively important category in Goldsworthy's theory because it constitutes the communicative link between speaker and hearer (or writer and reader). However, because the pragmatics of interpretation depend on circumstantial judgements about the intended meaning of a sentence, utterance meaning is more in the nature of an ideal towards which interpretation is directed, rather than a meaning that can always be grasped flawlessly. Not only is there the possibility of gross errors in interpretation, it seems impossible, in the nature of the case, to demonstrate a perfect identity between speaker's meaning, utterance meaning and reader's meaning.[27]

[25] J Goldsworthy, 'Constitutional Implications Revisited' (2011) 30 *University of Queensland Law Journal* 9, 19–21.

[26] A reader might also mischievously or deliberately misconstrue a communication, pretending that it means something other than its utterance meaning, properly construed.

[27] Goldsworthy sometimes writes as if speaker's meaning were directly knowable (eg, Goldsworthy, 'The Case for Originalism' (n 1) 49). He offers examples of where our interpretation of sentences varies, depending on whether

As Goldsworthy says, the evidence on which we have to rely in order to grasp the utterance meaning of a sentence is probabilistic, not demonstrative. But that does not mean that utterance meaning is not the goal at which we should aim.

III. Scales of Meaning

Questions of constitutional interpretation arise at different scales. We can ask coherent questions about the meaning of particular words, phrases, clauses and sentences of constitutions; we can also ask them about entire paragraphs, chapters and divisions. Our questions can concern individual sections and sub-sections; they can also concern the relationships between the various parts and chapters of a constitution, understood in the context of the constitution as a whole. We can even ask questions about the meaning of a written constitution in the context of other constitutional instruments and documents, such as the various imperial statutes that continue, in some way, to regulate the constitutional status and powers of former British colonies.[28]

To which of these kinds of interpretive question is Goldsworthy's general theory primarily directed? The general statements of theory encountered in his work, consonant with much philosophy of language, most often refer to the meaning of individual words, phrases and sentences. However, Goldsworthy has frequently applied his approach to the interpretation, not only of individual words and sentences, but also of entire paragraphs, chapters and, indeed, constitutions. Thus his general theory seems, in principle, applicable at all of these varied scales, even if its general articulation tends to focus on its narrower application at the level of individual words, phrases and sentences.

This can be understood in the first instance by reflecting on the scale at which semantics, syntax and pragmatics ordinarily operate. On first analysis, we might say that semantics concerns the meanings of particular words, and syntax enables us to construct the meaning of particular phrases, clauses and sentences, while pragmatics contributes to the meaning at all of these scales, from individual words to entire sentences. But, on further reflection, it is apparent that, considered together, semantics, syntax and pragmatics contribute to the meanings we attribute to texts at all of these scales and beyond, including larger units of communication, such as paragraphs, chapters and divisions of entire constitutions. This is so for two reasons. First, the larger linguistic structures are necessarily composed of the smaller ones, and so it is not possible to comprehend the larger ones without comprehending the

we are interested in ascertaining the speaker's meaning or the meaning of the utterance as such. However, what really makes the distinction is how much information we have about the speaker's intentions. What the examples demonstrate is that the alignment between our apprehension of the meaning of a sentence and the speaker's meaning depends on the quality and quantity of information that we have. An interpretation of a sentence based on very little, if any, contextual information will be so bereft of context that it will come very close to being identical with bare sentence meaning; whereas an interpretation based on a very intimate and extensive knowledge of the speaker and the context will bring us very close to the speaker's meaning, so close, that we might be inclined to identify our interpretation with the speaker's meaning. This does not mean, however, that we ever have direct knowledge of a speaker's actual subjective meaning. We always have only utterance meaning, based on the best evidence available to us of the speaker's meaning. That is, unless we get into some very complex metaphysics: J Arthos, *The Inner Word in Gadamer's Hermeneutics* (Notre Dame, Indiana, University of Notre Dame Press, 2009).

[28] For example, in Australia, consider the successive effect of the *Colonial Laws Validity Act 1865*, *Commonwealth of Australia Constitution Act 1900*, *Statute of Westminster 1931* and *Australia Act 1986*.

smaller ones as well. We all have to read one word, phrase and sentence at a time. Accordingly, the semantic, syntactical and pragmatic meaning of individual words, phrases and sentences necessarily contributes to constitutional meaning on the larger scales of paragraphs, chapters, divisions and constitutions as a whole. Second, pragmatics is especially pertinent to the apprehension of meaning at the larger scales, because it brings into focus the context of the constitution as a whole, together with all of the commonly shared beliefs and values relevant to the apprehension of its meaning.

The point can be seen in Goldsworthy's engagement with questions of interpretation arising at all of these scales. For example, Goldsworthy has applied his general theory to the meaning of the word 'marriage',[29] the phrase 'for the peace, order and good government',[30] and the sentence in section 117 of the *Australian Constitution* which guarantees the rights of citizens of other states.[31] He has also written on the implications of entire paragraphs, such as those that appear in sections 7, 24, and 128 of the Constitution,[32] and entire chapters, such as chapters I, II and III,[33] and the structural relationships between them.[34] In addition, Goldsworthy has written extensively about the general principles that may be said to be presupposed or implemented by the Constitution, such as the supremacy of parliament, the rule of law, equality before the law, judicial review, federalism, responsible government, the separation of powers, and so on.[35]

Put this way, a question arises concerning the relationship between Goldsworthy's general theory and the various modalities or methods of constitutional argument which Bobbitt has called textual, structural, historical, ethical, prudential and doctrinal. A question also arises about the relationship between Goldsworthy's theory of interpretation and those which give priority to one or another of these particular modalities, such as Jeremy Waldron's textualism,[36] Charles Black's and Laurence Tribe's structuralism,[37] Larry Alexander's and Richard Kay's intentionalism,[38] Ronald Dworkin's ethical interpretation,[39] Richard Posner's pragmatism,[40] and David Stauss's emphasis on doctrine,[41] to name just a few.

[29] Goldsworthy, 'Interpreting the Constitution' (n 9) 699–701.

[30] Goldsworthy, 'Interpreting the Constitution' (n 9) 681–83.

[31] Goldsworthy, 'The Case for Originalism' (n 1) 173.

[32] Goldsworthy, 'The Case for Originalism' (n 1) 179. J Goldsworthy, 'Constitutional Implications and Freedom of Political Speech: A Reply to Stephen Donaghue' (1997) 23 *Monash University Law Review* 362.

[33] J Goldsworthy, 'Kable, Kirk, and Judicial Statesmanship' (2014) 40 *Monash University Law Review* 75.

[34] Goldsworthy, 'Implications' (n 1) 172. See also J Goldsworthy, 'Justice Windeyer on the Engineers' Case' (2009) 37 *Federal Law Review* 363.

[35] Goldsworthy, 'Implications' (n 1) 172–78; J Goldsworthy, 'Interpreting the Australian Constitution: Express Provisions and Unexpressed General Principles' (2012) 24 *Giornale di Storia Costituzionale* 117; J Goldsworthy, 'Structural Judicial Review and the Objection from Democracy' (2010) 60 *University of Toronto Law Journal* 137; J Goldsworthy, 'Abdicating and Limiting Parliament's Sovereignty' (2006) 17 *King's College Law Journal* 255.

[36] J Waldron, *Law and Disagreement* (Oxford, Oxford University Press, 1999).

[37] CL Black, *Structure and Relationship in Constitutional Law* (Baton Rouge, Louisiana State University Press, 1969); LH Tribe, 'Taking Text and Structure Seriously: Reflections on Free-Form Method in Constitutional Interpretation' (1995) 108 *Harvard Law Review* 1221.

[38] See Larry Alexander, 'Goldsworthy on Interpretation of Statutes and Constitutions: Public Meaning, Intended Meaning and the Bogey of Aggregation' in chapter 2 of this volume; RS Kay, 'Adherence to the Original Intentions in Constitutional Adjudication: Three Objections and Responses' (1988) 82 *Northwestern University Law Review* 226.

[39] RM Dworkin, *Freedom's Law: The Moral Reading of the American Constitution* (Oxford, Oxford University Press, 1996).

[40] RA Posner, 'Constitutional Law from a Pragmatic Perspective' (2005) 55 *University of Toronto Law Journal* 299.

[41] DA Strauss, 'Common Law Constitutional Interpretation' (1996) 63 *University of Chicago Law Review* 877.

Goldsworthy's theory is self-consciously originalist, but that does not mean he advocates the use of historical evidence regarding the intentions or understandings of the framers without giving close attention to the relevant text of the constitution as well. It is only to the extent that the historical intentions of the framers are in some way inscribed into the text of the constitution that they become part of the law. This is because, as explained above, sentence meaning is a constituent element of utterance meaning. Pragmatic considerations can modify one's conclusions as to the meaning of a text understood at a sentence meaning level, but what they modify are the deliverances of semantics and syntax applied to the same text. Utterance meaning is not something independent of sentence meaning; sentence meaning delivers the substratum of meaning upon which utterance meaning must build. Accordingly, whatever might be the content of the wider context and shared beliefs that give shape to utterance meaning, the semantic meaning of the actual words used and the syntactical import of their particular arrangement in a sentence can never be ignored. Utterance meaning is a product not only of pragmatics, but of semantics and syntax applied to the literal text.

But if the text of the constitution is an indispensable component of meaning, this text cannot be limited to particular words, phrases, clauses and sentences. It must also embrace larger structures of the text: the paragraphs in which sentences are located, and the divisions, parts, and chapters of the constitution in which those paragraphs are located. Even at a sentence meaning level, the meaning of individual phrases and clauses is often dependent on other phrases and clauses contained in the same sentence. Likewise, the meaning of particular sentences is often affected and qualified by other sentences, sometimes located in the same paragraph, sometimes in a paragraph elsewhere in the constitution. This interdependence of meaning, which can span many different parts of a constitution, is a persistent characteristic of constitutions, statutes and other legal instruments. And if such interconnectedness can be demonstrated to exist at the level of sentence meaning, it must a fortiori exist at the level of utterance meaning as well.

It is through the interrelatedness of these varying linguistic units that powers are granted, rights are conferred and institutions created by a constitution. This is well illustrated, for example, by Chapter I of the *Australian Constitution*, the provisions of which establish the Parliament, define its component parts and confer legislative powers upon it. These sections, and the parts into which they are organised, are pervasively interdependent in meaning. Some provisions describe the institutions at high levels of generality, while others describe progressively finer details, and yet others confer powers by which even more specific legal requirements can be enacted from time to time. Thus, for example, the very first section of the constitution provides that there shall be a Federal Parliament, and stipulates that it shall consist of the Queen, a Senate and a House of Representatives. Subsequent sections provide that the Senate is to be composed of senators for each State, that these senators are to be directly chosen by the people of the State, and that the people of each State are, in the first instance, to vote as one electorate, subject to Parliament's power to prescribe otherwise. The individuals who are entitled to vote in such elections is similarly prescribed by the Constitution (by adopting the rules applying at a state level), but this is subject to the power of Parliament to provide otherwise, a power that Parliament has exercised.[42]

[42] See *Australian Constitution*, ss 1, 7, 8, 30.

It is not possible to understand the full meaning of any one of these provisions without taking into consideration the others. The progressively more specific provisions stipulate with increasing precision the particular character and features of the institutions established by the constitution, while the more general descriptions of the institutions as a whole are necessary to make contextual sense of the details. Even at a sentence level, the semantic meaning of the terms and their syntactical relations convey that a set of interrelated institutions and sub-institutions is being established. But it is difficult, when it comes to institutions, to distinguish easily between the semantics and the pragmatics that are at play, for the semantic definition of terms such as 'parliament', 'senate' and 'elector' cannot easily be separated from the pragmatics of our shared understandings of what these institutions are, what they are meant to do, and how they are intended to operate. Much is left to implicit assumptions about the kinds of institutions that are intended to be created. The *Australian Constitution* includes only a very minimal definitions clause to specify the meanings of its terms.[43] Many of the words used are terms of art, the meaning of which is determined, to some extent, by the conventional understandings of the subsisting legal and political culture.

It does not follow, however, that the conventional understandings of our contemporary culture offer an adequate or controlling context for the interpretation of the constitution. While there may be some very important continuities between our culture and the culture of those who first drafted the constitution, to the extent that there are differences, it was their culture, in their time and place, that shaped the content of the constitution. The text and structure of the constitution is a product of their time, not ours. For this reason, there is an inherently close connection between the deliverances of the modalities of text, structure and history that is liable to be overlooked when attempts are made to interpret the constitution in accordance with contemporary understandings and values. The text and structure of the constitution are products of its particular history. Closely examining its history can help to illuminate its text and structure, just as closely examining the text and structure of the constitution can illuminate its history. The deliverances of all three modalities have the tendency to illuminate and reinforce each other.

This is where a mediating account of the relationship between textual, structural, and historical modalities of interpretation, as well as the ethical and the pragmatic, is needed. Textualism focusses attention on the literal meaning of the words actually contained in the constitution. Its virtue is the discipline of the text itself,[44] understood in its conventional semantic meaning, and according to the ordinary rules of syntax. However, textualism, when artificially separated from the other modalities, offers little guidance when we encounter unconventional semantic or syntactic usages, historically specific references to particular institutions or contexts, or terms or concepts, the value of which is deeply contested. The meaning attributed to such textual elements, when divorced from the other modalities, is liable to reflect the dispositions of the interpreter more than any consensus about their conventional meanings, let alone the intentions of the framers. The other modalities, especially the structural and the historical, are needed to both discipline and illuminate the bare text of the constitution. The other modalities discipline textualism by

[43] *Commonwealth of Australia Constitution Act 1900*, covering cl 6.
[44] For a powerful account of textualism's virtues, see Waldron (n 36).

inhibiting the interpreter from introducing his or her own personal preferences into the equation. The other modalities illuminate textualism by bringing to light structural interrelationships and historical intentions and purposes that help to explain and make sense of textual details. Without this discipline and illumination many provisions of the constitution would otherwise be opaque to the understanding and liable to be filled by the untethered imagination of the interpreter. As a consequence, the structural and historical modalities help to guard against both under- and over-interpretation. They illuminate and discipline bare textualism.[45]

Much the same can be said of each of the other methods of interpretation when their use is artificially separated from the others. Structuralism, for example, is actually incoherent without textualism, because the specific text is the essential substratum out of which structural relationships between parts of a constitution are constructed. The structure cannot be grasped without also grasping the text, just as the text cannot fully be grasped without also grasping its structural context. Moreover, structuralism, when undisciplined by the strictures of history and text, is also apt (like untethered textualism) to generate fanciful over-interpretations. The maxim *generalia specialibus non derogant* is an important principle in all domains of legal interpretation. When structuralist arguments are undisciplined by text and history, they have a tendency to breach this maxim unjustifiably.

Even history needs to be disciplined and illuminated by the other modalities. Historical intentions, understandings and events that occurred or existed at the time a constitution was enacted into law are of no relevance to its interpretation except to the extent they illuminate its meaning. It is only when the deliverances of history shed light on the Constitution's text and structure, or its underlying ethical principles and prudential compromises, that history is relevant. Accordingly, it is the enactment history of the constitution that matters: the history of how the constitution became this particular document with all of its specific textual and structural features. This requires us to understand the constitution as the product of a particular drafting, ratifying and enacting process engaged in by purposive individuals whose intentions were to make a constitution that would function as a binding and authoritative document with the particular features that it has. For this reason also, the private or subjective intentions of individuals who played a role in the making of a constitution are relevant to its meaning only when they have a demonstrable influence on some feature or features of its text and structure, its ethical principles and its prudential compromises. The disciplining of history by text and structure implies that what is relevant in history is not the framers' subjective intentions, expectations or understandings per se, nor even the understandings of the political and legal culture of the time considered in themselves, but the relationship between those intentions, expectations and understandings, and the constitution's text and structure. Indeed, considered in this light, the disciplining of history by the other modalities helps to resolve the hoary old question of whose intentions or understandings are relevant: the drafters, the convention delegates, the state legislatures or the ratifying voters? The answer is this: it depends on an historical account of who and what demonstrably shaped the

[45] For a succinct illustration (using somewhat different terminology) which demonstrates the inadequacy of pure textualism, see R Ekins, *The Nature of Legislative Intent* (Oxford, Oxford University Press, 2012) 103–107.

substantive content of the constitution, particularly in terms of its text and structure. For it was not only individual actors who shaped the constitution, but also legislative procedures, voting rules and so on.[46]

Ethical reasoning is similar. Undisciplined by the deliverances of the textual, structural and historical modalities, ethical reasoning invites the interpreter to inject into a constitution his or her personal evaluations of what the constitution should have said, or should now be taken to say, rather than what it actually says. However, that does not mean that ethical reasoning can have no legitimate role in constitutional interpretation, provided it is disciplined and illuminated by the other modalities. The texts of constitutions undoubtedly contain morally-laden terms, such as: 'good government', 'just terms', 'fair compensation', 'equal protection' and so on. The structures of constitutions also evoke morally-infused institutions, such as: 'representative government', 'federalism', 'separation of powers' and so on. Textualism and structuralism demand that these features of constitutions be given their due effect. But without the discipline supplied by the historical modality, these morally rich terms and concepts are liable to be filled by the interpreter's own preferences. The historical modality helps to clarify and specify the sense in which such terms and concepts were used in the constitution. And it does so in a way that enlists the insights offered by textualism to both discipline and illuminate what we understand to be the structure of the constitution, as well as by enlisting the insights offered by structuralism to discipline and illuminate the text. In this way it is possible, in principle, to discern the extent to which, and the particular way in which, the constitution gives effect to some particular morally-laden concept or institution. It is in the combined application of textual, structural and historical modes of inquiry that ethical interpretation is most effectively and appropriately applied. This enables the moral purposes and principles which the constitution really does prescribe to be given their full effect, without allowing ethical reasoning to displace the text and structure of the constitution – the constitution as it was actually enacted into law.

Much the same can be said of prudential reasoning. Constitutions are by their nature not only instruments of ethical governance, but also contain provisions that are the outcomes of prudential compromises between conflicting points of view and clashing material interests. Whatever we may think ethically about these compromises, they are part of the text and structure of the constitution, and products of the history that brought

[46] Elsewhere, I have argued that federal constitutions in general, and the *Australian Constitution* in particular, can most comprehensively be explained and are therefore best understood as the products of a particular kind of enactment history. This enactment history includes prevailing assumptions about the authoritative sources of the constitution and the locations of effective constitutive power that shaped the drafting, ratifying and enacting process. These authoritative sources and locations of effective constitutive power will necessarily be plural in an integrative federation and more unified in a devolutionary one. The exact configuration of these elements has a demonstrable influence on the text and structure of federal constitutions and, indeed, of all constitutions. It is the context in which the constitution is drafted, ratified and enacted into law. See N Aroney, *The Constitution of a Federal Commonwealth: The Making and Meaning of the Australian Constitution* (Cambridge, Cambridge University Press, 2009); N Aroney, 'Formation, Representation and Amendment in Federal Constitutions' (2006) 54 *American Journal of Comparative Law* 277; N Aroney, 'Constituent Power and the Constituent States: Towards a Theory of the Amendment of Federal Constitutions' (2017) 17 *Jus Politicum: Revue de droit politique* 5; N Aroney, 'The Formation and Amendment of Federal Constitutions in a Westminster-Derived Context' (2018) 16 *International Journal of Constitutional Law* 17.

it into being. The authoritative status of the constitution demands that they be given effect.[47] Indeed, the conflicts and tensions which gave rise to the need for such compromises may well continue to exist, perhaps in somewhat altered form, in contemporary life; and so the contemporary application of those compromises may therefore contribute to the amelioration of such conflicts in our present time. However, this does not mean that untethered pragmatic considerations play a legitimate role in constitutional interpretation. Pragmatism, like the other modalities, needs to be disciplined and illuminated by the other modalities.

Although they are not named as such in Bobbitt's list of modalities, comparative law and international law can also function as categories of modality in constitutional interpretation. However, the use of comparative law and international law must be disciplined and illuminated by the other modalities. Although it is sometimes thought that textualism and originalism are inherently opposed to the use of comparative law and international law, this is not quite so. A constitution may demonstrably have been influenced by the example of some other national constitution, or it may deliberately have incorporated language derived from some international instrument or principle of international law. In addition, a constitution may, as a matter of its text and structure, contain elements that are relevantly similar, or relevantly different from, the text and structure of other constitutions. The examination and interpretation of those other constitutions can help to illuminate the interpretation of one's own constitution, provided that the similarities and differences are kept in mind and discipline the lessons that are learned. Only a careful assessment of the history of a constitution, combined with close attention to its text and structure, as well as its ethical principles and prudential compromises, can deliver a precise answer about the extent to which, and the respects in which, a constitution may have been influenced by, or contain elements that are relevantly similar to – or different from – the constitutional law of another country or the body of international law recognised by other countries. Provided that they are illuminated and disciplined in this way, comparative and international law can play a legitimate role in constitutional interpretation.[48]

Lastly, we come to the doctrinal modality – potentially the most difficult one to address, because doctrine is the direct product of the exercise by courts of their own authoritative interpretation and application of the constitution. While all the modalities are ways in which the authoritative meaning of the constitution can be brought to light, and therefore each of the modalities can draw attention to aspects of the authoritative meaning of the constitution, judicial decisions have a special authority of their own, derived from the jurisdiction of courts to determine disputes over the constitution's meaning and application. Does this mean that the doctrinal modality falls into a category of its own? Does it possess an authority that trumps the deliverances of the other modalities? My answer is no, not when it comes to the interpretation of a constitution. There are several related reasons for this.

[47] That is, on the assumption that such provisions are not so morally offensive that a decision-maker cannot, in good conscience, implement them. See J Goldsworthy, 'The Limits of Judicial Fidelity to Law' (2011) 24 *Canadian Journal of Law and Jurisprudence* 305. See also HLA Hart, 'Positivism and the Separation of Law and Morals' (1958) 71 *Harvard Law Review* 593, 620: '[I]f we … make our protest against evil law in the form of an assertion that certain rules cannot be law because of their moral iniquity, we confuse one of the most powerful, because it is the simplest, forms of moral criticism. If … we speak plainly, we say that laws may be law but too evil to be obeyed.'

[48] See N Aroney, 'Comparative Law in Australian Constitutional Jurisprudence' (2007) 26 *University of Queensland Law Journal* 317.

The first and most basic reason is that the authority of judges derives from the constitution itself. The texts and structures of constitutions routinely provide for the establishment of courts, the appointment of judges, and the conferral of judicial power upon them. The decisions of judges only have authority to the extent that their determinations involve exercises of power that are authorised by the constitution.

The constitutional authority of judges to make decisions is limited in various ways. Judicial decisions have a specificity that distinguishes them from the generality of constitutions and statutes. This is especially true in common law jurisdictions such as Australia and the United States where the jurisdiction of courts under the constitution is limited to the resolution of specific disputes between particular litigants.[49] The principle of *stare decisis* requires that lower courts in the judicial hierarchy follow the decisions of superior courts, but the binding force of precedent is limited to the particular facts, issues and *ratio decidendi* of the case at hand. The principle of *res judicata* also supports the authoritative finality of judicial decisions, but it only bars actions brought by the same parties, based on the same set of facts, and raising the same set of issues. For these reasons, judicial decisions have a specificity which contributes to our nuanced understanding of the constitution by forcing us to grapple with its meaning and application with respect to particular issues that would not necessarily occur to us on the basis of a merely abstract consideration of its text and structure.

When making decisions, courts accordingly have to apply the general words of constitutions to the specific circumstances of particular cases. This requires courts to specify the meaning of the relevant provisions of the constitution, and they frequently do this by articulating specific tests which seek to elaborate the meaning and facilitate the application of those provisions to the issues before them. These specifications of meaning are part of the legitimate interpretive functions of courts, giving rise to a body of doctrine that provides authoritative guidance for the determination of cases in the future. According to the principle of *stare decisis*, not only must lower courts adhere to the determinations of higher courts, but courts of highest jurisdiction tend to follow their previous decisions. However, this is not strictly adhered to, especially in constitutional cases. It is admitted in all common law countries that courts of highest jurisdiction have the authority to depart from their previous determinations. The real point of contention concerns the basis on which such departure is justified. In constitutional cases, departure from precedent is typically supported by arguments that appeal to the other modalities of constitutional interpretation and argument. Considerations of text, structure, history, ethics and prudence are assessed against considerations of precedent and doctrine. In this way, the specification of meaning produced by decisions of courts is always subject to assessments of whether those specifications are constitutionally justified, and such assessments turn on consideration of the other modalities of constitutional interpretation. Indeed, such is the importance of these other modalities of constitutional interpretation that, at the highest level, judges sometimes adhere to their own preferred views of the meaning and application of the constitution despite being, and continuing to be, in the minority. When judges persistently dissent in

[49] The advisory jurisdiction that is exercised in Canada and India only arises in relation to particular questions of law or fact. While the advisory opinions delivered by the Canadian and Indian courts are practically authoritative, there remain hesitations about according them formal binding authority on account of their advisory and abstract nature.

this way, they typically appeal to one or more of the other modalities as the ground on which they justify their prolonged disagreement with the majority. This is because no-one thinks that the decisions of courts have precedential authority if they flagrantly disregard the constitution. Constitutional judges do not have authority simply to make things up. Judges always present their constitutional decisions as acts of interpretation of the constitution, and they routinely justify their interpretations by reference to all of the modalities: text, structure, history, ethics, prudence, doctrine and, on occasion, comparative and international law.

For these reasons, I think it can be said that the doctrinal modality plays a role similar to the others: it offers insights into how a constitution can and should be understood; it offers a set of particular judgements about the meaning and application of the text and structure of the constitution, best understood in the light of its history and its underlying ethical principles, as well as its prudential compromises. Like the other modalities, however, the doctrinal modality needs to be disciplined by the others, in the sense that, when we come to interpret a constitution, the opinion of a particular judge or court may be very illuminating; it may even be binding if the same circumstances should arise in a subsequent case. However, judicial decisions can also prove to be *per incuriam*; they may fail to take into consideration some relevant feature of the constitution which one or more of the other modalities brings to light. Thus, in sum: despite the special authority vested in judges to determine the cases that come before them, and the requirement that they adhere to the doctrine of precedent when doing so, the best interpretation of a constitution is arrived at when doctrine is considered together with all of the other modalities, in a mutually disciplining and illuminating way.

The key, therefore, is that each modality disciplines and illuminates the others. For each of the individual modalities, when pursued in isolation, can tend to produce divergent interpretive results. Indeed, when pursued in isolation, none of the modalities is able to produce a coherent interpretation of the constitution, for they each fail to explain those elements of the constitution that are especially brought to light by the other modalities. What makes such approaches more or less viable in practice is that their proponents do not, in fact, treat their preferred set of considerations as the sole determinant of constitutional meaning. In practice, they always rely to some extent, either openly or covertly, on the other modalities to provide the necessary illumination and discipline. The key question is *how* this mutual disciplining and illuminating can best be put into practice.

IV. Explanatory Power

This brings me finally to explanatory power, the master concept that I propose offers a coherent and defensible way of bringing all of the modalities into a mutually illuminating and mutually disciplining relationship.

The concept of explanatory power is derived from the philosophy of science. The basic idea is that a theory has explanatory power in so far as it can explain a relatively large and complex array of facts with a relatively simple set of concepts or ideas. The simpler the concepts used to explain the data, and the larger and more complex the array of facts explained, the greater the explanatory power of the theory. On this view, explanatory power is the prime desideratum of a successful scientific theory.

The explanatory power of a theory is a function of its simplicity, its descriptiveness and its consilience with other theories. The greater the simplicity, descriptiveness and consilience of a theory, the greater its explanatory power. Simplicity concerns the economy of entities or concepts that are postulated by a theory: a theory is called parsimonious when it posits a relatively small number of explanatory entities, and a theory is elegant when it posits a relatively small number of explanatory concepts. Simplicity in this sense is opposed to the intricacy of a theory. Theories possessing a high level of explanatory power are relatively simple rather than intricate. And yet, a theory often needs to be adequately intricate in order to provide a sufficiently detailed and precise account of the data under consideration. Descriptiveness concerns the range and complexity of the things that a theory purports to explain. It is relatively more difficult for a theory to explain phenomena over a relatively wide range, as it is to explain a relatively complex set of phenomena in a highly specified way. The extent to which a theory can explain highly specific and detailed features of a phenomenon, as well as a wide array of such phenomena, contributes to its explanatory power. The more that is explained, in terms of both the specificity and the generality of the explanation, but with an economy of concepts or entities, the greater the explanatory power. The consilience of a theory – its coherent integration with other theories – is also a desirable attribute, for consilience between theories contributes to their explanatory power as a group. Consilience can occur when a relatively general theory provides a broad explanation of phenomena that coheres with more specific theories, or when a specific theory provides a particular explanation that coheres with the broader explanations of a more general theory. It can also occur when two theories of similar explanatory specificity or generality offer explanations that are coherent with each other, and which may even contribute to the explanations offered by each other.

How might this account of explanatory power be applied to constitutional interpretation?[50] The explanatory power of a particular interpretation of a constitution will be maximised in proportion to the simplicity of the concepts it uses, the specificity and generality of the constitutional data that it explains, and the consilience of the theory with cognate interpretations that deal with other aspects of the constitution. What then is the constitutional data that needs to be explained? The text and structure of the constitution is the basic datum. This text and structure consists of the many words, phrases, clauses, sentences, paragraphs, parts and chapters of which the constitution is composed. The specificity of an interpretation is measured by its capacity to give weight to each particular word, each particular phrase, and each particular sentence, in the context of the whole, while the generality of an interpretation is measured by its capacity to give weight to the structure of the constitution as a whole, considered in terms of its organisation into particular chapters, paragraphs, sentences and so on.

Text and structure are in this sense relative terms. A particular word can be seen as an aspect of the text of the constitution, while the phrase or sentence in which that word is contained is its immediate structural context. The meaning of the word is dependent on

[50] I assume here that explanatory power is applicable, by analogy, to legal interpretation, including constitutional interpretation. Space does not permit a detailed consideration of the question, but elsewhere I have argued that the features of law that distinguish it from the physical sciences – its social and human character, its normativity, its linguistic nature and its historical contingency – do not pose insurmountable obstacles to the application of explanatory power as prime desideratum to theory formation within the field of law. See Aroney, 'Explanatory Power' (n 6).

the meaning of the sentence as a whole, just as the meaning of the sentence is dependent on the meaning of the words, phrases and clauses that compose it. Likewise, but on a larger scale, a particular sentence or paragraph of a constitution is itself a textual feature of the constitution located within a larger structure consisting of the divisions, parts or chapters that compose the constitution as a whole. Again, the meaning of each paragraph is dependent, to an extent, on the meaning of the division or chapter in which it is contained, just as the meaning of the chapter is dependent on the paragraphs or parts that compose it. Understood in this way, the specificity and generality of the explanations offered by an interpretation of a constitution are correlative to each other. The explanatory power of an interpretation depends on its specificity and generality. An ideal interpretation will account in some way for every relevant word, phrase, sentence, paragraph and chapter in the constitution, either on its own account, or because of its consilience with other interpretations that focus on other aspects of the constitution.

This might seem to suggest that the explanation of specific, textual features of a constitution should be subordinated to the explanation of its more general, structural features. But this would be to misunderstand two things. First, the disciplining and illuminating functions of the textual and structural modalities work in both directions. Neither is subordinated to the other. Second, there is an implied criterion of relevance to be taken into consideration. Constitutional interpretation is focussed on particular questions that need to be resolved. The particularity of these questions requires that close attention be given to those features of the constitution that are specifically relevant to the question. If the matter in question is addressed in a particular provision of the constitution, then if a constitutional interpretation offered in response to that question does not give full weight to the specificity of the relevant provision, that interpretation will be explanatorily inadequate no matter how many considerations supposedly derived from the wider structures of the constitution may be adduced in its support. The maxim *generalia specialibus non derogant* applies.

In arriving at an interpretation of the text and structure of a constitution that has explanatory power, an understanding of its enactment history is essential. While some may like to think that constitutions can be interpreted adequately and convincingly solely by attending to their text and structure, it seems hardly likely that any convinced textualist or structuralist could actually approach a constitution with absolutely no knowledge or sense of its enactment history. That knowledge inevitably colours and informs the interpretation, elevating it from a mere sentence meaning interpretation based solely on semantics and syntax into an utterance level interpretation through consideration of the pragmatics of the communication. The illumination of history works at all the scales at which constitutional questions arise and constitutional interpretations are developed. It not only sheds light on the meaning of individual words, phrases, sentences and paragraphs, but also on entire divisions, parts and chapters of the constitution. History contributes to the explanatory power of an interpretation by illuminating our understanding of the constitution's most specific characteristics as well as its most general structural features. Many characteristics of text and structure that might otherwise be overlooked are often highlighted, and illuminated, through an understanding of the history of the constitution. Once seen in this light, it sometimes becomes apparent that the constitution contains shades of textual meaning and important structural interrelationships that would not otherwise have been recognised. But at the same time, history serves to discipline considerations of text and structure, by helping to ensure that meanings are not attributed to that text and structure as a result of the interpreter's personal preferences and predilections. In this way, considerations of text, structure and history have a mutually disciplining and illuminating effect on each other.

The ethical and pragmatic dimensions are relevant here too, provided they are mutually disciplined and illuminated by the other modalities. From the specific words and phrases used to the most general structural features of a constitution, considerations of history can shed light on the motivating ethical goals and principles, as well as the prudential compromises, to which those who drafted the constitution intended to give effect. Indeed, ethical and prudential considerations, when disciplined and illuminated in this way, can contribute not only to the specificity and generality of the explanations offered by an interpretation of a constitution, but also to their simplicity or elegance. It is no coincidence that constitutional law is suffused with references to broad ethical institutions or concepts such as the rule of law, federalism, representative democracy and the separation of powers. Provided they are appropriately disciplined, these institutional concepts are simplifying and yet illuminating ideas, for they can be used to propose, with some elegance, an interpretation of the constitution that accounts for many of the specific and general features of the constitution in a coordinated and coherent way. In other words, they can contribute to an interpretation of the constitution that has explanatory power. But they can only do this when disciplined by the other modalities, so that the content ascribed to the general principles is not allowed to become more, or to imply more, than is warranted when the specificities of the text, structure and history of the constitution are taken fully into account.[51]

International law and especially comparative law can also illuminate the meaning of a constitution, again provided any insights derived from them are disciplined by the other modalities. This can occur, for example, when a constitution's drafters deliberately modelled their document on another constitution in some particular respect. Understanding the constitution in this comparative context can illuminate its meaning because it can help to explain why the constitution has the particular textual and structural features that it has. The illumination can go in the opposite direction as well. The framers may have drafted their constitution deliberately to avoid what they considered to be pitfalls in another constitutional model, or they may have thought that some of its features were inappropriate for their circumstances or inconsistent with their aspirations. In such instances, historical knowledge of such a decision can help to explain why the constitution does not have certain features, but rather other features instead. And comparison can illuminate even when no historical relationship between constitutions can be identified at all. When two constitutions have certain features in common, interpretation of one can provide insights for the interpretation of the other. When they have features that are different, interpretation of one can shed light on the significance of those differences for the interpretation of the other.

[51] Because constitutions implement both ethical principles and prudential compromises, these two modalities also have a mutually illuminating and disciplining relationship. A constitution may give effect to a certain ethical principle, but not necessarily in a manner that is entirely consistent, perhaps due to the need to secure other ethical objectives, or because there is disagreement over competing ethical principles, or because the constitution has had to secure some kind of pragmatic compromise between competing interests.

The doctrinal modality plays an important role here as well, but in its own characteristic way. For just as the ethical and prudential modalities can (provided they are appropriately disciplined) bring to light relatively simple ideas that possess general explanatory power, so the particular issues that arise in contested cases, and the forensic scrutiny applied to those issues in the course of litigation, can bring to light specific features of a constitution that need to be understood and applied. As a consequence, the decisions of the courts contribute very significantly to the specificity of our engagement with the constitution. Cases often bring up issues that have not been thought about by even the most considered commentators and experts. Unanticipated problems of vagueness, ambiguity, inconsistency and incoherence arise not infrequently. Courts often have to adopt constitutional interpretations of sufficient specificity to address the particular questions that come before them. Due to the open-textured nature of constitutions, it may in some instances be difficult to decide between alternative constructions of constitutional meaning. In these sorts of cases, the principle of *stare decisis* plays an important role in contributing to the certainty of the law as applied by the courts. There is good reason for the courts to adhere to established doctrine in this interstitial sense. Departure from precedent is justified, however, if a different interpretation can be shown to have superior explanatory power when the other modalities are taken into account in a mutually illuminating and disciplining way.

This does not mean that such decisions will always be easy or uncontroversial. Constitutions are not perfect documents. They are as fallible as the people who create and interpret them. The problems that arise in litigation, and which are determined by the courts, force us to grapple with the particularity of our constitutions alongside their most overarching structures and general features. Constitutional interpretation is not, for this reason, an exact science, but the standards of explanatory adequacy that apply to the sciences apply also to our interpretations. The doctrinal modality contributes to the explanatory power of our interpretations by forcing us to grapple not only with big picture questions, but also with the very minute details of our constitutions. For the capacity of a particular interpretation of a constitution to account for the very specific and precisely-defined issues that arise in litigation is a significant measure of its explanatory power.

V. Conclusions

Close and careful analyses of text, structure and history, when rigorously pursued, tend to reinforce the findings of each other, and can help to disclose the ethical principles and prudential compromises that demonstrably motivated the making of a constitution. In hard cases, of course, reasonable minds may differ about what the most appropriate interpretation of the constitution will be. But, just as Goldsworthy has shown that the insights of the philosophy of language point to the rational attractiveness of an interpretation that seeks to identify the framer's intentions in drafting a constitution, so I have argued that the insights of the philosophy of science point to the rational attractiveness of an interpretation that offers the best explanation of a constitution. This suggests that the goal of constitutional interpretation is, and should be, to maximise the explanatory power of our interpretations – in as exhaustive and inclusive a manner as possible.

The explanatory power of a constitutional interpretation turns, I have argued, on standards of rationality that are common to all kinds of explanatory theories. Explanatory power is maximised when an interpretation uses a relatively simple set of concepts to account for a wide and yet detailed array of features of a constitution, from the meanings of individual words, phrases, clauses and sentences, all the way up to the structural relations between the divisions, parts and chapters of the constitution as a whole. Insights from the philosophy of language help us to understand how the semantic meaning of individual words and the syntactical meaning of entire phrases, clauses and sentences combine with the pragmatic considerations of the factual context, the conventional norms governing communication generally, and shared beliefs and values, to produce a rationally intelligible interpretation. Insights from the philosophy of science suggest that an interpretation will have explanatory power in proportion to its simplicity, its descriptiveness, and its consilience with other interpretations. They also suggest that the descriptiveness of an interpretation concerns the extent to which it offers a rationally satisfying explanation of both the specifics of the text and the generalities of the structure of the entire document.

I have argued that in order to secure an interpretation of a constitution that has superior explanatory power, the modalities of text, structure, history, ethics, prudence and doctrine, as well as those of comparative and international law, must be brought into a mutually illuminating and disciplining relationship. When this is done, the explanatory power of our interpretations is maximised. This is because considerations of text force us to grapple with the specifics of the constitution down to its most minute details; considerations of structure force us to grapple with the generalities of the constitution right up to its most comprehensive and universal features; considerations of history enable us to discern the particular meanings and purposes intended by the framers when they drafted the constitution, enabling us to make better sense of its text and structure; and considerations of ethics and prudence, provided they are disciplined and illuminated by the other modalities, offer us relatively simple concepts by which the complexity and variety of the constitution's textual and structural features can best be understood and explained. Judicial doctrine plays a key role as well, not only by virtue of its authoritative rulings, but because litigation forces us to grapple with questions of interpretation that might otherwise not occur to us, and the decided cases usually involve the resolution of very specific issues, which require a very minute examination of the constitution's finest details – its text and its structure, read in the light of all the other modalities. Even the interpretations of foreign constitutions by foreign courts can be illuminating, provided careful attention is given to the ways in which constitutions can in some respects be very similar in language and design, while in other important respects very different.

It is in the mutually disciplining and illuminating functions of text, structure, history, ethics, prudence, doctrine and comparison that the explanatory power of our interpretations can be maximised. This does not mean that there are always bright lines or easy answers to all questions. Obviously, this is not the case. Constitutions can be ambiguous and vague, and in the latter case, sometimes deliberately so. And judges and commentators often disagree about the best interpretation to be placed upon them. This is, in part, because the various elements of what makes for a theory possessing explanatory power are somewhat in tension with each other: it is difficult to arrive at a theory that is maximally simple and which is also maximally descriptive; and it is difficult to arrive at a theory that can explain both fine details and broad features of phenomena equally well. The various desiderata of explanatory power can tend to pull in different directions. However, the idea of explanatory power remains helpful even in such instances. Put simply: Theory A may offer a detailed explanation of an admittedly small range of data but at a very high level of specificity, whereas Theory B may offer a broad explanation of a very wide range of data but only at a relatively high level of generality. In these circumstances, we will have difficulty deciding which of the two theories has greater explanatory power, and we may well conclude that both theories are equally explanatory but for different purposes. However, if Theory C offers an explanation as detailed and specific as Theory A, yet as general and extensive as Theory B, we will conclude that Theory C has more explanatory power than either of the other two, and we will rationally prefer it to them. Theory C has the attributes to which all our theorisation is rationally inclined.

Theories about constitutions are the same. It is the interpretation of the constitution that most adequately explains its text and structure, together with its underlying ethical principles and prudential compromises, that is to be preferred. The enactment history of constitutions is of large significance in such inquiries, not only because it sheds light on the framers' intentions and understandings in themselves, but because those intentions and understandings help to bring to light textual details, structural relationships and motivating purposes which together help us to make sense of the document as an integrated whole composed of many parts. In genuinely hard cases, no interpretation is without its anomalies, and it is not always easy to decide between competing explanations. Sometimes interpreters are very candid about anomalies that cannot be resolved on their preferred interpretation, and they admit that an element of choice is involved. Other times, the anomalies are either avoided, or presented in a way that tries to downplay the force of the inconsistency. Critics routinely draw attention to these anomalies and present them as reasons to reject the interpretation. But, as is so often the case, the theories of the critics are also not without their anomalies. This is essentially because the law, although it aspires to consistency and coherence, is as imperfect as the human beings who make and interpret it. But this does not mean that the maximisation of the explanatory power of our interpretations is not the goal to which we should, and do, aspire. The fact that critics draw attention to these anomalies demonstrates, in fact, our shared commitment to the principle of explanatory power.

7

The Moral Motivations for Moderate Originalism

HEIDI M HURD*

I. Introduction

Jeffrey Goldsworthy is among the most thoughtful, illuminating and nuanced jurisprudential theorists of the past century. Among his many admirable talents is his unique ability to identify and defend previously unrecognised intellectual space between the polar positions of those engaged in long-running philosophical debates. By advancing fresh solutions that claim the advantages of both poles while avoiding their disadvantages, Goldsworthy has staked out jurisprudential positions that are both theoretically novel and more philosophically comfortable than are their competitors. His work honours Plato's claim that law lies at the junction between thought and action, for it seeks principled solutions to legal puzzles that enable lawmakers and adjudicators to interpret and apply laws in ways that realise, in practice, the deep-seated values that underpin our political institutions.

Goldsworthy's knack for staking out unoccupied middle ground is made particularly vivid within the long-running debate about the appropriate objectives of legal interpretation.[1] Indeed, in this context, Goldsworthy has made himself surprisingly comfortable between what many would think of as a philosophical rock and a jurisprudential hard place. On one hand, he has staunchly rejected what he has alternatively called

* My great thanks to Lisa Burton Crawford, Patrick Emerton and Dale Smith for making possible this scholarly celebration of Jeff Goldsworthy's important and impactful portfolio of work, and for co-organising the wonderful July 2017 symposium at which this piece got its first workout. Thanks also to Jonathan Crowe for his thoughtful reflections on this piece at that symposium, and to Dale Smith for his insightful comments during the editorial process. I am grateful to Larry Alexander and Larry Solum for informing the piece through helpful lessons on the distinctions between strong originalism, moderate originalism and public meaning originalism. And I am particularly grateful to Jeffrey Goldsworthy for extensive early comments that were designed to rescue me from various misstatements and misinterpretations. Lastly, I would like to thank Donald Zheng (Illinois Class of 2018) for his expert research and editorial assistance on this piece, as well as Professor Heather Simmons and the larger research team within the University of Illinois College of Law Library who provided invaluable research support.

[1] 'There are moderate versions of "intentionalism" and "originalism" that reject the excesses of more extreme versions. To completely deny the reality and utility of legislative intentions is to throw the baby out with the bathwater. … [At the same time] indeterminacies must be resolved by judicial discretion, which may be guided by values and goals very different from those of the lawmaker': J Goldsworthy, 'Legislation, Interpretation, and Judicial Review' (2001) 51 *University of Toronto Law Journal* 75, 82, 85.

'strong',[2] 'radical',[3] 'extreme',[4] or 'subjective'[5] intentionalism, arguing that an adjudicator engaged in legal interpretation should proceed, not by seeking to discern and comport with the subjective intentions of a text's authors, but rather by discerning the text's more objective 'utterance meaning'. On the other hand, Goldsworthy has sought to preserve a role for those authorial intentions by defining 'utterance meaning' as the speaker's subjective meaning that would have been assigned to the text by readers who were possessed of all publicly available textual, and non-textual, evidence of the speaker's subjective intentions, including sentence meaning, the context of enactment, then-prevalent political values and presuppositions, etc.[6] In short, legal interpretation should proceed not by seeking authorial intentions, but by seeking the informed beliefs about those intentions that the law's original audience would have reasonably entertained. Goldsworthy has further maintained that by 'moderating' originalism to allow judges not only to 'clarify' the meaning of obscure legal provisions, but to engage in forms of 'creative construction' that supplement, and sometimes correct, gaps and other flaws within laws that were apparently unintended, his theory of interpretation can claim the advantages of originalism while shedding its disadvantages. He thus claims to have comfortably wedged his theory of 'moderate originalism' between the unforgiving extremes of strong originalism and non-originalism.[7]

Just why would adjudicators do better – as a conceptual, practical and moral matter – to prefer *apparent* original authorial intentions to *actual* original authorial intentions when seeking to fix the meaning of legal language? And why would they be licensed to ignore certain objectively apparent intentions when they cannot ignore others, or to supplement or even correct texts in ways that would surprise, and sometimes dismay, their drafters?

[2] J Goldsworthy, 'Moderate versus Strong Intentionalism: Knapp and Michaels Revisited' (2005) 42 *San Diego Law Review* 669.

[3] J Goldsworthy, 'Marmor on Meaning, Interpretation, and Legislative Intention' (1995) 1 *Legal Theory* 439; J Goldsworthy, 'Dworkin as an Originalist' (2000) 17 *Constitutional Commentary* 49.

[4] J Goldsworthy, 'Originalism in Constitutional Interpretation' (1997) 25 *Federal Law Review* 1; J Goldsworthy, 'Constitutional Implications and Freedom of Political Speech: A Reply to Stephen Donaghue' (1997) 23 *Monash University Law Review* 362.

[5] J Goldsworthy, 'Subjective versus Objective Intentionalism in Legal Interpretation' in HM Hurd (ed), *Moral Puzzles and Legal Perplexities: Essays on the Influence of Larry Alexander* (Cambridge, Cambridge University Press, 2018).

[6] '"Utterance meaning," as distinct from "sentence meaning," is determined by contextual as well as textual factors – information concerning when, where, by whom, and for what apparent purposes the words were uttered. … Utterance meaning is sentence meaning, modified or supplemented only by contextual evidence of the speaker's meaning which is readily available to the intended audience': Goldsworthy, 'Constitutional Implications and Freedom of Political Speech' (n 4) 362.

[7] Goldsworthy defines originalism broadly. 'The core thesis of originalism is that the meaning of a constitution [or statute] is fixed at the time it is enacted or adopted, and can be lawfully changed only through the procedures for amendment prescribed by the constitution itself': J Goldsworthy, 'Interpreting the Australian Constitution: Express Provisions and Unexpressed General Principles' (2012) 24 *Giornale di Storia Costituzionale* 117, 118. Notice that this allows for multiple competing accounts of what exactly fixes the meaning of the law at the time of its enactment, and thus multiple competing theories that legitimately claim to be 'originalist'. Is it the subjective intentions of those who wrote or voted on the law, as a strong originalist would argue? Is it the intentions of those who wrote or voted on the law that were publicly-evidenced, as Goldsworthy's moderate originalism holds? Is it the conventional meaning of the text's sentences at the time of enactment, as public meaning originalists would argue?

The first question demands proof that Goldsworthy's moderate originalism can overcome the problems that have been raised in response to the subjective intentionalism of strong originalists. The second question demands a normative theory that has the resources to make Goldsworthy's brand of 'indirect intentionalism' morally compulsory, while also licensing his particular departures from publicly decipherable authorial intentions. The breathing room here has to be tight, because one cannot help but suspect that many accounts of why we should interpret present laws by reference to past facts about their authors will favour a version of subjective intentionalism; and, alternatively, many accounts of why we should look to factors beyond subjective authorial intentions will favour a theory of interpretation that parts ways with originalism altogether.

As my means of honouring Goldsworthy's distinguished scholarly legacy, I propose to take up this two-part project. In section II., I shall examine the principal points of departure between the subjective intentionalism of strong originalists and the objective intentionalism that defines Goldsworthy's moderate originalism. Inasmuch as a theory can often be defended by demonstrating its superiority over its alternatives, I shall ask whether a theory that looks to the appearances of authorial intentions and admits of a more generous understanding of what counts as honouring those apparent intentions escapes the problems that have beset interpretive theories that look to actual authorial intentions. To the extent that Goldsworthy's moderate originalism parts ways with strong originalism at points at which strong originalism invites practical or philosophical difficulties, we will have grounds for preferring it to its cousin, at least if it does not invite fresh problems of its own. In section III., however, I shall suggest that arguments against strong originalism are insufficient to ground Goldsworthy's moderate originalism, and that his reliance on arguments predicated on the rule of law, the nature of interpretation, and the values of democracy and federalism, fall short of providing an adequate moral account of both the pro-originalist and anti-intentionalist components of his interpretive theory. In section IV., I shall proffer an alternative account that promises fertile means of both vindicating originalism and motivating Goldsworthy's moderation of its traditional intentionalism. As I shall argue, if Goldsworthy either fessed up to having, or otherwise embraced, explicitly Burkean political commitments, he could provide his theory of interpretation with a secure philosophical home that would make non-contradictory his allegiance to, and periodic departures from, objective intentionalism. Of course, homes that sit on solid foundations come at a price; and this one would come at the price of defending foundational political presuppositions that are themselves morally contentious.

II. Does Moderate Originalism Succeed where Strong Originalism Fails?

Let us begin by asking whether Goldsworthy's moderate originalism alters intentionalism in interpretation, so as to escape the theoretical and practical problems that can be levelled against strong originalists. Inasmuch as strong originalists are not all of one mind, it would be unfortunate to treat them as though they were. In seeking the points of departure between Goldsworthy's moderate originalism and strong originalism, I shall thus explicitly lean on the version of strong originalism espoused by Larry Alexander and Emily Sherwin, for theirs is the most virile version of subjective intentionalism that has been defended to date by philosophically able originalists.

Strong originalists like Alexander and Sherwin take the meaning of legal terms and phrases within constitutional and statutory provisions to be given by the meaning that was subjectively intended by their authors. If the original intentions of lawmakers with regard to the meaning of an enactment cannot be gleaned, then the enactment is effectively meaningless, and the fact that its provisions have a conventional meaning should not confuse anyone into thinking otherwise. For to substitute conventional meaning for the speakers' meaning is to substitute what others would mean for what the drafters in fact meant; and this, according to strong originalists, is not to treat laws as communications at all.

There are at least three reasons why strong originalists embrace a communicative theory of law, and thus locate the meaning of a legal text in the subjective intentions of its authors. First, Alexander and Sherwin take their strong originalism to follow ineluctably from the law's authority. In their view, if we appreciate why law has authority at all, we will appreciate that it demands an investigation of its authors' intentions in cases in which its meaning is in doubt. 'We select legislators, administrators, and judges in large part based on our assessment of their moral expertise, that is, their ability to craft rules that represent moral improvements over the status quo ante.'[8] Inasmuch as expertise resides within the beliefs and intentions of experts, the expertise of law – its superior ability to guide action in accordance with morality – must reside within the beliefs and intentions of lawmakers. And if law possesses its authority by virtue of reflecting the moral expertise of its authors, then to honour the basis upon which it properly binds our actions today, judges must interpret its provisions in light of the intentions possessed by its original authors.

Second, many believe that the values served by democracy and the separation of powers demand allegiance to legislative intentions when assigning meaning to democratically crafted enactments. They fear that in the guise of interpreting statutory language, judges will invent and apply laws that were never, in fact, passed by democratically elected representatives. As Robert Bork famously insisted, policy-making within a democratic system devoted to the separation of legislative, executive and judicial powers is the sole province of elected legislators. The only interpretive theory that prevents judges from engaging in illicit legislation is that of subjective intentionalism, for such a theory transforms all adjudicative questions into empirical ones (concerning the psychology of past lawmakers), and so converts all apparent opportunities for judicial moralising into fact-finding exercises.

Third, many strong originalists fear that in the constitutional context, a departure from the subjective intentions of the framers will constitute a violation of the social contract that is the foundation of a constitutional democracy. As Richard Posner argued when discussing Bork's constitutional originalism, the *US Constitution* represents a great covenant by which Americans entered into society and defined their rights and duties vis-à-vis the state.[9] Just as they must seek the intentions of the drafters in standard contract cases, so judges must seek the intentions of the Constitution's drafters on pain of effectively tearing up the

[8] L Alexander and E Sherwin, *Demystifying Legal Reasoning* (New York, Cambridge University Press, 2008) 139.
[9] RA Posner, 'Bork and Beethoven' (1990) 42 *Stanford Law Review* 1365, 1372.

contract that was, and still is, the consensual basis upon which Americans trade individual liberty for the benefits of cooperative citizenship.

A great deal of ink has been spilled over the question of whether strong originalists have a coherent account of the objects to which they are referring when they insist that legal interpretation must proceed by reference to the subjective intentions of the framers, or legislators, who were responsible for codifying the specific provisions that constrain our actions.[10] As I have suggested elsewhere, there are at least five possible intentional states to which strong originalists might be referring when they equate the meaning of legal provisions to their 'speaker's meaning', and none of these possibilities prove problem-free for strong originalists.[11] After I tick through these, the question for our purposes will be whether Goldsworthy does not have the same obligation to identify which of these five intentional states he believes should be the locus of an adjudicator's evidentiary quest when enquiring about the intentions that an original audience would have reasonably assigned to lawmakers.[12] If so, then the follow-up question will be whether his moderate originalism somehow makes this choice easier for him than it is for strong originalists.

First, strong originalists might think that the meaning of a lawmaker's words should be fixed by the exemplars to which lawmakers subjectively adverted when employing those words. If, when prohibiting vehicles from the park, lawmakers consciously pictured automobiles but not farm equipment, then the word 'vehicles' within their regulation should be interpreted to mean cars and to exclude tractors. Robert Bork opted for this version of intentionalism when he insisted that the Equal Protection Clause should be read narrowly to prohibit only racial discrimination, for its drafters had in mind at the time of its enactment the Black Codes of the Reconstructionist South, but not instances of discrimination based on gender, religion, sexual orientation, age or disability.[13] While Bork was drawn to this parsimonious understanding of intentionalism precisely because it maximally emasculated judicial review, most strong originalists are embarrassed by the fact that the law rapidly runs out if the meaning of its terms is confined to the exemplars subjectively contemplated by its authors. To take a case even more obvious than Bork's own example, if when prohibiting vehicles in the park, city council members all had in mind a white Ford that was recently involved in a park accident, then it would seem that the prohibition would only exclude white Fords from the park, and not blue Chevys or pink Cadillacs. In order to avoid such silliness, strong originalists are anxious to insist that intended meanings extend well beyond the particular exemplars that authors conjure in their heads when they are

[10] A substantial quantity of this ink, some of which I have myself strewn, goes to the conceptual coherence and practical decipherability of 'group intentions' of the sort that are assigned to legislatures and groups of constitutional framers by originalists who subscribe to some version of intentionalist interpretation. I am not going to engage with this line of criticism, although to the extent that Goldsworthy defends against scepticism regarding the authorial intentions of past lawmakers (and thus, the ability of publicly-available evidence to, in fact, evidence actual things), he is well aware of the burden he faces in providing an account of such collective mental states. See, eg, J Goldsworthy, 'Legislative Intention Vindicated?' (2013) 33 *Oxford Journal of Legal Studies* 821; J Goldsworthy, 'Legislative Intentions, Legislative Supremacy, and Legal Positivism' (2005) 42 *San Diego Law Review* 493.

[11] HM Hurd, 'Interpretation Without Intentions' in G Pavlakos and V Rodriguez-Blanco (eds), *Reasons and Intentions in Law and Practical Agency* (Cambridge, Cambridge University Press, 2015) 52–71.

[12] As Goldsworthy wrote in very helpful comments on this piece, 'I think – and I suspect that most strong originalists would agree with me – that the relevant intentional state is an intention to communicate something – whether an assertion, instruction, request, or whatever – either expressly, impliedly, or both.'

[13] R Bork, 'Neutral Principles and Some First Amendment Problems' (1971) 47 *Indiana Law Journal* 1.

drafting legal provisions. As Alexander and Sherwin maintain, for example, '[t]he relevant intent must be something more than intent to govern the particular cases to which the rule-maker adverted'.[14]

The most obvious way of understanding how lawmakers might have interpretive intentions that extend beyond their adverted-to exemplars is by taking them to intend their words to mean what their words conventionally mean. On this second understanding, 'speaker's meaning' is identical to 'word meaning', where this is given by dictionaries that sum up sociological facts about common usage. If a lawmaker's use of the term 'vehicles' is rightly captured by the class of objects summed up in a dictionary definition, then it will include any power-driven means of transportation, including a combine, a tank and an airplane, whether the lawmaker subjectively anticipated that extension or not. Yet, as I earlier anticipated, strong originalists insist that to equate what speakers mean by their words with whatever their words conventionally mean abandons the communicative enterprise altogether, and with it, the interpretive enterprise. As Alexander and Sherwin maintain, '[t]he result is not interpretation of the lawmaker's rule. Rather the interpreter is constructing a rule out of materials provided by the original lawmaker, and in so doing, is acting as a lawmaker in his or her own right'.[15]

The third understanding of what constitutes the relevant authorial intentions to which adjudicators should look when fixing the meaning of words, and sentences, in legal texts construes those intentions as hypothetical. Adjudicators should fix the meaning of an enactment by asking what intentions lawmakers *would have had* with regard to a given application *if* they had adverted to it. Thus, if lawmakers would have intended to include manned aeronautics within the meaning of the word 'vehicles' had they ever adverted to the possibility that such machines would threaten entry into the park, then the word 'vehicle' should be interpreted to include a Twin Otter, but not a drone. Yet strong originalists have refused this offering, because they take it to induce doubts about 'the facticity of intentions' – doubts which lead to 'intention skepticism'.[16] As Alexander and Sherwin write: 'We believe that there are real, not hypothetical, intentions about matters not specifically adverted to.'[17] Thus, the question of what past legislators intended with regard to a situation to which they never adverted is quite different from the question of what, counterfactually, they would have intended had they adverted to that situation. It is the former question, not the latter, that must be asked, and according to strong originalists like Alexander and Sherwin, there is a fact of the matter (not a counter-factual) which makes that question answerable.

The fourth category of intentional objects that strong originalists might mean to pick out, when referencing the authorial intentions of lawmakers, is comprised of those things that lawmakers subjectively believed to be denoted by the words they used, in light of their subjective beliefs about the connotations of those words. As Goldsworthy explains, 'the denotation, reference, or extension of a term is comprised of all the things in the world which the word refers to; its connotation, sense, or intention consists of

[14] Alexander and Sherwin (n 8) 151.
[15] Alexander and Sherwin (n 8) 138–39.
[16] Alexander and Sherwin (n 8) 163.
[17] Alexander and Sherwin (n 8) 165.

the criteria which define it, and thereby determine its denotation'.[18] Thus, if given their subjective understanding of its connotation, lawmakers understood the word 'jury' to denote a panel of male fact-finders, it would be illicit for a contemporary judge to interpret the word to allow for female jurors. As Goldsworthy makes clear, it is the adoption of this thesis that makes many strong originalists both resistant to the notion that America's founding document is a 'living constitution',[19] and hostile to the claim that the meaning of statutory provisions can change, evolve and adapt to new circumstances without explicit legislative modernisation.[20] Yet Alexander and Sherwin reject the view that strong originalism entails that legal language denotes only those things believed to be denoted by its authors. They argue, for example, that while lawmakers might take a residential prohibition against bears to denote only black bears and grizzlies, it might well be within their intentions to denote Malaysian sun bears, even though they never knew such a species existed.[21] But how can the class of things denoted by a word be expanded beyond the class subjectively contemplated by a speaker without making that class co-extensive with the word's conventional extension? It must be that an author's subjective beliefs about the connotation of a word (rather than the rules of usage that sum up the conventional connotation of the word) allow for the extension of that word to things that would surprise the author. But if the conventional connotations of the author's words are not doing the work, what could justify the extension of those words to things beyond the author's knowledge?

By way of answer, the fifth category of intentional objects that might serve to define what strong originalists mean when they urge judicial searches for authorial intentions is comprised of the goals or larger purposes possessed by lawmakers. On this understanding, judges should disambiguate legal language by asking what lawmakers meant to achieve – what moral purpose they sought to advance – by passing the law in question. Thus, if a concern for pedestrian safety motivated the prohibition against vehicles in the park, the term 'vehicles' should be construed in ways that will advance that goal, and as such, it ought to be thought to denote bicycles, skateboards, and Segways, but not drones. If, on the other hand, the concern was for noise pollution, then bicycles and skateboards ought to be exempted from the class of things denoted by the word 'vehicles', but drones ought to be included. Yet strong originalists like Alexander and Sherwin very typically resist this reach to the morally plausible background motives that make sense of particular provisions within constitutional or statutory texts. This is because they are convinced that to move

[18] Goldsworthy, 'Originalism' (n 4) 31. See also J Goldsworthy, 'Clarifying, Creating, and Changing Meaning in Constitutional Interpretation: A Comment on András Jakab, "Constitutional Reasoning in Constitutional Courts – A European Perspective"' (2013) 14 *German Law Journal* 1279, 1293.

[19] For an oft-cited defence of the 'living tree doctrine', see LC Marshall, 'Contempt of Congress: A Reply to the Critics of an Absolute Rule of Statutory Stare Decisis' (1990) 88 *Michigan Law Review* 2467, 2478 ('Consistent with the notion of the Constitution as a living document, definitions and applications of terms like "due process", "cruel and unusual punishment", and "unreasonable search and seizure" evolve over time. The specter of judges inserting content into these phrases is not an unfortunate or inevitable by-product of the framers' poor drafting or lack of foresight; it is a critical part of the process of breathing life into a document originated by those long dead.')

[20] Goldsworthy, 'Originalism' (n 4) 30–35.

[21] 'If the rule maker had in mind particular tokens of keeping bears near private residences when he enacted his rule, but would reply affirmatively if asked whether his rule prohibits other tokens that were not in his mind at the time, his intended meaning, and thus the meaning of his rule, is that those latter tokens of keeping bears are prohibited': Alexander and Sherwin (n 8) 150.

from specific rules to more general background values, or goals, is to lose the value of rules altogether. As they argue: 'If the meaning of rules is derived from the moral principles that the rules were designed to serve, there are, in effect, no rules and no means for curbing moral error.'[22]

Yet if the relevant authorial intentions for strong originalists are neither occurrent mental exemplars, nor counter-factual constructs, nor subjective denotations, nor background motivations, nor the conventional extensions of their chosen words, what might they be? The sole remaining possibility is that they are unconscious interpretive intentions that can be later discovered to have been governing at the time of a law's enactment. On this thesis, lawmakers possess semantic intentions about which they are not conscious at the time when they enact given rules (for example, that drones – of which they never heard – should count as 'vehicles' under park rules). These unconscious intentions can, at least in principle, be reliably evidenced after the fact, so that it can be true to say that lawmakers intended their prohibition of 'vehicles' in the park to include Segways but exclude drones, even though they never consciously imagined that such things would exist, never had occurrent thoughts about them, and never consciously entertained the question of whether they should be included in the extension of their reference to 'vehicles'. To make out such an account of the intentions made material by exercises in legal interpretation, strong originalists would have to first make sense of the very notion of unconscious intentions (ie, unwilled choices), and they would then have to defend the claim that among those intentions is a set that concerns how words should be interpreted in unforeseen and unforeseeable circumstances. And they would further have to explain how these unconscious interpretive intentions have a greater claim to judicial deference than do other means of legal interpretation which are both more publicly available and more normatively relevant.

As I hope this survey reveals, it is not enough for strong originalists to insist that judges must fix the meaning of legal terms by the interpretive intentions of their authors. For such a formula masks a menu of intentional states, no one of which is obviously defensible, and all of which have been rejected by at least some strong originalists. One is left at a loss for what strong originalists like Alexander and Sherwin think they mean when they speak of a text's speaker's meaning, given their rejection of all the proffered candidates above, and their refusal to advance a clear and consistent alternative. That strong originalists do not have a clear and clearly defensible theory of the nature of the subjective intentions that fix the meaning of legal terms is, thus, a reason to doubt the coherence and practicality of strong originalism. For those wedded to some version of originalism, it is also a reason to hope that Goldsworthy's moderate originalism either escapes altogether the need to make a choice among this menu of options, or allows one to make the choice with greater ease than can strong originalists. It is to these alternative sources of optimism that I now turn.

Unlike strong originalists, Goldsworthy maintains that what fixes the meaning of a legal text is evidence of the lawmakers' intentions that was readily available to the lawmakers'

[22] Alexander and Sherwin (n 8) 151.

intended contemporary audience at the time of enactment;[23] not evidence of the lawmakers' intentions that, at the time of enactment, remained private:[24]

> The meaning of a law, like that of any other utterance, is something public, not hidden. It is partly determined by what its intended audience knows, or can be reasonably expected to know, about its author's intentions, but not about concealed intentions.[25]

Thus Goldsworthy maintains, until formally amended, 'statutory provisions mean what they meant when they were enacted',[26] and what fixes what they meant when enacted is what their audience would have taken their legislatively intended meaning to be. This, he claims, constitutes the 'objective intention' of a law.[27] According to Goldsworthy, those engaged in legal interpretation should elevate the intentions that could objectively be assigned to original drafters by then-contemporary readers above the drafters' actual intentions when the two are not in accord: and this is true even if the drafters' actual intentions are known with confidence.[28] Thus, if it would never have occurred to the constitutional framers' contemporary audience that the word 'jury' was used by the framers to mean 'a fact-finding panel of men', rather than a 'fact-finding panel representative of the community', then the proper intention to assign to the framers today is an intention to impanel women jurors, even *if we now know with confidence that this interpretation is not, in fact, in keeping with the subjective intentions of the framers.*

Goldsworthy's moderate originalism thus requires judges to see through a glass darkly – to seek original authorial intentions through the beliefs about those intentions that can reasonably be ascribed to then-contemporary audience members given evidence that was then publicly available. Notice that this formulation raises the same question as strong originalism does: About which subjective mental states should judges be seeking objective evidence so as to fix what a then-contemporary audience would reasonably have believed?[29] Should contemporary judges inquire into the intended exemplars that

[23] I shall resist the temptation to dwell on the apparent regress embedded in this formulation. But, if it is the case that in order to identify a law's intended audience, a judge must ask which audience a reasonable audience would believe was the intended audience, given publicly available evidence, then the judge will need to know how to identify *that* audience. If the answer turns on what the lawmakers intended, with regard to the audience whose beliefs would fix the identity of the reasonable audience to which its provisions were intended, the regress becomes infinite.

[24] While this form of what one might think of as 'indirect intentionalism' elevates perceptions of authorial intentions above those intentions themselves, it does not do so on the basis of any scepticism about there being determinate, knowable intentions on the part of framers or legislators, either individually or as groups. For a critique of sceptical rejections of intentionalism within interpretation, see R Ekins and J Goldsworthy, 'The Reality and Indispensability of Legislative Intentions' (2014) 36 *Sydney Law Review* 39.

[25] Goldsworthy, 'Originalism' (n 4) 20. As Goldsworthy explains, 'the irrelevance of hidden legislative intentions … follows from the political ideal known as "the Rule of Law". The law can only provide a practicable framework for social interaction if its meaning is made public … and imposing penalties or costs for a failure to comply with hidden intentions is obviously unfair': J Goldsworthy, 'Constitutional Interpretation: Originalism' (2009) 4 *Philosophy Compass* 682, 686.

[26] Goldsworthy, 'Originalism' (n 4) 9.

[27] Ekins and Goldsworthy (n 24) 48.

[28] Goldsworthy, 'Moderate vs Strong Intentionalism' (n 2) 671.

[29] Goldsworthy resists this conclusion. In his very helpful comments on this piece, he wrote: 'I think – and I suspect that most strong originalists would agree with me – that the relevant intentional state is an intention to communicate something – whether an assertion, instruction, request, or whatever – either expressly, impliedly, or both. This could be called a "communicative intention." In the case of a law, what is intended to be communicated

then-contemporary citizens would have attributed to past lawmakers given publicly available evidence? Should they instead attribute to then-contemporary citizens the view articulated by Alexander and Sherwin – namely, that 'intended meanings extend well beyond the particular images contained in authors' mental states',[30] so as to seek out then-contemporary perceptions of intentions that surpassed the exemplars that would reasonably have been attributed to lawmakers? If so, would it be legitimate for today's judges simply to assign, to original audience members, a belief that the words used by the lawmakers of their day were meant to be interpreted in accordance with their then-contemporary conventional meaning? And if this illicitly substitutes a theory of public meaning for what he means by moderate originalism, can Goldsworthy instead maintain that the relevant meaning to be assigned to legal texts is driven by what original audience members would have taken the words of those texts to denote, given their reasonable beliefs about the lawmakers' intended connotations? If fixing an interpretation in one of these ways generates results at odds with the lawmakers' apparent purposes in passing the legislation to begin with, can judges substitute an interpretation that better serves the morally-intelligible motivations that original audience members would reasonably have assigned to the law's authors? And if not any of these, then should judges be seeking to understand the unconscious intentions at work within past legislative choices, as gleaned through the beliefs about those unconscious forces that would have been reasonable at the time, given available objective evidence?

Goldsworthy does not explicitly address all of these alternative possible constructions of his moderate originalism, but he addresses some of them, and it is not hard to surmise what he would say about others. Let us work through those that allow us to decipher whether Goldsworthy's moderate originalism has a leg up on strong originalism. To begin, surely Goldsworthy does not take the evidentiary quest for the intentions that an original audience would have assigned to the authors of a given law to be a quest for beliefs about the exemplars, to which the lawmakers likely adverted when crafting the law's constraints. Very often those subjective exemplars would be sufficiently idiosyncratic to evade expression within the public record; and if they were apparently available to then-contemporary audience members (because the law was crafted to prevent the recurrence of a particular incident vivid in the minds of lawmakers and laypersons alike at the time), I am betting that Goldsworthy would attribute to the law's original audience, an appreciation of the need for laws to reach beyond salient examples. One would thus expect Goldsworthy to

is (usually) the enactment of a law, which is why I sometimes speak of "enactment intentions"': J Goldsworthy, Comments to the Author, 20 December 2017 (copy on file with author). Yet Goldsworthy's conviction that we (or a past original audience) can fairly readily establish the nature of the communication that legal authors intend to convey – its status as a law, request, assertion, question, etc – does not touch the question of its content. How are we – or how was the original audience to an enacted statute or ratified constitutional provision – to decipher what specific terms should be taken to mean? When the announced rule is, 'No vehicles in the park', no light is cast on what a 'vehicle' should be taken to mean by the discovery that the City Council had 'enactment intentions'. Goldsworthy does not think, by itself, that it does. He goes on to insist that all of the five candidates of relevant authorial mental states that I have canvassed are *evidential* of the question; none are dispositive. But then, the question is: What precisely are these evidential of? What is the thing as to which evidence is sought? What is the thing as to which an audience's beliefs based on publicly-available evidence is sought? To say, the authors' 'enactment intentions', is not an answer; for we need to know what fixes those intentions when there are at least five competing contenders. It is on this basis that I take the ensuing discussion to remain apt.

[30] Alexander and Sherwin (n 8) 142.

vest original audience members with the assumption that lawmakers intended their laws to apply to things beyond their mind's eye.

The most obvious means of projecting speakers' interpretive intentions beyond those exemplars, to which they explicitly adverted, is to attribute to them the intention to refer to the *class of things* to which the terms they used conventionally extend. On this account, we would ascribe to a law's original audience, the belief that what a speaker meant by his words is identical to what his words conventionally meant. But such a view collapses speakers' meaning into conventional meaning, and thereby sacrifices the distinction to be drawn between versions of public meaning originalism and Goldsworthy's unique understanding of moderate originalism. On the former theory, judges today ought to interpret the words in legal texts in light of their statistically common usage at the time those words were employed, as evidenced by their definitions within then-contemporary dictionaries.[31] In Goldsworthy's view,

> [t]he authors of legal documents, whether contracts, wills, statutes or constitutions, inevitably fail to express themselves with perfect clarity and comprehensiveness. To limit the meaning of their document to the literal meanings of its words maximizes indeterminacy, absurdity, and the frustration of their intentions or purposes.[32]

Moreover, original audience members might have assigned interpretive intentions to lawmakers that parted ways with the interpretive conventions of the day; and if they did, it is those non-conventional intentions that should govern the meaning of the terms they used, and not a now-outdated dictionary. In other words, the public meaning of a law (construed as its conventional meaning at the time it was drafted) is not identical to its utterance meaning, for its utterance meaning derives from evidence-based assessments of its speaker's meaning, and what its speakers meant may depart quite considerably from what their words conventionally meant.

Goldsworthy says little that would allow us to discern, with confidence, exactly what he would say if assigned the view that the quest for the public evidence of a speaker's meaning is tantamount to a hypothetical, rather than an empirical, enterprise. There is a sense in which it would seem that this is precisely his view. For the mandate of moderate originalism is to seek the beliefs that a then-contemporary audience *would have been reasonable* in forming concerning the operative intentions behind a newly crafted law. This exercise by itself appears to be a counter-factual inquiry, for it appears indifferent to whether any audience at the time actually formed any real beliefs about such authorial intentions. Yet I take it that Goldsworthy thinks that the intentions which are the objects of this counter-factual inquiry are not themselves counter-factual.[33] So, while the subjective intentions possessed

[31] Larry Solum, who famously defends a version of public meaning originalism, insists that 'the notion that originalists rely on dictionary definitions to determine the communicative content of the constitutional text' is a misconception. As he argues, 'although dictionaries may play some role, the better approach emphasizes primary evidence such as that provided by corpus linguistics', as well as by 'the investigation of context': LB Solum, 'Originalist Methodology' (2017) 84 *University of Chicago Law Review* 269.

[32] Goldsworthy, 'Constitutional Interpretation' (n 25) 684.

[33] Goldsworthy very explicitly rejects judicial references to 'objective legislative intentions' which presuppose that legislatures should be treated 'as if' they had intentions or 'as if' they were reasonable agents. As he writes: 'It might be suggested that an objective intention is an intention that *would* be imputed to the actual legislature by reasonable readers … *if it were* capable of having an intention. But what would be the point of pretending that a legislature has an intention, if in fact it does not and cannot have one? Another possibility is that an "objective"

by framers or legislators might part ways with the intentions reasonably assigned to them on the basis of publicly available evidence, the point of consulting such evidence is to get as close to actual, not hypothetical, subjective intentions as is reasonably possible. And such an exercise is not then co-extensive with asking what legislators would have counter-factually intended, if they adverted to the fact that a law might be called upon to address a circumstance to which they did not, in fact, advert.

How then should we understand the nature of the subjective mental states to which adjudicators ought to seek publicly-available evidence? Should we ask for the class of things that the public record suggests were denoted by the authors' use of a word within a text? Or should adjudicators look for public evidence of the belief that legal authors had concerning the connotation of their words? According to Goldsworthy, on pain of giving up originalism, altogether moderate originalists cannot allow the intended connotation of textual language to change (as understood through what a reasonable contemporary audience would have perceived that to be). But they can readily admit that what textual language *denotes* changes over time. Thus statutes that concern 'carriages' can properly be read to apply to Ferraris and Segways, and regulations regarding the telegraph can properly be read to apply to cellular telephones.[34] Of course, the denotation of enacted terms is fixed by their connotation, and their connotation is fixed by the criteria that a reasonable audience would take to have been subjectively assigned by legal authors to those terms, given the available public record on the matter. So, *if* a then-contemporary audience would have attributed to legislators, the belief that being male was a constitutive criterion of being a juror, then a judge today should not interpret the statutory use of the term 'juror' to apply to anyone who is not male.

Goldsworthy makes what I take to be the same point in a different but illuminating way, which captures the licence that he takes moderate originalism to afford judges. In his view, strong originalism precludes judges from applying legal language in ways that achieve results which are different from those intended by the drafters of the text. In other words, according to strong originalism, judges must think of themselves as constrained by the 'application intentions' of lawmakers – intentions that I take to be coextensive with lawmakers' subjective beliefs about the denotation of their terms. On this view, for example, judges are bound to deny homosexuals entry into the United States under the 1952 law that prohibits access to all persons having 'psychopathic personalit[ies]', because when this law was enacted, Congress expected (or would reasonably have been thought to expect) that it would result in the exclusion of homosexuals.[35] Goldsworthy maintains, in contrast, that moderate originalists can properly limit themselves to enforcing lawmakers' 'enactment intentions': they need not seek to fulfill the further 'application intentions' with which lawmakers laboured when crafting laws. Thus, he says, while legislators may have expected that the term 'psychopathic personality' would always be interpreted to include homosexuality, the phrase which they employed reasonably suggests that they intended it to connote conditions about which

intention is whatever a "reasonable legislature" or "ideal legislature" would have intended had it enacted the statute. But that would be an entirely imaginary intention': Ekins and Goldsworthy (n 24) 49 (emphasis in original; citation omitted).

[34] Goldsworthy, 'Originalism' (n 4) 32.

[35] Goldsworthy draws this example from L Lessig, 'Understanding Changed Readings: Fidelity and Theory' (1995) 47 *Stanford Law Review* 395, 415–19.

psychologists might change their views over time. If contemporary psychology does not consider homosexuality to be psychopathic, then judges should refuse to honour the application intentions of lawmakers when interpreting the phrase. Similarly, writes Goldsworthy, while the framers of the *US Constitution* may not have believed that flogging was cruel or unusual, 'they enacted a moral principle forbidding cruelty, not their own beliefs about the application of the principle in particular instances'.[36] According to moderate originalism, then, judges are entitled to conclude that what constitutional and statutory terms denote today, given their (original and unchangeable) connotations, differs from what their authors took their terms to denote.[37]

Not only is Goldsworthy willing to allow that the denotation of constitutional and statutory terms can change over time, consistent with an appropriate allegiance to publicly evidenced authorial intentions regarding the connotation of those terms, but he is also willing to part ways with strong originalists over their refusal to consult the background goals that motivated constitutional or legislative changes. Strong originalists, recall, insist that, on pain of engaging in illicit policy-making, judges must not substitute a quest for lawmakers' larger purposes for an inquiry into the intended connotation and denotation of particular words. As a result, strong originalists are prepared to say, for example, that inasmuch as Article I, Section 8 of the *US Constitution* grants Congress the power to raise and regulate 'Armies' and 'a Navy', but makes no mention of an Air Force, the power to form and support such a military force is not constitutionally protected – notwithstanding the fact that it would advance the purposes of the framers to read the Constitution so as to permit Congress to raise and regulate all possible sorts of military forces (including those we cannot now imagine).

Goldsworthy recognises that sometimes the task of interpreting law demands more than mere 'clarification' – that is, more than elucidating a publicly-evidenced intended meaning 'that despite being previously obscured was possessed by the text all along'.[38] In the interests of resolving disputes, judges are sometimes required to repair gaps within laws by engaging in 'creative construction'.[39] And, in some instances, they are required to go even further – to repair or improve laws that, by their clear terms, threaten undesirable results. In such instances, judges are called upon to correct obvious drafting errors, insert 'implied terms', and otherwise adopt interpretive strategies that resolve disputes in ways which honour the objectives or larger purposes that can be reasonably attributed to lawmakers.[40] While these latter exercises in judicial draftsmanship are 'a dangerous liberty,

[36] Goldsworthy, 'Originalism' (n 4) 30.

[37] See also JM Balkin, 'Alive and Kicking: Why No One Truly Believes in a Dead Constitution' (*Slate*, 29 August 2005) www.slate.com/id/2125226/ (last accessed 12 November 2018). ('Original meaning does not mean original expected application. For example, the Constitution bans cruel and unusual punishments. But the application of the concepts of "cruel and unusual" must be that of our own day, not 1791.')

[38] Goldsworthy, 'Clarifying, Creating, and Changing Meaning' (n 18) 1280.

[39] '[I]mplications may be added to the Constitution by construction, but only when necessary to fulfill its underlying purposes or principles. These must be its original purposes or principles, because otherwise, anything at all could be added to the Constitution': J Goldsworthy, 'Constitutional Cultures, Democracy, and Unwritten Principles' (2012) 3 *University of Illinois Law Review* 683, 708.

[40] One is entitled, it seems to me, to push on the distinction that Goldsworthy needs between the 'application intentions' of lawmakers and their larger 'purposes'. Why are judges not simply consulting lawmakers' application intentions when they seek to serve their larger goals or purposes in enacting a provision to begin with?

not lightly to be resorted to',[41] they are, in Goldsworthy's view, well within the ambit of legal *interpretation*, so long as they are guided by 'the expectations or desires' of those who crafted the laws in question.[42] Thus, judges may read the US Constitution to empower Congress to mobilise an Air Force, because in so doing, judges honour the purposes that the framers publicly evidenced when crafting Article I, Section 8, far better than they would if they limited themselves to the specific permissions of that text. Such a licence allows judges to 'adjust the Constitution's words so that the founders' purposes are not thwarted by changes in social facts, but it does not permit them to adjust those purposes themselves, in accordance with changed social values'.[43]

We thus need not resort to a journey into the unconscious in order to understand what Goldsworthy takes to be the relevant interpretive intentions that inform the notion of a lawmaker's 'utterance meaning', and that thus constitute the legitimate objects of the judicial quest for relevant contemporaneous public evidence. According to his moderate originalism, judges must ask what a reasonable audience at the time a law was passed would have believed about the intentions of its drafters, with regard to the connotations of the terms employed in the law and the larger, morally plausible goals its enactment would achieve. Judges are not bound to constrain the meaning of a law to the apparent exemplars to which lawmakers adverted when crafting the law, nor are they limited to applying the law to the objects that lawmakers denoted, given the apparent conceptions that lawmakers possessed concerning their words' connotations. Thus, in many cases, judges are entitled to reach interpretive conclusions that would surprise, and even appall, the drafters of the texts in question. As Goldsworthy sums it up, 'to properly apply a provision incorporating a moral or other evaluative principle, judges must decide what the principle requires, rather than what the law-makers may have believed it requires'.[44] Thus, if the phrase 'the right to marriage' is reasonably believed to connote a morally-informed relationship, a contemporary judge employing contemporary conceptions of the social meaning and value of marriage may rightly extend it to include gay marriage, even if that extension would surprise and dismay the lawmakers who first employed the phrase. As Goldsworthy anticipates, in many hard cases, the connotation/denotation distinction is very difficult to draw,

[41] Goldsworthy, 'Clarifying, Creating, and Changing Meaning' (n 18) 1281, quoting Learned Hand, *The Bill of Rights* (Cambridge, Harvard University Press, 1958) 29.

[42] Goldsworthy hesitantly goes even further by conceding the possibility of 'truly exceptional and extreme cases' in which more aggressive judicial activism – what he calls 'statesmanship' – is licensed, indeed required, in order to avoid injustice. J Goldsworthy, 'Kable, Kirk, and Judicial Statesmanship' (2014) 40 *Monash University Law Review* 75, 114. Whether he thinks of such rare instances of legitimate judicial activism as being in keeping with his theory of interpretation, or as simply a morally justified departure from what constitutes interpretation altogether, is unclear. See also J Goldsworthy, 'The Limits of Judicial Fidelity to Law: The Coxford Lecture' (2011) 24 *Canadian Journal of Law and Jurisprudence* 305; J Goldsworthy, 'Should Judges Covertly Disobey the Law to Prevent Injustice?' (2011) 47 *Tulsa Law Review* 133.

[43] Goldsworthy, 'Originalism' (n 4) 34. As Goldsworthy argues, 'there is clearly a point, even if it is unclear just where it lies, at which flexible and purposive interpretation becomes amendment. At that point interpretivism shades into non-interpretivism': J Goldsworthy, 'Realism about the High Court' (1989) 18 *Federal Law Review* 27, 38 (fn omitted). For example, Goldsworthy has forcefully condemned the High Court of Australia for its discovery of an unwritten, but implied freedom of political communication, as well as for its recognition of an implied requirement that state courts pass a strict 'character test' in order to exercise federal jurisdiction. Such exercises in judicial 'supplementation' part ways with interpretation altogether, in his view. See J Goldsworthy, 'Constitutional Implications Revisited' (2011) 30 *University of Queensland Law Journal* 9; Goldsworthy, 'Judicial Statesmanship' (n 42).

[44] Goldsworthy, 'Originalism' (n 4) 30.

for it may be impossible to know whether a given criterion (eg, the genders of the parties seeking marriage) is constitutive of, or incidental to, the drafters' intended meaning. In such a case, a court is entitled, indeed required, to repair to (publicly available evidence of) the larger goals that lawmakers were pursuing to 'choose the connotation which best reflects the purpose behind the provision in question'.[45]

Thus, unlike strong originalism of the sort defended by Alexander and Sherwin, Goldsworthy's moderate originalism promises originalists that they can have their cake and eat it too. They can reject the non-originalist view that the meaning of constitutional provisions and statutory enactments changes over time, so as to keep pace with changing concepts, values and goals. But they can take advantage of the distinctions upon which Goldsworthy puts weight (distinctions between enactment and application intentions, connotation and denotation, and literalism and purpose-responsive non-literalism), so as to permit the law sufficient flexibility to respond to new circumstances, technologies, discoveries and social values. As Goldsworthy describes it, moderate originalism wins out over strong originalism, because it better allows judges to 'find the boundary between legitimate interpretive flexibility, and illegitimate judicial amendment; to identify the ways in which the meaning or application of a statute or constitution in some sense change, consistently with the fundamental principle of original, intended meaning'.[46]

III. Does Moderate Originalism Make Moral Sense?

We might conclude that Goldsworthy's moderate originalism makes gains where strong originalism does not and that, as between the two, we thus have reason to prefer his theory of originalism to that of strong originalists who subscribe to a muscular version of subjective intentionalism. But we might still think that considerably more must be said before Goldsworthy's moderate originalism wins the day against theories of interpretation that part ways altogether with the intentions of legal authors or the beliefs of their original audiences. For example, what background principles justify Goldsworthy's moderation of originalism? What theoretical presuppositions make sense of his willingness to temper originalism in the ways that he does? On the one hand, Goldsworthy's means of moderating originalism make significant concessions to non-originalist theories. On the other hand, his continued refusal to allow judges to abandon the perceived intentions of lawmakers altogether precludes him from invoking the most obvious rationales for those concessions – rationales that entail just such an abandonment. In this section, I shall canvass reasons to think that Goldsworthy's unique brand of originalism is indeed in need of justificatory enrichment – that its points of departure from strong originalism are insufficiently motivated, and that without explicit appeal to larger political values that demand such departures, Goldsworthy's signature 'moderation' within the debate about legal interpretation is in danger of being ad hoc.

[45] Goldsworthy, 'Originalism' (n 4) 32. To take one of his examples: 'In 1900, when only those over 21 years of age were recognized by law as adults, was the connotation of the words "adult person", in s 41 of the Constitution, "person over 21 years of age", or "person recognized by law as of mature age"? If the former, the words cannot even today apply to persons between 18 and 21 years of age, despite legal reforms according them adult status for other purposes; but if the latter, they can.'

[46] Goldsworthy, 'Originalism' (n 4) 29.

Consider, for example, the concessions that Goldsworthy makes which bring him very close to a non-originalist plain meaning theory of the sort that Fred Schauer has defended[47] or, perhaps more accurately, that threaten to collapse his theory into the public meaning originalism that Larry Solum has defended.[48] On a plain meaning theory, judges should interpret legal texts according to their plain – ie, conventional – meaning, regardless of whether such a meaning was subjectively intended by the lawmakers who drafted the texts. According to public meaning originalism, judges should interpret legal provisions according to their historical plain meaning – that is, according to the conventional meaning they had at the time they were enacted, and upon which the beliefs of then-contemporary audience members surely traded. By categorically fixing the content of lawmakers' intentions by their then-contemporary audience's beliefs about those intentions, Goldsworthy's moderate originalism comes within a hair's breadth of public meaning originalism. After all, audiences regularly and reasonably presume that lawmakers intend their language to mean what it conventionally means. Hence, if 'statutory provisions mean what they meant when they were enacted',[49] then their meaning is seemingly best given by their plain meaning – the conventional public meaning that would have been employed by then-contemporary audience members – at the time of passage. For the conventional public meaning of a provision is the best measure, if not the definition of, the meaning that a reasonable audience at the time would take lawmakers to have intended.[50]

In view of how little light there is between Goldsworthy's moderate originalism and historical plain meaning theories of interpretation,[51] why is Goldsworthy prepared to leave the subjective intentions of lawmakers for the subjective beliefs of then-contemporary audience members concerning those lawmakers' intentions? And why, if he is prepared to go as

[47] See, eg, F Schauer, 'Easy Cases' (1985) 58 *Southern California Law Review* 399; F Schauer, 'Statutory Construction and the Coordinating Function of Plain Meaning' (1990) 7 *Supreme Court Review* 231.

[48] See, eg, LB Solum and RW Bennett, *Constitutional Originalism: A Debate* (Ithaca, New York, Cornell University Press, 2011); LB Solum, 'The Fixation Thesis: The Role of Historical Fact in Original Meaning' (2015) 91 *Notre Dame Law Review* 1; LB Solum, 'Constitutional Texting' (2007) 44 *San Diego Law Review* 123.

[49] Goldsworthy, 'Originalism' (n 4) 9.

[50] In Goldsworthy's defence, Dale Smith has suggested that there may be instances in which reasonable audience members would not conclude that lawmakers intended to adopt the conventional connotation of a word or phrase. In such instances, that audience would elevate its perception of lawmakers' semantic intentions above the then-contemporary plain meaning of the provision in question. This is an important reminder that there is, indeed, a difference between Goldsworthy's moderate originalism and public meaning originalism; and it is a difference, that will make a difference, if there ever is a case of the sort that Smith contemplates. D Smith, Correspondence with the Author, 25 April 2018 (copy on file with author). But see Solum, 'Originalist Methodology' (n 31) 275–76, where Larry Solum works through the publicly available evidence which contemporaneously suggested that the framers of the *US Constitution* intended their meaning to be 'accessible' to the public.

[51] Goldsworthy takes exception to the suggestion that his theory comes perilously close to those of plain meaning theorists and public meaning originalists, as I have construed them. As he maintains, 'the need to accommodate implied meanings is a major plank in my theory and so it will never collapse into original conventional meaning': J Goldsworthy, Comments to the Author, 20 December 2017. But for Goldsworthy to suggest that plain meaning theorists (and those whose theories trade on the conventional meaning of language at the time of authorship) do not, and cannot, make use of the notion of implied meaning is to make these theoretical foes into straw opponents. To take his own example, in giving the Australian Commonwealth Parliament the power to make laws 'with respect to taxation', section 51(ii) of the Australian Constitution does not commit those for whom plain (ie, conventional) meaning is dispositive to the conclusion that the Commonwealth Parliament can affect State taxation. What makes the meaning of legal language plain – what fixes its conventional content – can surely be things other than semantics – eg, the context which provides the pragmatics of utterance. Those things that Goldsworthy thinks of as sources of implied meaning are available to plain meaning theorists and public meaning originalists, whose theory is one of utterance meaning, rather than sentence meaning.

far as that, does Goldsworthy not abandon the interest in lawmakers' intentions altogether, as plain meaning interpretivists and public meaning originalists would both have him do?

Consider, as a second example, how much Goldsworthy concedes to the non-originalist natural law theory of interpretation defended by Michael Moore. Moore has argued that constitutional and statutory terms should be interpreted in light of our best moral and scientific theories concerning the nature of the things referred to by those terms.[52] While the equal protection clause of the American Constitution may have been intended by its authors solely to abolish the Black Codes of the reconstructionist South, our best theory of the nature of equality, in light of which the clause should be read, requires the extension of this constitutional protection to all morally equal persons – including, for example, women, the elderly, and members of the LGBTQ community.

When insisting that moderate originalism requires judges to fulfill the enactment intentions, but not necessarily the application intentions, of lawmakers, Goldsworthy makes claims very similar to those of Moore:

> The United States Constitution arguably includes many moral principles … [T]o apply [any one of those principles], judges today must make a moral judgment … not a factual judgment about the founders' beliefs. This may be true of many of the most controversial clauses of the American constitution, such as the 'equal protection' clause of the Fourteenth Amendment.[53]

Such claims remain originalist for Goldsworthy, because they constitute a means of honouring the subjective (enactment) intentions of the framers. In his view, then-available evidence made reasonable, the belief that the framers intended to enact a moral principle, and that they thus intended judges to engage in moral decision-making in light of contemporary moral beliefs. If we were to discover (via evidence that was publicly available in 1868) that the framers did not mean to enact a principle requiring equal treatment, generally, then judges would not today be entitled to extend the equal protection clause to women.

But if Goldsworthy is prepared to ignore lawmakers' application intentions, why is he so anxious to honour their enactment intentions? Why does he not link arms with Moore in recommending that whenever texts employ moral or scientific language, judges should interpret that language in light of the best moral and scientific theories of the day, regardless of whether the lawmakers who invoked such language intended such theorising or not?[54] After all, if the framers had had any idea that the equal protection clause would be read to require school desegregation or equal voting rights for women, they might well have

[52] MS Moore, 'A Natural Law Theory of Interpretation' (1985) 58 *Southern California Law Review* 277; MS Moore, 'Justifying the Natural Law Theory of Constitutional Interpretation' (2001) 69 *Fordham Law Review* 2087; MS Moore, 'Liberty and the Constitution' (2015) 21 *Legal Theory* 156.

[53] Goldsworthy, 'Originalism' (n 4) 30.

[54] To be clear, Goldsworthy does allow contemporary science to drive the interpretation of scientific language when he is confident that the language is properly interpreted as conveying a legislative intent that the language be so interpreted. See J Goldsworthy, *Parliamentary Sovereignty: Contemporary Debates* (Cambridge, Cambridge University Press, 2010) 256–61. But, as he cautions, 'what if they use ostensibly scientific language in a non-scientific sense [as in the case of *Nix v Hedden*, 149 US 304 (1893)] … where "vegetable" was said to have been used in an ordinary, everyday sense rather than in a scientific sense, so that tomatoes should be classified as vegetables not as fruit? Determining communicative intention seems to me critical in establishing what kind of language has been used': J Goldsworthy, Comments to the Author, 20 December 2017. And this is where he departs from Moore, who would certainly allow the context and purpose of the law to inform the interpretive question (in *Nix v Hedden*, that of setting different tariffs on fruits and vegetables), but who would not allow objectively-evidenced authorial intentions to settle the question of how words ought to be interpreted.

refrained from enacting such a general moral principle. Indeed, one might plausibly think that inasmuch as laws are enacted as a means of curing contemporary social ills, lawmakers formulate their enactment intentions in light of their application intentions. To honour the former over the latter is to invert the priority that lawmakers would assign to their own intentions – and the priority that then-contemporary audience members would assign to those intentions. If Goldsworthy is prepared to be as non-originalist as to reverse the priorities with which lawmakers craft laws, why is he not willing to part company with the intentions of lawmakers altogether?

Goldsworthy himself invokes concerns for the rule of law as grounds for rejecting non-originalist theories of interpretation.[55] Indeed, he appears to take it to be a conceptual truism that adherence to the rule of law entails adherence to (some form of) originalist interpretation.[56] On this view, to be constrained by law at all, is to be constrained by past choices of lawmakers that may no longer reflect the choices that present citizens or lawmakers would make. As Goldsworthy puts it, an argument against originalism

> is really an argument against having a constitution, or indeed any law, at all, since it is of the essence of law that decisions are governed by norms laid down in the past. Taken to its logical extreme, it is an argument not only that judges should ignore the law, but also that everyone else should ignore the judges, who owe their authority to laws laid down by 'the dead hand of the past'.[57]

He further maintains that 'everyday notions of meaning and methods of interpretation' presuppose that legal interpretation functions as 'a specialised case of linguistic interpretation', and as such, '[t]o say that a law no longer means what it meant when it was first enacted, is to say that it is no longer the same law'.[58]

If Goldsworthy were able to demonstrate, first, that the very concept of law presupposes originalism,[59] and second, that the sort of originalism it presupposes is his moderate sort, then his interpretive theory would surely need no further defence. Yet both of these hurdles would seem insurmountable. First, while the rule of law conceptually implies that the choices made by citizens and officials are constrained in a way that they would not be otherwise, such constraints are made possible by theories of interpretation that are indifferent to the intentions, or the perceived intentions, or the original public meaning, with which laws were originally authored. A judge who is faithful to the rule of law – so as to protect liberty, fairness, equality and the salience of coordination solutions – cannot think of herself as the umpire who insists that 'it ain't nothin' 'til I call it'. Rather, she has to think that there is some fact of the matter that is the measure of her call, so as to credibly avow that 'I call it as I see it'. But all of the major non-originalist theories of interpretation purport to constrain

[55] As he writes, 'if we were to discard all the contextual, historical evidence of what the provisions of the Constitution were originally intended to mean, … the scope, and indeed the need, for judicial creativity would be massive': Goldsworthy, 'Originalism' (n 4) 38.

[56] See, eg, Ekins and Goldsworthy (n 24) 67 ('[T]he constitutional grant of legislative authority … entails that interpreters must strive to find and give effect to the legislature's lawmaking intentions.').

[57] Goldsworthy, 'Constitutional Interpretation' (n 25) 687.

[58] Goldsworthy, 'Originalism' (n 4) 39.

[59] Goldsworthy is anxious that I do not overstate his commitment to the claim that originalism is required by the very concept of law. As he maintains, his case for moderate originalism is neither purely conceptual, nor does it rest on a single line of argument. Rather, as he writes, 'I now think that my moderate originalism is best supported on a variety of grounds … – legal interpretive conventions (at least in Australia), popular understandings of "interpretation" and "meaning", philosophy of language on the nature of communication and communicative intentions, and norms of political morality (the rule of law, etc)': J Goldsworthy, Comments to the Author, 20 December 2017.

judges so as to prevent them from thinking of themselves as moral and legal demi-gods. If judges must interpret legal texts according to their plain (ie, conventional) meaning at the time of their decisions, then they are constrained from implementing their own judgments. If judges must interpret legal texts in accordance with their 'spirit' – that is, the purpose to which they can best be put within the existing fabric of the legal system[60] – then judges are estopped from putting laws to their own ends. And if judges must interpret legal texts by consulting our best moral and scientific theories about the nature of the things to which those texts refer, then judges are precluded from conceiving of themselves as inventors rather than discoverers. Judges thus need not be originalists in order to find themselves constrained by their role within a system that honours the rule of law.

Moreover, even if Goldsworthy were able to muster arguments sufficient to persuade us that the rule of law required interpretive originalism, it is hard to imagine that he could extract from such arguments, reasons that distinctly favour his efforts to moderate it. After all, strong originalists standardly make the same conceptual claims that Goldsworthy has made, insisting that theories which reject intentionalism are, effectively, theories that reject law itself.[61] Thus Alexander and Sherwin write: 'If one is interpreting one is seeking the author's intended meaning. When one is constructing a meaning that may not be the meaning intended by the author … one is not interpreting but establishing a rule.'[62] For Goldsworthy to invoke conceptual arguments concerning the nature of law to justify his moderate originalism, he would have to persuade us that law conceptually requires judges to seek the original appearances of authorial intentions, not those intentions themselves. Perhaps he can do this. But I suspect that conceptual arguments about the nature or authority of law under-determine the choice between strong and moderate originalism, and certainly lack the means to rule out one altogether while fully validating the other. For moderate originalism to win out against strong originalism, Goldsworthy must be able to draw upon justifications that both justify originalism and justify its moderation. Any argument that does only the former falls short of the task. And any argument that favours moderation by drawing on claims that better justify the abandonment of originalism altogether is also a false friend.

Goldsworthy is not without arguments that take a distinctly normative turn; and indeed, as he argues today, his arguments against strong originalism 'include arguments about (a) the nature of language and communication; (b) political morality (the rule of law, etc); and (c) current legal interpretive conventions'.[63] Specifically, in his view, not only does the rule of law require allegiance to the law's original meaning; so too do the principles of democracy and federalism. Out of respect for the electors of today, judges are not entitled to change the law through the guise of interpretation, for by doing so, they usurp the authority presently

[60] Lon Fuller defended this interpretive theory – one that is quite distinct from intentionalist, plain meaning, and natural law theories of interpretation. See LL Fuller, 'Positivism and Fidelity to Law: A Reply to Professor Hart' (1958) 71 *Harvard Law Review* 630. His use of the term 'purpose' to capture the notion of a law's highest and best function within the larger web of statutory rules undoubtedly invites confusion. As Goldsworthy himself maintains, 'statutes – like other inanimate objects – do not have purposes; only the people who make or use them do. … It is self-contradictory to dismiss legislative intentions as fictions but to keep talking about statutory purposes': Ekins and Goldsworthy (n 24) 57. Fuller would have disagreed, insisting that it is perfectly meaningful to talk about a law's spirit or functional role (its purpose, in his lexicon) without in any way referencing the mental states of its authors.

[61] L Alexander, 'Telepathic Law' (2010) 27 *Constitutional Commentary* 139.

[62] Alexander and Sherwin (n 8) 139.

[63] J Goldsworthy, Comments to the Author, 20 December 2017.

possessed by the majority to give itself its own laws.[64] Inasmuch as judges change the law, if they depart from the meaning it had at the time that it was democratically enacted, democracy dictates an originalist theory of meaning. While the constitution's provisions, and the corpus of legislatively-enacted laws, may no longer perfectly suit the needs and values of state's or nation's citizens, it is the prerogative of those who find them outdated to revise them through democratic means. For judges to 'presume[e] to divine the "contemporary needs and values" of the nation', and to tailor their legal interpretations in the service of those divinations is to defy the substantive moral demands of democracy.[65]

Yet, while this set of claims provides moral muscle to his originalism, it provides no unique defence of the particular interpretive departures that comprise Goldsworthy's signature moderation. Other originalists – both strong originalists and public meaning originalists – lay equal claim to the principles of democracy and the separation of powers in defending their competing accounts. What Goldsworthy requires is a more discriminating normative theory that justifies his unique theory of interpretation – both his originalism and his moderation of its constraints – the legal match of its moral commitments.

I have argued in the past that Goldsworthy might gain justificatory mileage from a political theory that has been out of vogue for some time, but that appears to have resources by which to make principled, the particular moderating features of his originalism.[66] And indeed, it would seem that Goldsworthy's moderate originalism may be precisely the theory that is required to give legal expression to this political theory. The theory I have in mind is Edmund Burke's political conservativism – or at least, certain interpretations of that theory. While I have no desire to make the full case again for the symbiosis that might properly characterise Burke's political conservativism and Goldsworthy's moderate originalism, it seems fitting in this context to re-motivate the thesis that Goldsworthy's theory of interpretation might find a noble niche within this historically important political tradition. If I am right, then Goldsworthy may have a far more secure foundation for his moderate originalism, than other originalists have for their insistence that the dead continue to have power over the living.[67]

IV. Can Burkean Conservatism Uniquely Motivate Moderate Originalism?

Inasmuch as Goldsworthy explicitly eschews suggestions that his interpretive theory derives from 'a form of "ancestor worship"',[68] he is likely deeply sceptical of the suggestion that

[64] J Goldsworthy, 'Interpreting the Constitution in Its Second Century' (2000) 24 *Melbourne University Law Review* 677, 683–84.

[65] ibid 684.

[66] HM Hurd, 'Living in the Past: Burkean Conservatism and Originalist Interpretation' in J Goldsworthy and T Campbell (eds), *Legal Interpretation in Democratic States* (Aldershot, Ashgate, 2002) 173–206.

[67] Goldsworthy disputes that his moderate originalism requires a more secure normative foundation than he has given it. And he denies that 'relying on Burke would greatly assist originalism': J Goldsworthy, Comments to the Author, 20 December 2017. It was the burden of section III. to cast doubt on his first claim; and it is the burden of section IV. to dispute his second claim.

[68] Goldsworthy, 'Interpreting the Constitution' (n 64) 683 (quoting M Kirby, 'Constitutional Interpretation and Original Intent: A Form of Ancestor Worship?' (2000) 24 *Melbourne University Law Review* 1.

Burkean conservatism might lend moral credence to the combined commitments of his moderate originalism. But it is as much a mistake to accuse Edmund Burke of ancestor worship, as it is to accuse Goldsworthy of it. So let me begin by providing a thumbnail sketch of the important philosophical tenets of Burke's conservatism. This will then allow us to explore the degree to which Goldsworthy might draw justificatory sustenance from alternative construals of Burke's central theses.

Burke believed that the powers of human reason are highly circumscribed. As he said,

> [w]e are afraid to put men to live and trade each on his own private stock of reason, because we suspect that this stock in each man is small, and that the individuals would do better to avail themselves of the general bank and capital of nations and ages.[69]

He further conceived of human society as a fragile achievement comprised of intricate relationships that are held together by traditions, social rules, collective expectations, reciprocal conventions, interpersonal loyalties, religious dogmas, cultural myths and economic forces that both individually and collectively defy human comprehension, let alone systematisation. It followed from these two presuppositions that Burke vested little stock in abstract theory which purported to advance universal moral or political truths. As JGA Pocock explains,

> [Burke's] account of political society … endows the community with an inner life of growth and adaptation, and it denies to individual reason the power to see this process as a whole or to establish by its own efforts the principles on which the process is based.[70]

While Burke vested little faith in the powers of individual rationality, he vested considerable faith in what he called society's 'prejudices' – 'the unexamined wisdom accumulated over generations'.[71] As Burke wrote: 'The individual is foolish. The multitude, for the moment, is foolish … but the species is wise, and when time is given to it, as a species, it almost always acts right.'[72] His faith in the organic accumulation of rational capital motivated him to talk of there being a 'social contract' – conceived of not as a real or hypothetical consensual agreement of the sort the liberal social contract theorists had imagined, but rather as a 'partnership' between the dead, the living, and those of future generations, the continuance of which 'is under a permanent standing covenant'.[73] The terms of this covenant are given by 'natural law' – not by the consent of those subject to it, nor by the will of the majority. As Burke wrote: 'Men without their choice derive benefits from association; without their choice they are subjected to duties in consequence of these benefits; and without their choice they enter into a virtual obligation as binding as any that is actual.'[74]

[69] 'Edmund Burke's *Reflections on the Revolution in France*' in J Waldron (ed), *'Nonsense Upon Stilts': Bentham, Burke and Marx on the Rights of Man* (London, Methuen, 1987) 77–118.

[70] JGA Pocock, 'Burke and the Ancient Constitution: A Problem in the History of Ideas' in *Politics, Language and Time: Essays on Political Thought and History* (London, Methuen, 1971) 202, 203.

[71] E Young, 'Rediscovering Conservatism: Burkean Political Theory and Constitutional Interpretation' (1994) 72 *North Carolina Law Review* 619, 648.

[72] E Burke, 'Speech on the Reform of the Representation in the House of Commons (1782)' in *The Works of the Right Hon. Edmund Burke*, Vol 2 (London, HG Bohn, 1841) 487.

[73] E Burke, 'Appeal from the New to the Old Whigs' in *The Works of Edmund Burke*, Vol 3 (London, George Bell and Sons, 1903) 78.

[74] ibid.

Burke was thus deeply sceptical of attempts to design constitutional blueprints, and he abhorred suggestions that societies should seek to remake themselves in accordance with abstract moral ideals: 'It is with infinite caution that any man ought to venture upon pulling down an edifice which has answered in any tolerable degree for ages the common purposes of society.'[75] We should prefer, he said, 'living, acting, effective constitution[s]' to 'scheme[s] upon paper'.[76] Yet despite his distaste for utopian efforts at social reform, he was not opposed to social and political change, and he himself carried impressive reformist credentials.[77] It was his recipe for change, not his opposition to it, which marked Burke as a conservative; for he believed that the only kind of good change was slow change. Progress consisted of evolution, never revolution. The present must be able to justify itself by its incremental innovations on past arrangements and the future must unfold by analogy to the present:

> By a slow but well-sustained progress, the effect of each step is watched; the good or ill success of the first, gives light to us in the second; and so, from light to light, we are conducted with safety through the whole series.[78]

On the basis of his faith in progress by precedent, Burke advocated the political leadership of traditional elites, for he believed that those who are born to the ruling class will, as a matter of inherited character, be a better fit to rule than those to whom such power is novel. Relatedly, Burke believed that there is no substitute for character in a nation's political leaders. Contrary to Madison's view that tyranny can be eliminated by carefully-devised institutional checks and balances, Burke believed that no system of laws, however extensive, can constrain those who are not disposed to abide by the law. It followed for Burke, as a final foundational principle, that 'the manners of the ancient world' – 'chivalry' and 'nobility' – play a crucial role in protecting social and political stability. While laws can guide conduct, the only thing that guarantees that people will be inclined to be so guided is their possession of dispositional virtues that make them aspire to honourable dealings with others. Such virtues develop as a result of 'affection' for one's society, and for its institutional and cultural trappings. As Burke maintained, '[t]hese public affections, combined with manners, are required sometimes as supplements, sometimes as correctives, always as aids to law'.[79] They are fragile achievements of a society that pays homage to entrenched traditions, socially-reinforced and reinforcing manners, institution-affirming pageantry and moralised social myths.

We come then to my hypothesis that we might acquire the particular justificatory rationales for Goldsworthy's moderate originalism from one or more interpretations of Burke's central theses. For we can extract, from the above overview, three general categories of claims that might be of use to Goldsworthy – claims that alternatively take Burke to be making psychological, moral and aesthetic arguments about the importance of adhering to the ways of the past. As I shall argue, there are reasons to interpret Burke as advancing

[75] Waldron (n 69) 106.
[76] Waldron (n 69) 106.
[77] For a summary of Burke's vigilant efforts to end the oppression of Catholics in Ireland, the slavery of African Americans in the US, and the exploitation of Indians by the British East India Company, see Young (n 71) 653–54.
[78] Young (n 71) 217.
[79] Waldron (n 69) 110.

each of these three categories, and there are grounds to think that some serve Goldsworthy's purposes better than others. Thus, whether Goldsworthy's moderate originalism receives a tailored defence from Burkean theory will turn on whether those interpretations most favourable to its terms are themselves amenable to a robust defence.

Let us begin with the psychological theses that can be extracted from Burke's claims. Two of these are epistemic theses that concern the ways in which deference to the past can redress the cognitive deficiencies of those in the present; and two are volitional theses that address the ways in which traditions can remedy motivational deficiencies.

The first epistemic thesis is directed at the cognitive limitations under which legal officials are thought to labour. On this thesis, the past is the most reliable heuristic guide to what is best in the present. Traditions amount to acquired wisdom – the accumulated experiences of the many that the few alter at their peril. If two heads are better than one, then the judgments of generations are better than the judgments of a small elite. And thus, both lawmakers and judges ought to defer to enduring social arrangements and political traditions as their best indication of what is morally optimal and practically possible.

Goldsworthy might maintain that this first epistemic thesis makes good sense of his conviction that the content of law should be fixed, not by the subjective intentions of lawmakers, but by the public's reasonable understanding of those intentions. Inasmuch as a reasonably-informed public is likely to assign traditional values to lawmakers, it is likely to assign intentions to lawmakers that are consonant with familiar past practices. Hence, judges who seek a reliable means of preserving traditional practices would do well to interpret laws in accordance with their authors' publicly understood intentions. Yet Goldsworthy must admit that, in many instances, lawmakers clearly intend to alter or abandon entrenched past practices (think of the Civil Rights Act), so that to abide by lawmakers' publicly understood intentions is to contribute to law's revolution, rather than to participate in its slow evolution. Since the first epistemic thesis that can be assigned to Burke would require judges to thwart lawmakers' intentions in such cases, it cannot be reliably invoked in support of Goldsworthy's originalism, however moderate it is made.

The second epistemic thesis that can be extracted from Burke promises more support for Goldsworthy's project. This thesis draws on the epistemic limitations characteristic of citizens, rather than legal officials. On this thesis, lawmakers can effectively govern only if those who are governed understand and endorse the wisdom of legal innovations. The psychology of citizens, however, is such that they cannot readily grasp and appreciate anything that is new if it is not put in familiar terms. That is, citizens cannot understand the need for, or wisdom of, changes in law that depart from the language and values entrenched in their legal past. Hence, judges must always interpret laws in ways that demonstrate their connections to traditions.

This argument might go a good distance towards justifying several of Goldsworthy's modifications of originalism. He might argue, for example, that such a thesis makes sense of why moderate originalists should fix the content of authorial intentions by reference to the expectations of the lawmakers' then-contemporary audience concerning those authorial intentions. For only by adhering to the public's expectations regarding those intentions can judges ensure that the law is interpreted to cohere with what the public then understood the law to provide. And inasmuch as the present expectations of the public derive from those of the past, only by cohering the law with what the public understood in the past can judges be assured that their interpretations will be understood and appreciated in the present.

Goldsworthy also might maintain that this epistemic thesis lends support to his claim that originalists should happily permit changes in the denotation (but not connotation) of legal terms. If legal innovations must be anchored in traditional assumptions, in order to be understandable to those who are subject to them, then it may be that they can permissibly occur by extending legal terms to all those new objects and practices that share in the publicly-perceived intended criteria of those terms. The public cannot be surprised by courts' willingness to interpret cars as carriages, cellular telephones as telegraphs, and gay marriage as marriage, because its members can readily appreciate that while the law's jurisdiction is being extended to new inventions and practices, the functional values realised by doing so remain unchanged.

Still, while this epistemic thesis makes Goldsworthy's moderate originalism more defensible than strong originalism, it most obviously dictates the abandonment of originalism altogether. If citizens can appreciate new laws or legal interpretations only by grasping their connections to past ones, then it would seem that judges should implement an interpretive theory that *directly* attends to what the public will perceive as an extension of the legal past. Clearly, a conventional meaning theory would best fit this bill. Thus, Goldsworthy's moderate originalism, with its indirect, and hence imperfect, ability to compensate for epistemic limitations on the part of citizens, can ultimately derive only weak support from this second Burkean thesis.

Let us then turn to the two volitional justifications for moderate originalism that belong to the category of psychological theses that can plausibly be attributed to Burke. On these two justifications, Burke's appeal to tradition was more motivational than epistemic. The first of these volitional theses holds that citizens cannot be subjectively motivated to abide by the law absent 'affection' for the institutions of government. To command the obedience of citizens, legal changes must incorporate enough of the old to generate a kind of 'carry-over affection' for the new.

While such an argument can be force-fitted to Goldsworthy's moderate originalism, this argument, like the previous two, lends far more support to theories of interpretation that more directly require judges to interpret legal language so as to preserve public perceptions of historicity. Thus, while this thesis might favour his moderate originalism over strong versions of originalism, Goldsworthy cannot, in the end, draw upon it to defend moderate originalism against the claim that he should abandon originalism altogether in favour of something like public meaning originalism. Since we seek from Burke both reasons to prefer moderate originalism to strong originalism, and reasons to prefer moderate originalism to non-originalism, arguments that provide only the former support ultimately fall short of our philosophical needs.

We come considerably closer to our goal when we take up the second volitional thesis that can be extracted from Burke's brand of conservatism. On this thesis, the role of government is to solve the problem of weakness of will. Citizens are, by their nature, susceptible to temptations to abandon their long-term interests for short-term gratification. It is the task of law to prevent these short-sighted trades. Lawmakers and judges must thus frequently refuse to make legal changes that accord with the popular will, on pain of violating the trust vested in them by a citizenry that self-paternalistically looks to the law's incentive-altering effects to counteract the whims of temptation.

It is possible to tease apart two versions of this general thesis that paternalism demands conservatism. On the first version, paternalism is properly exercised by lawmakers at the time that laws are crafted, so as to effectively tie us to the mast of the past when we are later tempted to pursue short-term goals that have long-term costs. On the second version, we engage in wise self-paternalism when we tie ourselves to the mast of the past by refusing to depart from what was legally required of us in the past, despite present temptations to pursue current, possibly short-sighted goals.

Both of these versions of Burke's second volitional thesis appear to support Goldsworthy's refusal to abandon originalism altogether. Indeed, Goldsworthy appears to invoke the former version of this thesis when he applauds Justice Scalia's claim that '[t]he purpose of constitutional guarantees … is precisely to prevent the law from reflecting certain changes in original values that the society adopting the Constitution thinks fundamentally undesirable'.[80] But if past constitutional framers and legislators knew our own interests better than we now know them, then it would seem that we are best served, not by moderate originalism, but by strong originalism – as Alexander and Sherwin argue. For the moderate originalism that Goldsworthy advances allows judges to interpret laws in accordance with (short-sighted) contemporary goals, and so appears contrary to the paternalism that checks our volitional short-comings. We would be more firmly tied to the mast of the past if judges were required to enforce lawmakers' application intentions in addition to their enactment intentions. Judges would then be prevented from interpreting moral terms by engaging in moral reasoning that realises the whims of the day.

So we are left, after exploring this second volitional interpretation of Burkean conservatism, with a reason to prefer Goldsworthy's originalism to forms of non-originalism; but we are not left with a reason to prefer his *moderation* of originalism to strong originalism. And this means that our quest for a tailored justification of moderate originalism continues. For the arguments that have helped to motivate Goldsworthy's originalism have tended to undermine his willingness to moderate it; and the arguments that have helped to motivate his moderation of originalism have tended to undermine Goldsworthy's commitment to originalism altogether. Let us then leave behind the psychological claims that are made available by Burke's political theory and turn, instead, to whether moral or aesthetic interpretations of Burkean theory might be of greater help in justifying moderate originalism.

There are at least four normative theses suggested by Burke's political conservatism that might lend justificatory support to Goldsworthy's moderate originalism. The first capitalises on the claim that deference to the past protects substantive rule of law values. It thus constitutes a normative complement to Goldsworthy's conceptual claim that the nature of law requires allegiance to its original meaning. If liberty is chilled whenever the consequences of conduct are unpredictable; if fairness demands the protection of citizens' reliance interests; if equality demands the like treatment of like cases over time; and if coordination problems can only be solved by solutions made salient by long-term stability – then the law should be changeless, or very slow to change. As Goldsworthy writes:

> A constitution laid down by a foundation generation empowers as well as restricts subsequent generations, by providing them with the incalculable benefits of an established and accepted set of procedures for making collective decisions binding on all their members. If some attempt to

[80] Goldsworthy, 'Originalism' (n 4) 43 (quoting A Scalia, 'Originalism: The Lesser Evil' (1989) 57 *University of Cincinnati Law Review* 849, 862).

> evade the restrictions, others may be tempted to follow suit, leading eventually to the collapse of the constitution and the loss of empowerment it provided.[81]

There is no doubt that non-originalist theories of interpretation confront their greatest obstacle when they are called upon to make clear just how they will provide for the legal stability required to protect the rule of law values. The challenge for Goldsworthy once again, however, is not to extract from this first normative thesis a defence of his originalism, but rather to defend why he is willing to part ways with the sort of strong originalism that most powerfully guarantees that legal interpretations will live on in perpetuity. Inasmuch as moderate originalism would appear to make law less certain (by licensing judges to be morally progressive, by permitting judges to apply laws in ways that were never contemplated by their authors, by granting that the denotation of legal terms changes over time, and by allowing judges to set aside clear language in favour of the authorial purposes behind it), Goldsworthy's theory would seemingly protect rule of law values less well than would the versions of strong originalism with which they compete.[82]

The second normative thesis that occasionally emerges from Burke's writings on political conservatism is that of the utilitarian: lawmakers should seek to maximise social utility by summing the preferences of their citizens and satisfying those that are collectively the weightiest. In Burke's hands, this thesis translates as follows: Given their settled expectations, citizens are made happiest by slow change, rather than revolutionary change; and this is true, even if the system that results would have made everyone happier sooner had it been possible to adopt it whole-cloth. Such a claim is reminiscent of RM Hare's argument that utilitarianism often requires the perpetuation of institutions and cultural trappings that do not maximise happiness, because the transitions to arrangements that would better secure happiness are more costly than the incremental gains that would result.[83]

Goldsworthy might put this Burkean thesis to work by arguing that what maximises social utility is adjudication in accordance with moderate originalism. Such an interpretive strategy honours settled expectations concerning the content of the law – expectations inherited from the audience that first interpreted the law in accordance with the lawmakers' perceived authorial intentions – while permitting the kind of slow change necessary to keep legal pace with newly-arising circumstances and public preferences.

Like any utilitarian argument, the proof is in the empirics. To rest moderate originalism on a utilitarian foundation, Goldsworthy would have to defend the claim that people are, in fact, made happier by denying them what they think will make them happy (namely, judicial interpretations that would promote present conceptions of welfare maximisation) in favour of enforcing against them arrangements that, at best, promoted the happiness of people in the past. His defence of such a counter-intuitive claim may require him to invoke familiar, but troubling, methods of laundering citizens' preferences so as to substitute those they should have for those they think they do have. If Goldsworthy is not eager to join modern-day utilitarians in their efforts to insist that 'nudging' citizens to have wants that

[81] Goldsworthy, 'Constitutional Interpretation' (n 25) 687 (citation omitted).

[82] This point has inspired some push-back, however. As Dale Smith has suggested, inasmuch as strong originalism would elevate 'secret intentions' over those that would be attributed to lawmakers on the basis of publicly-available evidence, strong originalism might be thought to make the law less certain and predictable than does moderate originalism. Perhaps so. D Smith, Correspondence with the Author, 25 April 2018.

[83] RM Hare, 'What is Wrong with Slavery?' (1979) 8 *Philosophy and Public Affairs* 103.

they do not, in fact, have can be both true to the tenets of utilitarianism and defensibly non-paternalistic,[84] then this avenue of argumentation may prove unattractive.

The third normative thesis suggested by Burke's conservatism holds that honouring tradition is a crucial means of enforcing the terms of the social contract. Recall that Burke rejected the liberal view that the terms of the social contract are those to which citizens agree.[85] In his view, its content is given by principles of natural law that are best evidenced by the traditions that are enduringly capable of uniting past, present and future generations. It follows from this view that judges honour the social contract if, but only if, they attend to and advance enduring social traditions.

Goldsworthy might be tempted, at first take, to replace Burke's unusual social contract theory with the more traditional, consent-based theory that Richard Posner invoked on behalf of radical originalism.[86] On this view, judges should read all laws as they would read all voluntary contracts – implementing, as best as possible, the intentions and expectations of those who authored them. But those who are bound by laws are not analogous to those who are bound by contracts; for how can persons who were not, in fact, party to the drafting of laws be bound by their terms in the same way as are those who, in fact, entered into consensual agreements? Contractarian liberals have, of course, laboured long and hard to make the metaphor do moral work. Some have invoked Lockean claims of implied consent,[87] others have mustered Platonic claims of gratitude,[88] and still others have called upon Rawlsian obligations of reciprocity.[89] But if any of these arguments were successful, they would reinstate a theory of strong originalism. What Goldsworthy needs from a social contract theory is what he has always needed: both a reason for originalism *and* a reason for pursuing it in moderation.

Goldsworthy might be wise, then, to embrace Burke's unconventional conception of the social contract as a covenant that unites past, present and future generations through timeless traditions. Wrote Burke:

> [W]herein by the disposition of a stupendous wisdom, moulding together the great mysterious incorporation of the human race, the whole, at one time is never old, or middle-aged, or young, but in a condition of unchangeable constancy, moves on through the varied tenor of perpetual decay, fall, renovation, and progression. Thus, by preserving the method of nature in the conduct of the state, in what we improve, we are never wholly new; in what we retain we are never wholly obsolete.[90]

This view that those who administer states ought to engage in a form of biomimicry,[91] crafting institutions that organically permit evolution through time so as to maximise their

[84] See, eg, RH Thaler and CR Sunstein, *Nudge: Improving Decisions About Health, Wealth, and Happiness* (London, Penguin, 2009); CR Sunstein, *Why Nudge: The Politics of Libertarian Paternalism* (New Haven, Yale University Press, 2014); CR Sunstein, *Choosing Not to Choose: Understanding the Value of Choice* (New York, Oxford University Press, 2015). See also HM Hurd, 'Fudging Nudging: Why "Libertarian Paternalism" is the Contradiction It Claims It's Not' (2016) 14 *Georgetown Journal of Law and Public Policy* 703.

[85] See above n 73 and accompanying text.

[86] See above n 9 accompanying text.

[87] See J Locke, *The Second Treatise on Government*, 3rd edn (Oxford, Basil Blackwell, 1976) 61.

[88] See Plato, 'Crito' in E Hamilton and H Cairns (eds), *The Collected Dialogues of Plato* (translated by H Tredennick) (Princeton, Princeton University Press, 1961) 27.

[89] See J Rawls, 'Justice as Fairness' (1958) 67 *Philosophical Review* 164, 179–83.

[90] Waldron (n 69) 100.

[91] See JM Benyus, *Biomimicry: Innovation Inspired by Nature* (New York, Perennial, 2002).

adaptation (and not their 'speciation' into new entities altogether), would give Goldsworthy an argument for both prongs of his interpretive theory. As a means of honouring commitments to those in the past, judges are obligated to honour the intentions of past lawmakers (who themselves were obligated, on this theory, to honour the intentions of those who came before them); but as a means of honouring commitments to those in the present and future, judges must incrementally accommodate laws to present needs and anticipated future changes. Originalism, coupled with the bases upon which it is to be moderated, permits judges to reconcile the obligations they owe to past generations with the obligations they owe to present and future generations.

So far, then, this is the strongest argument for Goldsworthy's unique interpretive theory. Its strength derives from the fact that the normative thesis from which it takes its leave – the need to conceive of human institutions as themselves kinds of species made distinct by their unity over time – comes close to making Goldsworthy's interpretive principles definitional of justice. If this is indeed the case, then we need search no further for a motivation to embrace moderate originalism. But, of course, to declare moderate originalism constitutive of justice on the basis of the above argument, Goldsworthy would need to be prepared to make more than metaphorical Burke's claim that there is a non-consensual covenant between generations that requires judges to honour the perceived intentions of past legislators, while making room for incremental innovations that meet the needs and values of current and future citizens.

The final normative thesis that might be extracted from Burke's conservatism concerns the importance of cultivating virtues and suppressing vices in citizens and officials alike. As I recounted above, in Burke's view certain virtues of character accrue only by means of repetitive behaviours that are cultivated by traditional practices and rituals. To sacrifice tradition, he believed, is to jeopardise the cultivation of important character traits on the part of those who govern and those who are governed. In turn, '[t]he worst of the politics of revolution is this: they temper and harden the breast, in order to prepare it for the desperate strokes which are sometimes used in extreme occasions', so that 'the mind receives a gratuitous taint'.[92]

This notion that adherence to tradition breeds virtue, while revolution breeds vice, might afford Goldsworthy some welcome support for his moderate originalism. Habit is best assured by conformity to stable and enduring laws, and laws are made most stable by a theory of interpretation that locks in their meaning at the time of their enactment. While it might be thought that this constitutes an argument best suited to strong originalism, Goldsworthy might plausibly go on to argue that the process of inculcating particular character traits may be impervious to small or incremental changes in the legal order. Indeed, it may be integral to breeding virtue that one permits those who acquire its attributes to seek incremental improvements in imperfect human institutions; for one could not possess the virtue of justice without seeking to alter legal and political institutions in ways that better realise its demands. Thus Goldsworthy might argue that, so long as habits of character are preserved, habits of conduct can (and perhaps must) change. Of course, inasmuch as the former are contingently dependent upon the latter, revolution remains inconsistent with the goal of inculcating virtue through habit. But inasmuch as legal evolution may be consistent

[92] Waldron (n 69) 102.

with the cultivation of virtuous dispositions, the best theory of legal evolution may be one, like Goldsworthy's, that both preserves elements of the past and permits changes in the present and future.

I take it that the worry with this Burkean line of argument is that it might commit Goldsworthy to a perfectionist theory of law – a theory that takes the cultivation of virtue and the suppression of vice to be the proper role of government. While such a goal might make plausible both originalism and the departures from it that Goldsworthy licenses, a defence of its merits is no small philosophical matter. Goldsworthy would surely enjoy some distinguished company were he to declare himself a political perfectionist;[93] but the price for this justification would extend far beyond the costs of declaring himself a Burkean conservative.

We come then to the final category of justifications that Burkean conservatism might afford Goldsworthy's moderate originalism – a category comprised not of psychological or moral claims, but of aesthetic claims. Burke's conservatism appears particularly indebted to aesthetic considerations, for Burke frequently insisted that the constitutional tradition of Britain deserved deference in perpetuity just because it possessed important aesthetic qualities. As he maintained, it provided 'a decent drapery for life'; it fostered 'pleasing illusions which made power gentle'; it 'harmonized the different shades of life and … by a bland assimilation, incorporated into the politics the sentiments which beautify and soften private society'; it 'cover[ed] the defects of our naked shivering nature'; and without it, citizens would sadly come to know that 'a king is but a man; a queen is but a woman; a woman is but an animal; and an animal is not of the highest order'.[94]

Burke was surely right that traditions and pageantry adorn both public and private life in ways that provide aesthetic experiences valued in their own right. Our affection for public rituals such as standing for national anthems, reciting pledges of allegiance, honouring 21-gun salutes, holding large public inaugurations of heads of state, conducting broadly publicised state funerals, turning out for parades, and holding fireworks displays on national holidays, attests to the fact that traditions are valued, in part, solely for their aesthetic enrichment and expression. But Burke may have been right in believing that traditions do more than adorn our lives; they may positively display attributes of our national character and institutions of which we are rightly proud. He may thus have been right to fear that sweeping social reforms might also sweep away traditions that are valuable aspects of our lives, leaving us poorer for the loss of sources of ritual and pageantry.

It may be that the aesthetic motivation for honouring the past best explains the conservative psyche. While little in Goldsworthy's writings suggests that he shares the nostalgia that seems characteristic of those who are anxious to ensure that the future does not dismantle the past, it may be that his unwillingness to free interpretation altogether from the bonds of the past is, on self-reflection, partially explained by a desire to preserve the aesthetic virtues of a legal system that ensures the preservation of legal traditions into the future. Certainly an aesthetic account of the value of the past could accommodate

[93] See, eg, J Raz, *The Morality of Freedom* (Oxford, Clarendon Press, 1986); T Hurka, *Perfectionism* (New York, Oxford University Press, 1993); G Sher, *Beyond Neutrality: Perfectionism and Politics* (Cambridge, Cambridge University Press, 1997); M Nussbaum, 'Perfectionist Liberalism and Political Liberalism' (2011) 39 *Philosophy and Public Affairs* 3.

[94] Waldron (n 69) 110–11.

both Goldsworthy's originalism and his moderation of its demands. By requiring judges to adhere to publicly perceived enactment intentions and by precluding judges from parting ways with the connotations of legal terms that original audience members took lawmakers to intend, Goldsworthy's originalism assures the perpetuation of many of our most entrenched commitments and traditions. Yet by also allowing judges to depart from drafters' application intentions, to conclude that the denotation of legal terms has changed with time, and to tailor their interpretation of legal provisions by the apparent background goals that motivated their enactment, Goldsworthy allows judges to gradually purge the law of what may be ugly or unworthy legacies that do not reflect aesthetically enriching attributes of our system.[95]

Goldsworthy's philosophical burden would be to make sense of conceiving of the law as an instrument of aesthetic expression. It would surely be tempting to convert the aesthetic argument for living in the past into a psychological or moral one – to elevate as aesthetically worthy those legacies that bolster psychological virtues (eg, courage, generosity, the capacity for delayed gratification) or advance conditions of justice (eg, eliminating wealth disparities, reducing racial discrimination). But to convert the aesthetic justification into either a psychological or moral one again invites the challenges that I previously anticipated when considering whether Goldsworthy could predicate his moderate originalism on psychological or moral interpretations of Burkean conservatism. If the aesthetic interpretation appeals at all, it may serve Goldsworthy's purpose best if it is defended as a free-standing justification.

V. Conclusion

I have argued that Jeffrey Goldsworthy's moderate originalism avoids a number of problems that, in my view, make strong originalism indefensible. But I have also suggested that his commitment to making originalism more moderate is under-motivated. And many arguments to which it is tempting to appeal achieve the goal of clothing only one leg of his theory, but not both. Either they justify Goldsworthy's originalism, but not his moderation of it; or they justify his moderation of it by virtue of being arguments that in fact demand his departure from originalism altogether. What Goldsworthy requires is a justification for moderate originalism that does double-duty – that vindicates his conviction that legal interpretation is rightly hostage to the original meanings of legal provisions, while also making principled his particular licences to depart from aspects of those meanings. Only by finding a justification that makes sense of both his originalism and his particular concessions to non-originalism can he lay claim to having a principled position that enjoys the strengths and avoids the weaknesses of both interpretive extremes.

I have returned in this chapter to a suggestion I made years ago, which is that Goldsworthy might succeed at this seemingly impossible justificatory task by tapping the political conservatism of Edmund Burke. While Burkean arguments that accord the past

[95] As John Hart Ely pointed out, there are many ugly traditions that do not deserve perpetuation. 'Lynching is a tradition, riding people out of town on a rail is a tradition, keeping blacks from voting is a tradition': JH Ely, *Democracy and Distrust: A Theory of Judicial Review* (Cambridge, Harvard University Press, 1980) 21.

value for psychological reasons tend to support either strong originalism or the abandonment of originalism altogether, those that accord the past moral or aesthetic value offer Goldsworthy a menu of promising means by which to defend both his commitment to originalism and his desire to make its constraints more moderate. But as I have argued, each of these justificatory options would come at a considerable philosophical price. To choose from this philosophical menu, Goldsworthy would seemingly have to defend a preference-laundering version of utilitarianism, or sign onto Burke's idiosyncratic non-consensual social contract theory, or embrace a form of political perfectionism, or predicate his theory on the sheer aesthetic rewards that derive from adhering to judicially-tempered traditions. Knowing Goldsworthy's knack for finding surprising space between rocks and hard places, however, my bet is that he could identify a solution that capitalises on the advantages, while avoiding the disadvantages of one or more of these alternative possibilities.

8

Authenticity, Ontology and Natural History: Some Reflections on Musical and Legal Interpretations

KEVIN TOH*

With Romantic artists, we reach a generation often disconcerted by implications or intentions of their own works.

— Charles Rosen, 'The Definitive Text' (1987)

We're not trying to reproduce the notation here. We're trying to get back to the inspiration that caused the notations to exist. … I think the score has only the suggestion of what the piece actually has in it.

— Michael Tilson Thomas in an interview with *The New York Times* (31 October 2017)

I. Prelude

While each had important precursors, both the originalist movement in constitutional law and the period instrument movement in classical music gathered momentum in earnest in the late 1970s and the early 1980s. The concurrent timing was perhaps not entirely

* I am grateful for comments and questions from audiences when earlier drafts of this paper were presented at the Julius Stone Institute of Jurisprudence at University of Sydney in July 2017, a conference in celebration of Jeff Goldsworthy's work and retirement at Monash University in July 2017, the Jurisprudence Discussion Group at Oxford University in October 2017, a UCL Laws Staff Research Seminar in November 2017, a Hart Seminar at the Surrey Centre for Law and Philosophy in February 2018, and a workshop on meaning and intention in literary and legal texts at the Institute of Philosophy, University of London in October 2018. Special thanks to: Larry Solum, a conversation with whom in Champaign, Illinois a long time ago provided a prompt for the line of thought pursued here; Michael Moore who provided very instructive commentary at the Monash 'Jeff-Fest'; and the composer Anna Thorvalsdottir, whose serious though sceptical engagements with the paper in Surrey were of special significance and gratification for me. I also thank Larry Alexander, Nick Allott, Raquel Barradas de Freitas, Mitch Berman, Elizabeth Coulter, Patrick Emerton, George Letsas, Paul Mitchell, Richard Moorhead, Jayani Nadarajalingam and Lukas Opacic for helpful suggestions and/or comments on earlier drafts. I regret that I was not able to follow up on many of the reading suggestions that these and other people gave me along the way. Given my unfamiliarity with many of the issues and literatures that this paper touches on, and the limited time I have had, I was able to cover only so much this time around. I very much hope, however, to make additional dents on the deficit in some related future works. Finally, it is a great pleasure and a particular honour to contribute to a volume in celebration of the career and works of Jeff Goldsworthy, whom I admire greatly and unreservedly.

coincidental. Something might have been in the cultural air then that prompted both movements.[1]

Jeff Goldsworthy is not only a leading originalist legal theorist, but I know from conversations with him that he is a terrific lover of music. Perhaps he would find it of some interest and diversion if I were to try to assess originalism in law by bringing up certain considerations from the philosophy of music. In particular, the key considerations I have in mind are those having to do with the tight relation between the ideal of authenticity in musical performance on the one hand, and the ontology of musical works on the other. What kinds of performances count as authentic, it would seem, depends on what properties are constitutive of musical works.[2] The legal analogue of this relation, I believe, should help us to think carefully about originalism, which involves a particular way of conceiving the ideal of authenticity in legal interpretation. I realise that 'authenticity' is not a term that is often used to talk about a virtue in legal or constitutional interpretation. What I mean by it is the quality or virtue of 'being true to' or 'being faithful to' the object of interpretation. Perhaps 'fidelity' is a more familiar term in legal discussions. But I opt to use 'authenticity' as a vehicle to push the analogy between musical and legal interpretations in which I am interested. I also realise that authenticity is not the only virtue of, or value in, interpretations, either in music or law. To be sure, there are many other virtues and values to be pursued and promoted. But given that authenticity or fidelity has taken pride of place among virtues in the discussion of legal originalists like Goldsworthy, I too shall focus on it in this chapter. But my exclusive focus on it should not be thought to imply or suggest an indifference to other virtues of or values in interpretations, or any opinion to the effect that authenticity always trumps other considerations.

Taking seriously the analogy between legal and musical interpretations in ways that motivate significant engagements with well-developed philosophical literatures about both, I believe, offers prospects of real progress in our legal philosophy. For one thing, a regrettable feature of the ongoing discussion about originalism in law is the extent to which it is fraught with politics.[3] No doubt, even philosophy of music, or at least music theory more generally, sometimes gets inflected by political considerations and manoeuvrings. But at the least, the political forces in play in the two discussions are quite different from each other. And I doubt that I am being naïve in thinking that politics plays a much bigger role in legal, and especially constitutional, theorising than in musical theorising. My hope then is that thinking about legal interpretation by way of an analogy to musical interpretation would help us to steer clear of at least some distracting politics infecting our thinking and discourse about legal interpretation. Second, although a number of other legal philosophers have taken notice, and sought to take advantage, of the analogy between legal and artistic

[1] Also roughly contemporaneous was the Iranian Revolution, about the timing of which I opine even less.

[2] As Stephen Davies has said, '[w]hat we require from an authentic performance of the work is a performance that is accurate in the sense that it truly represents that in virtue of which the work is the individual it is'. S Davies, 'The Ontology of Musical Works and Authenticity of their Performances' (1991), reprinted in S Davies, *Themes in the Philosophy of Music* (Oxford, Oxford University Press, 2003) 64.

[3] In making this remark, I am not saying that Goldsworthy's own work in constitutional theory appears motivated by his political commitments, about which I know next to nothing. The closest I have gotten to learning about his political leanings was reading his criticisms of research grant mania in Australian academia. See J Goldsworthy, 'Research Grant Mania' (2008) 50 *Australian Universities' Review* 17.

interpretations (especially literary interpretations), they for the most part have relied only on their intuitive or folk understandings of artistic interpretations, rather than on anything that has been developed by philosophers working in aesthetics.[4] Artists, scientists and lawyers usually make wretched aestheticians, philosophers of science and legal philosophers, respectively. And I do not think that legal philosophers have any special advantage in being aestheticians unless they rely on well-developed thinking in aesthetics proper. Second-order thinking about any domain of thought is a hard and tricky business. And for the vast majority of us, going down a ladder to climb another is not any easier than climbing a ladder from the ground up. In so far as there is any prospect of benefiting from thinking about artistic interpretations, it seems to me, we should try to take advantage of the developed and disciplined literature on artistic interpretations.[5]

II. A Carve-Up

Musical works and musical performances clearly have divergent properties. For example, performances are events that take place in a particular time and space, whereas works are not. A performance that is aesthetically disastrous may be of a work that amounts to a great aesthetic achievement. The ontological status of a musical performance is relatively unproblematic. It is a concrete particular, a physical item, that occupies a particular location in time and space.[6] In this respect, it is like a physical copy of a novel. The ontological status of a musical work, on the other hand, is anything but simple and has instigated controversies among philosophers. In this respect, it is like a novel and unlike a painting or a building.

One initially tempting way of thinking about the ontological status of musical works is to identify them with scores.[7] Here, we immediately see a need to distinguish between at

[4] See, eg, R Dworkin, 'How Law is Like Literature' (1982), reprinted in R Dworkin, *A Matter of Principle* (Cambridge, Massachusetts, Harvard University Press, 1985) 146; R Dworkin, 'On Interpretation and Objectivity' (1983), revised and reprinted in Dworkin, *Matter of Principle*; R Dworkin, *Law's Empire* (Cambridge, Massachusetts, Belknap Press, 1986) Ch 2; J Raz, 'Interpretation Without Retrieval' (1995), reprinted in J Raz, *Between Authority and Interpretation: On the Theory of Law and Practical Reason* (Oxford, Oxford University Press, 2009) 241; J Raz, 'Interpretation: Pluralism and Innovation' (2009), reprinted in Raz, *Between Authority and Interpretation* (n 4) 299; A Marmor, 'Constitutive Conventions' (1998), revised and reprinted in A Marmor, *Positive Law and Objective Values* (Oxford, Clarendon Press, 2001); A Marmor, *Social Conventions: From Language to Law* (Princeton, Princeton University Press, 2009) chs 2–3.

[5] For similar and overlapping thoughts meant to encourage sustained theoretical thinking about games and sports, and making inferences about law, see MN Berman, '"Let 'em Play": A Study in the Jurisprudence of Sport' (2011) 99 *Georgetown Law Journal* 1325, 1328–31.

[6] By 'item', I mean to include events as well as things. And by saying that a performance occupies a particular time and space, as a novel does (as I go on to say in the next sentence in the text), I do not mean to suggest that the relevant occupations are of the same variety. There are important differences in types of instances depending on the genres of works. See the illuminating general discussion about the relation between works and instances across different genres of art in N Wolterstorff, 'Toward an Ontology of Art Works' (1975) 9 *Noûs* 115. Thanks to Patrick Emerton for pressing me to make these two points.

[7] Davies points out that this is a view that often, inaccurately, gets attributed to the Nelson Goodman of *Languages of Art: An Approach to a Theory of Symbols*, 2nd edn (Indianapolis, Hackett Publishing Company, Inc, 1968/76). See S Davies, *Musical Works and Performances: A Philosophical Exploration* (Oxford, Clarendon Press, 2001) 102.

least two things we could mean by 'score'. As we distinguish between a word-type and its tokens, and between a sentence-type and its tokens, we can distinguish between a score-type and its tokens. While types are abstract and unique, tokens are concrete particulars.[8] Score-tokens are quite easy to distinguish from musical works, for the two kinds of things have obviously different properties. For example, as Nick Zangwill once remarked in private communication, one cannot hear a score-token unless it is ripped or dropped. We can also buy a score-token at Foyle's, and inadvertently leave one in a taxi, whereas we cannot do either with a musical work.

Score-types are trickier to dismiss as identical to musical works, but still I think they should be distinguished. First, there is the possibility of mistakes in score-types. Here, of course, I do not mean mistakes in any individual copies of the score of a particular musical work that copyeditors or typesetters may make (or even in a master or autograph copy made by a composer or publisher), but instead in the score-type of that work. Second, there are works without corresponding scores. Before the advent of recordings, most musical works in the world were handed down, if at all, orally or by demonstration.[9] Only works belonging to the Western classical tradition, starting in the eleventh century, have been preserved and transmitted from generation to generation through notated instructions. And it was only in the eighteenth century that the notations began to take on the complexities and precision that are expected in scores today.

Third, the scores of even recent classical works are far from complete, in the sense of not containing instructions for some aspects of performances that would have to be there for them to count as performances of the relevant works. For one thing, the familiar notation system currently in use does not fully specify all aspects of performance, and some that are left out are thought important enough to be considered non-optional if the performances are to count as performances of the relevant works. Many such aspects are matters of 'expression' or 'phrasing', and are only imperfectly captured by stock Italian terms such as 'forte', 'cantabile' and 'vivace'. Many others are transmitted only through example, instruction and imitation, in addition to written instructions in scores. Ecosystems of such example, instruction and imitation could be conceived as making up traditions or conventions that regulate both what composers include and exclude in their scores, and also how performers perform the works thus conveyed.[10] As Davies has pointed out, in some cases, such elements of the ecosystem not only supplement, but also supplant some details of the written scores.[11]

[8] See L Wetzel, 'Types and Tokens' (*Stanford Encyclopedia of Philosophy*, 28 April 2006) s 3 https://plato.stanford.edu/entries/types-tokens/ (last accessed 13 November 2018).

[9] The information in this and the following few sentences are taken from the illuminating discussion in C Rosen, 'From the Troubadours to Frank Sinatra' (*The New York Review of Books*, 23 February 2006) s 1; C Rosen, 'From the Troubadours to Sinatra: Part II' (*The New York Review of Books*, 9 March 2006) s 3.

[10] See Davies, 'The Ontology of Musical Works' (n 2) 70–71.

[11] S Davies, 'Authenticity in Musical Performance' (1987), reprinted in Davies, *Themes in the Philosophy of Music* (n 2) 81. Along a similar line, Paul Mitchell, who is an amateur composer as well as a noted private law theorist and historian, told me that in his experience creation of a score oftentimes disciplines and formalises the relevant work in a way that is not entirely comfortable. In such cases, he said, he hopes that performing musicians will sort of 'see past' the notation. This characterisation of the experience of composing chimes with what the conductor Michael Tilson Thomas has said about performing in the second of the two quotes at the beginning of this chapter.

For another, as Kendall Walton has observed, a performance of a musical work invariably conveys multiple sound patterns, and not just the one approximated by a composer's score.[12] The sound pattern that is approximated by a modern score is one that requires a sound event that contains certain notes but not others, and also certain dynamics, tempos, phrasings, accents, etc. In addition to such a sound pattern, a performance would likely convey other patterns, including a simple note pattern and a figured bass pattern, to be explained presently. A score for a simple note pattern would lack particular dynamics, tempos, phrasings, accents, etc.; and consequently would resemble the scores that predated the eighteenth-century developments in specifications of these performance aspects. A figured bass pattern requires a sound event that contains certain bass notes ('root positions') and some harmonic structure at specified intervals above the designated bass notes. A score for such a figured bass pattern would have the bass line written out, along with figures (ie, numbers) for intervals written under each bass note that occupies a root position. (In its under-determination of many aspects of performance that modern classical scores would specify, such a score would resemble 'lead sheets' used by jazz musicians as bases for improvisation.) Walton's point is that although a modern classical score usually specifies only a complex note pattern of the sort described above, a performance of a piece of music is likely to have the function of presenting multiple sound patterns, including a figured bass pattern, a simple note pattern and others. He goes on to observe: 'It would seem arbitrary to identify a musical work with any single pattern, the pattern indicated by its score, for example, if its performances have the function of presenting other patterns as well'.[13]

III. More Carving

Both a word-type and word-tokens can be distinguished from the meaning of that word. And a sentence-type and sentence-tokens can be distinguished from the meaning of the sentence. Similarly, we can distinguish a score-type and score-tokens of a particular musical work from the *meaning* of that score.

An issue that I cannot delve into in detail here is what kind of meaning musical scores have. Nelson Goodman influentially conceived scores as providing *descriptions* of musical works, which he conceives as classes of performances.[14] An implication is that 'compliant' musical performances do not exactly *follow* or are *guided by* musical scores, but instead simply *match* them. For the reasons that Davies enumerates,[15] and without argument here, I shall assume throughout this chapter a different conception, according to which the meanings of musical scores are *prescriptive*. Musical scores (in tandem with performance traditions or conventions) *prescribe* and *mandate* certain kinds of performances from musicians, rather than describing them.

[12] KL Walton, 'The Presentation and Portrayal of Sound Patterns' (1988), reprinted with a postscript in KL Walton, *In Other Shoes: Music, Metaphor, Empathy, Existence* (Oxford, Oxford University Press, 2015) 230.
[13] ibid 244–45.
[14] Goodman (n 7) 128, 177–92, 210.
[15] Davies, *Musical Works and Performances* (n 7) 135–49. See also generally S Davies, *Musical Meaning and Expression* (Ithaca, Cornell University Press, 1994).

Now, a question arises as to whether a musical work is to be conceived as identical to, or wholly constituted by, the meaning of the score of that work as thus conceived. It might be thought that at least some of the considerations discussed in the preceding section clearly indicate that musical works ought not to be identified with even the meanings of scores. Once again, not all musical works come with scores. Moreover, scores are invariably incomplete for the reasons that were enumerated above. But the following line of thinking should give us pause before a quick dismissal of the identification. Linguists and philosophers of language often distinguish between what a speaker says and what he conveys to the audience, where the former notion is explained in terms of the semantic meaning of the sentence that a speaker utters, and the latter is explained in terms of the various contextual or 'pragmatic' factors that together with the sentence meaning enable the communication between the speaker and his audience to take place. It may then be argued that although the meanings of written scores do not correspond to musical works, because the scores are invariably incomplete, the 'pragmatically-enriched' information – ie, the meanings of written scores specified and supplemented by the traditions or conventions governing interpretation and performances of the relevant music, and any in-person instructions or tips – may very well correspond to, or wholly constitute, the works. Whatever sound patterns that a work's performances have the function of presenting, can be thought to be conveyed by such a pragmatically-enriched meaning of the score of that work. We moreover can think of the admittedly very common cases in which musical works come without scores as akin to, or perhaps as just special instances of, those cases in which speakers communicate without saying anything – eg, by gestures, pictures, standing mutual understandings, etc. There would still be meanings conveyed in such wordless communication. Alternatively, perhaps what is warranted, in light of these considerations, is that we expand our notion of a score, and include in it not just written notations, but also the traditions or conventions for performance, and also the in-person demonstration and oral instructions that supplement whatever written instructions are contained in written scores.[16] Meanings of scores, thus widely conceived, perhaps should be conceived as amounting to or constituting musical works.

Yet, we would do well, I believe, to resist this last identification as well. For there is logical room for thinking that a performance of a work that takes some liberties with the score, even in the pragmatically-enriched or widely-conceived sense discussed in the preceding paragraph, can be truer or more faithful to the relevant musical work, more authentic, than any that would adhere strictly to such a score. To put the point into a sharp relief, what I am arguing for is the possibility of what could be called 'radically authentic musical performances', or 'RAMPs' for short:

(1) Let 'RAMP' $=_{\text{def.}}$ a musical performance of a work that (a) departs from the pragmatically-enriched meaning of the score of that work, and (b) partly because of that departure,[17] is truer or more faithful to the work than any performances that strictly adhere to the pragmatically-enriched meaning of the score.

[16] This is suggested by Davies, 'The Ontology of Musical Works' (n 2) 71: 'Because it is contingent whether or not some particular part of the work (or of the manner of its performance) is recorded in the notation, I believe there is no reason for insisting on a sharp division between the score and the conventions controlling performance practice with respect to such scores, no reason for confining the work to what is notated and dismissing the rest as a matter of style that could play no essential part in shaping the identity of the individual work.'

[17] Nick Allott convinced me of the need to add this clause that ties the two requirements together in a way that excludes *accidentally* authentic performances.

In asserting the possibility of RAMPs, I am likely making a controversial claim. But consider the following possible (I think) scenario. The composer of a musical work and his audience had formed certain anticipations for performances of a work of his based on what he wrote, what the performance traditions or conventions for the relevant kind of work had been up to that point, and the instructions and tips that the composer had given to some musicians earlier. Then a new musician or ensemble comes along and delivers an electrifyingly new, even revolutionary interpretation. All, including the composer, are initially scandalised. The newcomers persist undaunted, however, and after a period of time, some critics, and the composer himself, are brought around. Eventually, the composer opines, and many agree, that the new interpretation is a 'revelation', and has enabled him and others to see the aspects or even the nature of the work that had hitherto eluded him and others.

This story is romantic, to be sure. But impossible? Nonsense? I hardly think so.[18] Musical performances, like musical compositions, are artistic products.[19] And artistic products in general are meant to solve certain problems or puzzles imposed by the artists themselves and/or the genres or traditions in which they work.[20] In a typical case, the tradition or the genre imposes certain constraints or puts up certain obstacles – eg, a multi-hued and dynamic four-dimensional event must be depicted monochromatically and on a two-dimensional surface, a musical improvisation must be unreliant on any idiomatic sound phrases – and the artist is supposed to negotiate those constraints or overcome those obstacles in a way that elicits and warrants aesthetic appreciation in the audience.[21] For musical performances, one set of constraints that musicians (the relevant artists) need to deal with has to do with being faithful to the (pragmatically-enriched or expanded) score. But there surely are other sets of constraints – some probably having to do with endowing the performances with vibrancy, spontaneity and creativity; some others possibly having to do with revealing the architectural organisation of the work; and certainly, likely encompassing all others, those having to do with the emotional expression of the work. A performance that excels in the first respect may be less successful in some of these other respects, and one that succeeds in these latter respects may have faults in the first respect. And there is no guarantee that the virtues of solving all the relevant sets of problems or puzzles would be readily combinable. It may very well be the case that pursuit of some of the goals hampers pursuit of some others.

[18] Lukas Opacic, a legal philosophy PhD student at the University of Sydney who used to be a professional classical pianist, related to me an anecdote that illustrates that RAMPs are more than mere logical possibilities. Sergei Rachmaninoff, upon hearing his third piano concerto performed by Vladimir Horowitz in a way that departed radically from the ways that it had been performed up to then by others (including presumably by Rachmaninoff himself), supposedly responded by remarking that that is how the work should have been performed all along. Opacic told me that this is a popular anecdote among classical pianists. I have not been able to track down this anecdote to any published record so far. But it seems to me that even the mere fact that it is a common lore among musicians is of some significance, and may even provide some support to my view that RAMPs are possible for the reasons I sketch in section VIII. below.

[19] Here, I intentionally avoid the term 'works' to avoid unnecessary confusion. But we could say that both musical compositions and musical performance are artistic works.

[20] Many philosophers of art have made this point. A modern *locus classicus* is KL Walton, 'Categories of Art' (1979), reprinted in KL Walton, *Marvelous Images: On Values and the Arts* (Oxford, Oxford University Press, 2008) 195.

[21] Once again, I am talking only about typical cases. There are many different kinds of atypical cases. See generally KL Walton, '"How Marvelous!": Toward a Theory of Aesthetic Value' (1993), reprinted in Walton, *Marvelous Images*, ibid 3.

I am here generalising a point that Peter Kivy has made in reaction to the period instrument movement in classical music. He observes:

> [W]e are creating a false dichotomy in contrasting *the* historical authenticity of (say) a musicologically correct performance of a Mozart sonata on one of Mozart's fortepianos with the historically *inauthentic* performance by Rudolph Serkin on a Steinway grand. And the question … is not which is better, but which is historically authentic. The answer is, *both* and *neither* … The musicologically correct performance on a period fortepiano is indeed historically authentic in ways in which Serkin's is not. The instrumental sound is more like the sound of Mozart performing it than the sound of a modern concert grand would be. And, let us assume, the phrasing, articulation, dynamics, ornamentation, balance, and "expression" are more like a Mozart performance too. In all these ways, then, the performance on the fortepiano by the musicologist-performer is more historically authentic than Serkin's on the Steinway. But in (at least) two very important ways, which result in a host of sonic features, Serkin's performance, on the modern piano, is more historically authentic than the musicologist's on Mozart's fortepiano. For, like Mozart, Serkin is giving a performance based not on historical judgment but on musical imagination, and all the rest of those "good things" that the great performer brings to the art of musical interpretation, on the instrument to which he was born. And, like Mozart's performance again, and unlike the musicologist's "reconstruction," Serkin's performance comes out of a living musical tradition, a laying on of hands, that gives such performances qualities of vibrancy and spontaneity that musicologically "correct" ones are felt to lack.[22]

The force of Kivy's particular observation here has dulled a bit in the ensuing years. Given the increasingly high number and quality of period instrument ensembles and performances since 1988, this movement too can now be considered a 'living musical tradition', and many contemporary musicians could be considered 'born into' period instruments. But Kivy's larger point still retains its edge. It is not implausible to think that authenticity for musical performances is a higher-order property made up of different combinations of realisations of incommensurate or incomparable values, so that any authentic performance involves trade-offs of realisations of such values.[23] The important implication for our discussion is that a performance that optimally adheres to the meaning of the score, however pragmatically-enriched or widely-conceived, may still be inferior in authenticity to some others that are less faithful to the score's meaning. And this in turn would be weighty evidence for thinking that a musical work is not identical to, or wholly constituted by, even the meaning of the score.[24]

[22] P Kivy, 'On the Concept of the "Historically Authentic" Performance' (1988), reprinted in P Kivy, *The Fine Art of Repetition: Essays in the Philosophy of Music* (Cambridge, Cambridge University Press, 1993) 117.

[23] This theme is further developed in P Kivy, *Authenticities: Philosophical Reflections on Musical Performance* (Ithaca, Cornell University Press, 1995).

[24] As Elizabeth Coulter pointed out to me, my case is further strengthened if we take into account musical works that have dramatic elements, such as operas. *The Marriage of Figaro* presents a nice illustration, and I thank Coulter for all the details that I am about to rehearse. In putting together their opera, Mozart and Da Ponte relied on a controversial and banned play by Pierre Beaumarchais that dealt with subversion of power and privilege. Modern-day performances of *Figaro* that scrupulously follow Mozart's score, Da Ponte's libretto, and contemporaneous stage directions and performance conventions invariably miss out on the political dimensions of the opera. Whereas ones that take certain liberties – as did those of Peter Sellars's production in the late 1980s, which moved the setting from eighteenth-century Spain to the modern day Trump Tower in New York City – would capture such dimensions much better. There is no reason to think that such radical performances could not be more authentic overall than the more traditionally authentic performances.

IV. Works and Meanings, Continued

The claim that a musical performance that adheres strictly to the meaning of the score, however pragmatically-enriched or widely conceived, could be less faithful to a musical work than some others that depart from the meaning of the score is bound to be controversial, or appear incredible, in the pejorative sense. And it could be protested that those of us (including I) who are not supremely knowledgeable and experienced in matters of musical performance are ill-placed to make any credible assessments. Perhaps this is the case. But what I am asking the reader to imagine and consider is something that is far less demanding on his musical culture, I think. Beethoven is reported to have disdained the short waltz that the publisher Anton Diabelli sent him in 1819, and only later and slowly came to realise that he could bring out from it variations that eventually made up the *Diabelli Variations*, often considered one of his great achievements.[25] It is difficult to think that Diabelli himself was mindful of the full potential of his theme. Similarly, the composer and band leader Misha Mengelberg saw in his orchestrations for a large jazz ensemble of various songs by Thelonious Monk and Herbie Nichols, the realisation of the full potential of those songs that Monk and Nichols appear never to have seen. We can also think of a director or an actor bringing forth an aspect or the overall shape of a play that the playwright and his contemporaries could not have grasped. Why could we not imagine a similar transcendence by musical performers of a composer's (or a composer and his contemporaries') own understanding of a musical work? The creative decisions that performers of written compositions make in their performances after all are not all that different from the decisions that composers make in composing variations on a given theme (as Beethoven did on Diabelli's waltz), and the decisions that improvisers make in improvising in real time on a theme (or a 'head', as it is often called in jazz). We delight in hearing interesting and novel decisions of the first kind as we do in hearing interesting and novel decisions of the other two kinds. Otherwise, frequenting of concert halls to listen to performances of the same work, or buying multiple recordings of the same work, would make little sense.

The pianist and critic Charles Rosen has reacted to Richard Taruskin's emphasis on the social determinants of classical compositions as follows:

> [A]s musical system changes over the centuries, possibilities of exploiting the musical language suggest themselves that are too fascinating to ignore, but the works inspired by this stimulus may possibly have to wait a long time for their exploitation. A musical system appears to have a logic of its own that can be inflected but not completely controlled by social pressures; it can act as an inspiration to composers, who often feel as if they were discovering rather than inventing. That is what the greatest of music critics, E.T.A. Hoffmann, conveyed when he wrote that Beethoven was not the wild, untamed genius that so many of his contemporaries thought, but the soberest of all composers, because everything he wrote came from the nature of music itself.
>
> Bach's great Mass in B minor was never performed during his lifetime: as a Catholic Mass, it could not be played in a Protestant church, and the use of an orchestra was forbidden in Catholic churches during Bach's lifetime, although he hoped it might eventually be possible. His "Goldberg" Variations is the most successful of all his works in concert performance today, yet the kind of

[25] See W Kinderman, 'From Parody to Transfiguration' (1989), booklet notes to A Brendel's recording of Beethoven's *Diabelli-Variationen* (Philips Classic Productions, 1990).

> concert in which it can be performed did not exist for another century, and it had to wait for recognition and acclaim for still another hundred years. Both these works fascinated many musicians during the long period before they could find a niche in the social world of performance. The first great set of works to become the staple of serious public piano performances was the thirty-two Beethoven piano sonatas: only two of these were played in a concert hall in Vienna during Beethoven's lifetime. To judge a work, as Taruskin often does, by how it sounded in the conditions that existed when it was written is useful and even necessary, but it can lead at times to profound misunderstanding. This is where the irritating contradiction between the work as written and the work as heard begins to rear its ugly head.
>
> In any case, many works of music like Beethoven's Great Fugue for String Quartet appear principally as a response to possibilities of the musical system of the time, possibilities that are irrelevant to any kind of contemporary social conditions, and the system itself developed both as a response to social pressures and in ways that are completely independent. No social history of music can succeed that does not acknowledge the partial independence of the musical language, the way it can offer abstract possibilities to the imagination irrelevant to the social and economic world of the musician, but often too tempting to turn down.[26]

Rosen is here focusing on a contrast, or perhaps more than one, somewhat different from the one with which we are concerned. He is concerned mostly with the contrast between a musical work as the composer composed it on the one hand, and the work as heard or consumed by the contemporaneous audience on the other. We on the other hand have been focusing on the contrast between what the composer meant on the one hand, and the musical work itself on the other. But several details in Rosen's discussion furnish some material for buttressing the latter contrast. In particular, Rosen speaks of the possibility of a musical system providing certain 'possibilities' and imposing 'a logic of its own', and certain musical works – he names Beethoven's *Great Fugue for String Quartet* in particular – that have the function of working out those possibilities or the logic. Could we not then imagine a performance of a work of such a sort in which the performers take some minor liberties with the score in ways that arguably better works out the possibilities or the logic of the musical system in play than any performance that strictly adheres to the score, and in so doing manages to be more authentic or faithful to the musical work in question?

In another context, taking notice of the fact that very frequently the early versions of the works by Romantic poets, produced when the poets were in their twenties, far surpasses in their powers and aesthetic values the later revised versions that the poets produced in their later years, Rosen observes:

> The Romantic belief in the importance of the unconscious will in artistic creation begins to appear more sensible and reasonable than we might be willing to acknowledge. Many an author has had the experience of creating a work that, as it grew, seemed to develop a logic and even a kind of will power of its own: the author carries out a plan of which he is only half aware. … The work at a certain point develops its own intention for which the author is only an agent. Even language had, for the Romantic artist, a momentum and an energy independent of the will of the artist.[27]

Here, again, the contrast that is of immediate concern to Rosen – that between the early versions and the later revised versions of poems – is somewhat different from ours.

[26] Rosen, 'Troubadours' (23 February 2006) (n 9) s 3.

[27] C Rosen, 'The Definitive Text' (1987), reprinted in C Rosen, *Romantic Poets, Critics, and Other Madmen* (Cambridge, Massachusetts, Harvard University Press, 1998) 26.

But again, the idea that a work may be aimed at working out 'a logic', 'a kind of will power', 'an intention', or 'a momentum and an energy' of its own appears to me to expose a logical space for distinguishing what an artist means (even in any pragmatically-enriched sense), and an artistic work itself.[28]

V. Legal Analogues

We made a variety of distinctions in the preceding three sections. There is the distinction between musical works and performances, and another between score-types and score-tokens. Neither of these last two are to be identified with musical works, and nor should the meanings of scores.

At least on first glance, analogous distinctions can and should be made with respect to law. There is the distinction between laws and legal interpretations. And when we have a text of a law, that text should be disambiguated between the type and tokens of that text. Both of these, as well as the meaning of the legal text, must be distinguished from the law that the text represents. And that would be the case no matter how pragmatically-enriched the relevant meanings, or how widely we conceive the legal texts. It would follow that, at least in some instances, the ideal of authenticity in legal interpretation may not be best served by adhering as strictly as possible to the meanings of the relevant legal texts. At least in some cases, in other words, lawyers and judges might be able to be truer to the relevant laws or legal norms themselves – the legal analogues of musical works – by departing from the meanings of legal texts, than by adhering strictly to such meanings.

These lessons would be no different if the legal texts in question were constitutional provisions. Once again, constitutional norms – ie, the norms that make up a constitution – must be distinguished from the meanings of constitutional textual provisions. At least in some cases, lawyers and judges might be able to be truer to the relevant constitutional norms – the constitutional analogues of musical works – by departing from the meanings of constitutional texts, than by adhering strictly to such meanings. These last implications of the preceding discussion unsettle some of Jeff Goldsworthy's conclusions about constitutional interpretation.

VI. Constitutional Clarifications

Goldsworthy's discussions of constitutional interpretation are straightforward, thorough, inclusive and fair-minded in enviable ways. In particular, his discussions clearly map out where and how much contemporary originalists and non-originalists agree with each other. Goldsworthy points out that both sides of the debate must recognise that pre-existing constitutional norms frequently underdetermine answers to constitutional questions that are brought before courts, and that in such instances judges must devise new legal

[28] To be fair, it should be noticed that Rosen (ibid 27) also warns against 'a certain kind of irresponsible editing, a descent back into the Dark Ages of publishing when an editor altered and repunctuated as he pleased and made up eclectic texts of all the little bits of different versions that he liked best'.

doctrines to fill-out and implement pre-existing norms.[29] A number of constitutional theorists, both originalists and non-originalists, have recognised such a *creative* judicial activity, and refer to it as constitutional 'construction' – to be distinguished from constitutional 'interpretation' proper, which is the activity of ascertaining pre-existing constitutional norms.[30] Goldsworthy refers to the two kinds of judicial activities as 'creative' and 'clarifying' interpretations, respectively, and observes that the dispute between originalists and non-originalists centres on the nature of clarifying constitutional interpretations.[31] Furthermore, Goldsworthy rightly highlights a point that both originalists and non-originalists ought obviously to endorse, but which often gets overlooked in dialectical shuffles; namely, that in some cases, judges and all others must flout laws in order to avoid unacceptable moral costs of complying with them.[32] It may even be the case, as Goldsworthy observes, that in some cases judges ought to flout existing laws surreptitiously – that is, pretend that they are merely clarifying the law when in fact they are changing it – when exigent moral considerations call for it. These and many other observations that Goldsworthy makes are extremely helpful in our avoiding mislocations of what is in contention between originalists and non-originalists.

Yet, if the discussion in the preceding four sections is on the right track, we have some reasons for thinking that Goldsworthy himself ultimately mislocates the focal point of dispute between originalists and non-originalists. As far as I can see, he conceives the dispute (again, about clarifying interpretations) as that between those (originalists) who advocate judicial fidelity to the textual meaning of the constitution, and those (non-originalists) who think that judges should be able to change the textual meaning.[33] This conception of the debate is premised on the assumption that the constitution is to be identified with the meaning of the constitutional text. And as we have seen, this is an assumption that we should be suspicious of when we consider the analogous relation between musical works on the one hand and the meanings of musical scores on the other.

[29] J Goldsworthy, 'Constitutional Interpretation: Originalism' (2009) 4 *Philosophy Compass* 682, 683; J Goldsworthy, 'The Case for Originalism' in G Huscroft and BW Miller (eds), *The Challenge of Originalism: Theories of Constitutional Interpretation* (Cambridge, Cambridge University Press, 2011) 42, 62.

[30] See, eg, K Whittington, *Constitutional Interpretation: Textual Meaning, Original Intent, and Judicial Review* (Lawrence, University of Kansas Press, 1999); MN Berman, 'Originalism is Bunk' (2009) 84 *New York University Law Review* 1.

[31] Goldsworthy, 'Constitutional Interpretation' (n 29) 683. Not all contemporary constitutional theorists draw the line between 'interpretation' and 'construction', or between 'clarificatory' and 'creative interpretation', at the same location. For a notable and influential detractor from how I characterise the location in the text, see LB Solum, '*District of Columbia v Heller* and Originalism' (2009) 103 *Northwestern University Law Review* 923; LB Solum, 'Originalism and Constitutional Construction' (2013) 82 *Fordham Law Review* 453. See a critical discussion of Solum's approach in MN Berman and K Toh, 'On What Distinguishes New Originalism from Old: A Jurisprudential Take' (2013) 82 *Fordham Law Review* 545. Also, while agreeing with Goldsworthy that the term 'interpretation' is often used to refer to both types of adjudicative activities, I find his use of the term 'clarifying' a bit unhappy. For the activity of devising new constitutional doctrines to implement pre-existing constitutional norms could very well be deemed as 'clarifying' such pre-existing norms.

[32] Goldsworthy, 'Constitutional Interpretation' (n 29) 698–99; Goldsworthy, 'The Case for Originalism' (n 29) 65–67.

[33] This formulation of Goldsworthy's position is a bit of simplification, as it overlooks four ways in which he explicitly recognises ways in which judges may depart from the original public meanings of constitutional provisions, and even change the constitution. I discuss those four ways in n 40 below, and point out some reasons for thinking that my simplification may be warranted.

A keen reader of Goldsworthy's writings may object to my attribution to him of an identification of a constitution with the meaning of the relevant constitutional text. For what he explicitly says are the following:

> A law necessarily means something – nothing meaningless can be a law – and its meaning is part of what it is. Therefore to change the meaning of a law is to change the law.[34]
>
> The meaning of a law is part (perhaps all) of what it is; therefore to change the meaning of a law is to change the law.[35]

These passages seem to indicate that Goldsworthy recognises the distinction between a law or a constitution on the one hand and the meaning of the relevant legal or constitutional text on the other, and that he thinks that the meaning of the text only *partly* makes up or constitutes the law or constitution. But his subsequent discussions strike me as warranting my attribution to him of the identification of the two.[36] It is not just the parenthetical in the second of the above-quoted passages that motivates this view. More important is Goldsworthy's subsequent discussion of constitutional interpretation, and more particularly of *clarifying* interpretation, which focuses exclusively on discerning the meanings of constitutional texts. If there were in his mind other constituents of constitutional law, then clarifying constitutional interpretations would surely have to delve into discerning those other considerations as well. For example, in reacting to 'pluralistic' non-originalism, 'which holds that a constitution's original public meaning is merely one among various relevant criteria that should guide its interpretation', Goldsworthy says: 'When the courts are engaged in clarifying interpretation, and are attempting to ascertain what the constitution means, it is hard to see how original public meaning could be merely one of many relevant considerations'.[37] He is willing to grant that pluralism makes sense when it comes to *creative*, rather than *clarifying*, interpretation[38] – that is, for what many others call 'constitutional construction'. The fact that Goldsworthy, by all appearances, conceives clarifying constitutional interpretation as consisting exclusively of discerning the meanings of constitutional texts is quite significant. The absence of any discussion of other considerations in that context appears to me to warrant an attribution to him of an identification of constitutions with the meanings of constitutional texts.

Unlike many other originalist constitutional theorists, Goldsworthy explicitly specifies that the meanings of constitutional texts that he is speaking of are pragmatically-enriched ones, and not merely the semantic meanings of the sentences in the constitutional texts.[39]

34 Goldsworthy, 'Constitutional Interpretation' (n 29) 688.

35 Goldsworthy, 'The Case for Originalism' (n 29) 42.

36 The second of the quoted passages in the text is one of the premises that Goldsworthy lays out in 'The Case for Originalism' (n 29), in an attempt to spell out his argument for originalism as explicitly as possible. For much of that paper, he argues for the soundness of the resulting argument by arguing for and clarifying each premise. Unfortunately, for the premise in question, he provides no argument or clarification, saying merely: 'This seems obvious and indisputable' (at 46).

37 Goldsworthy, 'Constitutional Interpretation' (n 29) 694.

38 Goldsworthy, 'Constitutional Interpretation' (n 29) 694.

39 Goldsworthy, 'Constitutional Interpretation' (n 29) 686–87; Goldsworthy, 'The Case for Originalism' (n 29) 46–51. Another philosopher who has recently emphasised the importance of pragmatic enrichment in the context of legal interpretation is Scott Soames. See S Soames, 'Interpreting Legal Texts: What is, and What is Not, Special About the Law' in S Soames, *Philosophical Essays: Natural Language – What It Means and How We Use It*, Vol 1 (Princeton, Princeton University Press, 2009) 403; S Soames, 'Deferentialism: A Post-Originalist Theory of Legal Interpretation' (2013) 82 *Fordham Law Review* 597.

For this reason, any available evidence of contemporaneous beliefs, evaluations, intentions and conventions that can be used to understand the contents of communication between the founders and their audience, Goldsworthy says, could be relied on for clarifying constitutional interpretations.[40] But my arguments in sections III.–IV. above was meant to cast doubt on the identification of laws or legal norms with even such pragmatically-enriched conceptions of meanings of legal texts. When it comes to musical performances, I argued, the ideal of authenticity or fidelity to musical works does not necessarily mean adhering strictly to the meanings of musical scores, however pragmatically-enriched those meanings, or however widely-conceived the notion of scores. A performance that is blameless in complying strictly with the meanings of the scores, plus any performance conventions prevalent at the time of the composition, and any orally-imparted tips and suggestions that the composer provided, may still be deemed less authentic or faithful to the relevant musical works than the performances that makes departures in those regards. I thus argued for the possibility of RAMPs.

Analogously, I am arguing, we should take seriously the possibility of what could be called 'RACIs', short for 'radically authentic constitutional interpretations':

(2) Let 'RACI' $=_{\text{def.}}$ a clarifying interpretation of a constitution that (a) departs from the pragmatically-enriched meaning of the relevant constitutional text, and (b) partly because of that departure, is truer or more faithful to the constitution than any clarifying interpretations that strictly adhere to the pragmatically-enriched meaning of the constitutional text.

[40] This is quite significant, even in ways that Goldsworthy himself may be overlooking. Goldsworthy attempts to soften the seemingly radical implications of originalism by taking note of four ways in which constitutions can be interpreted 'flexibly' even by originalist judges. See Goldsworthy, 'Constitutional Interpretation' (n 29) 688–91; Goldsworthy, 'The Case for Originalism' (n 29) 61–65. First is the creative interpretation, or 'constitutional construction' as many call it, that is to be contrasted with clarifying interpretation, or 'constitutional interpretation' proper in many others' terminology. Second, the operation of the principle of stare decisis can sometimes perpetuate interpretations that are initially inconsistent with the requirements of meanings of constitutional texts. Third, literal meanings of constitutional texts can be set aside when they conflict with clearly discernible original intentions of the founders. Fourth and finally, what originalism demands fidelity to are the meanings of constitutional texts, and not the applications of those texts expected or anticipated by the founders – the latter can be set aside or ignored. These are four ways, according to Goldsworthy, in which judges may *change* the constitution without running afoul of the strictures of originalism. It is unclear, however, that the last three of these four ways need to be mentioned when one fully takes into account the phenomenon of pragmatic-enrichment in one's conception of the meaning of constitutional texts. With respect to the second, surely, in the United States and Australia, for example, the principle of stare decisis was something that both the founders and their audience took into account in their communication of the meanings of the constitutional texts. With respect to the third, Goldsworthy is quite clear from the get-go that the meanings of constitutional texts that are relevant for understanding the strictures of originalism are not literal meanings, and that the framers' intentions may need to be taken into account to figure out the original public meanings of constitutional texts. (Perhaps what Goldsworthy has in mind when he discusses the third way are the intentions that are different from and conflict with those that determine the original public meanings of constitutional texts.) Furthermore, the fourth way also appears problematic. The meaning-application distinction that is widely relied on in constitutional theory literature becomes uncertain when pragmatic enrichment is taken into account. What a speaker conveys to the audience may be a *de dicto* meaning or a *de re* meaning, and which it is is something that the interpreter would determine in light of the relevant contextual factors. Restricting the notion of original public meaning to the (*de dicto*) meanings and not to the expected applications would then appear ad hoc, designed merely to allow freedom to judges in order to sidestep inconvenient implications of originalism.

Larry Alexander, reacting to an earlier version of this chapter, argued that it would be odd for a person who has been given a shopping list by his spouse to think and act as if he can be truer to that list by departing from the meaning of the list. In reaction, I note that, first, it is not obvious to me that what could be called 'RASPs', or 'radically authentic shopping performances', are impossible. Second, even if RASPs were impossible, there would be a good question to ask as to where in the spectrum, with shopping performances at one end and musical performances at the other, clarifying constitutional interpretations should be located. My sense is that they are more like musical performances. And if my arguments about the possibility of RAMPs are on the right track, then I would think that we should give credence to the possibility of RACIs as well, so long as we cannot bring up considerations that block or problematise the argument by analogy that I am pushing.

VII. Disanalogous?

So far, I have argued that musical works (or more generally, works of art) are not identical to the meanings of scores (or what artists meant, more generally); and that laws, or constitutions more particularly, are not identical to the meanings of legal texts, or of constitutional texts. For the dialectical purposes of this chapter, we can weaken these claims by modalising them as follows. Instead of the non-modal claims above, we can go for: musical works (or more generally works of art) are not *necessarily* identical to the meanings of the scores (or what the artists meant, more generally); and laws, or constitutions more specifically, are not *necessarily* identical to the meanings of legal texts, or of constitutional texts. The last claim would exclude a very strong claim – namely, that laws or constitutions necessarily are identical to the meanings of legal or constitutional texts. This strong claim is what Goldsworthy and other originalists in effect appear to espouse. Perhaps it is the sheer strength or immodesty of this last claim that motivates Goldsworthy to hedge when he says that meanings of constitutional texts are *partly* constitutive of constitutions, even when he appears to identify the two in the rest of his discussion.

One possible reaction to this chapter's line of thinking thus far is to doubt the analogy that I have been pushing. Perhaps there are significant differences between music and law that would block the argument by analogy that I have been outlining. Goldsworthy argues that laws and art works are fundamentally different in ways that should be reflected in our assessments of interpretations of the two kinds of things.[41] He approvingly quotes[42] in part the following diagnosis of 'a basic difference between art-works and legislation' that Joseph Raz has offered:

> This fundamental feature of art, that artworks are meant to carry meaning to people who have no interest in their creator, makes the intentions of the artists relatively unimportant. What counts is the work of art. …

[41] J Goldsworthy, 'Raz on Constitutional Interpretation' (2003) 22 *Law and Philosophy* 167, 186–92. Goldsworthy's argument on this point is a part of his general criticism of Joseph Raz's thinking about legal interpretation, and I am unsure how much of what Goldsworthy says about both law and art are mere temporary adoptions of Raz's commitments, in service of ad hominem arguments against Raz's overall position. But I shall assume in the text that Goldsworthy is endorsing those commitments of Raz's that he does not explicitly criticise and reject.

[42] ibid 190–91.

> An enactment, on the other hand, is binding not because its content is exceptional, but because it was promulgated by this person or body, which is endowed with authority to legislate. Legislation is to be interpreted in accordance with convention because this is the way of establishing the intention of the law-maker. Art is to be understood independently of the private context of its creation because what counts is its public meaning. If this meaning is the one intended by the artist, so be it. But if the work brings out something in the artist which even he is unaware of, and the expression of which is publicly perceived, and becomes crucial to the interpretation, that is to the common understanding of the work, this belittles neither this understanding of the work nor the work's merit.[43]

The contrast is between a set of objects (art works) for interpretations of which creators' intentions are of little or no importance, and another set of objects (laws or legislations) for interpretations of which creators' intentions are all-important. Perhaps this contrast in interpretations could be conceived as resulting from the different natures of the two kinds of objects that are interpreted. Perhaps we could even go so far as thinking that, whereas art works should not be conceived as necessarily identical to the contents of artists' communication, laws should be conceived as necessarily identical to the contents of lawmakers' communication.

Not only is this last conclusion exceedingly strong, but the initial impetus for it that Raz's discussion provides, which Goldsworthy appears to endorse, can be undercut, I believe. For Raz's contrast both overestimates the importance of lawmakers' intentions for legal interpretation, and underestimates the importance of artists' intentions for artistic interpretation. It is Raz's general conception of the nature of law that yields the former. The central and distinctive premise of that conception is that necessarily laws are meant to be authoritative, or that necessarily the members of a community with laws (at least pretend to) treat their laws as authoritative.[44] And Raz conceives authority in such a way that requires positing of agents ('authorities') who mediate between people ('subjects') and the reasons that apply to them. According to this 'service conception of authority',[45] the norms or directives issued by the authorities are authoritative if the subjects are more likely to comply with the moral

[43] J Raz, 'Why Interpret?', reprinted in Raz, *Between Authority and Interpretation* (n 4) 223, 248. There are complications in Raz's discussion of interpretation that makes straightforward understanding and assessment of the above-drawn contrast challenging. For one thing, what he means by 'public meaning' of an art work appears to be contrasted with what the work means to the artist who created the work: at 243–46. At least initially, the distinction here does not seem all that different from the distinction that Goldsworthy emphasises between what a speaker intends to mean, and the meaning that is publicly communicated between a speaker and his audience – ie, between 'speaker's meaning' and 'utterance meaning' in Goldsworthy's terminology. See Goldsworthy, 'Constitutional Interpretation' (n 29) 686–87; Goldsworthy, 'The Case for Originalism' (n 29) 47–48. If Raz's and Goldsworthy's distinctions were to coincide, then the contrast between art works and laws that Raz is drawing would be quite thin. For both art works and laws, what matters would be public meanings that are to be contrasted with private meanings. Another complication is the systematic ambiguity in Raz's uses of the term 'meaning'. Sometimes, the term is used to mean the content of communication, and at other times, it is used to mean something like 'importance' or 'significance'. See, eg, the first full paragraph in Raz, 'Why Interpret?' (n 43) 244. In many places, Raz's discussion seems to be marred by implicit trafficking back and forth between these two senses of 'meaning'. In any case, in my subsequent discussion in the text, I will assume that Raz only has in mind the communicative content sense of 'meaning'; and furthermore, that by 'public meaning' of an art work, he means something more than merely publicly accessible meaning (or 'utterance meaning'). I realise that there is tension between these two stipulations.

[44] The classic statement of this view, and the arguments for it, are provided in J Raz, 'Authority, Law and Morality' (1985), reprinted in J Raz, *Ethics in the Public Domain: Essays in the Morality of Law and Politics* (Oxford, Clarendon Press, 1995) 210.

[45] ibid 198.

reasons that apply to them anyway by treating the norms or directives as preemptive and content-independent reasons. Given this conception of the nature of law, it is unsurprising to find Raz arguing that legal interpretations must be aimed at reflecting lawmakers' intentions.[46]

Obviously, this is no place to attempt a systematic assessment of Raz's conception of the nature of law.[47] Let me make just two points. First, it is very far from clear that people living in communities with laws need to treat their laws (or at least pretend to treat them) as authoritative in the very thick sense that Raz articulates – that is, as directives issued by morally authoritative legislators that enable those who treat them as preemptively binding to comply more effectively with the moral reasons that apply to them anyway than they would be able to otherwise. A much more modest, or theoretically less expensive, conception according to which people merely treat their laws as reason-giving is likely to do much better in its explanatory economy.[48] Second, in requiring the positing of authoritative legislators, Raz's conception of the nature of law is in a significant respect a throwback to the command theories of law proposed by the likes of Hobbes, Bentham and Austin; and it incurs some of the characteristic costs. In particular, it encounters difficulties accounting for customary laws.[49] It is unsurprising to see Raz admit that his account of legal interpretation does not apply to customary laws.[50]

The supposed unimportance of artists' intentions for interpretations of art works also strikes me as exaggerated in Raz's discussion. It is true that Monroe Beardsley long ago influentially warned us against conflating art works with artists' intentions, even implicit

[46] See, especially, J Raz, 'Intention in Interpretation' (1996), reprinted in Raz, *Between Authority and Interpretation* (n 4) 265, 274–76. The conception of laws as purporting to be authoritative eventually motivates Raz to adopt a view about legal interpretation that is more complicated. See Raz, 'Interpretation Without Retrieval' (n 4); Raz, 'Why Interpret?' (n 43); Raz, 'Intention in Interpretation' (n 46); J Raz, 'On the Authority and Interpretation of Constitutions: Some Preliminaries' (1998), reprinted in Raz, *Between Authority and Interpretation* (n 4) 323; Raz, 'Interpretation: Pluralism and Innovation' (n 4). According to that view, newly enacted laws are presumed to issue from lawmakers who have moral authority, and the interpretations of such laws must be aimed at recovering or reflecting the intentions of such morally authoritative lawmakers. As time passes, the moral authority of the lawmakers with respect to the laws that they enacted diminishes, but considerations having to do with the value of continuity warrant interpretive practices that are partially motivated by continued deference to the intentions of the lawmakers. But such considerations must be combined and balanced with considerations of equity and needs for change. In the later years, innovative interpretations of a law are sometimes warranted by shifts in balance among the considerations of authority, continuity, equity and the need for change. Goldsworthy has objected to this view by arguing that such shifts in balance among the four considerations are shifts in balance between, on the one hand, reasons for paying attention to the law, and on the other hand, reasons for changing it: Goldsworthy, 'Raz on Constitutional Interpretation' (n 41) esp 191–92.

[47] I attempted something like it in K Toh, 'Some Moving Parts of Jurisprudence' (2010) 88 *Texas Law Review* 1283.

[48] An even more fundamental problem with Raz's position here is that he assumes that to treat something as reason-giving or normative is necessarily to treat it as moral-reason-giving or morally normative. Goldsworthy's otherwise admirably keen and judicious article, 'The Self-Destruction of Legal Positivism' (1990) 10 *Oxford Journal of Legal Studies* 449, appears to me to suffer from the same faulty assumption. I criticise the assumption in some detail in K Toh, 'Raz on Detachment, Acceptance and Describability' (2007) 27 *Oxford Journal of Legal Studies* 403, 414–21; and Toh, 'Some Moving Parts' (n 47) 1291–95. See also D Wodak, 'What Does "Legal Obligation" Mean?' (2018) *Pacific Philosophical Quarterly*, doi:10.1111/papq.12230, which marshals some compelling linguistic evidence against moralised readings of legal obligations claims.

[49] This issue is discussed in Toh, 'Some Moving Parts' (n 47) 1298–1301, where I criticise Raz, and also Andrei Marmor ('Authorities and Persons' (1995), revised & reprinted as 'Authority and Authorship' in A Marmor, *Positive Law and Objective Values* (n 4) 89), who tries to shore up Raz's position on this issue.

[50] Raz, 'Why Interpret?' (n 43) 276, 289.

ones; and argued that philosophers who treat artists' intentions as finally authoritative in interpreting works of art are guilty of what he called 'the intentional fallacy'.[51] But many philosophers of art have subsequently faulted Beardsley for his categorical denial, and have provided some compelling arguments to show that artists' intentions may be partly constitutive of works of art, and that appeals to such intentions hence may be legitimate ways to interpret many works.[52] As Walton has influentially argued, for example, what genres or categories a work belongs to determines which of its non-aesthetic properties are 'standard' or 'non-standard', and which of its non-aesthetic properties are 'standard' or 'non-standard' in turn determines its aesthetic properties.[53] And artists' intentions are at least partly determinative of the genres or categories to which their works belong.[54] Philosophers like Walton do not disagree with Beardsley that the nature of individual works of art may ultimately diverge from the respective artists' intentions, but they would take issue with Raz's facile denial of the relevance of artists' intentions for interpretations of art works.

In sum, I am unworried by Raz's case, which Goldsworthy appears to endorse, for thinking that works of art and laws are radically or sufficiently disanalogous as to undermine our argument from analogy. We are entitled to retain the thought that, as there is a distinction to be observed between musical works and the meanings of the relevant scores, so there is a like distinction to be observed between laws and the meanings of the relevant legal texts.

VIII. Ontologies?

That last conclusion does not deny the larger point that Raz and Goldsworthy can be seen as making – namely, that the nature or aim of interpretations is dependent on the nature of the objects interpreted. And for all I have said so far, it may still turn out to be the case that the nature of law is such that legal interpretations must be aimed centrally or even exclusively at reflecting the meanings of legal texts.

Going back to the philosophy of music, there has been a lively debate in the last 40 years or so about the ontological status of musical works. There appears to be a broad agreement among the participants in the debate that musical works are to be distinguished from musical performances, and that musical works are abstract objects. But several key

[51] See WK Wimsatt and MC Beardsley, 'The Intentional Fallacy' (1946) 54 *The Sewanee Review* 468; WK Wimsatt and MC Beardsley, 'The Affective Fallacy' (1949) 57 *The Sewanee Review* 31; MC Beardsley, *Aesthetics: Problems in the Philosophy of Criticism*, 2nd edn (Indianapolis, Hackett Publishing Co, 1981) ch 1.

[52] See, eg, Walton, 'Categories of Art' (n 20); R Wollheim, 'Criticism as Retrieval' in R Wollheim, *Art and its Objects*, 2nd edn (Cambridge, Cambridge University Press, 1980); J Levinson, 'Intention and Interpretation: A Last Look' (1992), reprinted as 'Intention and Interpretation in Literature' in J Levinson, *The Pleasures of Aesthetics: Philosophical Essays* (Ithaca, Cornell University Press, 1996) 175; S Davies, 'Beardsley and the Autonomy of the Work of Art' (2005) 63 *The Journal of Aesthetics and Art Criticism* 179.

[53] Walton, 'Categories of Art' (n 20).

[54] For a similar argument, see M Sagoff, 'On Restoring and Reproducing Art' (1978) 75 *The Journal of Philosophy* 453. An outrageously impish illustration of the point is made by JL Borges, 'Pierre Menard, Author of the *Quixote*' (1939), reprinted in JL Borges, *Fictions* (translated by A Hurley) (London, Penguin Books, 1998) 33. Walton's arguments are criticised in N Zangwill, 'Feasible Aesthetic Formalism' (1999) 33 *Noûs* 610; N Zangwill, 'In Defence of Moderate Aesthetic Formalism' (2000) 50 *The Philosophical Quarterly* 476; N Zangwill, 'Defusing Anti-Formalist Arguments' (2000) 40 *British Journal of Aesthetics* 376.

issues, reflective of some wider debates in aesthetics and philosophy more generally, divide philosophers of music. There are roughly two camps. On the one hand, there are philosophers who adhere to relatively thin conceptions of musical works as sound structures or patterns.[55] On the other, there are those who opt for somewhat thicker conceptions according to which musical works are sound structures or patterns created within specific musico-historical contexts, and with specific means of performance or sound production (eg, instrumentation).[56] What the ideal of authenticity demands in performances of a musical work depends crucially on presuppositions about the ontology of musical works.[57] If a musical work were conceived thinly, merely as a sound pattern, then many different ways of performing the sound pattern regardless of the instrumentation could count as authentic ways of performing that work; whereas a thicker conception requiring a certain instrumentation would permit a far narrower range for authenticity.

What I have argued in the preceding sections, especially in sections III.–IV., is that the meanings of musical scores are unlikely to be identical to or constitutive of musical works. In other words, even if we were to side with the proponents of the thicker conception of musical works, and thereby see musico-historical contexts of composition and the means of sound production as constitutive of musical works, the meanings of scores, however much pragmatically-enriched, are unlikely to be wholly constitutive of musical works. But there are two lines of thought that may warrant softening of that conclusion. First, one might question the primacy of the ontological status of musical works, and agree with Walton, who argues that metaphysical questions must be treated in tandem with aesthetic ones, and more particularly that a conception of the nature of musical works must mesh in revealing ways with insights about the aesthetic values of music.[58] Similarly, Davies observes that the dependence between ontological status of musical works and the ideal of authenticity does not run just in one direction.[59] Our conception of the ontology of musical works, he opines, should depend on what kinds of performances of works we deem authentic.

The second line of thinking is not unrelated to the first. Davies is of the view that performances of a work belonging to the Western classical tradition are more authentic the more they are faithful to the intentions that are publicly expressed in musical scores.[60] This is a view that is supportive of the period instrument movement in classical music, and is analogous to legal originalism of the sort that Goldsworthy has advocated, which I sought to resist in my arguments in the preceding sections. But Davies has also argued that things become much more complicated when a wider perspective – that is, wider than that of the music of the Western classical tradition – is taken. He observes:

> If we take a wider perspective and consider the way an interest in music might range from a concern with music making in the absence of musical works, through an interest in music making

[55] See, eg, Wolterstorff (n 6); P Kivy, 'Platonism in Music: A Kind of Defense' (1983), reprinted in Kivy, *The Fine Art of Repetition* (n 22) 35; P Kivy, 'Platonism in Music: Another Kind of Defense' (1987), reprinted in Kivy, *The Fine Art of Repetition* (n 22) 59.

[56] See, eg, J Levinson, 'What a Musical Work is' (1980), reprinted in J Levinson, *Music, Art, and Metaphysics: Essays in Philosophical Aesthetics* (Ithaca, Cornell University Press, 1990) 63; J Levinson, 'What a Musical Work is, Again' in Levinson, *Music, Art, and Metaphysics* (n 56) 215; J Levinson, 'Authentic Performance and Performance Means' in Levinson, *Music, Art, and Metaphysics* (n 56) 393; Walton, 'Sound Patterns' (n 12); Davies, *Musical Works and Performance* (n 7) pt I. *cf* Walton, 'Categories of Art' (n 20).

[57] See Walton, 'Sound Patterns' (n 12) 235; Davies, 'The Ontology of Musical Works' (n 2).

[58] Walton, 'Sound Patterns' (n 12) 250–51.

[59] Davies, 'The Ontology of Musical Works' (n 2) 75.

[60] Davies, 'Authenticity in Musical Performance' (n 11) 81–82.

> with musical works minimally important and the stress on the improvisational skills of the performer, and finally to music making with a complex, more or less determinate musical work as the primary object of interest and the music making the means by which that work is presented, what emerges, I think, is the realization that the notion of authentic performance has no single, fixed essence. The more it is that the musical work drops out of account – for example, because it exists as no more than a cipher the performers must expand and develop in the creation of a performance – the more it will be the case that authenticity in performance is concerned with faithfulness to the types of playing rather than to the work itself. The more it is that the musical work is sufficiently complex and stable to become the focus of attention – for example, because it is recorded by means of a sophisticated notation or because conventions for performance are sufficiently complex and detailed to allow for the preservation of the individuality of long pieces – the more it will be the case that authenticity in performance is concerned with faithfulness to a determinative text. Moreover, because musical conventions are mutable, as are complex systems of notation, what it is that can be determined by the composer and the conventions as the text of a musical work will be relative to the time of the work's composition. Accordingly, what it is that can be required in the name of faithfulness from a performance of a given work will depend very much on the work's period.[61]

Davies concludes by declaring: 'The totality of musical works from culture to culture and from time to time do not have any single ontological character. Some musical works are thick with properties, others are thinner.'[62]

Even when he is discussing works belonging to the Western classical tradition, Davies is much more conservative than I want him to be. As I have been arguing, I do not think that authenticity of performances, of even the works belonging to that tradition, should be measured solely or even primarily in terms of how faithful they are to the meanings of their respective scores. But the point that he is making, that there may not be any single ontological character of musical works as such, combined with the view that he and Walton share, that what ontology we assume for a musical work should depend on or mesh with our interests in and evaluations of the relevant tradition or episode of music making, are quite suggestive and even compelling. If they are right, then what properties performances of a work must have to be authentic depends on what properties of the work should count as constitutive of that work, and what properties of a work should count as constitutive of that work in turn depends on what we find aesthetically valuable and interesting about that work or works of that type. This is an especially intriguing suggestion given that both the philosophical issue about the ontology of musical works and the aesthetic issue of what counts as authentic performance are fraught with controversies. And perhaps what is warranted in thinking about law is something similar. There too, we can think, what properties interpretations must have to count as accurate or authentic should be thought dependent on what properties of a law should count as constitutive of that law, and what properties of a law should count as constitutive of that law in turn should be thought to depend on what we find valuable or important about that law or laws of that type. And evaluative considerations of

[61] Davies, 'The Ontology of Musical Works' (n 2) 76.

[62] Davies, 'The Ontology of Musical Works' (n 2) 77. Related observations about the relation between authors and works of literary art may be apt. Notice that Rosen's discussion, examined briefly at the end of section IV. above, of possible gaps between literary works on the one hand, and authors' own understanding on the other, concerned Romantic poetry primarily.

this last sort may well motivate a conception of interpretive authenticity that gives a pride of place to the meanings of legal texts.

Perhaps something like this last line of reasoning is what Goldsworthy is getting at when he opines that the originalist approach to clarifying constitutional interpretation, as he conceives that approach, adheres to the ideal of rule of law, the principle of popular sovereignty, and the principle of federalism in countries like the United States and Australia.[63] I am, however, uncomfortable with the way that such moral values, principles or ideals are invoked in Goldsworthy's discussion, and in many other originalists' exposition of their positions. For originalists often complain about their opponents' allowances for moral values, principles and ideals in the process of legal adjudication; and it is unclear why invocations of values, principles and ideals are legitimate in one context while they are illegitimate in the other.[64] In general, it seems to me, we want some way to regiment the ways in which values, principles and ideals can be brought in to discipline our conception of the ontology of laws, which in turn would determine what properties legal interpretations must have to be deemed faithful to the laws that they interpret.

IX. Interlude

In the balance of this chapter, I will propose a particular way of accomplishing such a regimentation. What I have in mind is the approach to explaining the nature of something by way of an imaginary history of how it came about. By talking about 'imaginary histories', I do not have in mind just those histories that are known or suspected to be false. Speculative histories that available evidence neither confirm nor refute would count as well. A particular species of such 'natural histories' or 'genealogies', as they were often called in the seventeenth to nineteenth centuries, are the state-of-the-nature narratives each of which specifies a certain initial situation, and then goes on to explain how certain human phenomena could have come about by operations of the forces that are specified to exist in such an initial situation.[65] The idea is to characterise the initial situation in a particular way, and to portray the human phenomenon in question as originating from people being motivated by a certain set of interests.

Such natural histories may be normatively vindicatory or debunking depending on the interests by which people in the initial position are characterised as motivated. If the interests in question were benign or salutary ones, then we would have a normative vindication of the phenomenon in question. This is what philosophers like Hobbes and Locke argued with respect to governments of certain sorts.[66] But a debunking natural history would be

[63] See Goldsworthy, 'Constitutional Interpretation' (n 29) 687–89; Goldsworthy, 'The Case for Originalism' (n 29) 57–60.

[64] This is a concern that is discussed in detail in Berman (n 30); Berman and Toh (n 31).

[65] For illuminating discussions of genealogical explanations, see generally B Williams, 'Naturalism and Genealogy' in E Harcourt (ed), *Morality, Reflection and Ideology* (Oxford, Oxford University Press, 2000) 148; B Williams, *Truth and Truthfulness: An Essay in Genealogy* (Princeton, Princeton University Press, 2002) ch 2; E Craig, 'Genealogies and the State of Nature' in A Thomas (ed), *Bernard Williams* (New York, Cambridge University Press, 2007) 181.

[66] The phenomenon that is thus shown as coming about need not be what exists here and now, but instead the ideal by appeal to which what exists here and now can be assessed. That was the approach taken by J Rawls, *A Theory of Justice* (Cambridge, Massachusetts, Harvard University Press, 1971).

warranted if the relevant motivating interests were discreditable. That is what we see in Hume's natural history of religion,[67] and Nietzsche's genealogy of morality.[68]

Somewhat different uses of natural histories could be made for more theoretical (as opposed to practical) purposes. By characterising the environment and the people (or creatures) in the initial situation in a particular way, using only the resources made available by certain disciplines, and by showing that the people (or creatures) so situated would have been motivated, and sufficiently equipped, to acquire certain additional characteristics, we can explain a target phenomenon in a non-mysterious way. Edward Craig, for example, has recently sought to explain knowledge by arguing that creatures with certain capacities, and with certain basic needs, including that of cooperation, would have been motivated to attribute a particular status – ie, what we would characterise as possession of knowledge – to those members among them who are particularly reliable sources of information on a given subject matter.[69] In Paul Grice's story of 'creature construction', we see an even more ambitious research programme to explain perception, belief and action by situating them together within a network of causal laws that it would make ethological and ecological sense to posit.[70] Debunking is possible for such theoretical natural histories as well. By his explanation of the origin of species by way of natural and sexual selections, Darwin in effect debunked any element of design.[71] Much closer to our concern is Lydia Goehr's partially debunking history of the concept of musical work.[72] Natural histories need not have exclusively practical or theoretical aims, but may have a mixture of the two kinds of aims or implications.

What, I believe, would be useful and illuminating is a vindicatory natural history or genealogy of non-originalism, or more precisely of a legal system with a judiciary that practices non-originalist constitutional interpretation. At one point, in the midst of discussing entrenchment provisions of constitutions – ie, those provisions that set out the exclusive means by which constitutions can be revised – Goldsworthy says:

> It would be possible, of course, for an entrenchment provision explicitly or implicitly to exempt judges from its prohibition of change other than by the procedures it prescribes. But it is surely unlikely that judges would be deliberately permitted to change a constitution that ordinary democratic procedures are forbidden to change. Such an institutional arrangement, if it exists anywhere, would be very unusual, and can be excepted from the argument that follows.[73]

[67] D Hume, *The Natural History of Religion* (1757) (edited by HE Root) (Stanford, Stanford University Press, 1956).

[68] F Nietzsche, *On the Genealogy of Morality* (1887), revised edn (edited by K Ansell-Person and translated by C Diethe) (Cambridge, Cambridge University Press, 2007).

[69] E Craig, *Knowledge and the State of Nature: An Essay in Conceptual Synthesis* (Oxford, Clarendon Press, 1990).

[70] HP Grice, 'Method in Philosophical Psychology (From the Banal to the Bizarre)' (1974) 48 *Proceedings and Addresses of the American Philosophical Association* 23. For further developments of the Gricean creature construction programme, see, eg, J Perry, 'Perception, Action, and the Structure of Believing' in RE Grandy and R Warner (eds), *Philosophical Grounds of Rationality: Intentions, Categories, Ends* (Oxford, Clarendon Press, 1986) 333; ME Bratman, 'Valuing and the Will' (2000), reprinted in ME Bratman, *Structures of Agency: Essays* (Oxford, Oxford University Press, 2007) 47.

[71] C Darwin, *The Origin of Species* (1859) (edited by W Bynum) (London, Penguin Books, 2009); C Darwin, *The Descent of Man, and Selection in Relation to Sex* (1871), 2nd edn (edited by AJ Desmond and JR Moore) (London, Penguin, 2004) pts II–III.

[72] L Goehr, *The Imaginary Museum of Musical Works: An Essay in the Philosophy of Music* (Oxford, Clarendon Press, 1992).

[73] Goldsworthy, 'Raz on Constitutional Interpretation' (n 41) 171.

I agree that such an institutional arrangement would be peculiar and their possibilities can be ignored. But, as I argued above, the divide between originalists and non-originalists is not aptly characterised as that between those who believe that judges must seek to reflect accurately in their interpretations the constitution, and those who believe that judges can change the constitution by way of their interpretations. Instead, I proposed, non-originalists are better characterised as those who are as committed to fidelity to the constitution as much as originalists, but who believe that the constitution that judges must accurately reflect is not wholly constituted by the meaning of the constitutional text. The phenomenon that a vindicatory natural history of non-originalism should explain then is not a legal system in which judges are permitted to change the constitution, but instead one in which judges seek to be faithful to the constitution that may not be accurately reflected in the constitutional text. In other words, it is a legal system in which judges, while aiming to reflect the constitution accurately, treat the meanings of constitutional text as not necessarily identical to the constitution of their system. Such a natural history would yield a conception of the ontology of constitutions, or of laws more generally, that would yield a conception of constitutional or legal authenticity that permits non-originalist adjudication, and at the same time meshes in the right and disciplined way with our normative interests. It would provide a legal analogue of what Walton and Davies have urged that we seek in our thinking about the ontology of musical works.

I suspect that I will not be surprising or disappointing the reader in confessing here that I do not have a worked-out vindicatory natural history of non-originalism to lay out in the remaining pages of this chapter. (The reaction is likelier to be relief!) What I have instead are some fragments of the beginning of such a natural history. More specifically, I will offer two fragments, one of which would be very familiar to students of legal philosophy, and an explanation of how the two are related. My hope is that the fragments offer some insights as to how a full-blown natural history would go. One of the fragments also offers the additional benefit of showing some reasons that have motivated me to think of law and art alongside one another.

X. First Fragment

In Chapter 5 of *The Concept of Law*,[74] HLA Hart offers what could be deemed a state-of-nature story of law. The initial situation he specifies is one that is much farther along in its development than the one that Craig specified in his history of knowledge, or even those that the classic political philosophers specified in their histories of governments. Not only do the creatures in it have the psychological makeup that makes them recognisably human, but they also accept and follow in their conduct a set of norms – what Hart calls 'primary rules of obligation'[75] – that may be community-specific. As is well-known to just about any student of legal philosophy, Hart observed that any community with a scheme of such primary rules alone would suffer from three types of problems: (i) those of uncertainty about the content and scope of the rules; (ii) those arising from the static character

[74] HLA Hart, *The Concept of Law*, 2nd edn (Oxford, Clarendon Press, 1994).
[75] ibid 91.

of the rules; and (iii) those arising from the lack of ways to definitively settle disputes that implicate the rules.[76] The remedy that such a community would eventually hit upon is the adoption of three kinds of higher-order norms, or 'secondary rules' as Hart calls them, that would govern operations of the primary rules that belong to the particular set that governs that community: (i) a 'rule of recognition' would specify the features the possession of which by a primary rule would be deemed an indication that the rule belongs to the relevant set; (ii) 'rules of change' would furnish ways to add new rules to the set, or to subtract existing rules therefrom; and (iii) 'rules of adjudication' would enable definitive adjudication of any disputes that implicate the rules of the set.[77] It is Hart's opinion then that the transition from the 'pre-legal' to the 'legal' stages of a community takes place with the adoption of these three types of secondary rules.[78]

Clearly, this natural history is not entirely normatively neutral. Other things being equal, it is better to have standing solutions to the three types of problems that Hart identifies, and law, according to Hart's story, provides, or more precisely amounts to, a solution to them. To that extent, we may opine, Hart's narrative provides a normatively vindicatory explanation of law. But as Hart observes at one point, in some situations when other things are not equal, a community equipped with a legal system may possess a much greater capacity for tyranny than one without it.[79]

More salient in Hart's narrative than any normative upshot is his explanatory economy, so to speak – ie, the resources he draws on, and how much gets explained by deploying those resources. Hart is not voluble in his description of the state of nature in Chapter 5, but we can surmise that it would not stray far from what he describes later in Chapter 9 to motivate what he calls 'the minimum content of natural law'.[80] The environment would be marked by limited resources, and people occupying it would be characterised by physical and psychological vulnerabilities, rough equality, limited altruism and limited understanding and strength of will. One thing that Hart does dwell on at length in Chapter 5 is the notion of 'the internal point of view'.[81] When rules are in play, as primary rules are even in the state of nature, one can take a mere 'external point of view' by which one observes regularities of thought and behaviour on the part of the members of the relevant community; or one could take an 'internal point of view', in the sense of treating thought and behaviour in accordance with the relevant rules as proper, appropriate or called for. People who 'accept' a rule take an internal point of view with respect to that rule. And as Hart earlier explains, acceptance of a rule consists of dispositions to follow the rule, to demand compliance with the rules, and to criticise others and oneself for non-compliance.[82] The relevance of all this to our current discussion is that people in the state of nature have and are motivated not only by beliefs and desires, but also by acceptances of rules. The key thought is that people

[76] ibid 92–94.

[77] ibid 94–98.

[78] For a quite similar conception of law as offering solutions to recurring problems posed by the pre-legal environment and human nature, see D Copp, 'Legal Teleology: A Naturalist Account of the Normativity of Law' in D Plunkett, S Shapiro, and K Toh (eds), *Dimensions of Normativity: New Essays on Metaethics and Jurisprudence* (New York, Oxford University Press, 2019).

[79] Hart (n 74) 117.

[80] Hart (n 74) 193–200.

[81] Hart (n 74) 89; *cf* ibid 84.

[82] Hart (n 74) 57.

living in an environment of limited resources; who are characterised by vulnerabilities, rough equality, limited altruism, and limited understanding and strength of will; and who are equipped with the psychological dispositions that amount to acceptances of primary rules would come to adopt a set of secondary rules that would turn their set of rules into a legal system. Nothing more complex or mysterious need be posited to explain law.

As Bernard Williams has observed, state-of-nature narratives often attribute functions to the target phenomena that they purport to explain.[83] And Hart's narrative fits the pattern. Law or a legal system has a particular function, according to the narrative – namely, that of solving the three aforementioned problems that invariably beset communities of primary rules only. The ambition is that, by attributing this function to laws or legal systems, we would be able to explain the most important non-contingent features of communities with laws or legal systems, or at least do a better job of explaining them than with any explanations that do not attribute such a function. And the theory of the nature of law that Hart motivates in large measure by his natural history has a legitimate claim to having fulfilled that ambition.

XI. Second Fragment

Let us go further back in time, to an earlier state of nature, in the hope of explaining something that is an even more fundamental feature of human culture than law. (The relevance of this second narrative to the first will be explained in the next section.) This time, the genealogy that I am about to discuss is more than an imagined narrative. It is instead a speculative sociobiological explanation proffered by the evolutionary psychologists John Tooby and Leda Cosmides.[84]

One apparently anomalous feature of human beings, from the standard evolutionary theoretical standpoint, is their propensity to seek out aesthetic experiences through works of fiction, and other exercises of imagination such as pretend play. Not only do people actively seek out such experiences – in various media including stories, paintings, films, sculptures and even music[85] – but they seem to treat them as intrinsically rewarding. In fact,

[83] Williams, *Truth and Truthfulness* (n 65) 31–32.

[84] J Tooby and L Cosmides, 'Does Beauty Build Adapted Minds? Toward an Evolutionary Theory of Aesthetics, Fiction and the Arts' (2001) 30 *SubStance* 6. *cf* L Cosmides and J Tooby, 'Consider the Source: The Evolution of Adaptations for Decoupling and Metarepresentation' in D Sperber (ed), *Metarepresentations: A Multidisciplinary Perspective* (Oxford, Oxford University Press, 2000) 53. As Williams has observed, given their highly speculative nature – about the nature of the environment, and about the characteristics of the relevant creatures – such sociobiological explanations could very well be deemed fictions: Williams, *Truth and Truthfulness* (n 65) 30. One key difference is that such explanations are susceptible to correction or corroboration by further empirical evidence, whereas those belonging more explicitly to the genre of philosophical state-of-nature narratives are not.

[85] There have been philosophical debates about whether at least some music – ie, what often gets called 'pure music', as opposed to 'program music' – is non-representational or non-depictive. See, eg, P Kivy, *Music Alone: Philosophical Reflections on the Purely Musical Experience* (Ithaca, Cornell University Press, 1990); P Kivy, 'The Fine Art of Repetition' in Kivy, *The Fine Art of Repetition* (n 22) 327; KL Walton, 'Style and the Products and Processes of Art' (1979), reprinted in Walton, *Marvelous Images* (n 20) 221; KL Walton, 'Projectivism, Empathy, and Musical Tension' (1999), reprinted in Walton, *In Other Shoes* (n 12) 118; Levinson, 'What a Musical Work is' (n 56); Levinson, 'What a Musical Work is, Again' (n 56); Levinson, 'Authentic Performance' (n 56). I find compelling Walton's and Levinson's position that even so-called pure music is representational or depictive, and that what they depict is how the sounds are produced.

while tendencies to store and deploy veridical information about the world are very likely fitness-enhancing, many if not most people display a decided preference for fictions over non-fictions in their spare hours, and our child-rearing practices are saturated with provision of fictions. This taste for aesthetic and other imaginative experiences is a cross-cultural, universal phenomenon that calls out for an explanation. The menu of explanatory options consists basically of three. First, in ways that are difficult to discern, human engagements with aesthetic and other imagined experiences are actually reproductive fitness-enhancing, and our propensities for such engagements are functional products of adaptations. Second, such propensities are accidental, functionless and not-too-harmful byproducts of adaptations. And finally, they are just evolutionary noise, produced by the chance spread of certain genes. It is in opting for, and fleshing out, the first explanatory option that Tooby and Cosmides could be seen as offering a state-of-nature narrative.

As Hart identified a set of problems, and construed law as a solution to those problems, Tooby and Cosmides identify a particular problem, and construe our propensities to seek out and immerse ourselves in aesthetic experiences as a solution to that problem. Humans are quite different from most other species in our abilities to adapt to and live in widely different types of environments. The state of nature that is relevant here then is one marked by varying sets of conditions. In order to thrive in different types of environments, we need to rely on contingently true information – ie, information that is true only in some locations, but not others, information that is true only momentarily, etc. We also need to rely on contingently useful skills – not just cognitive skills, but also affective and practical ones. The problem for creatures relying on such contingently true information and contingently useful skills is one that is posed by the greatly expanded risk of misapplication that such reliance brings.[86] The information and skills that may be useful when one set of conditions obtain may be false, harmful and even fatal when other sets obtain. The creatures then need some way of *decoupling* or *quarantining* bodies of information and sets of dispositions that amount to skills from each other. They will need to activate a body of information and a set of skills, while suspending commitments to other bodies of information and sets of skills, all the while having them ready for activation should actual conditions change.

Tooby and Cosmides argue that our propensities to consume fictions and to engage in other imaginative activities actually amount to an adaptation that has the function of developing and maintaining a psychological architecture that in turn develops and maintains various bodies of information and sets of skills in decoupled states, each ready to be tapped when conditions change appropriately. Such developmental and maintenance activities would likely have been drudgeries. But natural selection appears to have hit upon a particular way of 'bribing' us to commit our free time to such self-improving activities by endowing us with propensities to feel a special kind of pleasure – ie, aesthetic pleasure – when we engage in such activities.[87] The situation is not dissimilar to the way that natural selection has found a way to 'bribe' us to seek out reproductive activities by endowing us with propensities to feel sexual pleasure. We have subsequently developed various means of obtaining sexual pleasures without taking part in reproductive activities, including 'protected' sex and

[86] Tooby and Cosmides, 'Does Beauty Build Adapted Minds?' (n 84) 19.
[87] Tooby and Cosmides, 'Does Beauty Build Adapted Minds?' (n 84) 16.

pornography. Similarly, we have developed various means – ie, various genres of art – of obtaining aesthetic pleasure without necessarily doing the work of psychological upkeep that Tooby and Cosmides argue is the function of aesthetic activities. It is quite unlikely that listening to Haydn's string quartets or viewing Giacometti's stick figures in particular is reproductive fitness-enhancing. But the point is that, in seeking aesthetic pleasures by engaging in such activities, we are exploiting propensities that nature has endowed us with so that we would be reliably motivated to do the kind of psychological upkeep that is fitness-enhancing.

XII. A Synthesis

Now, what do the two fragments have to do with each other? Notice to begin that both law and art, according to the two stories, are adaptations – cultural in one case, and biological cum cultural in the other – for living in changing environments. But there is a tighter connection. We can think of our legal practice as reliant on the same psychological infrastructure that makes our aesthetic and other imaginative experiences possible.

According to Tooby and Cosmides, human beings maintain different bodies of information and sets of skills, and have a single body and one set activated to deal with the conditions at hand, while holding others in suspension, in decoupled form. We can sometimes call on such suspended information or skills to deal with some tasks at hand, and this is what happens when we engage in counterfactual reasoning – ie, reasoning about what would be the case if things were different from the way they actually are.[88] Not only beliefs, but also feelings, desires and other motivation-laden psychological states can be held in suspended and decoupled states, according to Tooby and Cosmides, and these are what we tap into when we consume and immerse ourselves in fictional and other imaginative experiences – eg, when we watch a horror movie. We can think of acceptances of norms or rules, which Hart highlighted in his explanation of law, as a type of motivation-laden psychological state that is susceptible to activation or suspension in such fashion. Once again, according to Hart, legal practices are partly made up of people's acceptance of rules, both primary and secondary. And an acceptance of a rule consists of dispositions to follow the rule, to demand compliance with the rule, and to criticise others and oneself for non-compliance. What Tooby and Cosmides's discussion makes salient is the distinction we can make between activated and suspended acceptances of rules.

As Hart conceives the notion of acceptance of rules, a person could accept rules of various different types. Some of the rules a person accepts may be moral rules, epistemic rules, etiquette rules, rules of grammar and notably legal rules. The notion of acceptance itself does not entail any particular type of rules that are accepted.[89] What this implies is the possibility of accepting simultaneously rules that are in tension or even conflict in some situations. An accepted etiquette rule may for example require a host to refrain from criticising a guest for his boorish behaviour, whereas an accepted moral rule may require criticism. Sometimes,

[88] Tooby and Cosmides, 'Does Beauty Build Adapted Minds?' (n 84) 20.

[89] This is a point that unsettles some central components of Raz's conception of the nature of law, as well as Goldsworthy's ('Self-Destruction' (n 48)), which is much influenced by Raz's writings. For criticisms of Raz on this point, see Toh, 'Raz on Detachment' (n 48) 414–21; Toh, 'Some Moving Parts' (n 47) 1291–95.

the tension or conflict between accepted rules may be more than just one-off, but ongoing or constant. In such cases, a person's acceptance of one of the rules may be suspended in the sense that Tooby and Cosmides are talking about, possibly held in abeyance until or unless some unordinary set of conditions obtain. Possibilities of such suspended acceptances of rules are especially acute when the relevant rules are in tension with moral rules. Moral rules, or at least the most fundamental ones, purport to be necessary or non-contingent in the sense of being applicable no matter the situation, and this feature of them introduces a standing possibility of tension or conflict that would necessitate suspension of acceptances of some other rules.[90] The adoption of secondary rules that the transition from the pre-legal to the legal world involves dramatically increases the possibility of tension or conflict with moral rules, and the need to hold some acceptances of rules in suspension. For a community's acceptance of a set of secondary rules of the sort that Hart discusses increases the opportunities for their acceptances of rules that are at variance with moral and other kinds of rules that the members consider non-contingently applicable and hence non-negotiable. A legislature may pass legislation, or a court may issue a ruling, that, while legally unimpeachable, is morally unacceptable. In such a case, the members of the community would be motivated to accept the rule implicated by the legislation or ruling in a suspended way, decoupled from their acceptances of the moral rules involved; or perhaps vice versa.

One may go so far as to liken the rules that make up any legal system to the information that makes up a work of fiction; and to liken our engagements with systems of law to our engagements with works of art. A sort of counterfactual thinking is involved in our engagements with a work of fiction, as Tooby and Cosmides argue; and likewise, we can think, a sort of counter-*normative* thinking is involved in our engagements with a body of law. The acceptances of rules that are involved in our legal engagements would be un-suspended or activated in those situations when legal rules line up in their implications with moral rules, but such lining-up is not a necessary feature of any body of laws. To make the point vivid, we can say that our engagements with, for example, a law that permits romantic relations and marriage between first cousins may be much like our engagements with a nineteenth century English novel that treats such relations and marriage as perfectly acceptable; and the two engagements likely rely on the very same psychological infrastructure.

We can find an echo of such way of thinking about law in Raz's conception of legal claims (which Raz traces to Hans Kelsen's work) as 'detached' normative claims.[91] Raz distinguishes between *committed* and *detached* normative claims. Whereas committed normative claims are those stating the contents of the norms that the speaker is committed to, detached normative claims are those stating the contents of the norms that the speaker only pretends or simulates commitments to.[92] If we were to resort to Hart's conception of normative claims as expressions of acceptances of rules, we can translate Raz's distinction as the distinction between expressions of activated and suspended acceptances of rules or norms, respectively. Raz's proposal is to conceive legal thinking and discourse

[90] Like things probably could be said for fundamental epistemic norms.

[91] See, eg, J Raz, *Practical Reason and Norms*, 2nd edn (Princeton, Princeton University Press, 1990) 172–77; J Raz, 'Legal Validity' (1977), reprinted in J Raz, *The Authority of Law: Essays on Law and Morality* (Oxford, Clarendon, 1979) 146; J Raz, 'The Purity of the Pure Theory' (1981) 35 *Revue International de Philosophie* 441.

[92] Raz conceives all committed normative claims as moral claims, and detached normative claims as pretended or simulated moral claims, but we need not follow him there. I take issue with this aspect of Raz's views in Toh, 'Raz on Detachment' (n 48). *cf* Wodak (n 48).

as essentially detached normative thinking and discourse. We can follow him in such a conception, and supplement it with the picture of the psychological infrastructure that enables such thinking and discourse. That psychological infrastructure is the one that Tooby and Cosmides posit in their explanation of our aesthetic and other imaginative dispositions and activities.

I ended the last section by discussing natural selection's finding a way to bribe us with aesthetic pleasures in order to motivate us to carry out certain works of psychological upkeep (quite similarly to its finding a way to bribe us with sexual pleasures in order to motivate us to engage in reproductive activities); and also our subsequent developments of various means to derive such pleasures without necessarily carrying out the tasks that such pleasures are meant to induce. Our implicit recognition of our propensities to seek out and immerse ourselves in aesthetic and other imaginative activities has actually prompted even more radical ways of 'co-opting'[93] such propensities. For example, we exploit these propensities in ourselves to convey information in easily accessible and retrievable ways, to advertise and market goods and services, to announce and maintain occupation of certain social statuses, etc. Such instances of co-option take advantage specifically of our desires for aesthetic pleasures. But other means of co-option may not tap into that particular aspect of our nature, but still take advantage of the psychological infrastructure that is developed and maintained by our dispositions to consume and immerse ourselves in aesthetic and other imaginative activities. We can think of our legal practices as relying on that infrastructure in so far as they make use of our abilities to hold in suspended and desegregated form different bundles of information and skills.

XIII. In Lieu of a Recapitulation

According to the partial and fragmented natural history that develops, legal thinking and discourse is much like critical thinking and discourse in being prompted by imagination or mental simulation. Judgments of constitutional interpretation are a species of legal judgment, and hence would be judgments of imagination or mental simulation. Walton has argued that art works can illuminatingly be conceived as props for imagination or make-believe, very much the way that say tree stumps are imagined to be bears by children playing a game of make-believe, and then are used to generate further imagined or fictional truths.[94] The rest of the projected full natural history would show how a working legal system could be sustained while its officials, and more particularly judges, try to coordinate their constitutional interpretations, or more specifically their clarifying interpretations, without necessarily ruling out possibilities of discrepancies between what the texts of their central props (ie, constitutions) say and what they imagine to be the case. I should think that it would be possible to tell it.

[93] To borrow a term that the authors of a recent study use to make similar points about our propensities to seek out mirth. See MM Hurley, DC Dennett and RB Adams, *Inside Jokes: Using Humor to Reverse-Engineer the Mind* (Cambridge, Massachusetts, MIT Press, 2011) 264–70. In my discussion in the text, I owe much to their fascinating and illuminating discussion.

[94] KL Walton, *Mimesis as Make-Believe: On the Foundations of the Representational Arts* (Cambridge, Massachusetts, Harvard University Press, 1990); KL Walton, 'Metaphor and Prop Oriented Make-Believe' (1993), reprinted in Walton, *In Other Shoes* (n 12) 175.

9

Populism and Parliamentary Sovereignty: The Goldsworthy Solution

ALISON L YOUNG

I. Introduction

It is often remarked that it is impossible to write an academic article which discusses parliamentary sovereignty without mentioning the work of Albert Venn Dicey. It is equally impossible to do so without mentioning the work of Jeffrey Goldsworthy. His groundbreaking work, *The Sovereignty of Parliament: History and Philosophy*, provides a detailed historical analysis of parliamentary sovereignty, furnishing clear evidential support for the claim that the sovereignty of Parliament is a key principle of the United Kingdom constitution.[1] Goldsworthy's work also provides a detailed evaluation of competing conceptions of sovereignty and its philosophical foundations, in addition to developing his own conception of sovereignty.[2] As such, when faced with a problem whose solution appears to turn on particular understandings of parliamentary sovereignty, it is important to ask not only what Dicey would do, but also, what would Goldsworthy do?

The aim of this contribution is to ask precisely this question with regard to a contemporary issue in UK constitutional law – the UK's exit from the European Union (EU). Brexit has already given rise to the so-called constitutional case of the century, *Miller*, in which the Supreme Court deliberated *en banc* to determine whether the notification of the UK's decision to exit the European Union was within the scope of the Government's prerogative powers.[3] The precise issue raised in *Miller* only touched indirectly on parliamentary sovereignty. The Supreme Court, by a majority decision of 8 to 3, concluded that the prerogative of foreign affairs did not include a specific power to notify the EU of the UK's intention to withdraw from the EU Treaties. In reaching this conclusion, the Government needed to find an alternative legal base for this power. This left only one real option – that of initiating legislation in Parliament to empower the Government to notify the EU. As such, the decision in *Miller* arguably enhanced parliamentary sovereignty. Parliament was given the ability both to discern whether the Government should be empowered to notify

[1] J Goldsworthy, *The Sovereignty of Parliament: History and Philosophy* (Oxford, Clarendon Press, 1999).

[2] See, in particular, J Goldsworthy, *Parliamentary Sovereignty: Contemporary Debates* (Cambridge, Cambridge University Press, 2010).

[3] *R (Miller) v Secretary of State for Exiting the European Union* ('*Miller*'). [2017] UKSC 5, [2018] AC 61.

the EU of the UK's decision to withdraw from the EU Treaties and, if so, whether there should be any conditions on the exercise of this power.[4]

However, underpinning this case was a deeper problem. To see this, we need to place the decision in its full historical and constitutional context. There had been no clear governmental policy to leave the EU. Rather, the then Conservative Government, led at the time by the then Prime Minister, David Cameron, had been elected on a manifesto commitment to hold an 'in-out' referendum on the UK's continued membership of the EU.[5] Following the success of the Conservative Party in the General Election, the *European Union Referendum Act 2015* was enacted to provide for the holding of a referendum. The referendum was held on 23 June 2016, with 51.9 per cent voting in favour of leaving the EU and 48.1 per cent voting in favour of remaining in the EU. The UK constitution was faced with divergence between the wishes of the Government and the legislature – the majority of whom had campaigned in favour of remaining in the EU – and the people, the majority of whom had voted to leave.

The use of referendums, with a potential for divergence between the wishes of the people and the wishes of Parliament, produces two distinct forms of challenge to parliamentary sovereignty. I will refer to these as the legal challenge and the normative challenge. The legal challenge focuses on the extent to which the existence of a referendum modifies legal principles. This chapter will focus on two legal challenges: the narrow and the broad. In *Miller*, a narrow issue arose as to whether the existence of a referendum meant that legal restrictions, which would apply to the use of prerogative powers, did not apply to the use of the prerogative to enact an instruction from the people as expressed in a referendum. The broader legal challenge, which did not arise in *Miller*, asks whether the existence of a referendum has an impact on the legal principle of parliamentary sovereignty. Could it be the case that a referendum requirement could effectively entrench legal provisions? The normative challenge is more abstract. It asks whether referendums, as an expression of direct democracy, challenge parliamentary sovereignty in a more fundamental sense. Is it the case that parliamentary sovereignty is best justified as an expression of popular sovereignty? If so, does this mean that, to the extent that there is a contradiction between the will of the legislature and the will of the people, the will of the legislature must always give way to the will of the people?

The chapter will argue that Goldsworthy's account of parliamentary sovereignty may be better able to ensure that referendums do not provide a means for populist movements to destabilise democracy. This is because of the way in which Goldsworthy's account permits Parliaments to bind future Parliaments as to procedure and form, offering a means of protecting long-term commitments, which could be used to protect pluralism, whilst ensuring that it is still possible for these long-term commitments to be changed where there is sufficient democratic will to do so – thereby minimising a potential cause of populist movements. In addition, Goldsworthy would only allow for the entrenchment of referendums where there was sufficient evidence of a modification of the rule of recognition to support a modification of parliamentary sovereignty, which would otherwise prevent the

[4] *European Union (Notification of Withdrawal) Act 2017.*

[5] 'Strong Leadership: A Clear Economic Plan: A Brighter, More Secure Future' *Conservatives* (2015) www.conservatives.com/manifesto2015 (last accessed 14 November 2018).

entrenchment of referendum requirements. This again may provide better protections against the potential dangers of referendums being used to further populist movements.

II. The Narrow Legal Challenge

The backdrop of the EU referendum gave rise to two arguments from the Government in the *Miller* case which were used to reinforce its claim that the Government did enjoy a prerogative power to notify the EU of the UK's decision to withdraw. Both of these suggested that the existence of a referendum modified the legal requirements that would apply in an identical legal situation where there had been no referendum. First, the suggestion was made that the 2016 referendum had taken place against an assumption that the outcome of the referendum would be decisive. More specifically, it was suggested that, through the enactment of the *European Union Referendum Act 2015*, Parliament had effectively delegated any decision as to whether the UK should remain within the EU to the people. As such, even if there were a role for the UK Parliament in reaching a decision to leave the EU, the Westminster Parliament had already exercised this role by enacting the 2015 Act.[6] It was therefore for Ministers alone to decide to act on the basis of the referendum outcome.[7] Second, it was argued that, any restrictions that may apply generally to the existence or scope of prerogative powers would not apply as regards the prerogative power to withdraw from the EU, given the context of the referendum. The restrictions that would apply to normal Ministerial decisions did not apply to those Ministerial decisions adopted in order to implement the decision of a referendum.[8]

The majority judgment of the Supreme Court rejected both of these arguments. The first was dismissed as unrealistic and was not fully developed before the Court. The second was rejected on the basis of an analysis of the status of a referendum in the UK constitution. It was recognised that the outcome of any referendum in and of itself was only politically advisory and not legally binding. This was not to dismiss the importance of any referendum outcome, but merely to recognise that, in the absence of a provision in a codified constitution, or in general legislation setting out the legal consequences of a referendum, its outcome would be dependent on the specific Act of Parliament governing the conduct of a particular referendum. The Referendum Act 2015, in contrast to other legislation enabling the holding of a referendum,[9] did not provide for a specific legal duty on the part of a Minister in response to the referendum outcome. Therefore, in the absence of any specific legal duty imposed in legislation, the referendum was only advisory as a matter of law. It did not impose any specific legal obligations in and of itself. Consequently, the outcome of

[6] *Miller* (n 3) [38]. See also Secretary of State for Exiting the European Union, 'Appellant's Case', Skeleton Argument in *R (Miller) v Secretary of State for Exiting the European Union*, UKSC 2016/196, 18 November 2016 [74]–[78] www.gov.uk/government/uploads/system/uploads/attachment_data/file/570778/Supreme_Court_Printed_Case_of_the_Secretary_of_State_for_Exiting_the_European_Union.PDF (last accessed 15 November 2018).

[7] *Miller* (n 3) [120].

[8] *Miller* (n 3) [116]–[125].

[9] See, eg, *Scotland Act 1978*, s 85; *Northern Ireland Act 1998*, s 1; *Parliamentary Voting System and Constituencies Act 2011*, s 8.

the referendum could not alter the legal position as to whether the Government enjoyed a prerogative power to withdraw from the EU.[10]

This section will argue that both Dicey and Goldsworthy would have reached the same conclusion as the UK Supreme Court on these issues. However, it is important to recognise that both would do so through a different route, requiring a more detailed balancing of the political sovereignty of the people with the legal sovereignty of Parliament. These more detailed arguments provide a better justification for why Ministers, and Ministers alone, should not have the power to implement the Brexit referendum without further Parliamentary involvement, as well as explaining why the existence of the referendum should not alter the legal principles that normally apply the control of the use of prerogative powers.

A. What Would Dicey Do?

The answer to this question would appear to be deceptively simple – surely Dicey would have reached the same conclusion as the majority of the Supreme Court in *Miller*? In reaching its conclusion that the legal requirements for the use of the prerogative did not alter when the prerogative was used to implement the outcome of a referendum, the Supreme Court drew on what would appear to be a classic Diceyan understanding of parliamentary sovereignty. The referendum is a means through which the electorate is able to express its will directly. As such, it can be seen as an exemplification of popular sovereignty. However, whilst the people may be sovereign in a political sense, the law does not recognise this sovereignty. Rather, the law recognises Parliament as the sovereign law-making institution. Parliament is the legal sovereign power. Courts deal with the law and not with politics. Therefore, even when there is a potential divergence between the will of the people and the will of the legislature, the court can only recognise the will of the legislature as expressed through legislation. It cannot recognise and enforce the will of the people. It is for Parliament to take account of the political sovereignty of the people. Any divergence between the will of the legislature and the will of the people should be resolved through political means – eg, through the holding of a general election, or through the legislature deciding to adopt and enforce the will of the people.

Dicey's theory of parliamentary sovereignty appears to mirror this analysis. Dicey describes the UK Parliament as enjoying unlimited parliamentary sovereignty, able to legislate on any subject matter that it pleases, save one – it is not able to legislate so as to bind its successors. In addition, legislation, once enacted, cannot be questioned in any court of law. Courts enforce legislation. They do not challenge the validity of legislation once enacted. Dicey's account also distinguished between legal and political sovereignty. For Dicey, the sovereignty of the UK Parliament was a legal fact, established through an analysis of case law. Political sovereignty, however, rested with the people. It was a political fact that the people elected members of Parliament.[11] As such the people, either understood on their

[10] *Miller* (n 3) [124].

[11] AV Dicey, *Introduction to the Study of the Law of the Constitution*, 10th edn (Basingstoke, MacMillan, 1959) 72–74.

own or expressed in terms of a combination of the wishes of the people as enacted by the Queen-in-Parliament, were the political sovereign. The wishes of the people expressed in a referendum would therefore be seen as an expression of political sovereignty. But the role of the court would be to determine the expression of the will of Parliament – the legal sovereign, – and not of the people – the political sovereign. The silence of Parliament in the *European Union Referendum Act 2015*, therefore, meant that the referendum outcome was purely politically advisory and not capable of influencing the law.

However, whilst the analysis of the Supreme Court mirrors a classic Diceyan account of parliamentary sovereignty, it does not provide a full account of how Dicey regarded referendums. Dicey's later work did advocate the use of referendums in certain circumstances.[12] In particular, he was concerned about situations that could arise when there was a divergence between the wishes of the electorate and legislation on issues of constitutional importance. Dicey regarded referendums as a potentially conservative force, which could hold a check on sudden constitutional change which may not match the wishes of the people. As such, he regarded referendums as playing a potentially positive role when they were held in response to a law reforming the constitution, with the referendum focusing on the specific question of whether this reform ought to be introduced. The referendum would need to be a peaceful and free vote in response to this specific question. However, even though the position is more complicated than the decision of the majority in *Miller* would suggest, it is still the case that Dicey would probably also have concluded both that the existence of a referendum vote did not mean that Ministers, and only Ministers, were required to implement the outcome of the referendum, and that the legal controls over the use of prerogative powers would not have been modified because the prerogative was being used to implement the outcome of a referendum.

There are a number of ways in which the Brexit referendum does not match the requirements of Dicey's normative account of the value of referendums. The referendum was not held in response to a law reforming the constitution. This is not to doubt the impact of the UK's withdrawal from the EU on the UK constitution. Rather, it is to point out the order in which the referendum arose. A referendum was not held in response to a clearly established policy which would lead to a precise form of constitutional change. It was, instead, used to determine whether constitutional change should be made in the first place. There was no clear account of the precise nature of the constitutional change that would occur following the UK's exit from the EU. Nor could there be – this would only become clear following negotiations with the EU establishing a Withdrawal Agreement. This lack of clarity also questions the extent to which the electorate was provided with a specific question on a specific issue. Although the question was specific in one sense – whether the UK should leave the EU or remain part of the EU – it was unspecific in terms of the precise nature of the UK's future relationship with the EU.

However, although these differences exist, this need not mean that Dicey would have concluded that the Brexit referendum should make a difference to the law controlling prerogative powers. These differences are more relevant to the determination of whether

[12] AV Dicey, 'Introduction' in *Introduction to the Study of the Law of the Constitution*, 8th edn (London, McMillan, 1931); AV Dicey, 'Democracy in Switzerland' (1890) 171 *Edinburgh Law Review* 113; AV Dicey, 'Ought the Referendum to be Introduced into England?' (1890) 57 *Contemporary Review* 489.

the UK should hold a second referendum; one where the precise constitutional changes had been set out in legislation, with the vote being as to whether this constitutional change should or should not be accepted. If we are to determine whether Dicey would have concluded that the existence of the referendum meant that it was for Ministers, and not Parliament, to implement the referendum, or that the existence of the referendum would have an impact on the law governing the use of prerogative powers, we need to explore Dicey's justification for the use of referendums.

There exists academic debate surrounding the extent to which Dicey's support of the use of referendums in his later work is a betrayal of his earlier theory, led by his strong opposition to home rule in Ireland,[13] or whether this is indicative of a dualist approach to constitutionalism. This dualist approach is one where the people play a bigger role in constitutional decision-making, focusing on the use of the House of Lords' veto of legislation which did not match the wishes of the electorate, thus forcing the dissolution of Parliament, and triggering an election focusing specifically on the legislation vetoed by the second chamber.[14] This latter approach was influenced by Dicey's growing distrust of the party system, leading to his concern that greater divergence would appear between the wishes of the electorate and the expression of these wishes in legislation by Parliament. Dicey's rationales for the use of referendums can be described as the conservative rationale and the constituent power rationale. The conservative rationale draws on Dicey's concern that Parliament could introduce a series of radical changes to the constitution through ordinary legislation. He saw referendums as a necessary, positive, conservative force. The constituent power rationale draws on the idea that major constitutional change involves a role for the people. As the political sovereign, the wishes of the people should be taken into account when faced with major constitutional change. Whilst the sovereign people may transfer ordinary lawmaking power to Parliament, this is not the case for constitutional legislation. That required a further check to ensure that constitutional change was in line with the wishes of the people, who, as the political sovereign, are the holders of constituent power.

Understood on its own terms, Dicey's account does not provide a clear answer to whether the referendum outcome was one that Ministers, and Ministers alone, had to comply with. Both the conservative rationale and the constitutive power rationale would appear to argue that there was no justification for this conclusion. This is because of the underlying justification provided by Dicey which motivated him to advocate the adoption of referendums. Dicey was concerned with the rise in parliamentarianism, which he saw as leading to the moral breakdown of parliamentary government. Dicey provided three reasons for why he believed that representative government was failing.[15] First, as representative government was adopted in more countries, this led to a loss of prestige in this form of government. It was clear from the range of examples that there was no necessary connection between representative government and, either economic prosperity, or wise and stable government. The greater use of representative forms of government provided a clear demonstration of how

[13] I McLean and A McMillan, 'Professor Dicey's Contradictions' [2007] *Public Law* 435.

[14] R Weill, 'Dicey was Not Diceyan' (2003) 62 *Cambridge Law Journal* 474; R Weill, 'We the British People' [2004] *Public Law* 380.

[15] AV Dicey, 'Will the Form of Parliamentary Government be Permanent?' (1899) 13 *Harvard Law Review* 67; AV Dicey, 'The Paralysis of the Constitution' (1905) 88 *Contemporary Review* 305.

representative governments could enact the folly as well as the wisdom of the electorate. Moreover, given the growing transparency of the decisions of representative government, these faults were laid bare for the electorate to see, leading to reactionary politics.

Second, representative governments did not always provide an account of the wishes of the nation. There were issues arising from the potential tyranny of the majority, when large majorities could override the wishes of smaller minority groups. Party politics meant that often it was not the case that a consensus was reached through deliberation, but rather that agreement could be forced through calling on party loyalty. The rise of the power of governments also meant that democratic discussion could be curtailed.[16] Third, representative governments were often performing tasks for which Dicey believed they were unsuited. Rather than representative governments focusing on laissez-faire policies, based on conceptions of individualism, governments were focusing more on producing communitarian policies, aiming to achieve the greater good in society. However, this often required broad sweeping changes, sometimes of a constitutional nature. Dicey was concerned that these changes should be brought about by the electorate as a whole and not through representative democracies.

Running through these criticisms is the concern at the lack of correlation between the wishes of the legislature, as expressed in legislation, and the wishes of the electorate. Referendums helped to perform a check on this divergence; whether as a conservative force, or as a means of ensuring that the sovereign people had a real say in constitutional change. To see referendums as meaning that it was the role of Ministers, and Ministers alone, to implement a referendum outcome could be interpreted as a means of ensuring that legislatures are further prevented from ignoring the wishes of the people. Ministers would be required to enact the wishes of the people, as expressed in the referendum, regardless of whether this was in line with the wishes of the legislature. As such, Ministers could ensure that the wishes of the electorate prevailed.[17]

However, a better understanding of Dicey would reach the opposite conclusion. Just because Ministers should act in line with the wishes of the people does not mean that only Ministers should then have the power to implement a referendum outcome. Moreover, to conclude that Ministers and only Ministers should implement the outcome of a referendum could further the problems of parliamentarianism. This is particularly true of the Brexit referendum, given that it was used to prompt the initiation of constitutional change, as opposed to being used to confirm a detailed plan of constitutional change. To give Ministers, and only Ministers, the power to act would give too much power to the executive, removing the ability of the legislature to play a role in determining when to implement the outcome of the referendum, or how to implement a referendum outcome that was not a mere expression of approval of detailed constitutional change that had already been set out for approval, or disapproval, by the electorate. This could further the problems of parliamentarianism, undermining the wishes of the electorate in the long-term, particularly if Ministers used this power to reject the need to hold a further referendum on a later, more detailed plan of constitutional change. On that basis, it is likely that Dicey would conclude

[16] See also, Weill, 'Dicey was Not Diceyan' (n 14) 484–86.
[17] Dicey, 'The Paralysis of the Constitution' (n 15) 315.

that the referendum did not provide a justification for Ministers alone to act to implement the referendum decision without further parliamentary involvement.

It is harder to reach a conclusion as to whether Dicey's account of referendums would require that the legal restrictions that control the use of prerogative powers would not apply as regards a prerogative power exercised in order to implement a referendum outcome. Similar difficulties arise given the divergence between the Brexit referendum and Dicey's normative account of referendums. An argument could be made that, had the referendum been a vote in favour of a fully debated detailed plan for constitutional reform, backed by the legislature, then there would have been a strong case for arguing that the legal restrictions on the use of the prerogative power would be modified. Here, the constituent sovereign – the people – would have had a say on a specific plan which modified the constitution so as to remove rights currently enjoyed in EU law, and to remove EU law as a distinct source of law. As such, there is a strong argument that, given the normative backing for these changes by the sovereign people, there was no further need for legal controls over the exercise of the prerogative. Indeed, to add legal controls might undermine the constituent sovereignty of the people, thus harming the constituent power justification for referendums.

However, this was not the case as regards the Brexit referendum. As such, it is arguable that Dicey's theory would require either that the legal controls over the exercise of the prerogative remained the same, or were strengthened in the face of a potential constitutional change. The latter is particularly true if we accept that Dicey adopted a dualist approach to constitutionalism, requiring a delineation between constitutional and ordinary legislation. As the use of the prerogative to withdraw from the EU would instigate constitutional change, but of a nature that had not yet been fully approved in detail by the people, then an argument could be made that at least the same, if not greater legal controls should be placed on the exercise of this prerogative power by the executive.

B. What Would Goldsworthy Do?

Goldsworthy's account of parliamentary sovereignty is similar to that of Dicey. In particular, Goldsworthy does not advocate that any one Parliament can bind future Parliaments as to the substance of legislation that it can enact. All Parliaments must be able to enjoy full lawmaking power, and be able to enact legislation on any subject which they choose. However, in contrast to Dicey, Goldsworthy concludes that Parliaments can bind their successors as to the form and procedure used to enact legislation.[18] However, Goldsworthy does not empower any one Parliament to place a procedural restriction on a future Parliament that would restrict its substantive lawmaking powers.[19]

Goldsworthy's theory focuses on choosing an account of sovereignty that maximises the lawmaking powers of Parliament. Dicey's theory prevents any Parliament from binding its successors as to manner and form. However, this means that Parliament is unable to make long-term commitments. To empower a Parliament to bind future Parliaments as to the form and procedure through which legislation is enacted empowers Parliaments

[18] Goldsworthy, *Parliamentary Sovereignty* (n 2) 181.
[19] Goldsworthy, *Parliamentary Sovereignty* (n 2) 174.

to make long-term commitments. It therefore provides for a greater sovereignty of Parliament, in the sense of a wider range of measures that can be validly enacted by Parliament. Not only can Parliament enact legislation on any subject matter it wishes, but it may also indicate that some matters are long-term commitments. This may make it harder for future Parliaments to legislate in that subject area, so as to preserve the long-term commitment. However, future Parliaments would still be able to overturn these long-term commitments, provided that they did so using a specific form and procedure. In order to ensure that the lawmaking power of future Parliaments is not overly limited, Goldsworthy's theory restricts the type of form and procedure mechanisms that may be used to create long-term commitments. These form and procedure requirements must not make it practically impossible for a future Parliament to overturn a long-term commitment. Moreover, form and procedure requirements cannot be used to redefine Parliament, including a body other than Parliament in the lawmaking process. As such, all Parliaments have no substantive restrictions on their lawmaking powers. This preserves the sovereignty of Parliament, as Parliament is sovereign when it has the ability to enact legislation on any subject matter that it wishes. Goldsworthy's theory would not enable Parliaments to bind future Parliaments as to a referendum requirement, as this would include the electorate, expressing its views through a referendum, in the lawmaking process. This would be to redefine Parliament, rather than to restrict a future Parliament as to the form and procedure through which to enact legislation.[20]

Despite the differences between Goldsworthy and Dicey, it is likely that they would have reached the same conclusion both as to whether it was the case that only Ministers were required to implement a referendum outcome, and as to whether the existence of a referendum would modify the law regulating the use of prerogative powers. Whether the referendum had such an impact would depend upon an analysis of the wording of the *European Union Referendum Act 2015*. As the 2015 Act was silent on this point, it is unlikely that Goldsworthy would reach the conclusion that Ministers, and Ministers alone, should enact the outcome of the referendum. To do so would require this to be read in to the legislation. In addition, to read the 2015 Act as removing Parliament's future role would be to effectively replace Parliament's role with that of the electorate, thus redefining Parliament. Yet, according to Goldsworthy's theory, that requirement could not bind a future Parliament that wished to have a say in the implementation, or not, of the referendum outcome.

Where Goldsworthy would differ from Dicey's account is as to whether the existence of the referendum could modify the legal requirements for the use of the prerogative power. It is hard to reach a definitive conclusion on this issue as it is not touched upon directly by Goldsworthy's theory. However, if legislation establishing a referendum would not be capable of binding future Parliaments, it would be odd if this were capable of modifying the legal controls over prerogative powers. Again, it is likely that Goldsworthy would answer this question by examining the provisions of the 2015 Act. In the face of legislative silence, an application of his theory would conclude that the referendum made no difference to the legal controls over prerogative powers. As such, it may well be that he would differ

[20] J Goldsworthy, 'Parliamentary Sovereignty and Constitutional Change in the United Kingdom' in R Rawlings, P Leyland and AL Young (eds), *Sovereignty and the Law: Domestic, European and International Perspectives* (Oxford, Oxford University Press, 2013) 50.

from Dicey's theory, which could be used to require stronger, as opposed to weaker, legal controls over the use of the prerogative to achieve a referendum outcome in order to avoid the dangers of the executive overriding the wishes of the legislature.

III. The Broad Legal Challenge

To set out the broad legal challenge, we need to imagine a possible scenario of the way in which Brexit could have taken place. For example, we could imagine that the *European Union Act 2011* (EUA) was worded differently. Section 2(1) of the EUA states that 'a Treaty which amends or replaces the TEU [Treaty on European Union] or the TFEU [Treaty on the Functioning of the European Union]' cannot be ratified unless this is done by an Act of Parliament and a referendum has been held where a majority of those voting in the referendum vote in favour of the ratification of the Treaty amending, or replacing, the TEU and the TFEU.[21] To this provision, we can add two further imaginary provisions. First, a statutory provision making it clear that the Withdrawal Agreement was a Treaty that would amend or replace the TEU or the TFEU. Second, a requirement that the referendum requirement in section 2(1) was itself protected by a referendum – ie, it was clear that section 2(1) could not be amended other than through an Act of Parliament and a referendum where a majority had voted in favour of repealing section 2(1). The question arises as to what would occur were Parliament to then enact legislation to implement the Withdrawal Agreement, without this having been agreed to by a referendum.

A classic reading of Dicey's theory would conclude that such a referendum requirement could itself be impliedly repealed by future legislation. However, this perpetuates a conundrum central to parliamentary sovereignty. If Parliament is sovereign because it reflects the will of the people, who are politically sovereign, should this not mean that any conflict between a referendum and legislation must be determined in favour of the referendum requirement? Michael Gordon's theory picks up on this tension, arguing that a better understanding of parliamentary sovereignty would enable referendums to be entrenched in this manner, such that future legislation could not be used to impliedly repeal a referendum requirement.[22] Goldsworthy's theory would appear to reach the opposite conclusion. A referendum requirement could not be entrenched as to do so would be to alter the composition of Parliament, and would be contrary to Goldsworthy's conception of parliamentary sovereignty. However, Goldsworthy's theory does admit of a possible means through which a referendum requirement could be entrenched; if there was sufficient evidence of a modification of the rule of recognition, such that the conception of Parliamentary sovereignty had been changed.

A. What Would Dicey Do?

As discussed above, Dicey's theory includes an argument in favour of adopting referendums, seeing this as a form of people's veto over important legislation. Understood in this

[21] The provision has now been overturned by the *European Union (Withdrawal) Act 2018*, Schedule 9.

[22] M Gordon, *Parliamentary Sovereignty in the UK Constitution: Process, Politics and Democracy* (Oxford, Hart Publishing, 2015).

manner, the referendum provides a counter-balance to the growing power of political parties, particularly those political parties that are able to command a large majority in the House of Commons. The withdrawal of the UK from the EU would easily be classified as important legislation given its constitutional significance. Moreover, a referendum on the withdrawal agreement, once designed and legislated upon by Parliament, would fit Dicey's pattern of the referendum operating as a people's veto. The people would be able to see legislation, deliberated on by Parliament, as well as the terms and implications of the Withdrawal Agreement, being therefore able to determine whether they did or did not want the legislation to be enacted in order to implement the Withdrawal Agreement.

Nevertheless, although Dicey wrote in favour of referendums, most of his writing focused on incorporating a referendum in a manner that would not result in Parliament binding its successors. For example, he advocated use of the veto power of the House of Lords as a means of achieving a result similar to referendums. Prior to the enactment of the Parliament Acts 1911–1949, it was possible for the House of Lords to veto legislation. The House of Commons were unable to respond to this veto by enacting legislation without the consent of the second House of the legislature. Dicey argued that the House of Lords should exercise its veto power to prevent legislation that was contrary to the wishes of the electorate, effectively forcing the House of Commons to dissolve and hold a general election focused on the legislation that the House of Lords had decided to veto. Although not ideal, given that such a general election would focus on issues in addition to the legislation which the House of Lords had vetoed, the UK constitution could nevertheless incorporate some of the values of the referendum. Dicey specifically advocated such a course of action with regard to Home Rule, arguing that the House of Lords should insert a clause into the Home Rule Bill that it should not come into force until it has received the approval of the majority of the electorate of Great Britain and Ireland.[23] In doing so, Dicey recognised that the use of a referendum in this manner would protect the principle 'which lies at the basis of English democracy – that a law depends at bottom for its enactment on the assent of the nation as represented by the electors'.[24]

Dicey also recommended that either House could petition the Queen to refuse to give assent to legislation, unless there is a general election in which the electorate can demonstrate its support, or rejection, of that legislation. Dicey also suggested that legislation could be enacted which would not come into force unless it is approved by a vote of the majority of the electorate within six months of its enactment. This could be achieved either by specific legislation on a case-by-case basis, or from a general Act of Parliament which prescribed that legislation enacted in certain subject areas could not come into force without a referendum.[25]

None of these provisions would undermine Dicey's traditional conception of sovereignty. Dicey did not originally advocate that any form of referendum requirement should itself be entrenched. Although recognising that this would mean that any general legislation requiring a referendum for the enactment of legislation in specific areas of the law could itself then be repealed, Dicey was confident that the requirement would command political

[23] AV Dicey, *A Leap in the Dark: A Criticism of the Principles of Home Rule as illustrated by the Bill of 1893*, 2nd edn (London, John Murray, 1911) 136–37.

[24] ibid 137.

[25] Dicey, 'Ought the Referendum' (n 12).

respect and would therefore not easily be ignored. This would not be the case, however, as regards our imaginary legal challenge, where a referendum would be required to approve the Withdrawal Agreement and where this requirement itself could only be removed by a further referendum. However, Dicey's recognition of the importance of democracy resting on the political sovereignty of the people could lead to the conclusion that conceptions of parliamentary sovereignty should allow for a referendum requirement to be entrenched in the manner suggested in our imaginary scenario.

Gordon's account of parliamentary sovereignty, which draws on Dicey, would provide an argument in favour of the entrenchment provision being unable to be removed through implied repeal by future legislation. Gordon provides an account of self-embracing sovereignty. In common with Goldsworthy, he argues that conceptualising parliamentary sovereignty in a manner other than Dicey's conception of continuing parliamentary sovereignty could enhance the sovereign power of Parliament, as it allows Parliament to make long-term commitments. Gordon further argues that conceiving parliamentary sovereignty in this way enhances democracy. As such, he advocates manner and form requirements, and not just form and procedure requirements, which could be used to entrench legislation. Gordon argues that manner and form restrictions are justified when they enhance democracy. Unlike Goldsworthy, he would approve of a manner and form provision which required a referendum to enact important constitutional modifications. For Gordon, this would enhance democracy through requiring a component of direct democracy. Moreover, these requirements may enhance the political restrictions on Parliament, helping the legislature to be aware of ensuring its legislation is in line with the wishes of the electorate.

It may not be the case that Dicey would argue that a requirement of a referendum for the approval of the Withdrawal Agreement, coupled with a referendum requirement to remove such entrenchment, could potentially be impliedly repealed. However, it could also be the case that, in order to enhance the principle on which parliamentary sovereignty is based, Dicey would agree with Gordon's modified account of parliamentary sovereignty, such that a requirement for a referendum could itself only be removed by a further referendum. Understood in this manner, the courts in our imaginary scenario would not give effect to legislation to implement the Withdrawal Agreement unless the referendum requirement had been fulfilled.

B. What Would Goldsworthy Do?

As with our inquiry with Dicey, it would appear to be deceptively easy to provide an answer to our imaginary scenario when applying Goldsworthy's account of parliamentary sovereignty. Goldsworthy does not regard the doctrine of implied repeal as central to the sovereignty of Parliament. Consequently, it is not the case that he would be forced to conclude that any later legislation would impliedly repeal the content of earlier legislation. However, Goldsworthy's theory only permits the entrenchment of procedure and form requirements that would not produce too great a restriction on Parliament's substantive lawmaking power. Not only would a referendum requirement go beyond a form and procedure requirement, making it too difficult for Parliament to then enact legislation to implement the Withdrawal Agreement, but it would also redefine Parliament, incorporating the electorate into the lawmaking process. As such, this would go beyond the form and procedure requirements that could be entrenched through an application of Goldsworthy's theory of the constitution.[26]

However, it is important to recognise that this would not be the end of the inquiry for Goldsworthy. In his later work, Goldsworthy does recognise the possibility of an entrenched referendum requirement. For such a requirement to succeed, there would have to be sufficient evidence of the repudiation of parliamentary sovereignty as a principle of the UK's unwritten constitution.[27] Goldsworthy's account of parliamentary sovereignty rests on regarding parliamentary sovereignty as an aspect of a Hartian rule of recognition.[28] As such, its content is determined by the acceptance of this principle by the officials in the legal system. For the courts to recognise a modification of this doctrine, therefore, they would have to be satisfied that the consensus amongst legislators as a whole had changed, moving from a consensus resting on parliamentary sovereignty, where a referendum requirement could not be entrenched, to a consensus where it was possible to entrench referendum requirements. Such a change would not occur where this was seen to be the imposition of a referendum requirement merely for political gain, or where this expresses the wishes of one particular political party but is not reflective of the legislature as a whole.

Goldsworthy argues that one particular indication of a referendum requirement representing a change in consensus would be the element of symmetric entrenchment – ie, that the requirement for a referendum was itself authorised by a referendum.[29] This aspect of symmetric entrenchment would provide clearer evidence that the referendum requirement was indicative of a modification of the doctrine of parliamentary sovereignty, having been approved by the electorate in addition to the legislature. In addition, it would provide a further moral justification for the judiciary to enforce the referendum requirement; this requirement itself having been approved by the electorate. In particular, this would demonstrate the backing of the sovereignty of the people for the entrenchment of the substantive principles that could only be modified following a referendum.[30] Goldsworthy refers to this as the consensual change thesis.

The criteria of the consensual change thesis are provided as indications of the evidence of a change, and as a justification for this change. As such, they are not necessary, although they may be sufficient to indicate a modification in the rule of recognition so as to allow the entrenchment of referendum requirements. It is hard to know how the courts would evaluate the situation in our hypothetical scenario. The answer may depend upon a range of factors. For example, although we have provided the scenario of Parliament wishing to enact legislation to implement the Withdrawal Agreement, we do not know whether this is the same Parliament as that which initially required a referendum, or whether this is a different Parliament with different political persuasions. Applied to current UK constitutional law, the EUA was enacted during the Conservative and Liberal Democrat Coalition. The hypothetical legislation to implement the Withdrawal Agreement without legislation

[26] Goldsworthy, *Sovereignty of Parliament* (n 1) Ch 7; Goldsworthy, *Parliamentary Sovereignty* (n 2) Ch 10; Goldsworthy, 'Parliamentary Sovereignty and Constitutional Change' (n 20) 66.

[27] Goldsworthy, 'Parliamentary Sovereignty and Constitutional Change' (n 20) 66–67.

[28] Goldsworthy, *Parliamentary Sovereignty* (n 2) Ch 10.

[29] Goldsworthy, 'Parliamentary Sovereignty and Constitutional Change' (n 20) 67.

[30] Goldsworthy, 'Parliamentary Sovereignty and Constitutional Change' (n 20) 67.

would either be enacted by the current Conservative minority Government, which holds a working majority courtesy of a confidence and supply Agreement with the Democratic Unionist Party (DUP), or a differently composed Government holding a working majority in the House of Commons. The difference in composition of the legislature could provide evidence that the referendum requirement had not modified the rule of recognition, given that future legislatures clearly did not feel bound by this requirement. However, it could also provide evidence of a politically-induced preference for not holding a referendum on this issue.

There was no referendum surrounding the enactment of the EUA and, as such, this lack of symmetric entrenchment may provide further evidence that there had been no modification to the rule of recognition. However, on the other hand, there is evidence of a move towards the use of referendums in the UK constitution, both in terms of the membership of the EU,[31] and in terms of issues which affect the constitutional structure of the UK.[32] There is also growing evidence of reference to referendum requirements in legislation.[33] Whilst this may provide evidence of a growing use of referendums, this may not be evidence of a modification of the rule of recognition. None of these provisions endeavour to entrench the referendum requirement itself. This may imply that, whilst there has been an acceptance of the use of referendums, there has not been a modification of the rule of recognition as regards a move away from parliamentary sovereignty.

Goldsworthy's theory of parliamentary sovereignty focuses on the ability of Parliaments to entrench procedure and form requirements, in order to make clear long-term commitments. For example, the UK Parliament could have enacted a procedure and form requirement to demonstrate its long-term commitment to the EU by, for example, requiring future legislation to expressly repeal requirements of EU law, or to be enacted with a specific clause explaining that the legislation in question was to take effect notwithstanding provisions of EU law. This would help to clarify the difficulties that would arise were the UK Parliament to enact legislation which conflicted with directly effective provisions of EU law. In this situation, it can be difficult to determine whether Parliament wished to enact legislation overturning its long-term commitment to membership of the EU, or whether Parliament had inadvertently enacted legislation which contradicted directly effective EU law. By requiring a notwithstanding clause, for example, Parliament has the ability to clarify its intention to legislate contrary to its long-term commitment to EU membership. As such, this furthers Parliament's lawmaking power. It ensures that future Parliaments do not inadvertently legislate contrary to their long-term commitments.

[31] *Referendum Act 1975.*

[32] Northern Ireland Border Poll 1973; the Scottish and Welsh Devolution Referendums in 1979; the devolution referendums in Scotland and Wales in 1997; the referendum in Greater London determining whether to establish an Assembly and an elected Mayor for London; the Good Friday Agreement Referendum in Northern Ireland in 1998; the North East England Devolution Referendum in 2004; the Welsh Devolution Referendum in 2004; the United Kingdom Alternative Vote Referendum in 2011; and the Scottish Independence Referendum in 2014.

[33] *Referendum Act 1975*; *Scotland Act 1978*, s 85; *Wales Act 1978*, s 80; *Referendums (Scotland and Wales) Act 1997*; *Greater London Authority (Referendum) Act 1998*; *Political Parties, Elections and Referendums Act 2000*; *European Union Act 2011*, ss 2, 3, 6, 11–13; *Northern Ireland Act 1998*, s 1; *Local Government Act 2000*, ss 34–36; *Localism Act 2011*, s 72; *Scottish Independence Referendum Act 2013*; *Regional Assemblies (Preparation) Act 2013*, ss 1–6 (repealed); *European Union Referendum Act 2015*.

The referendum requirement envisaged in our hypothetical example could be understood as one designed to make a long-term commitment to the preservation of the status quo. It focuses on ensuring that changes to the UK's membership of the EU require a referendum. There is no evidence of the backing of the sovereignty of the people to this long-term commitment. Moreover, it is arguable that the Brexit referendum provides the backing of the public for the rejection of this long-term commitment. As such, the courts could conclude that there is no normative justification for upholding the referendum requirement. Not only is there evidence of the wishes of the electorate in favour of upholding the UK's long-term commitment to its current membership of the EU, but more importantly, there is evidence of the electorate wishing to break this long-term commitment. However, there are other justifications for a referendum requirement in this situation. First, it could be argued that, although there is evidence of a move away from a long-term commitment to EU membership, there is no general consensus of the electorate as to the nature of the future relationship with the EU. As such, it could be argued that there are good normative reasons for upholding the referendum requirement, and for requiring a referendum in favour of the Withdrawal Agreement. Second, there are other normative reasons for upholding the referendum requirement, focusing on the importance of referendums when introducing constitutional change, particularly one which would have an impact on individual rights.

Whilst it may be hard to predict how Goldsworthy would evaluate these competing arguments, what is clear is that Goldsworthy's approach to the resolution of this issue differs from that of Dicey, and that of Gordon building on Dicey. Dicey's theory prefers referendum requirements which do not require entrenchment, although this may mean that the legal sovereignty of Parliament is preserved over the political sovereignty of the people. Gordon's account would uphold the referendum requirement, preferring to uphold the political sovereignty of the people over the sovereignty of Parliament, given that Parliamentary sovereignty is itself justified through the preservation of democracy and the sovereignty of the people. Goldsworthy's account is more subtle, requiring a more detailed assessment of whether the political facts have changed, such that the UK constitution is no longer based on parliamentary sovereignty. In addition, it would require an evaluation of normative arguments in favour of accepting a modification of the rule of recognition allowing for the entrenchment of referendums, focusing on the legitimacy of the manner in which the referendum requirement was entrenched.

IV. The Normative Challenge

The Brexit referendum raised a deeper normative challenge concerning the conception of democracy in the UK constitution. It touches on deeper tensions that run through democracy; these tensions being ones that are also reflected in accounts of populism. This chapter is not the place to provide a detailed definition of populism – a concept that has eluded precise definition, referred to as a 'difficult and slippery concept';[34] a concept that is circular,

[34] PA Taggart, *Populism* (Buckingham, Open University Press, 2000) 2.

fundamentally elusive and contradictory;[35] and as an essentially contested concept.[36] Difficulties arise when aiming to provide a clear definition of populism given that there is a lack of a historical, ideological or social commonality running through the examples of populism or populist movements,[37] as well as the fact that populism can be used to describe a movement, a group or an ideology.[38] Moreover, those who are described as populist do not adopt the term themselves. Rather, the term is often used to criticise a movement, or as a term of abuse.[39] Its definition can also be subject to modification in order to demonstrate either that all forms of populism are damaging to democracy,[40] or to delineate between good and bad populism; the former being seen as a corrective to, and the latter as damaging democracy.[41] The focus of this section is to evaluate deeper tensions in democracy, and to consider how different conceptions of parliamentary sovereignty may provide a better, or worse, means of resolving these tensions and avoiding the perils of populism; where populism acts not as a corrective to democracy, but as a path to authoritarianism.

In order to evaluate this issue, we need first to provide an account of the perceived problems in democracy that fuel a populist response, or which leave a space for the emergence of populist movements. Political theorists point to two main issues: the boundary problem;[42] and the tension between liberalism and democracy in conceptions of liberal democracy, which leads to a questioning of the authority of courts to strike down democratically-enacted legislation in order to protect liberal principles.[43] Both of these difficulties can give rise to populist movements which may, or may not, harm democracy. This section will argue that Gordon's account of parliamentary sovereignty may appear to provide a better means of resolving the boundary problem, and the difficulties which arise when courts strike down legislation in order to protect liberal principles, as it favours the outcome of referendums over legislation and would enable entrenchment of liberal principles only when this enhances democracy. However, this conclusion fails to take account of when populist movements may enhance – and when they may undermine – liberal democracies. Dicey's and Goldsworthy's accounts provide a better means of channelling populism's ability to correct failings in democracy without giving rise to instances when populism may undermine democracy.

A. The Problems with Liberal Democracy

We argued above that liberal democracies face two problems: the boundary problem, and the difficulty of determining when liberal principles should override democratic legislation.

[35] E Laclau, *On Populist Reason* (London, Verso, 2005).

[36] C Mudde and C Rovira Kaltwasser, *Populism: A Very Short Introduction* (New York, Oxford University Press, 2017) Ch 1.

[37] M Canovan, *The People* (Cambridge, Polity, 2005) 79.

[38] Mudde and Rovira Kaltwasser (n 36) Ch 1.

[39] Canovan, *The People* (n 37) 79; M Canovan, 'Trust the People! Populism and the Two Faces of Democracy' (1999) 47 *Political Studies* 2.

[40] J-W Müller, *What is Populism?* (London, Penguin Books, 2017).

[41] R Howse, 'Populism and its Enemies' (Unpublished) www.trendsmap.com/twitter/tweet/967766744902393857 (last accessed 15 November 2018).

[42] C Rovira Kaltwasser, 'The Responses of Populism to Dahl's Democratic Dilemmas' (2014) 62 *Political Studies* 470, 472–74; Taggart (n 34) Ch 8; M Canovan, '"People", Politicians and Populism' (1984) 19 *Government and Opposition* 312; M Canovan, 'Populism for Political Theorists?' (2004) 9 *Journal of Political Ideologies* 241, 247–50; Canovan, *The People* (n 37) Ch 4.

[43] Canovan, *The People* (n 37) Ch 5; Taggart (n 34) chs 9–10; Rovira Kaltwasser (n 42) 474–77; Canovan, 'Trust the People!' (n 39).

The boundary problem occurs because, although democratic theory regards the people as sovereign, it is difficult to define what is meant by the people. Moreover, the definition of the people cannot be achieved by democratic means. Democracy may require lawmaking power to rest with the people or their representatives, but does not explain who the people are to whom lawmaking power is to be given. Other arguments need to be provided for defining the people who enjoy political sovereignty in any particular legal system. This may be either through merely accepting a particular definition of the people as a fact – eg, the people living in the territory of the United Kingdom, or of Australia – or through an evaluation of normative arguments to determine the identity of the people.

Populism can often be used as a means to plug this gap. A common theme running through accounts of populism is the identification of a particular section in society as 'the real people', whose wishes have been ignored by those in power.[44] This can be expressed through a referendum on a particular issue, as well as via a broader political movement. Populism responds to the lack of a clear identification of the people by challenging reality, and arguing that those in power are not 'the real people'. This may be either because there is a perception that those in power fail to recognise a particular minority group in society, or a perception that those in power focus so much on the rights and interests of minority groups that they fail to recognise the wishes of the 'silent majority' of the people. However, populist theories frequently fail to provide an alternative justification for defining the people in a particular manner, either in terms of the factual accuracy, or the normative desirability of a particular account of the people. Rather, populist theories make an ideological claim, focusing on the identity of one particular group and asserting that this group, and this group alone, are 'the real people', often defined in an homogenous manner to the exclusion of others.

Liberal democracies strive to achieve two apparently competing aims. They recognise the need to protect liberal principles, particularly those aiming to protect minority rights, from erosion by actions of the majority. In addition, they recognise the legitimacy of democratic lawmaking institutions. Tensions arise when non-democratically accountable institutions – eg, courts – enforce liberal principles so as to restrict the activities of democratically accountable lawmakers. If democracy rests on an understanding of the sovereignty of the people, is it right for a non-democratic body to challenge measures enacted by a democratic lawmaking body? If the courts are drawing on principles in a constitutional document, how can we be sure that the liberal principles which the courts rely upon are the liberal principles that a democracy would wish to protect? Populism challenges the right of non-democratic elite institutions to protect liberal principles in this manner. In particular, it sees these principles as out of touch with those that the people would want to protect; it being the job of the people and not the liberal elites to define and protect these principles.

The tension between political and parliamentary sovereignty draws on both of these difficulties. They were also illustrated in the specific example of the Brexit referendum. Concerns were expressed that the UK people were not properly represented in Europe, and that the UK's membership of the EU was limiting the sovereign lawmaking power of the UK Parliament. Moreover, it was claimed that this meant that European values were being

[44] Mudde and Rovira Kaltwasser (n 36) Ch 1; Taggart (n 34) Ch 8; Canovan, *The People* (n 37) Ch 4; M Canovan, *Populism* (London, Junction Books, 1981).

used to override the values of the British people. This is not to suggest that the Brexit referendum is a clear example of a populist movement. Such a claim would be almost impossible to prove, given both the difficulties in providing an accurate definition of populism, and the many motives of those who voted both in favour of leave or remain in the EU referendum. Nor is it to suggest that every referendum is an example of an expression of populism. Rather, it is to recognise that the tensions which can give rise to populist movements were present in the Brexit referendum, and that referendums may be a means of communicating the wishes of the people. Referendums can, but need not, be a means of furthering a populist agenda.

Is there a solution to the tension between the political sovereignty of the people and the legal sovereignty of Parliament, which is less likely to give rise to a situation in which a populist movement capitalises on a referendum, or where the potential damage to democracy that may be caused by populist movements is minimised? At first glance, it would appear that Gordon's approach provides the best solution. His theory ensures that, to the extent there is a conflict between the sovereignty of the people as expressed in a referendum, and the sovereignty of Parliament, the referendum prevails. This preference may alleviate tensions, thereby potentially reducing the opportunity for populism. In addition, Gordon's theory provides a possible resolution of the problem of the identification of the people. The people are able to assert their constitutive sovereignty, and can thereby place a limit on the activities of Parliament. If the courts enforce these limits, they are doing so in order to ensure that the legislature acts within the bounds of its power as established by the people. This would seem to provide an effective channel through which to resolve the tensions that arise in the identification of the people, and in ensuring that institutions which protect rights do so in order to protect the rights as required by the people. This is not the case in Dicey's or Goldsworthy's accounts of sovereignty. Dicey's account of sovereignty prioritises parliamentary sovereignty over the sovereignty of the people. Goldsworthy's account of parliamentary sovereignty does the same, albeit recognising that it may be possible for the rule of recognition to change, allowing for the sovereignty of the people to override parliamentary sovereignty.

However, there are problems with this initially attractive conclusion. The obvious problem is that it provides a solution which tips the balance in one direction; that of favouring the wishes of the people over those of Parliament, and thereby preferring direct to representative democracy. However, if we are to regard populism as emerging when there is a perceived imbalance between the two, how can we be sure that a resolution which always favours the outcome of a referendum is the best means of dealing with this perceived imbalance? It could be that the referendum helps to correct flaws in democracy, ensuring that a group which has been ignored is able to have better democratic representation. However, it could also potentially harm democracy if this leads to the homogenisation and stultification of the will of the people, this being definitively equated with the outcome of the referendum.

If we return to the example of the Brexit referendum, the outcome in that referendum was close. Critics of the referendum outcome may challenge the extent to which the referendum represents the wishes of the people, especially when outcomes can be determined by a relatively small percentage of the votes cast. Those in favour of remaining in the EU, for example, may feel that their view is a better representation of the wishes of the people, perhaps focusing on the extent to which the referendum vote did not represent the wishes of the people in a specific component part of the UK – eg, Scotland or Northern Ireland – or that it did not represent an account of a majority of all of those who could have voted in the referendum. This criticism may be even stronger if the referendum result is always to prevail over legislation. It may fuel, rather than temper, the flames of populism.

More fundamentally, this solution fails to take account of the relationship between populism and democracy. As intimated above, it is not the case that populist movements always undermine democracy. Rather, populism can work as a corrective to, as well as a corruption of, democracy. Adopting a constitution that may channel expressions of the will of the people through referendums, rather than through public protest or even potentially violent protests, may minimise the need for populist uprisings. However, this may not be sufficient to ensure that populist sentiments operate effectively to correct failings in democracy without thereby undermining democracy. To evaluate whether the respective approaches of Gordon, Dicey or Goldsworthy to potential conflicts between popular and parliamentary sovereignty survive this normative challenge, we need to investigate further the extent to which populism may undermine democracy. There are two main themes. First, populism may undermine democratic debate. Second, populism may undermine pluralism. Whilst Dicey's account of parliamentary sovereignty provides a means of responding to the first potential challenge posed by populism, Goldsworthy's account also provides a response to the second of these challenges.

B. Populism and Democracy

Populism may undermine democratic debate by challenging representative institutions which aim to facilitate the formation of consensus. Taggart identifies the mistrust of representative institutions as one of the core features of populism.[45] Populist movements challenge the representative nature of institutions by calling into question the extent to which these institutions represent the wishes of the people. Populism calls for a move away from mediated politics, where political viewpoints are formed through the mediation of political parties, to unmediated politics, where political demands are expressed directly by the people.[46] One theme that appears to be common to differing accounts of populism is a mistrust of elites. This is demonstrated not just through a criticism of the ability of elites to represent the wishes of the people, but also through the way in which populism focuses on the politics of simplicity, drawing on strong dichotomies as opposed to encouraging mediation and co-operation.[47] This undermines the ability of political institutions to reach a consensus, by hollowing out political institutions.[48] These problems are exacerbated when those in power adopt populist positions.[49]

[45] Taggart (n 34) 2.

[46] J Hayward (ed), *Élitism, Populism, and European Politics* (Oxford, Oxford University Press, 1996).

[47] C Pinelli, 'The Populist Challenge to Constitutional Democracy' (2011) 7 *European Constitutional Law Review* 5; Taggart (n 34); Hayward (n 46).

[48] F Decker, 'The Populist Challenge to Liberal Democracy' [2003] (3) *Internationale Politik und Gesellschaft* 47 http://library.fes.de/pdf-files/ipg/ipg-2003-3/artdecker.pdf (last accessed 15 November 2018).

[49] C Mudde and C Rovira Kaltwasser, 'Populism and (Liberal) Democracy: A Framework for Analysis' in C Mudde and C Rovira Kaltwasser (eds), *Populism in Europe and the Americas: Threat or Corrective for Democracy?*

Dicey's account of referendums illustrates that he was aware of these difficulties, albeit that these were not expressed specifically in terms of a desire to avoid populism. Dicey was concerned that referendums could result in the views of the ill-informed replacing those of the informed. This is not to criticise the relative knowledge, or ignorance, of politicians or the electorate. Nor is Dicey aiming to glorify the role of politics and political parties – a mistrust of political parties having motivated Dicey to advocate the use of referendums to prevent institutions enacting important or constitutional legislation without the consent of the people. Rather, it is to recognise the role that political institutions can play in terms of providing detailed deliberation, drawing on different viewpoints to facilitate consensus and collaboration. Dicey's solution was to require a referendum as a veto to legislation that had already been deliberated upon. This enabled the electorate to benefit from political deliberation, minimising the risk that referendums would facilitate the politics of simplicity, or the focus on strong dichotomies, whilst still enabling the people to correct instances when important or constitutional changes would be made without this being according to the wishes of the people.

In addition, Dicey's account of the way in which the wishes of the people were to be taken into account minimises the ability of those in power to adopt populist positions. Dicey saw the House of Lords as playing a prominent role here, refusing to grant assent to legislation when it was felt that those in power were not reflecting the wishes of the people, thereby forcing a general election. Similarly, Dicey advocated that those in power could call upon the Monarch to refuse to give assent to legislation unless, and until, this was approved in a referendum. These mechanisms could minimise the extent to which populism could be used by those in power. If these were the only means through which a referendum could be used, it would not be possible for a government to use its majority in Parliament to call for a referendum on a particular issue, thus using a populist movement to extend its power.

Goldsworthy's account of parliamentary sovereignty may also help to prevent a referendum from leading to the damaging effects of populism. First, although Goldsworthy's account of parliamentary sovereignty does allow for entrenchment, it only permits the entrenchment of procedure and form requirements and would not allow Parliament to redefine itself by incorporating the wishes of the people, expressed through a referendum, as a component of Parliament. This can also serve as a means of preventing populism from being used by those in power. Second, Goldsworthy's theory would only give rise to a situation in which a referendum could be entrenched if there was evidence of a modification of the rule of recognition, which would require evidence not just from whichever government was in power, but an analysis of the behaviour of officials in the system as a whole. For a government to call for a referendum in a particular area may not be sufficient to demonstrate a general move to the entrenchment of referendums, meaning that the requirement of a referendum could be overturned by a future legislature, minimising the extent to which the use of referendums might facilitate the use of populism by incumbent governments. Where Goldsworthy's account of parliamentary sovereignty may provide a further deterrent effect is as regards the second danger of populism – the undermining of pluralism.

(Cambridge, Cambridge University Press, 2012) Ch 1; C Mudde and C Rovira Kaltwasser, 'Populism, Corrective *and* Threat to Democracy' in Mudde and Rovira Kaltwasser, *Populism in Europe and the Americas* (n 49) Ch 10.

C. Populism and Pluralism

Populism undermines pluralism by homogenising the will of the people.[50] It characterises the will of the people as a single, homogenous expression of one will; this will being that of 'the real people', which must therefore be protected over and above other conceptions of the people or conceptions of the public good which are not shared by 'the real people'. This in turn may undermine the protection of civil liberties, as protected liberties are often those of minorities, which do not form part of 'the real people'. There may therefore be calls for these rights to be removed.[51] These pressures become evident in particular when there is a perceived inequality in the distribution of rights and benefits.[52] Mudde and Rovira Kaltwasser argue that these dangers of populism are less likely to occur in States with consolidated, as opposed to unconsolidated, protections of civil liberties and minority rights – ie, those where there are constitutional protections of rights.[53]

Goldsworthy's theory furnishes a means of providing for long-term commitments through the expression of procedure and form requirements. As such, it may be possible for societies that adopt Goldsworthy's account of sovereignty to provide for a stronger protection of minority rights than is provided in systems which provide a traditional, Diceyan protection of sovereignty where long-term commitments to individual rights may be accidentally eroded by later legislation. However, Goldsworthy's account of sovereignty would not permit any one Parliament to bind a future Parliament in such a way that would limit the substantive law-making capacities of that future Parliament. Whilst a future Parliament may have to use a specific form and procedure to clearly illustrate its intention to legislate contrary to a long-standing commitment, it is still able to legislate contrary to these commitments. This may enable a protection of civil liberties that does not stray too far from the wishes of the people, thereby preserving aspects of pluralism and equality. There would need to be a clearer expression of Parliament to remove these long-term commitments.

In addition, Goldsworthy's account would only allow for the entrenchment of the referendum requirement when certain conditions were met: where the entrenchment of a referendum requirement is itself found in a referendum, and when there is clear evidence of a change in political facts; changing the conception of parliamentary sovereignty into a conception which allows for substantive limits to be placed on future Parliaments; or one which recognises a redefinition of the legislature to include the electorate, as expressed through a referendum. We discussed above how this evaluation could make it harder for populist movements to gain government control, or for governments to rely on populism as a means through which to further their own objectives. In addition, courts would take account of the normative justifications provided in support of a move towards a conception of sovereignty which allows entrenchment through referendums. These justifications may be stronger when referendums are required to make broad constitutional changes, or to

[50] Decker (n 48); Mudde and Rovira Kaltwasser, 'Populism and (Liberal) Democracy' (n 49).

[51] P Alston, 'The Populist Challenge to Human Rights' (2017) 9 *Journal of Human Rights Practice* 1.

[52] Mudde and Rovira Kaltwasser, 'Populism and (Liberal) Democracy' (n 49).

[53] Mudde and Rovira Kaltwasser, 'Populism and (Liberal) Democracy' (n 49). See also D Laycock, 'Populism and Democracy in Canada's Reform Party' in Mudde and Rovira Kaltwasser, *Populism in Europe and the Americas* (n 49) Ch 3.

modify civil liberties. As such, this may provide an extra means of ensuring that the conflict between popular and parliamentary sovereignty is not always resolved in a manner which may facilitate the damaging effects of populism on democracy. Courts will not automatically resolve this tension in favour of either parliamentary or popular sovereignty. Rather, normative justifications will play a part in determining whether referendum requirements should be entrenched or not. However, although this may minimise some of the damaging effects of populism, this is achieved indirectly as opposed to directly. There may be no direct means of preserving pluralism, and preventing the homogenisation of the will of the people being expressed through a referendum.

V. Conclusion

There is no easy answer to the potential conundrum between parliamentary and popular sovereignty. The attraction of Goldsworthy's solution is its recognition of this fact. Whilst his theory favours the sovereignty of Parliament over the sovereignty of the people, it does so in a manner that enables Parliament to make long-term commitments, potentially providing conditions in which constitutional systems can preserve protections of pluralism and liberal principles, whilst at the same time enabling these commitments to be changed more easily than when they are constitutionally entrenched. In addition, Goldsworthy's theory may also provide a means through which to entrench referendum requirements, albeit one which requires an analysis of political facts and normative justifications in favour of a modification of the rule of recognition to permit the entrenchment of referendum requirements.

However, it is also important to recognise ways in which even Goldsworthy's account of parliamentary sovereignty may leave constitutional systems vulnerable to the potentially damaging impact of populism on democracy. There is no direct connection between the arguments relating to whether referendums should take priority over legislation, and the need to protect against the homogenisation of the will of the people, or the over-simplification of politics which detracts from deliberative democracy. These dangers are only protected indirectly – either through Parliament wishing to preserve these elements in legislation- regulating referendums, or through factors that may influence whether there are justifications for accepting a modification of the rule of recognition such that referendum requirements can be entrenched. To this extent, a better solution would be to incorporate some of the arguments from Dicey – in relation to the potential advantages and disadvantages of referendums – into the normative arguments used to determine whether courts should accept a modification of the rule of recognition allowing for the entrenchment of referendum requirements. Moreover, it may be better if this is done on a case-by-case basis, rather than being used as a justification for a general modification of the rule of recognition.

The Brexit referendum brought these issues to the fore because of the divisive nature of the referendum, and the way in which the referendum outcome reflected how populism may both facilitate and undermine democracy. There were those who voted in favour of leaving the EU, at least in part, because they felt that their needs had been ignored for a long time in the UK. These votes reflected the belief that decisions of Parliament had failed to take account of the interests or needs of those in lower income brackets, particularly those in constituencies far-removed from Westminster. However, there has also been criticism as to misleading statements provided by some on either side of the campaign, in addition to suspicion that charismatic politicians and campaigners were aiming to present a simplistic account, rallying around an homogenised will of the people, and preferring emotional assertions to rational arguments.

An application of Dicey's arguments may provide support for the holding of a second referendum, allowing the people to vote on whether to accept the specific withdrawal agreement, which emerges from discussions between the UK and the other 27 EU Member States. However, whilst there may be sound constitutional reasons for doing so, unless this referendum is accompanied by rational arguments, and recognises the legitimate range of views represented in the will of the people, a second referendum may pose an even greater danger that further populist movements may undermine as opposed to reinforce democracy. Applying Goldsworthy's approach, taking account of the extent to which referendum outcomes may merely be furthering the homogenisation of the will of the people and over-simplifying, and eroding, the political process, may provide a better means of understanding the extent to which we should prioritise referendums; helping to determine whether there are good reasons for the sovereignty of the people to override the sovereignty of Parliament.

10

Democracy, Mixed Government and Judicial Review

RICHARD S KAY*

I. Introduction

Jeffrey Goldsworthy has been a formidable scholar in public law and legal theory, notably in connection with the relationship between courts and legislatures in the creation and interpretation of law. His *The Sovereignty of Parliament: History and Philosophy*[1] is a near definitive explanation of the development of and the justifications for parliamentary sovereignty. Under that doctrine, a legally unlimited power to make and change rules of positive law is vested in a politically accountable legislature. Such a system may be contrasted with those – much more common these days – in which politically accountable lawmaking institutions may be checked and limited by decisions of unelected constitutional courts. The arguments for one or another of these models resonate with a central concern of American constitutional theorists; namely the propriety of constitutional judicial review that may thwart the actions of elected decision-makers. This is the famous 'counter-majoritarian difficulty'; the assumption that judicial review must be a 'deviant institution' in a country committed to democratic government.[2]

Commentators on this issue usually take it for granted that, presumptively, collective decisions should be made democratically; that is, decided in a way that respects the preferences of the population to be affected by those decisions. Any departure from this practice – in this case, the right of unelected judges to intervene – demands special justification. Apart from a bare assertion that the only 'morally supportable' government was based on consent,[3] Alexander Bickel, who coined the phrase 'counter-majoritarian difficulty', made no attempt to explain why democracies were superior to any other kinds of government.

* I am grateful for helpful suggestions from James Allan, Dale Smith and Scott Stephenson. I received essential research assistance from Anastasiya Collins.

[1] J Goldsworthy, *The Sovereignty of Parliament: History and Philosophy* (Oxford, Oxford University Press, 1999). In a subsequent volume, Goldsworthy collected his later writing responding to critical evaluations of his positions: J Goldsworthy, *Parliamentary Sovereignty: Contemporary Debates* (Cambridge, Cambridge University Press, 2010).

[2] AM Bickel, *The Least Dangerous Branch: The Supreme Court at the Bar of Politics* (Indianapolis, Bobbs-Merrill Company, 1962) 16, 18. See B Friedman, 'The History of the Countermajoritarian Difficulty, Part One: The Road to Judicial Supremacy' (1998) 73 *New York University Law Review* 333, 334 (The counter-majoritarian difficulty is the 'central obsession of modern constitutional scholarship'.).

[3] Bickel, ibid 20.

It may never have occurred to him that such an explanation was necessary.[4] Usually when we speak of democratic government, we mean what Christopher Achen and Larry Bartels have called the 'folk theory' of democracy in which the preferences of the population determine social decisions.[5] That theory assumes that legislatures are the 'faithful mirrors of the popular will' and the 'responsible delegates of average citizens'.[6] Democracy, that is, is understood to be government 'by the people', as well as 'of' and 'for' the people.[7]

In section II., I will summarise what many observers have found to be the virtues of democratic government. I will then raise some difficulties associated with the decision-making competence of voters, difficulties which may have been exacerbated in recent decades. I conclude this part by describing factors that may be thought to have 'perfected' democracy, causing it to reflect more accurately the preferences of the population. In section III., I return to the institution of judicial review and suggest that, if we put aside its traditional justifications, its interaction with the elected departments of the state resembles a 'mixed government'; one in which power is shared among institutions representing different interests. I raise the possibility that such a government's attraction may lie exactly in its tendency to check the decisions made by faithful representatives of the people. In section IV., I raise certain caveats concerning the costs and benefits of this judicial review version of mixed government, noting that, whatever its merits, it may lack the best qualities claimed for both mixed government and the constitutional state.

II. The Majoritarian Difficulty

A. Virtues and Vices of Democracy

These days the unique desirability of democratic government appears axiomatic.[8] Several virtues are identified with it. It operationalises the idea that human beings should only be subject to constraints to which they have consented.[9] Just government, therefore, requires that the people subject to it have a say in approving the measures it imposes. Goldsworthy quotes the sixteenth century cleric, Richard Hooker: a 'law is the deed of the whole body politic, whereof if you judge yourselves to be any part, then is the *law even your deed* also'.[10] A corollary to this is that each member of society, all of whom are subject to its laws, has a right to have his or her desires counted equally in the making of collective decisions.[11]

[4] For a more recent and astute discussion of judicial review sharing the same assumptions, see MJ Perry, *Constitutional Rights, Moral Controversy, and the Supreme Court* (Cambridge, Cambridge University Press, 2008) 41–47, 169–87.

[5] CH Achen and LM Bartels, *Democracy for Realists: Why Elections Do Not Produce Responsive Government* (Princeton, Princeton University Press, 2016) 1.

[6] L Hilbink, 'Beyond Manicheanism: Assessing the New Constitutionalism' (2006) 65 *Maryland Law Review* 15, 21 (referring to the 'many ways in which public representation can and does break down in the legislature'.).

[7] RA Dahl, *Democracy and Its Critics* (New Haven, Yale University Press, 1989) 233.

[8] See EL Rubin, 'Getting Past Democracy' (2001) 149 *University of Pennsylvania Law Review* 711, 725 ('Democracy … is virtually a synonym for good or desirable in modern political and academic discourse'.).

[9] *United States Declaration of Independence* (4 July 1776) para 2.

[10] Quoted in Goldsworthy, *Sovereignty of Parliament* (n 1) 263 (emphasis added).

[11] See Goldsworthy, *Sovereignty of Parliament* (n 1) 263; J Waldron, *Law and Disagreement* (Oxford, Oxford University Press, 1999) 283.

Apart from this intrinsic merit, democracy is praised for its consequences.[12] Some of these are intangible. It is supposed to make better citizens. Participation in the political process fosters an appreciation of the benefits of community and sharpens the important social skills of communication and cooperation.[13] Decisions concurred in by the greater part of the population might also be better decisions in terms of social welfare. Condorcet argued that the more people assent to a group decision, the more probable that the decision will be 'right'.[14] More concretely, there is ample evidence that democratic societies have, in fact, been successful in ways that human beings generally value. They are, on the whole, more prosperous, more peaceful and more respectful of the rights of individuals.[15]

Although '[t]he folk theory of democracy celebrates the wisdom of popular judgments by informed and engaged citizens. The reality is quite different'.[16] As a matter of history, its place of honour is fairly recent. The vaunted – and often misrepresented – democracy of Athens was, after all, the system that put Socrates (himself, a consistent critic of democracy) to death for corrupting Athenian youth.[17] Plato believed that public decisions were best committed to the few men who were versed in the 'royal science'.[18] In *Gorgias*, he assumed that the ignorance of the 'mob' ended up vesting demagogues with dangerous power. He criticised the rhetorician as someone ignorant about the subject matter of his arguments, who acted 'not by teaching but by persuading', so that 'one who does not know … will be more persuasive than the one who knows among those who don't know'.[19] The later Greek historian, Polybius, of whom we will have more to say, was sure that 'every multitude is fickle, full of lawless desires, unreasoned passion, and violent anger'.[20]

Little in the ensuing centuries discredited this sceptical view. Certainly, it was alive and well by the eighteenth century when British statesmen began to think self-consciously about parliamentary government. As Goldsworthy notes, its defenders were at pains to distinguish it from government actually determined by the views of the 'people'. The essayist, Joseph Addison, defended the sovereignty of Parliament but warned against the 'tumultuary rabble', stating: '[N]othing can be more contemptible and insignificant, than the scum of a

[12] Goldsworthy calls these 'goal-based' grounds for democracy: Goldsworthy, *Parliamentary Sovereignty* (n 1) 211.

[13] See Goldsworthy, *Parliamentary Sovereignty* (n 1) 263.

[14] Condorcet's proof was based on probability theory. It has been shown that the hypothetical conditions on which it is based are usually unrealistic in practice. See, eg, Achen and Bartels (n 5) 40–41; PH Edelman, 'On Legal Interpretations of the Condorcet Jury Theorem' (2002) 31 *Journal of Legal Studies* 327. Aristotle had come to a similar conclusion. 'Even though none of the many is individually a man of excellence, nevertheless they can be better when they are all together … With each of the many having a part of excellence and intelligence, when they join together they become like a single person': Aristotle, *Politics* (translated by H Rackham) (Cambridge, Massachusetts, Harvard University Press, 1944) ss 1281a–1281b.

[15] See generally MH Halperin, JT Siegle and MM Weinstein, *The Democracy Advantage: How Democracies Promote Prosperity and Peace*, revised edn (New York, Routledge, 2010) (documenting superior economic growth in developing countries that adopt democratic government).

[16] Achen and Bartels (n 5) 9.

[17] Plato, *The Apology of Socrates* (translated by DF Neville) (London, FE Robinson & Company, 1901) 67–71.

[18] Plato, *Statesman* (revised by M Oswald and translated by JB Skemp) (Indianapolis, Hackett, 1992) 7.

[19] Plato, *Gorgias and Phaedrus: Rhetoric, Philosophy, and Politics* (translated by JH Nichols) (Ithaca, Cornell University Press, 1998) 458e, 459b.

[20] Polybius, *The Complete Histories of Polybius* (translated by WR Paton) (LaVergne, Tenn., Digireads, 2009) 364.

people, when they are instigated against a king, who is supported by the two branches of the legislature'.[21] It is worth noting that Addison was a Whig, the more 'popular' party.[22]

Similar doubts about democracy were widely shared among the governing classes in North America when constitutions started being written, in the late eighteenth century. John Adams, the principal author of the *Massachusetts Constitution of 1780*, whose writing influenced many of the era's constitutions, wrote to Thomas Jefferson in 1815: There had to be 'a democratical branch in the Constitution', but only a 'branch'. He warned that, when unrestrained, the 'people' 'have been as unjust, tyrannical, brutal, barbarous, and cruel, as any king or senate possessed of uncontrollable power'.[23] The debate on 31 May 1787, at the Philadelphia Convention that drafted the *United States Constitution*, considered the composition and selection of the houses of the proposed national legislature. When it was moved that one of the houses be directly elected by the people of the states, Elbridge Gerry of Massachusetts complained that, '[t]he people do not want virtue, but are the dupes of pretended patriots. … [T]hey are daily misled into the most baneful measures and opinions by the false reports circulated by designing men'.[24] George Mason, a proponent of the proposal, 'admitted that we had been too democratic but was afraid we should incautiously run into the opposite extreme'. The danger was reduced by pairing this body with an *indirectly* elected second chamber that would hedge against the risks of popular government. According to Edmund Randolph of Virginia, the Senate would help 'to provide a cure for the evils under which the United States labored [arising from] the turbulence and follies of democracy'.[25] The authors of *The Federalist Papers*, advocating ratification of the Convention's Constitution, agreed. In *The Federalist No 59*, Alexander Hamilton asserted that the more numerous the assembly, 'the greater is known to be the ascendancy of passion over reason … [and] the greater will be the proportion of members of limited information and of weak capacities'.[26] In defending the Senate, Madison praised the intervention of 'some temperate and respectable body of citizens' to delay actions of the people who necessarily will sometimes be 'stimulated by some irregular passion, or some illicit advantage'.[27]

Even today, occasional challenges to democracy still appear, and are based on grounds similar to the historical arguments cited. They depend, that is, on assertions about the ignorance and incompetence of the population, and its vulnerability to deception and manipulation. The classic statement of the modern critique is Jose Ortega y Gasset's *The Revolt of the Masses*, published in 1930. Ortega detailed the evils that could be predicted from the 'accession of the masses to complete social power'.[28] As 'civilization becomes

[21] Quoted in Goldsworthy, *Sovereignty of Parliament* (n 1) 177.

[22] See also Goldsworthy, *Sovereignty of Parliament* (n 1) 177 (quoting Walpole and Burke).

[23] Quoted in GS Wood, *The Creation of the American Republic, 1776–1787* (Chapel Hill, University of North Carolina Press, 1969) 578.

[24] M Farrand (ed), *The Records of the Federal Convention of 1787* (New Haven, Yale University Press, 1911) Vol 1, 48.

[25] G Hunt and J Brown Scott (eds), *The Debates in the Federal Convention of 1787: Which Framed the Constitution of the United States of America* (New York, Oxford University Press, 1920) 32–34.

[26] A Hamilton, 'The Federalist No 59' in C Rossiter (ed), *The Federalist Papers* (New York, New American Library, 1961) 360.

[27] J Madison, 'The Federalist No 62' in Rossiter, ibid 384.

[28] J Ortega y Gasset, *The Revolt of the Masses* (New York, WW Norton, 1932) 11.

more complex and difficult', the 'number of people whose minds are equal to [its] problems becomes increasingly smaller'.[29] In these circumstances, 'command over public life' had been turned over to 'the intellectually vulgar'.[30]

A few contemporary critics still rehearse these themes, notwithstanding developments that might appear to have made voters smarter and better informed. There has been a substantial increase in educational attainment. In 1940, one fourth of the United States population had received a high school diploma. By 2015, that number had risen to 88 per cent. In the same period, the percentage of adults with college or university degrees rose from less than five per cent to 33 per cent.[31] The availability of information relevant to political decisions has also dramatically increased. This can be observed in the multiplication of broadcast sources, including 24-hour news channels. And, of course, the Internet has made it spectacularly easier and cheaper to access, and to disseminate news and opinion of every kind.

Still, there is reason to doubt that these developments have translated into more capable voters. We are all familiar with surveys demonstrating that a substantial part of the population cannot answer even basic questions about government and society.[32] There is even reason to doubt that much of the public holds positions which might be translated into political opinions. Voters, that is, may not 'really know what they want'.[33] This not only prevents voters from choosing candidates who will translate their opinion into policy, it also undermines the 'retrospective theory' of accountability whereby the population rewards or punishes elected officials who enhance or diminish their well-being. Research suggests that voters as a whole are largely incapable of measuring the performance of incumbents or, indeed, of evaluating whether their welfare has improved or declined.[34] Moreover, there is reason to believe that political choice is influenced far more by a voter's identification with certain social groups including, but not limited to political parties, than it is by any ideological or policy preference.[35] For reasons to be considered, this tendency may have been dramatically intensified by developments in information technology.

Ilya Somin has suggested a structural explanation for political ignorance. Since the probability of any individual's vote altering the outcome of an election is very close to zero, the 'benefits of devoting more than minimal time and effort are greatly outweighed by the costs'.[36] If correct, this calculation is unlikely to change even in the face of new tools and resources. In fact, as Somin reports, 'political knowledge in the American electorate has

[29] ibid 90.

[30] ibid 70.

[31] CL Ryan and K Bauman, 'Educational Attainment in the United States: 2015' (*US Census Bureau*, Current Population Report P20-578, March 2016) www.census.gov/content/dam/Census/library/publications/2016/demo/p20-578.pdf (last accessed 19 November 2018).

[32] For one example among many, see T Jensen, 'Democrats and Republicans Differ on Conspiracy Theory Beliefs' (*Public Policy Polling*, 2 April 2013) www.publicpolicypolling.com/wp-content/uploads/2017/09/PPP_Release_National_ConspiracyTheories_040213.pdf (last accessed 19 November 2018) (finding, inter alia, that 28% of Americans believed that 'a secretive power elite with a globalist agenda is conspiring to eventually rule the world though an authoritarian world government').

[33] Achen and Bartels (n 5) 30. See also 30–37.

[34] Achen and Bartels (n 5) 91–175.

[35] Achen and Bartels (n 5) 213–66, 297–301.

[36] I Somin, *Democracy and Political Ignorance: Why Smaller Government is Smarter*, 2nd edn (Stanford, Stanford University Press, 2016) 74.

increased only modestly, if at all since the beginning of mass survey research in the late 1930s'.[37] The problem with this situation 'is that behavior that is individually rational may have major negative effects on society as a whole'.[38]

There are two reasons to think, in fact, that the problem of political incapacity in the general population may be getting *worse*. First, the information revolution has not just failed to improve the judgement of voters, it may also have increased the confidence with which they hold their unfounded positions. Second, both legal and non-legal rules, practices and institutions associated with political decisions have changed in ways that cause those decisions more accurately to mirror the uninformed preferences of the population.

B. The Competence of the Electorate

The drastic increase in the volume of available information may have been matched by an at least equal increase in the share of that information taken up by erroneous propositions. The result is captured in the quip that, 'it's better not to know quite so many things than to know so many things that ain't so'.[39] The competition for a mass audience in both print and electronic media has created incentives for slick presentation and simplified material. Thomas Nichols has commented that:

> [E]veryone involved in the news industry knows that if the reports aren't pretty or glossy or entertaining enough, the fickle viewing public can find other, less taxing alternatives with the click of a mouse or the press of a button on a television remote.[40]

The defects are most obvious on Internet sites, which are often unfiltered and unedited, and therefore notoriously prone to inaccuracy, if not downright falsehood. In a much-quoted depiction of a blogger, Jonathan Klein, a former television network news executive, described 'a guy sitting in his living room in his pajamas writing what he thinks'.[41] The problems may be aggravated by the ability and inclination of online publishers to promote the most popular posted items. One study found that stories on the 'most read' list were kept longer on the 'front pages' of major newspaper sites.[42] The massive amount of available data, both true and false, requires time, care and judgement to sort out. Such resources are simply unavailable in sufficient quantity to the average citizen. The result, as Nichols points out, can be a 'chaotic mess that does not inform people so much as it creates the illusion of being informed'.[43]

[37] ibid 21. See also 198–99.

[38] ibid 75.

[39] This line has been attributed to many people, most commonly to Mark Twain. For an exhaustive survey identifying the nineteenth century humourist, Josh Billings, see 'It Is Better to Know Nothing Than to Know What Ain't So' (*Quote Investigator*, 30 May 2015) www.quoteinvestigator.com/2015/05/30/better-know/ (last accessed 19 November 2018).

[40] TM Nichols, *The Death of Expertise: The Campaign Against Established Knowledge and Why It Matters* (New York, Oxford University Press, 2017) 22.

[41] A Barlow and R Leston, *Beyond the Blogosphere: Information and Its Children* (Santa Barbara, Praeger, 2012) 31.

[42] J Bright and T Nicholls, 'The Life and Death of Political News: Measuring the Impact of Audience Agenda Using Online Data' (2014) 32 *Social Science Computer Review* 170. The authors controlled for the fact that longer lasting articles were, for that reason alone, more likely to be read: at 178.

[43] Nichols (n 40) 129.

As noted, people's political behaviour is often more a result of group identification than of considered views on public issues. This manifests itself in the way people pattern their consumption of information, and results in the abundance of information reinforcing rather than testing their political preferences. Achen and Bartels note that: 'Once inside the conceptual framework, the voter finds herself inhabiting a relatively coherent universe. Her preferred candidates, her political opinions, and even her view of the facts will all tend to go together nicely'.[44] People seek out news providers with whom they are already well acquainted, thereby walling out unfamiliar and challenging opinion.[45] Modern research has shown that the evaluation of new information is 'biased by the apparent consistency of that evidence with the perceiver's theories and expectations'.[46] People even find it easier to learn new material if it will fit into their pre-established preferences.[47] This 'confirmation bias' is intensified by algorithms employed in popular websites, which lead readers to sources most resembling material they have already read. The result has been called a 'filter bubble'. According to one website owner, '[t]he danger is that increasingly you end up not seeing what people who think differently see and in fact not even knowing that it exists'.[48]

It gets worse. In addition to favouring information conforming to their existing preferences, people instinctively resist contrary information when they do encounter it. In the modern information environment, that is, opinions harden. In many people, the activity of watching hours of reports from all-news television channels, or of clicking through massive volumes of online material, fosters the illusion that they understand political issues.[49] One experiment showed that, when presented with factual reports which conflicted with their prior opinions, readers were not just unconvinced, but perceived the conflicting accounts as unfairly biased.[50] Another study showed that, when a subject confronted reports that contradicted his or her deeply held beliefs, there was a 'backfire effect'. The original beliefs were clung to with even greater force.[51] Given this research, it is no surprise that a 2017 Gallup Poll found that 88 per cent of Donald Trump voters reported that media criticism

[44] Achen and Bartels (n 5) 268.

[45] MS Hindman, *The Myth of Digital Democracy* (Princeton, Princeton University Press, 2009) 73, 90.

[46] CG Lord, L Ross and MR Lepper, 'Biased Assimilation and Attitude Polarization: The Effects of Prior Theories on Subsequently Considered Evidence' (1979) 37 *Journal of Personality and Social Psychology* 2098, 2099.

[47] J Jerit and J Barabas, 'Partisan Perceptual Bias and the Information Environment' (2012) 74 *The Journal of Politics* 672, 673–74.

[48] Eli Pariser quoted in 'The Reason Your Feed Became an Echo Chamber – And What to Do About It' *National Public Radio* (24 July 2016) www.npr.org/sections/alltechconsidered/2016/07/24/486941582/the-reason-your-feed-became-an-echo-chamber-and-what-to-do-about-it (last accessed 19 November 2018). The marginalisation of novel opinions is reinforced by the tendency of Internet users to follow links that are seen to have been most frequently accessed by others: F Manjoo, 'I Ignored Trump News for a Week. Here's What I Learned' *The New York Times* (22 February 2017) www.nytimes.com/2017/02/22/technology/trump-news-media-ignore.html?_r=0 (last accessed 19 November 2018).

[49] See Nichols (n 40) 129–30.

[50] RP Vallone, L Ross and MR Lepper, 'The Hostile Media Phenomenon: Biased Perception and Perceptions of Media Bias in Coverage of the Beirut Massacre' (1985) 49 *Journal of Personality and Social Psychology* 577.

[51] B Nyhan and J Reifler, 'When Corrections Fail: The Persistence of Political Misperceptions' (2010) 32 *Political Behavior* 303, 307. The remarkable impact of Internet use on political beliefs is demonstrated by a 2015 study which concluded that people who had been using Internet search engines were more confident in their beliefs not only with respect to the materials they were searching, but also in connection with questions *unrelated to those searches*: M Fisher, MK Goddu and FC Keil, 'Searching for Explanations: How the Internet Inflates Estimates of Internal Knowledge' (2015) 144 *Journal of Experimental Psychology: General* 674.

of the President reinforced their conviction that he was 'on the right track'.[52] Even more alarming, it appears that the least informed citizens seem to be most confident about their views.[53] This is a special case of the general proposition that incompetent people may, amongst other things, lack the competence to know the limits of their own capacity.[54] In sum, to an alarming extent, people are misinformed, confident of the correctness of their inaccurate beliefs, and resistant to education or correction.[55] As Nichols concludes, 'alone in front of the keyboard but awash in websites, newsletters, and online groups dedicated to confirming any and every idea, the Internet has politically and intellectually mired millions of Americans in their own biases'.[56]

C. Democracy Perfected

The second reason to think that democratic decision-making may be becoming riskier concerns the ways in which the rules of political participation have changed. The word 'democracy' covers a wide range of government arrangements. A direct vote of the actual population on every mooted issue has, for obvious reasons, rarely been attempted. Ancient Athenian democracy did briefly rely on the deliberation and vote of every citizen, but the voting citizens were a fairly small percentage of the governed population.[57] As a practical matter, the choices of a population can only be exercised indirectly though some kind of representation. In modern states, moreover, a variety of specialised institutions will usually be established to carry out public functions skillfully and efficiently. Generally, all of these institutions will be answerable to the governed population, but only periodically and indirectly. In such societies, the democratic will is transformed as it passes through these intermediate bodies and is directed into established channels. What emerges will differ significantly from application of the initial raw popular preference.[58] One consequence of this structure and process is that expert, elite opinion will exert a powerful influence. According to Robert Dahl, 'expertise is so important that our systems of government have sometimes been called a mixture of democracy and meritocracy'.[59]

[52] G Sargent, 'Trump's Lies Are Working Brilliantly. This New Poll Proves It' *The Washington Post* (27 April 2017).

[53] JH Kuklinski and others, 'Misinformation and the Currency of Democratic Citizenship' (2000) 62 *The Journal of Politics* 790. There is little comfort in the fact that another study concluded, that 'the most knowledgeable voters tend to be more biased in their evaluation of new evidence than those with less prior political information': Somin (n 36) 95.

[54] This is sometimes referred to as the Dunning-Kruger effect, because of its articulation in a 1999 article: J Kruger and D Dunning, 'Unskilled and Unaware of It: How Difficulties in Recognizing One's Own Incompetence Lead to Inflated Self-Assessments' (1999) 77 *Journal of Personality and Social Psychology* 1121.

[55] Kuklinski and others (n 53) 795, 810.

[56] Nichols (n 40) 121.

[57] K von Fritz, *The Theory of the Mixed Constitution in Antiquity: A Critical Analysis of Polybius' Political Ideas* (New York, Columbia University Press, 1954) 342. '[N]ot only were women excluded (as of course they continued to be in all democracies until the twentieth century), but also long-term resident aliens (*metics*) and slaves. Since the requirement for Athenian citizenship from 451 onward was that both parents must be Athenian citizens themselves, citizenship was for all practical purposes a hereditary privilege based on primordial ties of kinship (though full citizenship was a privilege inheritable only by males)': Dahl, *Democracy* (n 7) 22.

[58] J Brennan, *Against Democracy* (Princeton, Princeton University Press, 2016) 171.

[59] Dahl, *Democracy* (n 7) 57.

One of the most striking changes in the operation of modern democracies, occurring in recent decades, is that the processes just described have deferred more and more to the unmediated preferences of the population. Of course, some developments appear to have taken the opposite direction. Most obvious has been the emergence of the administrative state. The day-to-day business of government is largely carried out by agencies removed from the direct influence of the people. This complicated bureaucracy effectively legislates and enforces rules that have only the scantest connection to policies enacted by elected legislatures.[60] The agencies, moreover, adjudicate disputed questions about compliance with those rules. Judicial oversight of these agencies is necessarily sporadic. Courts, moreover, are often at a loss to evaluate administrative decisions in highly specialised fields. While it is undeniable that the administrative state has inserted a distinctly undemocratic element into modern government, it is worth noting that Bickel still found judicial review to pose a qualitatively greater counter-majoritarian difficulty. Conceding that 'admirals and generals and the members, say, of the Federal Reserve Board or of this or that administrative agency are not electorally responsible', he insisted that the system as a 'whole operates under public scrutiny and criticism'. So 'the essential majority power is there and is felt to be there'.[61]

Whatever reduction the advent of modern bureaucracy has worked on the influence of democratic choice must be evaluated in light of the opposite tendency which arises from the erosion of other legal obstacles to the expression of popular will. The suspicions of many of the American founders regarding democratic government have already been noted. The set of institutions created in the original Constitution of 1787–89 could barely be said to amount to a democracy at all. In his celebrated argument against 'faction', in *The Federalist No 10*, James Madison was most concerned with the dangers of a *majority* faction whose position would enable it to subordinate the public good to 'its ruling passion'. This, he thought, was a genuine risk in democracies constituted in societies 'consisting of a small number of people'. That danger was reduced in the proposed government of the United States. It would be established over a large population and extended over a vast territory, making the coalescence of a majority faction difficult. But Madison also stressed the reassuring fact that political power would be held by only 'a small number of citizens elected by the rest'. This setup would

> refine and enlarge the public views by passing them through the medium of a chosen body of citizens, whose wisdom may best discern the true interest of their country … Under such a regulation

[60] See A Vermeule, 'The Administrative State: Law, Democracy, and Knowledge' in M Tushnet, MA Graber and S Levinson (eds), *The Oxford Handbook of the US Constitution* (Oxford, Oxford University Press, 2015) 259, 267–68.

[61] Bickel (n 2) 18–20. See also EL Rubin, *Beyond Camelot: Rethinking Politics and Law for the Modern State* (Princeton, Princeton University Press, 2005) 116–24. The transfer of governmental power from national to supranational organisations may present another example of apparent reduction of democratic authority, at least if the relevant *demos* continues to be defined on the national level. The expansion of the jurisdiction of the European Union is the most obvious example. In so far as EU institutions themselves are not answerable to elected representatives, this 'democratic deficit' is aggravated. The classic statement is set out in JHH Weiler, UR Haltern and FC Mayer, 'European Democracy and Its Critique' (1995) 18(3) *West European Politics* 4. The ultimate supervisory power of national public opinion, in this case, is dramatically demonstrated by the 2016 Referendum in which voters in the United Kingdom expressed their preference for withdrawing from the European Union. See E Mavrozacharakis, SI Tzagkarakis and A Kamekis, 'Brexit: A Consequence of the European Social and Democratic Deficit' (University of Crete, Working Paper, 2017) www.ssoar.info/ssoar/handle/document/51586 (last accessed 19 November 2018).

> it may well happen that the public voice, pronounced by the representatives of the people, will be more consonant to the public good than if pronounced by the people themselves.[62]

This philosophy was built into the new government. Most of the American founders believed that a 'republican' government had ultimately to be grounded in popular choice, but they wanted that choice to play out only after reconsideration and refinement by wiser and more responsible minds. The executive was to be chosen by an electoral college consisting of members deputed by each state 'in such manner as the legislature thereof may direct'.[63] There would be two houses of the legislature with one, the Senate, consisting of two representatives from each state who would serve six-year terms and who would be selected by that state's legislature. Only in the second legislative chamber, the House of Representatives, do we find officials who are to be 'chosen every second year by the people of the several states'. The powers of the direct representatives of the people, that is, were to be hedged on every side by institutions staffed with people who had been carefully insulated from the direct choices of ordinary voters. Madison thought that direct and frequent election of the lower house was essential to take into account the preferences of the people, but he thought it equally important to balance that house's power with the smaller Senate, indirectly chosen for longer terms, and consisting of older and presumably more thoughtful men.[64]

The subsequent history of constitutional institutions in the United States can be seen as a sustained disassembly of the Constitution's democracy-limiting institutions. There has been, that is, a persistent movement in the direction of establishing the actual choices of the governed population as the principal ingredient in public decision-making.[65] The most obvious development has been the expansion of the franchise. At the time of the Constitution's adoption, seven of the 13 states required voters to have some interest in real property, two allowed intangible property to suffice, and four demanded that voters pay specified sums in taxes. By the 1840s, pretty much all these financial qualifications had been abandoned and, with some narrow exceptions, all adult white males could vote.[66] These changes were made state by state. Thereafter, the broadening of the right to vote was affected nationally by amendments to the *United States Constitution*. In 1870, in the wake of the Civil War, states were barred by the Fifteenth Amendment from limiting the right to vote on account of race. Under the Nineteenth Amendment, ratified in 1919, neither the states nor the United States could withhold the vote because of sex. In 1961, the Twenty-Third Amendment expanded the right to choose presidential electors to residents of the District of Columbia. The Twenty-Fourth Amendment, ratified in 1964, prohibited conditioning the right to vote for federal office on the payment of a tax. Finally, in 1971, the Twenty-Sixth Amendment expanded the constitutional right to vote in state or national elections to all persons who had reached the age of 18. The cumulative result was that, as matter of law, the potential electorate was very nearly co-extensive with the adult population of the United States.[67]

[62] J Madison, 'The Federalist No 10' in Rossiter (n 26) 81–82.

[63] *United States Constitution*, art II, § 1, para 1.

[64] See J Morrow, *The History of Political Thought: A Thematic Introduction* (London, Macmillan Press, 1998) 245.

[65] See Achen and Bartels (n 5) 53 (citing Bruce Cain).

[66] A Keyssar, *The Right to Vote: The Contested History of Democracy in the United States* (New York, Basic Books, 2000) 328–29.

[67] The formal constitutional changes did not always translate into an effective right to vote, especially with respect to discrimination on account of race. The *Voting Rights Act of 1965, Pub L No 89-110, 79 Stat 437*, created

In addition to the expansion of the franchise, the Constitution's scheme of independent mediating institutions was largely dismantled. The Seventeenth Amendment, adopted in 1913, established the direct election of Senators 'by the people'. The selection of electors for President is still constitutionally committed to state legislatures. But as a matter of practice, by 1832, every state but one provided for popular elections of presidential electors who were pledged to vote for certain presidential candidates.[68] Thus, although the electoral college still results in some anomalies, all of its participants represent choices made by voters in presidential elections. Decisions of American governments are also more accurate reflections of the preferences of the people, due to holdings of the United States Supreme Court requiring legislative districts to be equal in population.[69] Most American states have taken the next logical step and provided for many public issues to be decided by direct consultation of the electorate in a referendum. (There is no machinery for submitting *national* lawmaking to a popular vote.) All states but one require a referendum to approve amendments to the state constitution. In 18 states, a sufficient number of signatures on a petition oblige the state to put a proposed constitutional amendment on the ballot. In 23 states, legislatures are authorised to put proposed statutes on the ballot and, in 21 states, legislation may be initiated by popular petition.[70] Hence, Achen and Bartels state that 'with a few fits and starts, American history has proceeded steadily away from the sophisticated notions of balance enshrined in the Constitution and inexorably toward a larger direct popular control as envisaged in the simplistic folk theory [of democracy]'.[71]

A final important development has been the emergence of political parties. Parties are not mentioned in the Constitution nor is there much in the debates surrounding its adoption that suggest it was the subject of much concern. But some form of political organisation is essential if democratic choices are to be translated into a set of representatives who will pursue any preferred programme.[72] For a long time, political parties also served a mediating function between voter sentiment and public policy but, in recent decades, the influence of party organisation and leadership has been reduced. Primary elections, in which voters directly choose the party's candidates, have played an increasingly important

legal rights and procedures that went a long way toward making that right effective. See CS Elmendorf and DM Spencer, 'Administering Section 2 of the Voting Rights Act after *Shelby County*' (2015) 115 *Columbia Law Review* 2143, 2144 ('Widely lauded as one of the most effective statutes ever enacted, the Voting Rights Act of 1965 finally made good on the promise of the Fifteenth Amendment'.). That law is still on the books, but its reach has been very significantly restricted by a 2013 holding of the Supreme Court, striking down one important requirement of the Act as an unconstitutional infringement of state sovereignty: *Shelby County v Holder*, 570 US 529 (2013).

[68] ZS Rosen, 'The Irony of Populism: The Republican Shift and the Inevitability of American Aristocracy' (2006) 18 *Regent University Law Review* 271, 284. The exception was South Carolina which did not conform to the general pattern until after the Civil War: DR Deskins, H Walton and SC Puckett, *Presidential Elections, 1789–2008: County, State, and National Mapping of Election Data* (Ann Arbor, University of Michigan Press, 2010) 3.

[69] An early significant ruling was *Reynolds v Sims*, 377 US 533 (1964). Every ten years with a new national census, the courts decide a rash of challenges to legislative redistricting. The resulting law is both messy and dense.

[70] See WB Fisch, 'Constitutional Referendum in the United States of America' (2006) 54 *American Journal of Comparative Law* 485. An up-to-date chart of the state of the law in American jurisdictions is available online at 'Initiative and Referendum States' (*National Conference of State Legislatures (NCSL)*, 2018) www.ncsl.org/research/elections-and-campaigns/chart-of-the-initiative-states.aspx (last accessed 19 November 2018).

[71] Achen and Bartels (n 5) 67.

[72] See RA Dahl, *How Democratic Is the American Constitution?* (New Haven, Yale University Press, 2001) 30. S Issacharoff, 'Democracy's Deficits' (2018) 85 *University of Chicago Law Review* 485, 488–90.

function, replacing conventions where experienced party leaders exercised more control. No presidential candidate of either major political party has been selected as a result of unbound delegate votes at a national convention since 1952.[73] These days, party primaries are conducted in such a way as to make them almost indistinguishable from general elections.[74] The result is to 'allow candidates to appeal over the heads of party leaders directly to the voters'.[75] Among other effects, intraparty contests have encouraged appeals to energised but narrow – and sometimes extreme – segments of the public, reinforcing the 'filter bubble' phenomenon already mentioned.[76]

Much the same story can be told in other jurisdictions. As in the United States, the first decades of the nineteenth century in the United Kingdom saw a substantial, although far from universal, extension of the right to vote for members of Parliament. The *Great Reform Act of 1832* strengthened the link between the population and Parliament: constituencies were redrawn to make their representation more consonant with their relative populations and their economic importance; property qualifications for voting were rationalised, although not eliminated. The Act resulted in an increase of almost 50 per cent in the total number of voters.[77] As the House of Commons became more representative of the larger population, the other, unelected elements of Parliament – the Crown and the House of Lords – were reduced in importance, receding into a subsidiary role in the effective constitution. The political predominance of the Commons eventually took legal form in the Parliament Acts of 1911 and 1949.[78] More recently, the United Kingdom has turned to direct referendums on important constitutional questions. These have included votes on the devolution of legislative authority to assemblies in Wales and Scotland in 1979 and 1997; on proposed preferential voting for Parliament in 2011; on independence for Scotland in 2014; and, most recently, on the termination of Britain's membership in the European Union in 2016.[79]

Taken together, the two trends just summarised should be disheartening. We have dispensed with the institutional obstacles and the built-in delays to the faithful effectuation

[73] D DeSilver, 'Contested Presidential Conventions, and Why Parties Try to Avoid Them' (*Pew Research Center*, 4 February 2016) www.pewresearch.org/fact-tank/2016/02/04/contested-presidential-conventions-and-why-parties-try-to-avoid-them/ (last accessed 19 November 2018).

[74] See Achen and Bartels (n 5) 61–66; S Issacharoff, 'Outsourcing Politics: The Hostile Takeover of Our Hollowed-Out Political Parties' (2017) 54 *Houston Law Review* 845, 875–79.

[75] DH Lowenstein, RL Hasen and DP Tokaji, *Election Law: Cases and Materials*, 5th edn (Durham, Carolina Academic Press, 2012) 415.

[76] See Isaacharoff, 'Democracy's Deficits' (n 72) 491–92.

[77] See C Seymour, *Electoral Reform in England and Wales: The Development and Operation of the Parliamentary Franchise, 1832–1885* (New Haven, Yale University Press, 1915) 2, 10–16, 25–28, 68, 71. EJ Evans, *The Shaping of Modern Britain: Identity, Industry and Empire, 1780–1914* (Harlow, Pearson Longman, 2011) 217. Evans also cautions, however, that the effect of the 1832 Act in democratising parliamentary representation was decidedly mixed: at 217.

[78] Dahl, *Democratic* (n 72) 46. CC Weston, *English Constitutional Theory and the House of Lords, 1556–1832* (Routledge Revivals) (London, Routledge & Kegan Paul, 2010) 1. See also *House of Lords Act 1999* reducing the number of hereditary peers in the House of Lords.

[79] A list of United Kingdom referendums – 'a relatively new feature of UK constitutional practice' – was given in the Supreme Court's judgment in *R (Miller) v Secretary of State for Exiting the European Union* [2017] UKSC 5, [2018] AC 61 [117]. See P Leyland, 'Referendums, Popular Sovereignty, and the Territorial Constitution' in R Rawlings, P Leyland and AL Young (eds), *Sovereignty and the Law: Domestic, European and International Perspectives* (Oxford, Oxford University Press, 2013) 145.

of the population's judgements. This means that the public is more directly empowered to choose the policies to be pursued by the government, and to select the individuals who will hold the public offices that formulate and execute those policies. If we were convinced of the accuracy of the ancient slogan, '*vox populi, vox Dei*', we might regard this as genuine progress in social organisation.[80] But the intractable political ignorance of the public at large, along with the exaggerated confidence with which political opinions are often held, may make us doubt that this is a cause for celebration. Those facts underline the value of a limited and mediated democracy; one in which popular opinion is an essential but not an exclusive source of decision. In such a system, popular beliefs need to be considered with respect, but such consideration must also take into account realities that the population may have missed or misunderstood. Such a process is more likely to enhance public welfare than is the direct working of a 'perfected' democracy in which majority opinion trumps every other source of judgement.[81]

Having come this far, someone is likely to recall the caution on this question expressed by Winston Churchill, that 'it has been said that democracy is the worst form of Government except all those other forms that have been tried from time to time'.[82] It is not so often remembered that this sentiment was expressed in a speech in which Churchill was speaking *in opposition* to a bill (later enacted as the *Parliament Act 1949*) which would have reduced the power of the House of Lords to delay legislation passed by the Commons.[83] It may also be worth remembering another aphorism usually attributed to Churchill, that '[t]he best argument against democracy is a five-minute conversation with the average voter'.[84]

III. Democracy and Mixed Government

If this sobering account of modern democracy is in any measure convincing, our initial concern over the relative roles of courts and legislatures in making public decisions may appear in a new light. The counter-majoritarian difficulty took the presumptive rightness of democratic decision-making more or less for granted. If we believed, as a matter of principle, that majorities ought to govern and that the people who constituted those majorities could safely be expected to use their political power to promote public welfare, then any restraint on their ultimate authority would need to be justified.[85]

[80] Scepticism of '*vox populi, vox Dei*' goes back a long way. One of the earliest documented uses was in a letter from the English scholar and cleric, Alcuin, to Charlemagne. He advised the Emperor to ignore the people who 'keep saying, the voice of the people is the voice of God, since the riotousness of the crowd is always very close to madness': JR Stone, *The Routledge Dictionary of Latin Quotations: The Illiterati's Guide to Latin Maxims, Mottoes, Proverbs, and Sayings* (New York, Routledge, 2005) 282.

[81] One recent study describes the 'constitutional assistance' activity of the European Commission for Democracy through Law (the Venice Commission) as aiming to establish 'counter-majoritarian democracy'. See V Volpe, 'Drafting Counter-Majoritarian Democracy: The Venice Commission's Constitutional Assistance' (2016) 76 *Heidelberg Journal of International Law* 811, 834. See further, discussion in text attached to n 136 below.

[82] HC Deb 11 November 1947, vol 444, cols 206–207.

[83] ibid.

[84] Quoted in M Deacon, 'Why Winston Churchill Will Always Be the Last Word in Political Wit' *The Telegraph* (22 November 2012) www.telegraph.co.uk/news/politics/9696402/Why-Winston-Churchill-will-always-be-the-last-word-in-political-wit.html (last accessed 19 November 2018).

[85] This is roughly the position of Jeremy Waldron. See generally J Waldron, 'The Core of the Case against Judicial Review' (2006) 115 *Yale Law Journal* 1346, 1349.

A. Constitutionalism and its Sceptics

The standard argument for granting courts the power to prohibit, or to cancel, actions of politically accountable legislatures is that it is essential to the 'rule of law'. Constitutions pre-establish rules for the operation of the state. The existence and enforcement of such rules allow individuals (and private groups) to know when their conduct is at risk from or immune to state regulation.[86] Although those rules themselves are usually the product of an intense democratic process,[87] the point of a constitution is to lock those limits in, prohibiting their modification by any government, no matter its democratic credentials. Even if we thought, notwithstanding the problems with modern democracy, that public welfare was otherwise best protected by a government responsive to popular opinion, we might still believe that predictability and stability – the peculiar constitutionalist values – could only be secured by a law-bound state.

It is essential in such a state to make provision for some mechanism to enforce the entrenched rules against political actors. The psychological assumption implicit in the maxim, *nemo judex in causa sua*, tells us that those actors cannot be trusted consistently to follow the constitutional rules on their own. Constitutionalism requires independent monitors with the power to declare when the rules have been violated and to demand that the government adjust its actions accordingly. The constitutional judge, therefore, appears to be part and parcel of any scheme for limiting democracy with constitutional rules. Critically, however, constitutionalism assumes such courts will exercise that authority only in conformity with the entrenched rules. Experience confirms the seriousness of this concern. What exactly it means to be faithful to a written constitution is itself a disputed question, but a fair examination of actual constitutional judgements is unlikely to convince many observers that those decisions closely match up with the rules in the constitutional text.[88] Some critics of judicial review go further. They contend that discretionary judgement is intrinsic to the enterprise of constitutional interpretation. The language of constitutions, they point out, is typically vague, especially in their individual rights provisions. Goldsworthy sums up this viewpoint when he notes that bills of rights consist 'of abstract and flexible principles of political morality, whose "interpretation" is indistinguishable from moral and political philosophy'.[89] Similarly, James Allan claims that many constitutional rules 'build in a value judgment … whose application is inherently contestable and over which smart, reasonable even nice people will differ and disagree'.[90] For reasons like these, Hans Kelsen excluded any declaration of individual rights from the *Austrian Constitution of 1920*.[91]

If we accept that many constitutional rules are not interpreted to yield determinate answers to concrete disputes, then the standard constitutionalist argument that democratic

[86] I described the benefits of constitutional government in RS Kay, 'American Constitutionalism' in L Alexander (ed), *Constitutionalism: Philosophical Foundations* (Cambridge, Cambridge University Press, 1998) 16, 17–27.

[87] See RS Kay, 'Constituent Authority' (2011) 59 *American Journal of Comparative Law* 715, 738–47.

[88] I do not, however, think that the promulgation of constitutional rules is, therefore, necessarily a futile endeavour. I explained my reasons in Kay, 'American Constitutionalism' (n 86) 39–50.

[89] Goldsworthy, *Sovereignty of Parliament* (n 1) 278.

[90] J Allan, *Democracy in Decline: Steps in the Wrong Direction* (Montreal, McGill-Queen's University Press, 2014) 48. See also Waldron, 'Judicial Review' (n 85) 1368–69.

[91] See M Patrono, 'The Protection of Fundamental Rights by Constitutional Courts: A Comparative Perspective' (2000) 31 *Victoria University of Wellington Law Review* 401, 403–405.

decision-making must be limited in order to maintain the rule of law state collapses.[92] In a significant number of cases, the courts act not on the basis of pre-existing rules, but according to their own evaluation of the public welfare. This is implicit in the historical experience of many jurisdictions and is explicit in much of the academic commentary including the extrajudicial writing of constitutional judges.[93] On this understanding, the judges effectively sit as another legislative chamber, albeit one with its own peculiar procedures and deliberation; and one whose concurrence is sometimes essential for the decisions of the elected legislature to be effective. So, Sir Stephen Sedley declared sovereignty in the United Kingdom to be 'bi-polar', divided between 'the Crown in Parliament and the Crown in its courts, to each of which the Crown's ministers are answerable – politically to Parliament, legally to the courts'.[94] Keith Whittington supposes that 'a key characteristic of a court is that it resolves disputes in accord with some pre-established set of legal rules', but that '[t]he justices [of the United States Supreme Court] have relatively little interest in resolving disputes, and they have little concern for pre-established legal rules'. Instead, they 'have in fact regularly exercised their "will" to set national economic, social, political, and legal policy even where no clear constitutional inconsistency exists'.[95] Adopting this view, Eric Segall, another American constitutional law scholar, has proposed that the Supreme Court should permanently consist of eight justices 'with four Republicans and four Democrats'.[96] It is on the basis of this perception of a 'wholesale transfer to the courts of some of the most pertinent and political controversies a democratic polity can contemplate' that Ran Hirschl characterised modern polities as 'juristocracies'.[97]

B. Mixed Government

Looked at this way, the practical functioning of 'constitutional democracies' involves a sharing of power between at least two kinds of agencies. The first is composed of individuals directly and frequently answerable to the people. The personnel of the second are chosen other than by election and hold office for a fairly long term. The first makes decisions that are, at least in large part, based on an appreciation of the desires of the voting public. The second decides according to its own view of the principles and values that ought to ground

[92] See RS Kay, 'Rights, Rules, and Democracy' in T Campbell, J Goldsworthy and A Stone (eds), *Protecting Human Rights: Instruments and Institutions* (Oxford, Oxford University Press, 2003) 117.

[93] See, eg, A Barak, 'The Constitutionalization of the Israeli Legal System as a Result of the Basic Laws and Its Effect on Procedural and Substantive Criminal Law' (1997) 31 *Israel Law Review* 3, 5, quoted in GJ Jacobsohn, *Constitutional Identity* (Cambridge, Massachusetts, Harvard University Press, 2010) 152, fn 44 (The judiciary 'must reflect the general public's conscience, the social consensus, the legal ethics and the value judgments of society …'). For other examples, see Kay, ibid 119–20.

[94] S Sedley, 'Human Rights: A Twenty-First Century Agenda' [1995] *Public Law* 386, 389.

[95] K Whittington, 'Is the Supreme Court a Court?' (*Law and Liberty*, 23 February 2017) www.libertylawsite.org/2017/02/23/is-the-supreme-court-a-court/ (last accessed 19 November 2018). An extended argument on the same point is contained in EJ Segall, *Supreme Myths: Why the Supreme Court Is Not a Court and Its Justices Are Not Judges* (Santa Barbara, Praeger, 2012).

[96] EJ Segall, 'Eight Justices are Enough: A Proposal to Improve the United States Supreme Court' (2018) 45 *Pepperdine Law Review* 547.

[97] R Hirschl, *Towards Juristocracy: The Origins and Consequences of the New Constitutionalism* (Cambridge, Massachusetts, Harvard University Press, 2004) 222.

public action. This arrangement brings to mind the ancient concept of 'mixed government'. The essential characteristic of such governments is that power is divided among independent agencies, each representing a different interest in society, and each operating and staffed in a way that reflects the peculiar attributes of these interests. I am not the first to observe the affinity between mixed governments and democracies with constitutional courts. In criticising such regimes, Goldsworthy suggested that the institution of constitutional courts may 're-insert[] an "aristocratic" element into the political process to check the ignorance, prejudice and passion of the "mob"', thus effecting 'a return to the ancient principle of "mixed government"'.[98] In a 1999 comment, John Hart Ely also re-imagined the United States Supreme Court as fulfilling the aristocratic function in a mixed government. While the capacity of the United States Senate to take on that responsibility was waning, 'the comparable role of the Supreme Court was symmetrically waxing'.[99]

Mixed government has been discussed and promoted by political theorists as far back as Plato and Aristotle, but the first fully worked out description is usually attributed to the Greek historian, Polybius, attempting to explain the success of the Roman republic.[100] Polybius borrowed from Plato the idea that there were three simple forms of government – rule by one (monarchy), by the few (aristocracy), or by the many (democracy). Each had its own virtues, but each was also prone to its own form of corruption; monarchy to tyranny, aristocracy to oligarchy and democracy to anarchy (or in another reading to ochlocracy, mob rule). These six forms of government always followed each other in a suspiciously symmetrical pattern.[101] The solution, exemplified by Lycurgus' Spartan constitution, was to reject each of the simple forms in favour of a combination of the three, 'so that none of the principles should grow unduly and be perverted into its allied evil'. So designed, 'the constitution should remain for long in a state of equilibrium like a well-trimmed boat'.[102] Polybius' basic scheme was adopted and elaborated by Cicero in *On the Commonwealth*, written in the last years of the republic.[103] Its main themes were reiterated in various forms in the medieval and early modern periods, turning up in the works of Thomas Aquinas, Machiavelli and James Harrington, among others.[104] It survived as a central theme in theoretical political writing into the nineteenth century, even as the priority of democratic decision-making began to swamp all competitors.

The attractions of mixed government were a function of the peculiar qualities of its components. There were two different but overlapping derivations of such a government's constituent elements. The first was worked out from particular institutional and procedural

[98] Goldsworthy, *Parliamentary Sovereignty* (n 1) 10–11.

[99] JH Ely, 'The Apparent Inevitability of Mixed Government' (1999) 16 *Constitutional Commentary* 283, 290. See also Somin (n 36) 214 (describing Supreme Court adjudication as a 'mechanism for allowing insulated experts to overturn the decisions of democratic processes'). Rosen (n 68) 292–95 (The Supreme Court can be seen as 'acting as an aristocratic legislature instead of in an adjudicatory role'.).

[100] See Morrow, *Political Thought* (n 64) 229–35; von Fritz (n 57) 60–83; CJ Richard, *The Founders and the Classics: Greece, Rome, and the American Enlightenment* (Cambridge, Massachusetts, Harvard University Press, 1994) 124–25.

[101] 'It is impossible … that each of these should not in course of time change into this vicious form': Polybius (n 20) 330–31. For a thorough study of the ahistoricity of Polybius' account, see von Fritz (n 57).

[102] Polybius (n 20) 335.

[103] MT Cicero, 'On the Commonwealth' in *Cicero's Tusculan Disputations* (translated by CD Yonge) (New York, Harper & Brothers, 1877) 330–31, 355.

[104] J Morrow, *History of Western Political Thought: A Thematic Introduction*, 2nd edn (New York, Palgrave Macmillan, 2005) 154–56.

characteristics which made certain bodies especially well equipped to deal with certain tasks, and to respond to certain risks. Although not often defended in exactly these terms, these qualifications seemed to follow from the number of people associated with each unit. Thus, most mixed government theorists claimed that the singular monarch displayed special 'order or energy'. The limited number of aristocrats could engage in careful deliberation and thereby add 'wisdom'.[105] The special contribution of the 'democratic' aspect was harder to pin down. For Charles I, it was 'courage and industry', while for John Adams, it was 'honesty or goodness'.[106] Second, and less frequently, the elements of mixed government were associated with certain economic and social interests in the population, each of which had its own strengths and weaknesses. This view, as Gordon Wood observed, relied on the value of involving 'in the government all of the social orders of the body politic. … [M]ixed government was not an institutional abstraction set apart from the society but indeed was the very embodiment of the society'.[107] Adams, whose descriptions of the constituent parts of government were not always consistent, insisted that the 'three branches of power have an unalterable foundation in nature. … and that if all of them are not acknowledged in any Constitution of government, it will be found imperfect, unstable, and soon enslaved'.[108]

The model of mixed government figured substantially in American constitutions at the end of the eighteenth century. Those founders saw an incarnation of the idea in the constitution with which they were most familiar, that of the United Kingdom. The English constitutional struggles of the seventeenth century had put paid to the idea – one never fully accepted – of the absolute authority of the monarchy. Historians have identified a critical moment in English political development in Charles I's issuance of his *Answer to the Nineteen Propositions*, in response to extravagant claims of authority by the Long Parliament. The *Answer*, described by Corinne Weston as 'one of the most influential [pronouncements] ever made on the nature of the English government', set out the three basic types of government and noted that they all have 'their particular conveniences and inconveniences'.[109] In England, the existence of King, Lords and Commons amounted to a 'mixture of these' resulting in the 'conveniences of all three, without the inconveniences of any one, as long as the balance hangs'.[110] 'The *Answer*', as one commentator noted, 'introduced the Polybian idea of balance to English constitutional theory'.[111] This 'classical theory of the English constitution' stirred Montesquieu's admiration and he, in turn, strongly influenced American constitution-makers.[112]

[105] Wood (n 23) 197–98 (citing John Adams).
[106] D Wootton (ed), *Divine Right and Democracy: An Anthology of Political Writing in Stuart England* (Indianapolis, Hackett Publishing Company, 2003) 171–74; Wood (n 23) 197. On Charles I's defence of mixed government, see text at nn 109–111 below.
[107] Wood (n 23) 199.
[108] Quoted in CM Walsh, *The Political Science of John Adams: A Study in the Theory of Mixed Government and the Bicameral System* (New York, GP Putnam's Sons, 1915) 57.
[109] Weston (n 78) 23–24, 263.
[110] Wootton (n 106) 171–74. On the significance of the *Answer*, see CC Weston and JR Greenberg, *Subjects and Sovereigns: The Grand Controversy over Legal Sovereignty in Stuart England* (Cambridge, Cambridge University Press, 1981).
[111] A Fukuda, *Sovereignty and the Sword: Harrington, Hobbes, and Mixed Government in the English Civil Wars* (Oxford, Clarendon Press, 1997) 29. See Weston (n 78) 10; Goldsworthy, *Sovereignty of Parliament* (n 1) 75, 200–201.
[112] Weston (n 78) 125–26.

Mixed government, consequently, featured prominently in the various projects of constitution-making in North America in the late eighteenth century. Whereas in earlier versions, mixed governments were conceived as alternatives to the unchecked power of a monarch, Americans admired them for their capacity to restrain the dangers of popular government.[113] According to the historian, Carl J Richard, '[t]he theory was still so axiomatic among all but a few absolute monarchists and radical Democrats that it was rarely questioned'.[114] A delegate to the North Carolina congress drafting a state constitution praised the British constitution for effecting 'the union of the three grand qualities of virtue, wisdom, and power as the characteristics of perfect Government'.[115] Opponents of the short-lived Pennsylvania constitution of 1776 objected particularly to the unchecked power vested in its legislature. According to Wood, the critics thought that '[w]hat was most needed was a Senate or upper chamber which could balance the basic honesty of the people with the knowledge and experience of the few men of education and leisure in the society'.[116] The concept was clearly on the minds of the drafters and ratifiers of the *United States Constitution of 1787–89*. In 1787, Thomas Jefferson sent a copy of Polybius to James Madison, then serving in the Philadelphia Convention.[117] And, in arguing for it in *The Federalist No 40*, Madison referred to the Convention's proposal as a 'mixed constitution'.[118] Probably the most assiduous proponent of mixed government among the American founders was John Adams. He was as worried about the corruption of democracy as he was about any tyrant or oligarchy.[119] He assumed that there were 'three different orders of men' with different talents and different interests.[120] Adams's *Thoughts on Government*, published in 1776, had a powerful influence on the drafting of state constitutions. Adams, himself, was the principal draftsman of the Massachusetts constitution of 1780, which directed that the right to vote for Senators in the state legislature was reserved for those holding more property than was demanded of the electors of members of the state House of Representatives. An even stricter qualification was required for the electors of the governor.[121]

As already noted, the original version of the *United States Constitution* could not reasonably be described as a democracy. Many of its framers were deeply sceptical, in fact apprehensive, about any government the decisions of which depended on the preferences of the general population. Edmund Randolph of Virginia, speaking in the Philadelphia Convention, said that 'every man' agreed that the troubles of the national government were all traceable to 'the turbulence and follies of democracy'.[122] One proposed check on this danger was a defeasible veto of legislation to be vested in a Council of Revision consisting of 'the national executive and a convenient number of the national judiciary';[123] an idea

[113] See Rubin (n 61) 114–15.
[114] Richard (n 100) 131. See also Wood (n 23) 232.
[115] Quoted in Wood (n 23) 202.
[116] Wood (n 23) 234.
[117] Richard (n 100) 157–58.
[118] J Madison, 'The Federalist No 40' in Rossiter (n 26) 247.
[119] CF Adams (ed), *The Works of John Adams, Second President of the United States: With a Life of the Author, Notes and Illustrations* (Boston, Little, Brown and Company, 1851) Vol 6, 10.
[120] Quoted in Wood (n 23) 575.
[121] Richard (n 100) 132–33.
[122] Farrand (n 24) 51.
[123] Farrand (n 24) 94.

borrowed from the New York constitution of 1777. Wood sees it as a response to 'the inherited dread of magisterial despotism and a fear of popular disorder'.[124] After the Convention narrowly rejected the Council, a veto was granted but exclusively to the President. The proponents of the Council had argued that this alternative would be an inadequate check on the legislature. 'The aid of the judges', said Oliver Ellsworth, 'will give more wisdom [and] firmness to the Executive'.[125] Madison, who favoured the Council, thought there was no risk that their combination would give too much power to the President and judges. The real danger was that the legislative branch would 'overmatch' the other two, given the 'powerful tendency in the legislature to absorb all power into its vortex'.[126] Even the executive veto shows that the drafters concurred with this sentiment. 'All agree', said Nathaniel Gorham, who opposed the Council, 'that a check on the Legislature is necessary'.[127]

In addition to the veto, framers of the *United States Constitution* put their faith in the Senate to check popular democracy. Influenced by the English model of King, Lords and Commons, Alexander Hamilton had hoped that the upper chamber would consist of members appointed for life. In notes made before the Convention, he echoed the classical understanding of the essential role of aristocracies in mixed governments, stating: 'Society naturally divides itself into two political divisions – the few and the many, who have distinct interests'. 'Nothing but a permanent body', he went on, 'can check the imprudence of democracy'.[128] While a hereditary aristocracy had little prospect of adoption, some of the constitution-makers hoped it would still be possible to rely on a 'natural aristocracy'.[129] Assuming that talent and wisdom generally resulted in material success, some states had limited the right to vote for members of the legislative upper houses to holders of some minimum value of property.[130] The Senate in the federal constitution, moreover, was designed in such a way as to increase the likelihood that its members would possess disinterested and careful temperaments. These Senators would be qualified to balance what Hamilton, at the New York ratifying convention, described as the 'intemperate passions, and regulate the fluctuations, of a popular assembly'.[131] In this respect, the Senate should be compared with the House of Representatives. Senators were to be selected by the state legislatures; Representatives elected by the 'people' of the states. The minimum age for Senators was 30, and only 25 for Representatives. Senatorial terms were six years, whereas Representatives had to face election every two years.[132] It was hoped that this 'dissimilarity in the genius of the two bodies',[133] would at least approximate a natural aristocracy that could restrain, if it could not stop, the 'irresistible force possessed by that branch of a free government,

[124] Wood (n 23) 433.
[125] M Farrand (ed), *The Records of the Federal Convention of 1787* (New Haven, Yale University Press, 1911) Vol 2, 74.
[126] ibid.
[127] ibid 79. See generally RL Jones, 'Lessons from a Lost Constitution: The Council of Revision, the Bill of Rights, and the Role of the Judiciary in Democratic Governance' (2012) 27 *Journal of Law and Politics* 459.
[128] Quoted in Richard (n 100) 141.
[129] Richard (n 100) 131. See also Wood (n 23) 246 (discussing the political views of Benjamin Rush).
[130] Wood (n 23) 246–49.
[131] Quoted in Wood (n 23) 557–58.
[132] *United States Constitution*, art I, §§ 1, 2.
[133] Madison, 'Federalist No 62' (n 27) 379.

which has the people on its side'.[134] This was exactly the reasoning of mixed government, and it is not surprising to learn that Madison's notes for his *Federalist* essays 'cited Aristotle, Polybius … and Cicero as his sources'.[135] The mechanism requiring the agreement of a less responsive institution before decisions of a more electorally sensitive chamber could be put into effect continues to attract the approval of some constitution-makers. A recent analysis of the work of the 'constitutional assistance' projects of the Council of Europe's Commission on Democracy Through Law (the Venice Commission) commends its promotion of bicameral legislatures exactly because 'it represents an effective check on the majoritarian principle', thus 'offer[ing] representation to groups, such as minorities, whose presence in the lower house is limited or absent'.[136]

We have already seen that the original plan of mixed government in the *United States Constitution* has been fundamentally altered by constitutional amendments, new legislation and reformed political practice; and that the pressure of public opinion is now a serious factor in almost every government decision. Supporting these developments was the prevalent conviction that political power was justified only in so far as it was traceable to some act of assent on the part of the people who were to be governed. At the same time, American political opinion increasingly embraced the basic equality of all citizens and, therefore, the unacceptability of vesting independent power in any special or privileged class.[137] The concept of mixed government depended on the existence of distinct social and economic classes, as well as the belief that popular preference should be only one element in the formulation of state policy. In the founding generation, a distinct tension arose between the apparent mixed government justification of the preferred constitutional architecture, and the ideology of the paramount rights of the people. Gordon Wood has supplied the definitive account of how many of the original constitution-makers resolved this tension in the period between independence in 1776, and the drafting of the federal Constitution in 1787. Bodies and procedures that had originally been understood as devices for harmonising the talents and interests of different social elements, came to be re-conceived as different techniques for expressing the choices of a sovereign 'people'. Wood cites a pamphlet of John Stevens, published during the 1787 ratification debates. Stevens criticised John Adams's defence of classical mixed government, but not

> the structure of government that Adams defended; [Stevens] was actually contesting Adams's reasoning and his justifications. For Stevens, the purpose of instituting an upper house was not to confine or embody the aristocracy, but rather to mitigate the inconvenience of having only a single House of Representatives. … For Stevens, the parts of the *government* had lost their social roots. All had become more or less equal agents of the people.[138]

The success of this new explanation of the components of government made more or less inevitable the changes we have observed that occurred over the next 200 years. The

[134] Madison, 'Federalist No 62' (n 27) 389.
[135] Richard (n 100) 140–41.
[136] Volpe (n 81) 834.
[137] Rubin (n 61) 114.
[138] Wood (n 23) 584. Wood quotes a 1778 statement of the Virginia Senate insisting that it ought not – like the House of Lords – be disabled from initiating money bills. '"In our legislature", declared the Senate, "can be perceived only the representatives of the people, separated into two bodies, and mutually endeavoring to exercise faithfully their delegated power"': at 241. See also 255: '[I]t was now somehow possible for the people simply through the electoral process, to have two different agents speaking for them at the same time'.

eighteenth-century rules came to be understood as defective vehicles for implementing the people's choices.

But what had been the point of constitutions requiring the participation of multiple institutions if all of them were meant to be 'more or less equal agents of the people?' Overlapping and sometimes confused with mixed government in the constitution-making period of the late eighteenth century, was the theory of 'separation of powers'. It depended not on pre-existing social or economic orders, but on the separation of government *functions* – executive, legislative, and judicial – each to be allocated to separate and independent institutions.[139] These departments were so designed that none would possess the means to disturb the liberty of the subject, and each would serve as a check on the others' natural tendency to abuse.[140] Proponents of mixed government going back to Polybius, of course, had argued that it too would be restrained by the mutual antagonism of its constituent parts.[141] Viscount Bolingbroke, writing in the first half of the eighteenth century, made this claim for the constitution of the United Kingdom. The result of the 'monarchical, aristocratical and democratical power ... balancing one another' was that

> wicked princes have been opposed, restrained, reformed, punished by parliaments; that the real, and perhaps the doubtful exorbitancies of Parliaments, have been reduced by the Crown; and that the heat of one House hath been moderated, or the spirit raised, by the proceedings of the other. Parliaments have had good effect on the people by keeping them quiet and the people on parliaments by keeping them within bounds which they attempted to transgress.[142]

Mixed government, therefore, as Kurt von Fritz argued, 'will always be a system of checks and balances'.[143] But there is a crucial difference between the two ideas. Decisions in a system of mixed government are made only upon the acquiescence of 'the one' and 'the few' in the desires of 'the many'. It is, therefore, an oxymoron to speak of a 'democratic mixed government'. A democratic regime observing the principles of separation of powers, and checks and balances, on the other hand, is perfectly coherent.[144] The value of mixed government is in the supposed superiority of the choices issuing from the 'triple mixture',[145] combining the wills of very different social interests with equal contributions from each. The result, according to Cicero, was

> by means of the just apportionment of the highest, middle, and lower classes, the State is maintained in concord and peace by the harmonic subordination of its discordant elements: and thus, that which is by musicians called harmony in song answers and corresponds to what we call concord in the State.[146]

[139] CdS Montesquieu, *The Spirit of the Laws*, rev edn (translated by T Nugent) (London, Colonial Press, 1900) Vol 1, 151–62.

[140] ibid 150. Weston's reading suggests that, when Montesquieu's admiration of the British constitution shifted from the different functions of government to the tripartite legislature of king, lord and commons, it 'had melted into the tradition of mixed government': Weston (n 78) 124–25.

[141] See Polybius (n 20) 339–40.

[142] H St John, 'A Dissertation upon Parties' in D Armitage (ed), *Political Writings* (Cambridge, Cambridge University Press, 1997) 1, 125–26.

[143] von Fritz (n 57) 184–85.

[144] See Morrow, *Political Thought* (n 64) 228.

[145] Weston (n 78) 10.

[146] Cicero (n 103) 330. See also W Lambarde, *Archeion, or, A Discourse Upon the High Courts of Justice in England* (first published 1635, CH McIlwain and PL Ward eds) (Cambridge, Massachusetts, Harvard University Press,

IV. Judicial Review as Mixed Government

If, as we noted in section III.A., courts exercising the power of constitutional judicial review are actually engaging in lawmaking, that practice takes us unavoidably in the direction of mixed government. Like every version of mixed government, such a system creates two or more different centres of political power that share in policy formulation.

Early forms of mixed government were understood to mitigate the dangers of concentration of power in a single person. They were, that is, 'the primary rival of absolute monarchy throughout the five centuries after Aristotle's *Politics* was translated into Latin'.[147] When, in the early eighteenth century, Bolingbroke praised what he saw as the mixed government of the United Kingdom, he described it as the means whereby 'wicked princes have been opposed, restrained, reformed, punished by parliaments'. Today, there are few monarchies still in need of a check from legislatures. We thus might put greater store by Bolingbroke's further assurance that the Parliament (which he saw as the 'aristocratical' element of government) 'had good effect on the people by keeping them quiet'.[148] That is also the principal way in which many American founders saw the problem of constructing a government, and it was an important factor in the creation of the 'aristocratical' Senate to balance the essential but dangerous House of Representatives.[149]

The developments described in section II. have resulted in a modern electorate that has both more power and less ability to use that power in ways that enhance general welfare. It is at least tempting to see constitutional courts as a salutary offset to the popular branches of government. Supporters of vigorous judicial review occasionally describe it this way, but its opponents do so more frequently. Allan objects to giving judges power to control public decisions based on 'the judges' views of what is reasonable and appropriate'.[150] Waldron points to the practice of majority decision-making in collegial courts as evidence of their essentially legislative character.[151] And Ely suggested that the United States Supreme Court had ended up keeping the law-making system 'within the bounds of what is acceptable to the reasoning class', thus discharging the function that many of the founders had expected from the aristocratic Senate.[152]

Modern constitutional courts appear to have attributes that might qualify them as a valuable counterweight to the enlarged power of the electorate. The judges of a constitutional court of last resort are typically appointed for life, until a fixed retirement age, or for a reasonably lengthy and non-renewable term.[153] They are, by design, insulated from

1957) 126 ('And this frame of Policie is both natural and harmonicall: Naturall, in that it hath an imitation of the natural bodie of man, truly called a *little World*; out of the three *Cells* whereof, namely the *Head, Breast* and *Belly*, the whole three *powers* of the Soule doe open, and utter themselves: and *Harmonicall*, because from such, and so well-tuned a *Base, Meane*, and *Treble*, there procedeth a most exquisite *consent*, and delicious *melodie*.').

[147] Rubin (n 61) 114.

[148] St John (n 142) 125–26.

[149] See text at nn 23–27 above.

[150] J Allan, *The Vantage of Law: Its Role in Thinking about Law, Judging and Bills of Rights* (Farnham, Ashgate, 2011) 137.

[151] J Waldron, 'Freeman's Defense of Judicial Review' (1994) 13 *Law and Philosophy* 27, 32, 36.

[152] Ely (n 99) 290.

[153] A Stone Sweet, 'Constitutional Courts' in M Rosenfeld and A Sajó (eds), *The Oxford Handbook of Comparative Constitutional Law* (Oxford, Oxford University Press, 2012) 816, 824–25.

the influence of popular opinion. They are chosen from groups markedly different from the average member of the electorate. They are 'comparatively old, well-educated, isolated, thoughtful, and wise'.[154] They are consequently less prone to the difficulties that afflict modern democracies outlined in section II. Therefore, the participation of these courts in collective decision-making may improve the ultimate outcomes for society, in the same way that the requirement of assent from elected parliaments provided a valuable check on the authority of powerful monarchs.[155]

Of course, this reconceptualisation of constitutional courts as discretionary decision-makers in a mixed government is a post hoc explanation. Although it may be a better description of what these courts actually do, it fits awkwardly with the forms and procedures under which they operate. The jurisdiction of these courts is established by laws that refer to the enforcement of a constitution. The courts' judgments often engage in close analysis of the constitutional text or the historical circumstances of its enactment. The disjunction between what these courts say they are doing and what they actually do must make it harder for them to achieve results that best promote the public welfare. If, therefore, they operate as part of a mixed government, it is an awkward, even a haphazard kind of mixed government. Usually, we think, planned human institutions work better than inadvertent ones.[156]

If constitutional courts were to respond to this problem by candidly aligning their rhetoric with their practice, a different problem would arise. Such an approach would subvert the legitimacy that these institutions enjoy in the eyes of the public. Unelected constitutional courts tend to enjoy a high regard from the population, but arguably this esteem is borrowed from the constitution; namely, the rules that the judges are understood to be executing. Were the mixed government version of judicial power openly embraced, then that text could no longer be called upon to bolster the judges' authority.[157]

Apart from questions of legitimacy, constitutional courts appear crudely designed to exercise useful functions in a mixed government. If our objective were to restrain democratic rule with a purpose-built institution, we would probably design something quite different. Legal training will be useful in the resolution of many public issues, but so would expertise in science, philosophy, history, engineering and many other fields. A more diverse set of skills and backgrounds would have much to commend it in such a body.[158] The procedures of courts would also fit uncomfortably with the kind of public policy matters with which a mixed government institution would be confronted. It is standard wisdom that courts lack the resources to adequately examine the kinds of disputed factual questions on

[154] Ely (n 99) 290. See Goldsworthy, *Parliament Sovereignty* (n 1) 10–11 (Judicial review is argued to 'shift[] power to people (judges) who are representative members of the highly educated, professional, upper-middle-class, and whose superior education, intelligence, habits of thought, and professional ethos are thought more likely to produce enlightened decisions'.).

[155] The courts, in this picture, fulfil, albeit crudely, some of the functions of the 'epistocratic veto' in a system of universal suffrage hypothesised by Jason Brennan: Brennan (n 58) 184–86.

[156] See RS Kay, 'Changing the United Kingdom Constitution: The Blind Sovereign' in Rawlings, Leyland and Young (n 79) 98, 112.

[157] Thus, one of the arguments of the opponents of the proposed Council of Revision at the Philadelphia Convention was that it was improper to conscript judges into a policy-making role. See Jones (n 127) 487–88; JT Barry III, 'The Council of Revision and the Limits of Judicial Power' (1989) 56 *University of Chicago Law Review* 235.

[158] See Allan, *Vantage of Law* (n 150) 54 ('*[L]legally* trained judges have no more moral expertise than plumbers or secretaries or teachers or CEOs of large companies or even bond traders'.).

which large scale collective decisions may turn.[159] It is also doubtful, at least in common law jurisdictions, that constitutional courts end up dealing with just those questions that might most benefit from independent scrutiny. These courts rely mainly on the initiative of private parties to determine the issues they decide. It would only be a fortunate coincidence if those parties' selections always included the matters of most importance to the polity.

In this, and in several other respects, however, constitutional courts organised along the centralised 'European' model may better fit the theory of mixed government. There is, in fact, some reason to think that those tribunals, mostly created in the second part of the twentieth century, were designed with something like that function in mind. Generalising, the dockets of these courts include issues referred by other political institutions – legislatures, executive agencies, sub-national units. (Until fairly recently, this was the *only* way a case could be presented to the Constitutional Council in France.)[160] In addition, these courts more often exercise 'abstract review', looking at the question without the distraction of a concrete dispute in which the parties' interests, rather than the public welfare, will influence what gets decided. In fact, abstract review is often carried out *before* a proposed law is promulgated. This makes the form (as well, we have assumed, the substance) of the courts' decision-making much more like that of a legislature.[161]

These European-style constitutional courts are indeed commonly regarded as participants in the lawmaking process. Hans Kelsen, the principal architect of the Austrian Constitutional Court established in the 1920 Constitution – generally credited with serving as the model for European-style courts – famously referred to such a court as a 'negative legislator'.[162] He believed its judgments had 'a constitutive, not a declaratory character'.[163] In keeping with this understanding, a decision by a European-style constitutional court holding a law invalid is not just binding on the parties to the litigation (*inter partes*). It has universal (*erga omnes*) effect. The 1920 Austrian Constitution also required any decision of the Constitutional Court that annulled a law to be promptly published in the official government gazette, in the same way that affirmative laws and regulations were published; and this practice has been followed in most other European constitutional tribunals.[164] Judgments of these courts invalidating a law, moreover, are usually held to have only *ex nunc* effect.[165]

[159] See, eg, A Vermeule, 'Common Law Constitutionalism and the Limits of Reason' (2007) 107 *Columbia Law Review* 1482, 1506–18.

[160] See P Pasquino, 'New Constitutional Adjudication in France: The Reform of the Referral to the French Constitutional Council in Light of the Italian Model' (2009) 3 *Indian Journal of Constitutional Law* 105, 117.

[161] For a collection of essays describing case selection in various constitutional courts, see RS Kay (ed), *Standing to Raise Constitutional Issues: Comparative Perspectives* (Brussels, Bruylant, 2005).

[162] H Kelsen, *General Theory of Law and State* (translated by A Wedberg) (Cambridge, Harvard University Press, 1949) 268. *cf* Brennan (n 58) 184 (The 'epistocratic council has no power to make law. … But it has power to unmake law'.). On Kelsen's contribution to the Austrian court, see S Lagi, 'Hans Kelsen and the Austrian Constitutional Court (1918–1929)' (2012) 9 *Revista Co-herencia* 273. On the influence of the Austrian court, see A Gamper and F Palermo, 'The Constitutional Court of Austria: Modern Profiles of an Archetype of Constitutional Review' (2008) 3 *Journal of Comparative Law* 64.

[163] H Kelsen, 'Judicial Review of Legislation: A Comparative Study of the Austrian and the American Constitution' (1942) 4 *The Journal of Politics* 183, 190.

[164] Venice Commission, 'Decisions of Constitutional Courts and Equivalent Bodies and their Execution' (17 May 2001) CDL-INF (2001) 9.

[165] ibid 13–14.

The law at issue will be treated as ineffective only from the date of the judgment and, in that respect, the decision is like the enactment of a repealing statute. This approach is inconsistent with the prevailing American assumption that all a court does in such a holding is identify an attempt at legislation which was ineffective *ab initio*.[166] In fact, European-style constitutional courts sometimes further emulate legislators by postponing the effective date of a judgment if it decides that immediate application would impose unacceptable costs on the parties affected.[167] The political character of these courts is further reflected in the way in which their judges are selected. In sharp contrast to the bureaucratic and apolitical selection adopted for ordinary courts in civil law countries, constitutional judges are chosen in a process that involves the highest organs of the state.[168] The peculiar nature of these bodies is underlined by the fact that they are assigned duties associated with the operation of the electoral system. They are often authorised to decide disputed returns.[169] The same courts are frequently given jurisdiction to try cases of presidential impeachment.[170]

These features of European-style constitutional courts make it easier to associate them with a non-democratic component in a mixed government. The job of such institutions 'inescapably involves questions of and choices about political morality'.[171] These characteristics would hardly be necessary if these courts were the simple law-appliers described in Chief Justice Marshall's decision in *Marbury v Madison*.[172] They do not decide 'constitutional issues', only as an unavoidable aspect of their obligation to adjudicate disputed cases.[173] In these jurisdictions, in fact, they do not even feature in the 'judicial' lines of the state's organisational chart. They are 'not really at the top of the "normal" judicial system but rather outside of it'. They inhabit a '"twilight zone" between law and politics'.[174] John Reitz has observed that, in the European system, a constitutional court resembles 'a sort of adviser and/or policeman to the other two branches. … [It] is more obviously part of the state machinery because it is charged with policing on behalf of important state interests'.[175] We have already reviewed a substantial literature arguing that once we look beyond their form and rhetoric, we see constitutional courts in common law jurisdictions doing much the same thing.[176]

[166] See *Norton v Shelby County*, 118 US 425 (1886) 442. After much back and forth, the Supreme Court has reaffirmed this basic view: *Harper v Va Dep't of Taxation*, 509 US 86 (1993) 97. For a survey of the American law, see RS Kay, 'Retroactivity and Prospectivity of Judgments in American Law' (2014) 62 *American Journal of Comparative Law* 37.

[167] Venice Commission (n 164) 14. See W Rupp-v.Brünneck, 'Admonitory Functions of Constitutional Courts' (1972) 20 *American Journal of Comparative Law* 387. This technique is also sometimes followed in constitutional courts in common law jurisdictions. See, eg, *Canada (Attorney General) v Bedford*, 2013 SCC 72, [2013] 3 SCR 1101. For a rare example from the United States Supreme Court, see *Northern Pipeline Construction Co v Marathon Pipe Line Co*, 458 US 50 (1982).

[168] See Hilbink (n 6) 22–23.

[169] See RS Kay, 'Standing to Raise Constitutional Issues: A Comparative Analysis' in Kay (n 161) 1, 33.

[170] ibid 34.

[171] See Hilbink (n 6) 22.

[172] *Marbury v Madison*, 5 US 1 Cranch 137 (1803).

[173] See Kay, *Constitutional Issues* (n 161) 33–38.

[174] RA Lorz, 'Standing to Raise Constitutional Issues in Germany' in Kay, *Constitutional Issues* (n 161) 163, 169. See Hilbink (n 6) 22–25.

[175] JC Reitz, 'Political Economy and Abstract Review in Germany, France and the United States' in SJ Kenney, WM Reisinger and JC Reitz (eds), *Constitutional Dialogues in Comparative Perspective* (Basingstoke, Macmillan, 1999) 62, 83.

[176] Political scientists have produced a huge literature treating common law courts as strictly political agencies. See Dahl, *Democracy* (n 7). TJ Peretti, *In Defense of a Political Court* (Princeton, Princeton University Press, 2001)

It is necessary to emphasise what this reading of judicial review as part of mixed government does and does not do. It conceives the constitutional court as an undemocratic body exercising occasional political monitoring of the acts of the more democratically responsive departments of government. It treats the conventional explanation of constitutionalist government – the enforcement of ex-ante legal rules on the conduct of the state – as largely defunct. It leaves in its place a process of ex-post review, according to uncertain and possibly idiosyncratic standards of public behaviour. It severs the activity of constitutional courts from the constitutional text. To that extent, it gives up on constitutionalism as the foundation of public power. The unique appeal of constitutionalism derives from the belief that it is possible to prescribe, in advance, and in understandable terms, a set of rules to be observed by the state. Whatever the benefits of a non-democratic, mixed government agency, they do not include marking out a knowable boundary between permissible and impermissible state acts. When all of its components act in concert, a mixed government is an unlimited government. It is true that by dividing state power among independent actors with different interests and outlooks, the state is likely to do fewer things. In that respect, mixed government, like rule-bound government, will appeal to those who fear the power of the state.[177] But reduced state power is only one of the attractions of constitutionalism. The other arguably more significant benefit is that it enables its citizens to make plans with confidence that certain things, at any rate, will not be subject to public interference.[178]

The consistent historical failure of constitutional courts to limit their decisions to the execution of pre-existing rules might cause us to despair of realising the peculiar constitutionalist advantages. If so, we will have to decide between different versions of unlimited government. One possibility is a government that attempts to execute the largely unmediated preferences of the population in something like the 'perfected' democracy described in this chapter. So far, however, intentionally or accidentally, modern states have instead balanced popularly responsive institutions with ones that consult other, perhaps longer-term, principles and values.[179] In maintaining and respecting constitutional courts, they have in effect chosen the model of mixed government.

Thinking about constitutional courts as constituents of a mixed government does not entail a rejection of democracy, broadly conceived. Democratic government is not an all or nothing proposition, and a great many state arrangements have claimed the democratic label. We can identify a spectrum of more and less democratic regimes. We can hypothesise, that is, a perfectly non-democratic state; one where no decisions are made based on any consultation of popular preference. At the other 'most democratic' end, we might place the short-lived democracy of ancient Athens, where every citizen voted on every question, and where every public office was rotated among all of the citizens.[180] Indeed, 'from classical

(arguing that the United States Supreme Court should openly embrace a political role). For a defence of the same position by an American legal academic, see Segall (n 95).

[177] See RS Kay, 'Substance and Structure as Constitutional Protections: Centennial Comparisons' [1989] *Public Law* 428.

[178] See Kay, 'American Constitutionalism' (n 86) 22–24.

[179] See Achen and Bartels (n 5) 303 ('[E]ffective democracy requires an appropriate balance between popular preferences and elite expertise'.).

[180] See Dahl, *Democracy* (n 7) 14–23. On the restrictive requirements for 'citizenship', however, see above n 57.

Greece to the seventeenth century, the possibility that a legislature might properly consist not of the entire body of citizens but of their elected representatives remained mainly outside the theory and practice of democratic or republican government'.[181] As late as the eighteenth century, Rousseau insisted that the people's authority had to be exercised in person.[182] Regular direct popular participation in collective decisions is impossible in modern states, but there are an infinite number of degrees of public participation.[183] And there is always some gap between the choices of the population and the choices made by representatives. The size of that gap will depend, amongst other things, on the rules for qualifying voters and candidates, selecting officials from among candidates, terms of office, the structure and procedures for state decision-making, as well as any enforceable substantive constitutional rules limiting the state's choices. According to Robert Dahl:

> It is a common practice for democratic bodies to impose procedures on themselves that help to ensure that they act carefully, not hastily; wisely, not foolishly. These procedures often delegate to some minority the authority to halt, delay, or modify what might otherwise be enacted by simple untrammeled majority rule.[184]

So, neither bicameralism nor the specification of supermajorities for certain decisions need be thought inconsistent with the essentially democratic character of states that adopt them.[185] Jeremy Waldron, who has insisted on the moral right of citizens to decide contested public issues for themselves, paints a picture of a 'broadly democratic system' that includes 'procedures for lawmaking [that] are elaborate and responsible, and incorporate various safeguards, such as bicameralism, robust committee scrutiny, and multiple levels of consideration, debate, and voting'.[186]

Consequently, we can say that constitutional government in the United States was 'democratic' even before the various 'perfecting' changes outlined in section II.C. If we also accept the argument, described in section II.B., that those developments have, in the context of the parallel changes in social institutions and communication technology, made the government less qualified to deal with collective problems, we should be at least open to the possibility that we have ended up with too much democracy. Reading fairly unrestrained constitutional judicial review as the operation of a non-democratic institution in a mixed government might make sense as a partial corrective to those changes. As noted, this appears quite plausible in European-style constitutional courts, but it is arguably true even when this power is exercised by courts designed on the American model. We would still be justified, moreover, in calling states so organised representative democracies: it would still be the case that the population is effectively engaged in deciding the course of public affairs and will garner the benefits associated with such involvement. These include the intellectual and moral benefits arising from 'participation in public debate … [thus] develop[ing]

[181] Dahl, *Democracy* (n 7) 28.

[182] 'Every law the people has not ratified in person is null and void': JJ Rousseau, *On the Social Contract, or, Principles of Political Rights* (translated by RM Harrington) (New York, GP Putnam's Sons, 1893) 158–62.

[183] See Dahl, *Democracy* (n 7) 161.

[184] Dahl, *Democracy* (n 7) 76.

[185] Dahl, *Democracy* (n 7) 185; Volpe (n 81) 834.

[186] J Waldron, *Political Political Theory: Essays on Institutions* (Cambridge, Harvard University Press, 2016) 143, 204.

important civic virtues',[187] as well as the material advantages of relative peace and prosperity that have been associated with modern democracies.[188] In jurisdictions exhibiting one of these forms of qualified democracy, the filters and obstacles erected to prevent the implementation of public opinion will, at most, delay its ultimate success. Modern commentators have described constitutional courts as engaged in a 'dialogue' with elected officials.[189] Dahl persuasively argued that the United States Supreme Court, sooner or later, ends up conforming its judgments to political convictions prevailing in society.[190] The constitutional scheme designed by the American founders at the turn of the nineteenth century was intended to separate the active machinery of government from the choices of the populace, so that the 'public voice, pronounced by the representatives of the people, will be more consonant to the public good then if pronounced by the people themselves, convened for the purpose'.[191] But it was also meant to provide machinery that could not long function in contradiction with deeply held desires of the population.[192] According to James Madison, it was sufficient that a republican government 'derives all its powers directly or indirectly from the great body of the people, and is administered by persons holding their offices during pleasure and for a limited period, or during good behavior'.[193] All our modern 'constitutional democracies', even those with constitutional courts that have slipped the bonds of the constitutional text, satisfy that definition.

[187] Goldsworthy, *Parliamentary Sovereignty* (n 1) 211.

[188] See generally Halperin, Siegle and Weinstein (n 15).

[189] See PW Hogg and AA Bushell, 'The Charter Dialogue Between Courts and Legislatures (Or Perhaps the Charter of Rights Isn't Such A Bad Thing After All)' (1997) 35 *Osgoode Hall Law Journal* 75; J Ferejohn and P Pasquino, 'The Countermajoritarian Opportunity' (2010) 13 *University of Pennsylvania Journal of Constitutional Law* 353, 365, 375; J Cameron, 'Collateral Thoughts on Dialogue's Legacy as Metaphor and Theory: A Favourite from Canada' (2016) 35 *University of Queensland Law Journal* 157.

[190] RA Dahl, 'Decision-Making in a Democracy: The Supreme Court as a National Policy-Maker' (1957) 6 *Journal of Public Law* 279.

[191] Madison, 'Federalist No 10' (n 62) 81–83.

[192] 'The Framers' ambition was to create a governmental structure that functioned, *as a whole*, in a manner that was both tied to popular control and simultaneously possessing a requisite distance from it': Jones (n 127) 498. See also Ortega y Gasset (n 28) 48–49 (lamenting the disappearance of the society where the masses were restricted to approving or disapproving the programme of one minority or another).

[193] J Madison, 'The Federalist No 39' in Rossiter (n 26) 241.

11

Models of (and Myths about) Rights Protection

RICHARD EKINS*

I. Introduction

The doctrine of parliamentary sovereignty is the centrepiece of the British constitutional order, an order in which Parliament is free to choose what should be law and in which courts enjoy no authority to quash statutes by reference to human rights law. Jeffrey Goldsworthy is today the foremost scholar of that doctrine, as was Albert Venn Dicey in an earlier age. The significance of Goldsworthy's work lies not only in its painstaking exposition of the historical and jurisprudential foundations of the doctrine, but also in its measured yet forceful defence of entrusting Parliament with responsibility for final lawmaking choice. This chapter evaluates and elaborates that defence, aiming to elucidate the constitutional architecture of representative self-government. It begins, in section II., by considering Goldsworthy's contingent case for legislative supremacy. The argument is powerful, but at times risks understating the strength of the case for the British model of rights protection, as Goldsworthy terms it. Like Goldsworthy, I argue that it is not for judges freely to choose how to protect rights: the positive law of the constitution settles whether they have authority to quash statutes. The chapter goes on, in sections III. and IV., to consider Goldsworthy's refutation of two myths: first, that there is an ancient common law constitution which transcends and disciplines parliamentary sovereignty; and second, that immanent within all democracies in the common law tradition is one model of rights protection. He refutes the second myth in part by noting the Canadian, British and New Zealand experiments in empowering courts in relation to human rights law, while preserving the capacity of legislatures to override judgments. The final part of the article, section V., considers Goldsworthy's argument that this hybrid model avoids the democratic critique of judicial review. I argue that the hybrid model is not a stable, attractive alternative to the British model that Goldsworthy's work does so much to explain.

* I am grateful to Lisa Burton Crawford, Grant Huscroft, Grégoire Webber, Paul Yowell and, especially, Jeffrey Goldsworthy for helpful comments on an earlier draft. The usual disclaimer applies.

II. Two Models of Rights Protection

In reflecting on how constitutions ought to be designed, Goldsworthy notes:

> From the late eighteenth century until recently, the common law world included just two alternative models for the protection of individual rights. The first, developed in Britain, is the model of parliamentary sovereignty, which reposes primary responsibility for protecting rights in parliaments. The second, developed in the United States, is the model of judicial review, which reposes that responsibility in courts of law.[1]

The British model has predominated throughout the common law world, notwithstanding the adoption of judicial review to police the federal compact in Australia and Canada. Each model is open to familiar objections, Goldsworthy argues: parliamentary sovereignty for endangering rights and judicial review for undermining democracy. The choice between the models turns on a judgment as to which of these alleged dangers is more to be feared.[2] Goldsworthy's enthusiasm for the British model is real but is tempered in the following way:

> My own opinion is that [the judicial enforcement of constitutional rights] may be highly desirable, or even essential, for the preservation of democracy, the rule of law, and human rights in some countries, but not in others. In some countries, a history of rampant corruption, populism, authoritarianism, or bitter religious, ethnic, or class conflict may make judicially enforceable bills of rights desirable. Much depends on culture, social structure, and political organization.[3]

Goldsworthy goes on to make the case for legislative supremacy in political communities like Australia, Canada, New Zealand and the United Kingdom. His argument is primarily grounded in the moral importance of

> the old democratic ideal of government by ordinary people, elected to represent the opinions and interests of ordinary people [who] have a right to participate on equal terms in the political decision-making that affects their lives as much as anyone else's, and should be presumed to possess the intelligence, knowledge, and virtue needed to do so.[4]

His faith in this ideal is not naïve. He recognises that there is no guarantee that this mode of government will never violate individual or minority rights. But he insists that, in the right social and political conditions, clear injustice will be rare and that the frequency of clear injustices will diminish over time.[5] The stress on clarity is important, for Goldsworthy follows Waldron in recognising that there will often be reasonable disagreement about what justice requires.[6] The cost of 'giving judges power to correct the occasional clear injustice is that they must also be given power to overrule the democratic

[1] J Goldsworthy, *Parliamentary Sovereignty: Contemporary Debates* (Cambridge, Cambridge University Press, 2010) 79.

[2] ibid 80.

[3] J Goldsworthy, 'Questioning the Migration of Constitutional Ideas: Rights, Constitutionalism and the Limits of Convergence' in S Choudhry (ed), *The Migration of Constitutional Ideas* (Cambridge, Cambridge University Press, 2006) 115.

[4] ibid 121.

[5] ibid 121; J Goldsworthy, *The Sovereignty of Parliament: History and Philosophy* (Oxford, Oxford University Press, 1999) 269.

[6] J Waldron, *Law and Disagreement* (Oxford, Oxford University Press, 1999).

process in the much greater number of cases where there is reasonable disagreement and healthy debate'.[7]

This is the core of Goldsworthy's argument for the British over the American model. However, he notes other relevant considerations, including the historical record, which reveals that countries governed by way of the British model are not obviously worse off than the United States or other countries in which courts overrule primary legislation by reference to constitutional rights.[8] The rule of law, Goldsworthy argues, does not require judicial review of legislation, and indeed that practice may come at a substantial cost to the rule of law ideal itself.[9] And democratically elected legislatures, with their access to vast amounts of relevant information, may be better placed than courts to make good decisions.[10] Again, Goldsworthy stresses that this is a limited, contingent advantage: courts see particular cases of alleged injustice and are detached from partisan political argument, which may be an advantage in one case and a disadvantage in another.[11]

There is much to admire in the careful, patient way in which Goldsworthy has defended the British model against its many detractors, in the academy and on the bench. However, it may be that this leads him at times to understate the force of the case for legislative supremacy. Consider the argument from the history of the common law world. Goldsworthy is right to deny Dworkin's extravagant claims that judicial review of legislation is the handmaiden of democracy and that the American example proves as much.[12] On the contrary, the historical record of parliamentary self-government in the common law world – in Australia, Canada, New Zealand and the UK – is on the whole an enviable record of decent government. The absence of constitutional rights adjudication in these jurisdictions (in Canada, before 1982) has not put individual freedom or constitutional government in peril. By contrast, the availability of judicial review in the United States cannot be said to have guaranteed rights protection, and indeed has often compromised it, not least by blocking legislative attempts to secure racial justice[13] or to address social and economic problems.

Consider next the argument from the rule of law. Goldsworthy's argument that the ideal in no way warrants rejection of legislative supremacy is powerful and persuasive.[14] But the shape of that argument supports the stronger conclusion that legislative supremacy is in general a much better way to secure the rule of law than is judicial supremacy.[15] Invalidating statutes after they have been enacted (often long after) is inimical to the ideal. Modern rights adjudication is ill-disciplined. It consists in the exercise of an often arbitrary power by courts, a power that overlays the statute book with an inconstant set of case law norms and puts in doubt the validity of legislation, thereby undercutting the contribution that

[7] Goldsworthy, 'Questioning the Migration of Constitutional Ideas' (n 3) 121.

[8] Goldsworthy, *Sovereignty of Parliament* (n 5) 277–78.

[9] Goldsworthy, *Parliamentary Sovereignty* (n 1) Ch 3 ('Legislative Sovereignty and the Rule of Law').

[10] Goldsworthy, *Sovereignty of Parliament* (n 5) 262.

[11] Goldsworthy, *Sovereignty of Parliament* (n 5) 262.

[12] Goldsworthy, *Sovereignty of Parliament* (n 5) 277–79; RM Dworkin, *Freedom's Law: The Moral Reading of the American Constitution* (Cambridge, Massachusetts, Harvard University Press, 1996).

[13] P Yowell, *Constitutional Rights and Constitutional Design: Moral and Empirical Reasoning in Judicial Review* (Oxford, Hart Publishing, 2018) 120–26; G Webber and others, *Legislated Rights: Securing Human Rights through Legislation* (New York, Cambridge University Press, 2018) 143–50.

[14] Goldsworthy, *Parliamentary Sovereignty* (n 1) 57–78.

[15] See R Ekins, 'Judicial Supremacy and the Rule of Law' (2003) 119 *Law Quarterly Review* 127.

positive law ought to make to our social life.[16] True, courts take care to minimise these ills, and legislators may enact overly vague or incoherent statutes. Goldsworthy is right to note that constitutional rights enforcement may uphold parts of the rule of law ideal and that this ideal is not fully capable of being upheld by courts alone.[17] It follows that there is an asymmetry of risk: judicial review of legislation does not address the risks that parliamentary sovereignty may otherwise pose to the ideal but judicial review itself constitutes a standing threat to the rule of law, partly by undercutting the legislature's capacity to secure it. Respect for the rule of law is a positive reason, all else equal, to support the British model.[18]

Finally, consider the argument from relative institutional expertise. Goldsworthy argues that legislators may be better placed than judges to make wise decisions, because the limits on rights will routinely turn on the interests of other members of the community and 'Parliament is often more able to gather the relevant facts, consult widely with all affected parties, and arrive at an overall balance or compromise of the competing interests at stake.'[19] On the other hand, he says, it is arguable that judges may be better placed than legislators to decide well because they are independent of popular prejudice. The truth of this proposition cannot be decided in the abstract, he maintains, but turns 'on difficult factual and normative questions, whose answers can vary from one country to another, depending on culture, social structure, and political organization'.[20] The importance of local conditions may lead Goldsworthy to underplay the force of the general argument from institutional competence. In contrast to courts, especially ordinary common law courts, legislatures are intelligently structured to decide what should be done.[21] They are able to handle relevant information; they involve a wide range of persons in their deliberations; they may change as much or as little of the law as there is good reason to change; they can approach questions directly.[22] Any particular statute may be unwise or unjust but the legislature is structured, especially in a democracy, to reconsider its decisions, to be open to criticism, and to repeal or amend its handiwork. None of this is true of courts, for the obvious reason that the defining point of a court is not to decide what the law should be, but rather to adjudicate a dispute fairly in accordance with settled law.[23]

In framing the argument from democratic principle, Goldsworthy rightly stresses that constitutional rights adjudication often seems to collapse to an open question about what should be done, about what justice requires.[24] Authorising judicial review of legislation thus transfers from the people (and their elected representatives) to the courts' ultimate authority

[16] R Ekins, 'Rights, Interpretation and the Rule of Law' in R Ekins (ed), *Modern Challenges to the Rule of Law* (Wellington, LexisNexis, 2011) 165.

[17] Goldsworthy, *Parliamentary Sovereignty* (n 1) 64, 71–72.

[18] *cf* Goldsworthy, *Parliamentary Sovereignty* (n 1) 78.

[19] Goldsworthy, *Sovereignty of Parliament* (n 5) 262.

[20] Goldsworthy, *Sovereignty of Parliament* (n 5) 262.

[21] R Ekins, *The Nature of Legislative Intent* (Oxford, Oxford University Press, 2012) 121–25; see also Webber and others (n 13) 96–101.

[22] G Webber, 'Judicial Power and Judicial Responsibility' (2017) 36 *University of Queensland Law Journal* 205; Yowell (n 13) 90–98, 108–14.

[23] J Finnis, 'Judicial Power: Past, Present and Future' in R Ekins (ed), *Judicial Power and the Balance of Our Constitution: Two Lectures by John Finnis* (London, Policy Exchange, 2018) 26–61; Yowell (n 13) 90–96.

[24] Goldsworthy, *Parliamentary Sovereignty* (n 1) 71–72.

judges that it would be lawful to revise (qualify, overturn) the doctrine. These claims cannot withstand Goldsworthy's exploration of the historical record,[43] which makes clear that there was no ancient common law constitution of the kind asserted, viz. no justiciable limits on the lawmaking competence of the King-in-Parliament, which was a body long understood to represent the whole kingdom, to bind it in lawmaking action, and to brook no rivals. The doctrine long pre-dates the tumult of the seventeenth century, let alone the eighteenth, and the constitutional settlement that marks the Glorious Revolution and its aftermath – while affirming the doctrine of parliamentary sovereignty – did not create or introduce that doctrine. Rather, the tragic conflict between King and Parliament was resolved by renewed commitment to the proposition that both warring sides always shared – that King-in-Parliament is sovereign. The settlement was authoritatively to limit the King's alleged powers to dispense with statutes or to levy taxes and, in practice (not law), to subject the King to the Houses of Parliament, especially the House of Commons.

The assertion that the doctrine is a common law rule, created by and open to change by the judges, is also false. It is historically absurd: the judges were the King's servants and it is inconceivable that they somehow had authority to empower the King-in-Parliament. Goldsworthy neatly disposes of the argument that all legal rules must be either common law or statute, such that parliamentary sovereignty, never having been enacted, must be a rule of the common law. The assumption, which would unravel the British constitution at a stroke, misses an alternative, namely that the doctrine is a fundamental legal rule which is constituted by a shared consensus. Following Hart, Goldsworthy locates this consensus in senior officials.[44] It would be better to say that the political community has long been committed to this centrepiece of its constitution, with the commitment manifested in the practice of senior officials but clearly shared by other officials and citizens too.[45] The breadth of the commitment is significant for it means that in attempting to undo the doctrine judges would not merely be betraying their peers and predecessors but would be overthrowing the constitution of the body politic, which makes our unity in self-government possible. Note that the point is not that parliamentary sovereignty is a good foundation for self-rule – although this is true – but rather that, because it is (and long has been) our law, it should not be unravelled.

The classification of the doctrine as a common law rule, which perhaps resonates with Wade's careless talk of 'a political fact in the keeping of the courts',[46] is intended to license judicial remaking, and thus abandonment, of the rule. It is just not true to say, as some judges and scholars do, that the doctrine is somehow uncertain or unstable.[47] What judges contemplate when they speculate about restoring the ancient common law constitution, or qualifying the common law rule that is the doctrine, is a radical, unilateral unsettlement of the constitution. Not every revolution is wrong but this revolution would be: it would overthrow the fundamental law of a mature democracy in order to establish minority rule, at least in relation to an important class of cases. It would also compromise the rule of law,

[43] Goldsworthy, *Parliamentary Sovereignty* (n 1) 18–47, 268–80; Goldsworthy, *Sovereignty of Parliament* (n 5) especially 229–35 ('Historical Conclusions').

[44] Goldsworthy, *Sovereignty of Parliament* (n 5) 253–59.

[45] R Ekins, 'Legislative Freedom in the United Kingdom' (2017) 133 *Law Quarterly Review* 582, 603–604.

[46] HWR Wade, 'The Basis of Legal Sovereignty' (1955) 13 *Cambridge Law Journal* 172.

[47] Ekins, 'Legislative Freedom' (n 45) 604.

both in lawlessly departing from settled law and in providing for statutes to be invalidated on uncertain grounds, with retrospective effect.[48]

Goldsworthy's magisterial study of parliamentary sovereignty should make it impossible to deny that Parliament has enjoyed and still does enjoy legally unlimited lawmaking power. If one thinks this is a lamentable state of affairs (like Goldsworthy, I think otherwise), one should argue clearly and publicly for the political community to revise its governing arrangements. The rule of law requires this course of action. That said, the whole premise of the argument for the American model, and thus for asserting a mythical common law constitution to which we might return, is that one cannot trust the people, or their representatives in Parliament, to act well. Thus, the premises of the argument against parliamentary sovereignty may incline many to indulge, or engage in, judicial myth-making in which one pretends that the doctrine is uncertain or has shallow foundations.

This mode of argument is sometimes justified with reference to the extraordinary career of Edward Coke in the seventeenth century, whose claims about the scope of royal power were not as well-grounded in the law of England as he asserted, but which were made true by being taken up by Parliament and others across the tumultuous century. There is, as Goldsworthy notes, a tradition of conservative, reluctant revolution, carried out in the name of our ancient liberties.[49] However, the constitutional law and practice of a mature democracy like the United Kingdom ought not to be unravelled by its judges, who cannot credibly cast themselves as latter-day Edward Cokes confronting overweening power and entitled to limit tyranny by remaking the constitution. The location of authority ought itself to be settled authoritatively.[50] Goldsworthy's work reminds us of the importance of law in the constitution, including the British constitution, and cautions against its dismissal.

IV. The Myth of the Homogenised Constitution

The lawmaking authority of the Westminster Parliament is not subject to a common law constitution, ancient or contemporary. Parliament legislates in the context of the constitution, which is formed by statute, common law, convention and principle, but retains authority to choose freely what the law should be. Likewise, the common law does not take the place of the Constitution of the Commonwealth of Australia or the Constitution of Canada, which make provision for legislative supremacy within a federal compact (in Canada now also subject to the Charter of Rights and Freedoms). The United States is a common law jurisdiction, but has plainly adopted a different form of government in which courts are free to invalidate legislation that they conclude breaches constitutional principle. It makes sense to speak of a shared common law constitutional tradition, but not at the cost of overlooking what distinguishes these jurisdictions. The myth of the common law constitution ignores history and asserts that parliamentary sovereignty simply cannot

[48] The problem of the retroactive effect of annulling statutes is acute even where constitutions explicitly provide for such a situation, as in Canada and Ireland. See Yowell (n 13) 159–61. It would be even greater in the absence of any constitutional authorisation for judicial review.

[49] Goldsworthy, *Parliamentary Sovereignty* (n 1) 2.

[50] J Finnis, *Natural Law and Natural Rights*, 2nd edn (Oxford, Oxford University Press, 2011) 249–50.

be the fundamental law it has otherwise been recognised to be. The myth of the homogenised constitution, which Goldsworthy also contests, is to think that something like the American model of judicial power must be immanent in the law of any mature common law democracy.

Trevor Allan argues that liberal democracies in the common law world share a fundamental constitutional similarity in that courts stand ready to protect constitutional principle and legislative supremacy is an illusion.[51] The shared foundation is said to be the ideal of the rule of law, which Allan takes to entail that reason has priority over will and thus that judges must prefer constitutional principle to (arbitrary) legislative will. With characteristic generosity, Goldsworthy has praised Allan's work as 'unquestionably an important contribution to legal theory and comparative public law'.[52] But he has also left no doubt that this line of thought is self-defeating, for it undercuts the authority of any institution, including the court. Reason requires the exercise of authority precisely to settle what should be done in circumstances when unity of action is otherwise impossible to secure; it is unreasonable to dissolve authority as Allan does. This denial of authority turns on a dubious idea of law, which conflates legal validity and moral legitimacy. This conflation would make it impossible for law to coordinate social life around public standards for action. More specifically, this understanding of law cannot explain and would unsettle the law's allocation of authority, which would dissolve government more generally. Positive law does not, and should not, operate in this way. Constitutional design requires lawmaking choice and these choices do not fade away because different political communities all aspire to be ruled by law.

The collapse of constitutional law to the principle of the rule of law is fatal to the ideal. The rule of law is realised by taking positive law seriously – not by dissolving that law and licensing whatever judicial action is thought fit to discipline *other* public power, as if judicial power was not in particular need of justification by reference to its adherence to positive law.[53] Reflection on the rule of law may well help judges discharge their adjudicative function, including by framing their inference about what Parliament is likely to have intended in enacting this or that statute, but judges go wrong if they take the ideal itself to be a justiciable master principle that qualifies all other norms. Allan attempts to discern the ideal's fundamental standing in the law of various common law jurisdictions. The attempt fails, as Goldsworthy records, with the positive law of the constitution affirming legislative supremacy, forbidding judicial review of legislation or, alternatively, licensing that review on some grounds (or by some courts) only. It would be very odd indeed to think that, say, the introduction of the Charter to Canadian law, or the Human Rights Act to UK law, did not change judicial responsibilities or bear on the balance of the constitution. Constitutional design matters, Goldsworthy reasons, which entails that while the common law world may share much, choices to make or change constitutional law will determine what judges are free to do.

The myth of the homogenised constitution is at work not only in Allan's distorted account of the rule of law, but also, in less stark fashion, in the widely shared assumption

[51] TRS Allan, *Constitutional Justice: A Liberal Theory of the Rule of Law* (Oxford, Oxford University Press, 2001).
[52] Goldsworthy, *Parliamentary Sovereignty* (n 1) 82.
[53] See L Burton Crawford, 'The Rule of Law' in R Dixon (ed), *Australian Constitutional Values* (Oxford, Hart Publishing, 2018) 77, 93.

that there is a common constitutional model, to which mature democracies now conform and to which all ought to conform. Goldsworthy considers this assumption in his work on judicial borrowings and constitutional convergence.[54] His main concern is to explain why it is wrong for courts to depart from settled law in order to bring about such convergence. I share the concern, but my focus here is on his analysis of the common constitutional model and his argument that it is premature to declare the end of history in relation to the development of constitutional government. In thinking about the phenomenon of constitutional convergence, Goldsworthy traces the outline of a 'common model' of liberal democratic constitutionalism, in which the legislature (and perhaps also the executive) is democratically elected, individual rights are guaranteed, an independent judiciary has authority to enforce the constitution including constitutional rights, and constitutional provisions can only be changed by special, more demanding procedures.

Goldsworthy argues that these elements are vague and may be implemented in many different ways, such that the model may fragment into a number of variations. This is true, of course, for the structure of legislature and executive, but also for the judiciary and for amendment procedures. Most interestingly, for his purposes (and mine), he notes that there are many alternative systems of judicial enforcement of rights, with differences concerning which rights to protect (only negative rights or also socio-economic rights?), which court to protect them (a special constitutional court or ordinary courts?), and how to protect them (perhaps only through interpretation and declaration as in the UK), with the freedom of legislatures to respond or pre-empt review (as in Canada) being relevant also. Goldsworthy's strategy is to splinter the assumed consensus around the judicial role in enforcing rights. He does not doubt that a 'rights revolution' has swept the world or that legal and political elites are increasingly enthusiastic about robust judicial review. However, the detail of constitutional practice in the common law world, especially the introduction of a hybrid model in Canada, New Zealand and the United Kingdom, suggests that the victory of the common model (the American model recast) is not yet assured.[55] The continuing variety of constitutional forms ought to be valued, Goldsworthy suggests, partly because the democratic challenge to judicial review is a serious one, but also because experimentation with different models avoids complacency. The Australian resistance to a bill of rights, for example, thus provides a control to the wider experiment in judicial review. If Australia turns out to be reasonably well-governed without constitutional rights, this would help vindicate the old democratic faith, subject to the usual cautions about local political conditions.

The argument from experiment is an interesting one and Goldsworthy's moderate, careful tone may be precisely what is needed to encourage enthusiasts for judicial review to think again. It may seem quixotic for constitutional arrangements to be designed with an eye on experimentation, and I doubt that Goldsworthy means that Australia should understand its decision to live without a bill of rights as an experiment. However, the introduction of a statutory bill of rights might itself be an experiment, enacted with an open mind as to

[54] Goldsworthy, 'Questioning the Migration of Constitutional Ideas' (n 3) 116–19.

[55] See G Williams and L Burton, 'Australia's Exclusive Model of Parliamentary Rights Protection' (2013) 34 *Statute Law Review* 58.

whether the innovation will succeed.[56] The history of the wider common law world is a history of experiments in self-government, with or without judicial review, a history which does not establish that the United States has been more justly ruled than Britain. Indeed, one might contrast the treatment of a racial minority in New Zealand, where the rights of Maori have been considered and advanced by political means,[57] with the American equivalent, where the courts have often been used to limit legislative efforts to provide justice for African-Americans.[58]

In view of its history, it is strange that the American model has such a hold on the modern legal imagination. Enthusiasts for judicial review often seem to take for granted that legislative supremacy has been tried and failed, with the fate of the Weimar republic often called in aid.[59] This is an odd reaction to the failure of Germany's immature pre-war democracy. The free peoples who fought the Nazis from the beginning to the end of the war – Australia, Canada, New Zealand and the UK – were mature democracies, governed in accordance with the British model. In these states, courts certainly enforce rights – English law is thick with legal rights – but rights that have been specified, often by legislation, which do not require lawmaking choice in the course of adjudication, and which do not limit the legislature itself.[60] Parliament enjoys the main responsibility to reason about what rights require and to choose how the law should secure the common good. There is much to be said for the British model, as Goldsworthy's scholarship confirms, but it is a fact that its merits are often disputed. Still, other facts suggest that it is premature to declare the victory of the common model: Australia remains stubbornly without a federal bill of rights,[61] and New Zealand and the UK remain robustly committed to parliamentary sovereignty.

V. The Hybrid Model

Goldsworthy takes it to be very significant that Canada, New Zealand and the United Kingdom have adopted a hybrid constitutional model, 'which allocate[s] much greater responsibility for protecting rights to courts, without altogether abandoning the principle of parliamentary sovereignty'.[62] The partial preservation of legislative supremacy is confirmed, he reasons, by section 33 of the Charter – the 'notwithstanding clause', which enables (partial) legislative override of constitutional rights. Parliaments in Westminster or Wellington remain competent to legislate inconsistently with the *Human Rights Act 1998* (HRA) or the *New Zealand Bill of Rights Act 1990* (NZBORA). Declarations of

[56] See also L Burton Crawford, 'A Failed Human Rights Experiment? The Human Rights (Parliamentary Scrutiny) Act 2011 (Cth)' in M Groves, J Boughey and D Meagher (eds), *The Legal Protection of Rights in Australia* (Oxford, Hart Publishing, 2019, forthcoming).

[57] M Hickford, *Lords of the Land: Indigenous Property Rights and the Jurisprudence of Empire* (Oxford, Oxford University Press, 2011) Ch 8.

[58] See above n 13 and CR Sunstein, 'Did Brown Matter?' *The New Yorker* (3 May 2004): 'Most of the time, the judiciary has been an obstacle to racial equality.'

[59] For example, see J Weinrib, *Dimensions of Dignity: The Theory and Practice of Modern Constitutional Law* (Cambridge, Cambridge University Press, 2016).

[60] Webber and others (n 13).

[61] The *Human Rights (Parliamentary Scrutiny) Act 2011* (Cth) seems rather different in kind.

[62] Goldsworthy, *Parliamentary Sovereignty* (n 1) 79.

incompatibility under the HRA do not invalidate legislation, but instead bring political pressure to bear on Parliament to consider changing the law.

It is important for Goldsworthy's argument against the myths of the common law constitution and homogenised constitution that there truly is a hybrid model, importantly distinct from the British or American model. It is also important that this model is intelligible and might warrant support. He notes that

> the hybrid models now offer the possibility of a compromise that combines the best features of both the traditional models, by conferring on courts constitutional responsibility to review the consistency of legislation with protected rights, while preserving the authority of legislatures to have the last word.[63]

This reads as an explanation of the promise of this model, not a conclusion that the promise is realised or that the model should be adopted. Goldsworthy is not an enthusiast for the model, I think, but he does defend it at least against some important criticisms. The defence is not persuasive and he would have done better to hew more closely to the British model.

The argument for the hybrid model is that it 'combine[s] the most attractive features of both models, while discarding their most objectionable features'.[64] More precisely, Goldsworthy takes the hybrid model plausibly to answer the main objection to judicial review, which is the argument from democracy, especially the right of participation. The attraction of judicial review on the hybrid model is thus that it introduces a further check on the political process without preventing legislatures in the end having the final say about what the law should be. It seems to me that Goldsworthy equivocates between reporting that it is plausible to think empowering judges is a useful constitutional innovation and concluding that such empowerment would be a reasonable check on the legislature (or at least would be a tolerable alternative to strong-form judicial review of legislation, which would otherwise be likely to be introduced). The equivocation is related to his view that what matters is that the legislature freely chooses to introduce the bill of rights and remains free to override judicial decisions explicating and enforcing the rights it enumerates. This focus allows Goldsworthy largely to avoid the question of whether the legislature *should* make this choice. Insofar as he answers this question, it is by recalling that constitutional design is contingent, that one size does not fit all, such that legislative supremacy may not be warranted in certain social or political conditions. This may be true, subject to the discussion above, but it does not explain quite how judicial empowerment, of the kind one sees in the hybrid model, is attractive. The judicial action which that model invites or authorises may vary widely from system to system – Canada, New Zealand and the United Kingdom are quite different – and may be expected to be an unhappy mix of law-application and lawmaking because the rights in question are underspecified and invite or require judicial elaboration in the course of adjudication.[65] But if legislative supremacy is broadly attractive, then why overlay it with judicial make-believe? The closest Goldsworthy comes to answering this, I think, is in saying that Canadians might reasonably trust their judges more than

[63] Goldsworthy, *Parliamentary Sovereignty* (n 1) 80.

[64] Goldsworthy, *Parliamentary Sovereignty* (n 1) 204.

[65] R Ekins, 'Human Rights and the Separation of Powers' (2015) 34 *University of Queensland Law Journal* 217, 224–32.

their elected representatives to make good decisions about rights. The arguments considered above, which go to judicial competence and the rule of law, suggest otherwise. Lawmaking by rights adjudication is an unattractive mode of government.

The question Goldsworthy focuses on is whether judicial review in the hybrid model is compatible with democratic principle. He argues that it is compatible because a legislative override power, like section 33 of the Canadian Charter, or the UK Parliament's authority to legislate notwithstanding convention rights, makes it the case that the right to participate remains intact – for defeat in the courts may be undone by victory in the political process. Thus, public deliberation about rights is not politically irrelevant – as one might say it is in the United States – for it may culminate in the use of the override power. That the power is rarely used is not fatal to the argument, Goldsworthy says, because the most likely reason why it is not used is that the electorate trusts judges more than legislators. He reasons that:

> It would not be open to [Waldron] to object that an ingenuous electorate is likely to be deceived by the specious objectivity of constitutionalised rights, or dazzled by the mystique of the judiciary – by a naïve faith in judges' expert legal skills, superior wisdom, and impartiality. That objection would reflect precisely the same lack of faith in the electorate's capacity for enlightened self-government that motivates proponents of constitutionally entrenched rights. They fear that a majority of voters, motivated by ignorance, prejudice or passion, might trample on the rights of minorities or individuals. Waldron objects that ordinary people should not be presumed to be ignorant, prejudiced or intemperate, because that would be inconsistent with the basis of their having rights in the first place. … But if a majority's opinion about the rights even of minorities and individuals are entitled to respect, surely their opinions about the exercise of their own rights – to political participation – is entitled to even more respect, because in that case there is even less danger of ignorance or prejudice. … If a majority of ordinary people strongly prefer that an override not be used, because in relation to rights they trust judges more than legislators – or perhaps even more than themselves – how can the rights-based theorist say they are wrong?[66]

I say the question is not whether the people should be free to decide to authorise judicial review subject to a legislative override. The enactment of a statutory bill of rights is a free choice to change the law. The question is whether a free people *ought* to choose this and, if they choose it, whether the form of government they have chosen maintains robust self-government over time.

It is important, of course, that this mode of judicial review is chosen, not imposed, and the continuing capacity to respond to judicial decisions is also important (so too is the capacity to undo the jurisdiction altogether, if such exists). But scepticism about the wisdom of adopting judicial review subject to an override does not entail self-contradiction.[67] The worry is not that voters lack the virtue necessary to exercise self-government, but rather that

[66] Goldsworthy, *Parliamentary Sovereignty* (n 1) 208.

[67] Compare P Craig, 'Judicial Power, the Judicial Power Project and the UK' (2017) 36 *University of Queensland Law Journal* 355, 361 ('There is something markedly ironic about a project that extols the virtues of deliberative choice, while deprecating the result thus made by countless nations, including the UK, which have expressly opted for rights-based review in a constitution or statute.') with R Ekins and G Gee, 'Putting Judicial Power in its Place' (2017) 36 *University of Queensland Law Journal* 375, 395 ('It is perfectly coherent to defend Parliament's law-making authority and democratic legitimacy and also to argue that it made a mistake in enacting the HRA and/or should in any case now amend or repeal that legislation.')

the hybrid model risks alienating them from that self-government.[68] At least in a mature democracy, it is a mistake for the people to trust judges more than legislators (or than themselves) to resolve fundamental lawmaking questions. Judges are not best placed to decide and in any case it is in answering these questions by way of their representative institutions that the people exercise self-rule. The legislative process provides a means to participate in one's government; the institution of judicial review does not.[69] One does not treat ordinary people as fools or bigots, or doubt their entitlement to a share in self-government, when one worries that judicial review will misrepresent the nature of the questions that require decision or, relatedly, will falsely imply that legal expertise is needed to handle them intelligently. The trust that voters have in judges rather than legislators may thus be based on a false premise.

Likewise, one does not abandon one's faith in democracy when one opposes lawmaking by referendum (at least in most cases), on the grounds that the electorate is not well structured to legislate.[70] The electorate should instead exercise self-government by way of representative institutions, which enable public deliberation and choice over time. One may see here a problem with Goldsworthy's reliance, noted above, on Waldron's static conception of democracy, which is inattentive to the ways in which the legislative process may form the will of the people.[71]

The problem recurs in Goldsworthy's discussion of delegation. He rightly notes that there is a major difference between (i) permanent surrender of power, (ii) indefinite surrender subject to possible reclamation, (iii) temporary surrender to a delegate followed by return of the power to the principal or its delegation to another, or (iv) delegation, whether indefinite or temporary, which is subject to power on the part of the principal to reclaim or cancel the delegation at any time.[72] Goldsworthy argues that representative democracy itself is an instance of (iii) and that lawmaking by the executive (and/or unelected officials) is legitimate if legislatures can disallow it if need be. This is not a good account of representative democracy, which is not a transfer or delegation of the people's inherent power, but rather is a means by which we act jointly to rule ourselves.

The analogy is strained, for what is contemplated in the hybrid model, especially in Canada as Goldsworthy understands it, is power to quash primary legislation, not power to make incremental or subsidiary choices subject to the supervision of legislatures or a responsible government. The common law, in its ordinary sense, may be closer to this picture, with judges developing the law in various fields, which legislatures may reasonably tolerate while always retaining freedom to intervene.[73] In the hybrid model, it is the legislature's own actions that are subject to challenge and interference. The capacity to resist interference is important, but does not render the initial judicial action unobjectionable, for it is a jurisdiction that presupposes that courts are the right forum to consider rights. (The argument that follows in this section suggests that in practice Canada is more like (ii) than (iii) or (iv).)

[68] See further Ekins, 'Human Rights and the Separation of Powers' (n 65) 222–24, 232–35.
[69] *cf* A Harel, *Why Law Matters* (Oxford, Oxford University Press, 2014), and Webber and others (n 13) 107–15.
[70] Ekins, *Legislative Intent* (n 21) 146–48.
[71] Ekins, *Legislative Intent* (n 21) 94–107, 149–54.
[72] Goldsworthy, *Parliamentary Sovereignty* (n 1) 209–10.
[73] Ekins, *Legislative Intent* (n 21) 121–23.

It is a mistake, Goldsworthy argues, to think that the democratic objection to judicial review centres exclusively on the right to participation. One might defend democracy on the grounds that 'widespread participation in public debate and decision-making, in which all are treated as equals, helps develop important civic virtues' – viz. self-respect and mutual understanding – which make possible cooperation and compromise, and encourage responsibility.[74] Goldsworthy reasons that the structure and dynamics of representative democracy may be important to these ends: deliberation in a representative assembly, in which legislators form coalitions and understand that they do not hold office forever, encourages 'mutual respect, moderation and compromise'.[75]

This is an intelligent, insightful discussion of the shape of a beneficial form of government. Goldsworthy goes on to ask whether the judicialisation of politics puts this dynamic at risk, noting that it is sometimes feared that it may foster apathy and irresponsibility, or extremism and intolerance. Whether judicial review in fact distorts politics, he says, turns on finely balanced sociological judgements about which one should not generalise. In relation to Canada, he speculates that legislators would be more likely to use section 33 if it were not likely to prove unpopular with the voters. He concludes that voters are not apathetic; they simply trust judges more than legislators, which may be reasonable. More generally, 'even goal-based democrats should have considerable faith in the inherent intelligence, knowledge and virtue of the electorate'.[76] It follows that they should respect 'the apparent opinions of Canadians that their rights are better protected by judges than legislators, and that the override clause should rarely be used'.[77] The argument that 'the electorate can be duped by the claim that a small group of people possess superior expertise or wisdom, and persuaded to defer unquestioningly to the judgments of that group' is equally an argument that they could be duped by demagogues – in which case constitutional rights might be warranted.[78]

This is not a convincing defence of the democratic merits of the hybrid model. The decision to institute the hybrid model may be rational and yet the operation of the model disastrous. One does not impugn the intelligence or integrity of voters when one concludes they are wrong, especially when their error is shared by legal and political elites and runs deep in the structure of their constitutional law. The hybrid model is premised on the false assumption that judges have a peculiar competence in relation to rights protection, viz. that rights are for judges and lawyers to decide. The model is designed to encourage voters and legislators to adopt this assumption, which readily explains why many voters and legislators are sceptical about an override power. The argument from demagoguery is neat but can be turned on its head: outsourcing one's moral judgment to judges and lawyers bears a structural similarity to reposing unearned trust in a demagogue. That said, the latter would require continuing political support; the former is relatively secure from interference.

The hybrid model is not an intelligent, stable compromise between the British and American models. It either collapses into the American model (in Canada) or weakens

[74] Goldsworthy, *Parliamentary Sovereignty* (n 1) 211.
[75] Goldsworthy, *Parliamentary Sovereignty* (n 1) 212.
[76] Goldsworthy, *Parliamentary Sovereignty* (n 1) 224.
[77] Goldsworthy, *Parliamentary Sovereignty* (n 1) 224.
[78] Goldsworthy, *Parliamentary Sovereignty* (n 1) 224.

the integrity of the British model (in New Zealand and the UK). In Canada, the Charter is constitutionally secure and cannot be dethroned save by constitutional amendment, which is all but impossible. The Canadian people chose the Charter (notwithstanding Quebec's concerns), but they lack the effective continuing capacity to choose again, which is hard to square with the argument that the Charter passes democratic muster. The Charter has instituted an aggressive form of judicial review of legislation, which persists despite the formal capacity of legislatures to immunise some legislation from at least some types of Charter review. Goldsworthy argues that the override power should be understood to be a way for legislatures to privilege their view of rights over that of courts. This understanding is attractive but, I fear, unreal. The override power is expressly framed as a power to dispense with rights rather than a power to prioritise legislative decisions about rights over judicial decisions.[79] This framing is apt to distort public deliberation and makes it very difficult to freely exercise the power. The Government will be slow to propose legislation that can so easily be misrepresented by media or opposition. It follows that the override power is not a discipline on Canadian judges; indeed, if anything, one might speculate that it emboldens them, for judges may tell themselves that they are not in the end responsible. Canadian courts are relatively free from real political constraint and seem to me even more self-confident than their American counterparts.[80] I conclude that judicial review in Canada is not a half-way house between the British and American models – it is instead a form of the latter. The override power is significant, for it provides a means by which, if the politics were to change, voters and legislators might attempt to resist judicial supremacy and, to this extent, judicial review in Canada may be the less constitutionally secure instance of North American judicial review. But courts in Canada just as much as in America are the decisive agents for choosing what rights require.

Happily, the situation in New Zealand and the UK is very different. Unlike the Charter, the HRA and the NZBORA are ordinary statutes and may be repealed or amended like any other statute; in the UK, in recent years, repeal of the HRA has been a live prospect. Parliament thus retains full legal authority to vary or cancel the scheme by which British or New Zealand courts subject legislation to rights review. In both jurisdictions, courts do not have authority to quash incompatible statutes, which remain valid, but are required to strive to interpret those statutes consistently with rights. This interpretive direction is a significant constitutional innovation, which does undermine the rule of law.[81] But it is importantly distinguishable from judicial review of legislation. In the United Kingdom, courts also have authority to declare legislation incompatible with rights. This does not invalidate the statute, but does trigger executive power to change the law and may also prompt Parliament to amend or repeal the relevant statute. Parliament retains authority to refuse to change the impugned law and the default is that the statute remains good law unless and until Parliament legislates. This default is vital and sharply distinguishes the UK from Canada.[82]

[79] Goldsworthy notes that the drafting of section 33 is a problem (Goldsworthy, *Parliamentary Sovereignty* (n 1) 219), and then goes on to consider whether a differently worded override power might be used more frequently (at 222–23).

[80] Consider, for example, *Canada v Bedford*, 2013 SCC 72, [2013] 3 SCR 1101; *Carter v Canada (Attorney General)*, 2015 SCC 5, [2015] 1 SCR 331; see also D Newman, 'Judicial Power, Living Tree-ism, and Alterations of Private Rights by Unconstrained Public Law Reasoning' (2017) 36 *University of Queensland Law Journal* 247.

[81] Ekins, 'Rights, Interpretation and the Rule of Law' (n 16).

[82] *cf* A Kavanagh, 'What's so Weak about "Weak-Form Review"? The Case of the UK Human Rights Act 1998' (2015) 13 *International Journal of Constitutional Law* 1008; for my part, I take the HRA to encroach upon legislative freedom but not to destroy it: Ekins (n 45) 595–97.

I mention in passing that I doubt Goldsworthy's argument that it lies within the power of Parliament to change the default by deeming statutes to be invalid if passed in breach of convention rights unless Parliament were expressly to legislate otherwise. This would not be analogous to how EU law is received into British law, for in that case each Parliament since 1972 has legislated on the premise that its enactments are to be read subject to contrary European law, as it is at the time of enactment and as it will be in the future.[83] Thus, membership of the EU has changed the context in which Parliament legislates, which bears on the intention of each new enactment. Goldsworthy envisages Parliament's intention to legislate inconsistently with convention rights failing to take effect unless and until it expressly cancels the default, established by an earlier Act of Parliament, that Parliament cannot legislate in breach of rights. But each Parliament enjoys continuing authority to make law and, if it manifests its intention to legislate, its intention is and should be decisive. Parliament could enact a prospective Henry VIII clause, authorising courts to amend legislation yet to be enacted, and in a sense this is how section 3 of the HRA sometimes operates. However, it could not prevent successive Parliaments from enacting the legislation they intend to enact by requiring express cancellation of the default that legislation cannot be enacted in breach of convention rights. Thus, I deny that Parliament in Wellington or Westminster has the capacity to enact an equivalent to the Charter.

Parliament retains a robust capacity to defy or ignore a judicial declaration of incompatibility. However, this capacity, while constitutionally vital, cannot properly be understood without noting the wider context in which the HRA operates, viz. the UK's membership of the *European Convention on Human Rights* (ECHR) and subjection to the jurisdiction of the Strasbourg Court. In many cases, a declaration of incompatibility reports or anticipates that unless the statute is changed the Strasbourg Court will be likely to hold the UK to be in breach of the ECHR. This holding cannot itself compel Parliament or change domestic law, but it does change the UK's obligations in international law. This international dimension reinforces the weight of a declaration, for Parliament comes under much pressure to conform to Strasbourg judgments or to avoid inviting adverse judgments. The pressure is a function not of the disapproval of voters, to whom defiance of Strasbourg will often (rightly) seem like good sense, but is a function instead of diplomatic complications and elite dissatisfaction, with many in the legal and political elite arguing that the principle of the (international) rule of law requires the UK to conform. Again, it remains important that Parliament may stand its ground, as it has done in relation to prisoner voting, but the HRA is nested within, and derives much of its force from, ECHR membership. In other words, rights adjudication in the UK is at least as much a function of international agreement as it is of domestic legislation. The latter may be repealed straightforwardly by Parliament; the Government may withdraw from the former, but this is costly and difficult. Rights adjudication in and over the UK follows from voluntary actions of the UK's representative institutions but cannot easily be undone and is designed to limit, and to some extent is effective in limiting, democratic freedom.

The NZBORA is relatively less important, and less controversial, than the HRA. This is partly because the international context is very different, but also because the NZBORA has not been taken to license radical statutory interpretation, and because it does not authorise judges to declare legislation incompatible with rights and freedoms. Strikingly,

[83] See further Ekins, 'Legislative Freedom' (n 45) 588–90.

New Zealand courts have recently assumed a power to declare legislation incompatible with the NZBORA, despite the absence of any statutory power to this end.[84] In this way, the NZBORA, itself the model for the HRA, is being reanimated in light of the HRA. This move on the part of the New Zealand courts is unjustified by law or principle and risks entangling the courts in controversies that ought not to be for them to decide. The blithe assumption that parliamentarians will (or should!) respond respectfully and patiently to such judicial interference, not required by statute, is unfounded.[85] However, the NZBORA clearly remains much less significant a limitation on Parliament's lawmaking freedom than the HRA, let alone the Charter.

It is clear that much separates New Zealand and the United Kingdom, on the one hand, from Canada on the other. Judicial review of legislation in Canada conforms to a North American model. Judicial review in New Zealand and the United Kingdom remains anchored in the British model. Neither the HRA nor the NZBORA are constitutionally secure and Parliament remains largely free, legally and constitutionally, to legislate as it chooses. Judicial review in these jurisdictions undermines constitutional principle, including by encumbering legislative freedom, but the constitutional cost is relatively muted when one considers the Canadian equivalent. The UK's membership of the ECHR is a distinct ground for problematic constitutional rights adjudication and the shadow of Strasbourg reinforces the domestic judicial role. ECHR membership is difficult to square with the British model, but importantly the UK and its representative institutions remain capable of defying Strasbourg. Thus, it is difficult to speak of a hybrid model that embraces Canada, New Zealand and the UK. One might say that all three polities share a partial loss of confidence in the British model, but this obscures more than it reveals. For, New Zealand and the UK remain robustly committed to parliamentary sovereignty, with rights adjudication important but not yet controlling, and with some public dissatisfaction with its scope.

VI. Conclusion

Goldsworthy's work illuminates the intellectual appeal and historical significance of the British model of parliamentary rights protection. His argument for legislative supremacy is powerful but risks understatement. It is true that how institutions should be designed, and powers separated, is to some extent unavoidably contingent. Still, there are good reasons for a general superiority of legislature over judiciary in relation to responsibility for choosing what the law should be. Whatever the merits of legislative supremacy may be, Goldsworthy reminds us that the constitutional law of Australia, New Zealand and the UK has long been committed to parliamentary sovereignty,[86] which it is not open to judges now to unsettle. It is not true that the common law has somehow always been our real constitution or that all common law polities are in the end committed to an American model of rights protection.

[84] *Attorney-General v Taylor* [2018] NZSC 104.

[85] Justice Glazebrook, 'Comment: Mired in the Past or Making the Future?' in Ekins, *Judicial Power and the Balance of Our Constitution* (n 23) 79, 84–86; cf J Finnis, 'Rejoinder' in Ekins, *Judicial Power and the Balance of Our Constitution* (n 23) 111, 114–15.

[86] In Australia's case, the commitment has of course been more to legislative supremacy subject to the limitations imposed by the federal compact.

These claims cannot be squared with our legal history, with sound legal philosophy, or with comparative constitutional law, as the diversity of law and practice across the common law world confirms. Goldsworthy's equivocation about the merits of the hybrid model, which he discerns in the law and practice of Canada, New Zealand and the UK, is a mistake. Authorising judges to oversee legislation by reference to a vague bill of rights is not consistent with democratic self-government. And, in practice, Canada collapses to the American model while New Zealand and the UK remain, not without struggle, instances of the British model, the historical foundations and continuing vitality of which are made vivid by Goldsworthy's masterful scholarship.

12

Political Obligation and Public Law

TRS ALLAN

I. Introduction

Discussions of political obligation usually proceed on the assumption that the law's requirements can be identified independently of questions about their moral bindingness. They can be identified, it is supposed, as a matter of social fact – what Parliament or courts have decided in exercise of their official authority. We can determine the law's demands, as dictated by statute or precedent or other appropriate source, and then inquire, as a separate matter, about whether or in what circumstances we have a moral obligation to obey. When the law is deeply unjust, or otherwise inimical to the public good, we may conclude that it exerts no moral force; we have no moral duty to comply and may be justified in resorting to civil disobedience.[1]

The premise, however, is controversial. It is not self-evident that the law can be identified in a morally neutral way, ignoring considerations of justice. The conception of law supported by legal positivism, focused on officially established sources of law, is open to challenge. In its reliance on official consensus as the ultimate basis for legal rights, duties and powers – the consensus described by Hart's 'rule of recognition' – the positivist conception lacks a convincing response to the important question of legitimacy.[2] While legal duties may be presented as 'obligations' only in a technical sense, as deriving from the contingent content of the rule of recognition, we may well feel that the analogy with moral obligations is more important than the Hartian vision allows. It is true, of course, that legality and legitimacy sometimes seem to be at odds: they are in obvious tension if we grant the 'legal' character of oppressive regimes that deny people their basic human rights. But we should make that concession with great care, if we make it at all. Legality connotes constraints on the exercise of power that have moral importance even when they fall short of the standards of governance to which we aspire.[3]

[1] For an eloquent defence of this view, see J Goldsworthy, *Parliamentary Sovereignty: Contemporary Debates* (Cambridge, Cambridge University Press, 2010) Ch 4, challenging the different thesis offered in my *Constitutional Justice: A Liberal Theory of the Rule of Law* (Oxford, Oxford University Press, 2001). See also J Goldsworthy, *The Sovereignty of Parliament: History and Philosophy* (Oxford, Oxford University Press, 1999) Ch 10, opposing the view that I defended in my *Law, Liberty, and Justice: The Legal Foundations of British Constitutionalism* (Oxford, Clarendon Press, 1993). I am very grateful to Jeffrey Goldsworthy for his careful and persistent critique of my work, thus obliging me to try to improve and clarify my arguments.

[2] HLA Hart, *The Concept of Law*, 2nd edn (Oxford, Clarendon Press, 1994).

[3] For a powerful critique of Hartian positivism, see NE Simmonds, *Law as a Moral Idea* (Oxford, Oxford University Press, 2007). I understand positivism as, in essence, the denial of any intrinsic connection between law

To invoke the status of law as a reason for compliance with a rule, or ruling, may readily be understood as making a certain kind of moral claim. The good citizen should be willing to accept the burdens and sacrifices involved in social and political cooperation when they come in the name of law – when the various demands of officials or fellow citizens carry the legitimacy that only a legal *imprimatur* can provide. To violate the law, correctly determined, is not fundamentally to flout an official consensus about the basis and consequences of the assertion of governmental power. It is rather to breach a moral duty of fidelity to the political community – to act *unjustly* by denying the rights of others as these are affirmed by the charter of justice that law, as the historical record of collaboration between equal citizens, provides.[4]

It may, of course, be controversial whether our own legal and constitutional order meets the necessary conditions. Its legitimacy is ultimately a matter of individual moral judgement. Each of us must decide whether, for all its demerits and deficiencies, the legal order nevertheless deserves allegiance – whether it can plausibly be treated as a charter of justice, properly respectful of individual human dignity. As Dworkin observes, however, we can honour a coherent, if imperfect, scheme of justice, conceived as a collaborative political endeavour, just as we may applaud the integrity of someone who adheres to a consistent and coherent moral outlook that we may think, in certain respects, misguided.[5] If we are reluctant to identify our institutional arrangements and requirements with *justice*, conscious of the ever-present tension between our political ideals and their practical implementation, we can nevertheless acknowledge the moral importance of the *quest* for justice. We can embrace a scheme of governance that aims to give systematic practical effect to a shared foundational premise – the equal dignity of all members of the community.

Legality and legitimacy are, accordingly, closely aligned. Legal obligations are moral obligations because they express our commitments as members of the political community – the commitments that arise from institutional arrangements and decisions to which we are party in virtue of that membership.[6] In granting the legitimacy of these arrangements (if we do), we acknowledge our obligation of obedience – obedience to law as it is correctly interpreted, in line with the fundamental rights and basic principles that underpin and justify our continuing allegiance. Law is not, on this view, to be equated with the demands of state officials, whatever their content. It is constituted, instead, by a persuasive interpretation of legal practice, viewed as a whole – an interpretation grounded in the political ideals that inspire and sustain our disposition to pursue the quest for justice, as embodied in legal and constitutional tradition.

In rejecting legal positivism, we must also challenge the standard approach to the issue of political obligation. When law is conceived as itself a moral idea, involving an

and morality, law being viewed as a tool for moral or immoral purposes. The separation of inquiry into law's nature from study of its justificatory force is a central feature of analytical legal positivism.

[4] The grounds of political obligation are, of course, contested and controversial. For the idea of fidelity, see GJ Postema, 'Law's Rule: Reflexivity, Mutual Accountability, and the Rule of Law' in Z Xiaobo and M Quinn (eds), *Bentham's Theory of Law and Public Opinion* (Cambridge, Cambridge University Press, 2014) 7; GJ Postema, 'Fidelity in Law's Commonwealth' in LM Austin and D Klimchuk (eds), *Private Law and the Rule of Law* (Oxford, Oxford University Press, 2014) 17.

[5] RM Dworkin, *Law's Empire* (London, Fontana Press, 1986) 165–66.

[6] Political obligation is associative, in Dworkin's view, by analogy with the responsibilities that we acquire towards other people in virtue of family or other relationships, as these are defined by social practice: ibid, 311–17.

interpretation of legal practice rooted in moral or political principle, we have good reason to suppose that it is normally morally binding. If considerations of justice are pertinent to our interpretation of the law's requirements – influential in guiding our reading of the rules and rulings apparently applicable to the matters in hand – we would expect to be morally bound by those requirements when correctly ascertained. If, in a generally benign regime, respect for human rights is ingrained in the political culture – perhaps even entrenched, to some degree, in a bill or charter of rights – any plausible interpretation of law will take account of them. Restrictions on liberty will be permitted only when they can be morally justified, even if that justification includes an appraisal of the wider public interest made by elected representatives or other suitably qualified officials.[7]

It is helpful to reflect on the nature of common law adjudication, which exemplifies an understanding of law at odds with legal positivism – a deliberative process guided less by determinate rules, marking out the boundary between law and morality, than by general principles blurring or even obliterating any such boundary. Common law rules are inherently defeasible, dependent on the applicability of underlying general principles to particular cases. While serving conveniently to summarise the implications of these principles, offering a degree of legal certainty in many cases, they are subject to qualification, reformulation or even abrogation by higher courts when the interests of justice so demand.[8] Admittedly, the interests of justice may be perceived by reference to legal principle – what is sought is typically consistency and coherence across the branch of law immediately in view – but there is normally a presumption that legal and moral principles converge. Law is treated as a path to justice, provoking argument about the right way to extend general principles, affirmed by practice and tradition, to new conditions or novel circumstances.

A common law judgment, applying the law to particular facts, strives to be both legally and morally correct. Based on legal principle, as exemplified by precedent, it purports to determine the requirements of justice – justice according to law. If, in practice, we often have doubts about a judgment's correctness, thinking it a departure from justice, our misgivings concern primarily the consistency of the law's administration. We think that a different decision on the facts of the case would better comport with the principles that provide the best moral account of our legal practice, viewed as a whole. We seek a high level of consistency, in the form of a deep principled coherence, to satisfy the basic idea of equality before the law. Everyone must be treated equally in accordance with legal principle, distinguishing between morally relevant and irrelevant features of his case. The distinctions made by legal rules or official decisions must be capable of justification by reference to the larger scheme of public justice. The public purposes that support these distinctions must themselves respect the constitutional rights that legal doctrine endorses. There is an interaction between practice and principle at every level. All governmental actions are vulnerable to challenge on the ground of inconsistency or arbitrariness – that they make distinctions between persons that do not reflect a genuine public interest, compatible with that general scheme of public justice.

[7] See further TRS Allan, *The Sovereignty of Law: Freedom, Constitution, and Common Law* (Oxford, Oxford University Press, 2013).

[8] Compare SR Perry, 'Judicial Obligation, Precedent and the Common Law' (1987) 7 *Oxford Journal of Legal Studies* 215, especially 234–57.

Dworkin's ideal of integrity captures the general idea of a unified scheme of public justice, constructed from an interpretation of legal practice, attuned to the demands of moral and political principle.[9] While justice is conceived as an ideal arrangement of the benefits and burdens of social cooperation, integrity is presented as its substitute in non-ideal conditions where people disagree about the requirements of justice. In Dworkin's account, integrity may depart so far from justice that, in certain cases, the normal obligation to obey the law may be overridden by a duty to resist injustice. While integrity entails a commitment to fundamental equality – government must treat its citizens with equal concern and respect – legal practice may exhibit a defective conception of equality. There may be genuine obligations of obedience, deriving from the community's commitments to equality and fraternity, which nonetheless conflict with requirements of justice, posing a moral dilemma for citizens and officials alike.[10]

It is doubtful, however, whether Dworkin's analysis can be sustained. A person who embraces the ideal of integrity is obliged to construct an account of legal practice that merits compliance. Practice commands allegiance, imposing a duty of obedience, only in so far as it is compatible with fundamental rights – the moral conditions of respect for human dignity. But the fundamental status of these rights, which give substance to the ideal of equality, will ensure that governmental action inconsistent with them lacks legal force or validity. Disobedience must therefore be understood as a demand for adherence to law as it is correctly interpreted. *Purported* rules or rulings are rejected as infringements of legal and constitutional principle: they cannot have the legal consequences that their authors or apologists claim. It makes no difference that the nature and scope of fundamental rights may themselves be controversial. Each interpreter must in good faith offer an account of these rights that both satisfies his conscience, enabling him to sustain his allegiance, and at the same time shows legal practice as a whole in its best light, *worthy* of such allegiance.[11]

Admittedly, the dissentient's arguments may fall on deaf ears: his own understanding may be rejected. But if that rejection is widespread and comprehensive, the would-be interpreter may succumb to scepticism.[12] Legal practice has proved resistant to a morally attractive interpretation; it deserves repudiation rather than allegiance. There is then no law at all in the moral or interpretative sense, pertinent to the ideal of integrity. But the conscientious citizen would be reluctant to draw that conclusion. It is usually more productive to seek common ground with one's fellow citizens, urging the incompatibility of morally offensive measures with the scheme of public justice that those citizens claim, in principle, to honour. Moral and political argument is then disciplined within mutually agreed parameters, invoking familiar paradigms.[13] Its focus is on a shared tradition that *constitutes* the community, forging an alliance between independent moral agents who must try to find, and then preserve, an honourable basis for continued cooperation.

[9] Dworkin, *Law's Empire* (n 5).

[10] For the alleged conflict between integrity and justice, see especially, Dworkin, *Law's Empire* (n 5) 202–206.

[11] For further argument, see TRS Allan, 'Law, Justice and Integrity: The Paradox of Wicked Laws' (2009) 29 *Oxford Journal of Legal Studies* 705; TRS Allan, 'Interpretation, Injustice, and Integrity' (2016) 36 *Oxford Journal of Legal Studies* 58.

[12] Compare Dworkin, *Law's Empire* (n 5) 76–85.

[13] For the role of paradigms in legal argument, see Dworkin, *Law's Empire* (n 5) 72–73, 88–92, 138–39.

Contrary, then, to the standard view, I shall deny that the law's requirements can be determined independently of the question of political obligation. Legal rights, duties, powers and immunities are dependent on an interpretation of legal practice grounded in moral or political principle. The assertion of state force on behalf of law must be morally justified; and the relevant justificatory argument is critical to the plausibility of any legal interpretation. It follows from a thoroughgoing interpretative approach, connecting legality with legitimacy, that legal obligations, correctly ascertained, are morally binding. They are the moral obligations that bind the citizen in virtue of his membership of the political community. While the law may differ from 'ideal' justice – the arrangements that anyone might like to write on a clean slate – it cannot differ from the scheme of justice that provides the most persuasive account of the legal record (statute and precedent). It cannot do so without undermining the interpretative endeavour, plunging the interpreter into scepticism. When the official sources of law, as these are widely understood, are wholly inimical to justice – violating any plausible understanding of equality or equal dignity – there are no genuine legal obligations. There are only official demands for compliance, which ought as far as possible to be resisted.[14]

Respect for – interpretative deference to – decision-making powers of officials, including elected members of the legislature, may entail limited and temporary departures from moral coherence. Conflict between the best theories of different parts of the law must be anticipated; we can hope to resolve such conflict, advancing towards a deeper overall coherence, in the evolution and refinement of precedent and principle. But grave injustice of a kind that threatens fundamental equality, infringing basic rights, is excluded by any plausible interpretation of law as a whole, regarded *as* a scheme of justice. It is excluded from the outset by the considerations of legitimacy that provide the taken-for-granted background to an interpretative judgement of law.[15]

When individual conscience is engaged in this way, we can offer a convincing account of public law. We can portray it as a flourishing debate over justice, disciplined by respect for past political decisions. The legal record is the basis for argument about how to translate our political ideals into a workable scheme, binding on all in spite of their doubts and disagreements. Its foundational commitment to justice – or at least the pursuit of justice – has important consequences. It precludes, in particular, the drawing of hard-and-fast lines between institutional spheres of control, independent of context. The legitimate scope of judicial review, or at least of interpretative ingenuity, depends on the nature and gravity of the threat to legal and constitutional principle. If the law is to be treated as morally binding, it must be correctly ascertained: it must be elaborated in accordance with the constitutional vision underpinning the allegiance that any interpretative judgement of law assumes. There cannot be governmental requirements or restrictions that operate

[14] Compare G Radbruch, 'Statutory Lawlessness and Supra-Statutory Law' (1946) (translated by B Litschewski Paulson and L Paulson) (2006) 26 *Oxford Journal of Legal Studies* 1, arguing that beyond a certain level of injustice, repudiating the fundamental demands of equality – the 'core of justice' – enactments can have no validity, amounting only to 'statutory lawlessness'. For relevant discussion, see TRS Allan, 'In Defence of Radbruch's Formula: Injustice, Interpretation, and Invalidity' in M Borowski, SL Paulson and J-R Sieckmann (eds), *Rechtsphilosophie und Grundrechtstheorie* (Tübingen, Mohr Siebeck, 2017) 87.

[15] See also R Alexy, 'A Defence of Radbruch's Formula' in D Dyzenhaus (ed), *Recrafting the Rule of Law: The Limits of Legal Order* (Oxford, Hart Publishing, 1999) 15; J Ebbinghaus, 'The Law of Humanity and the Limits of State Power' (1953) 3 *The Philosophical Quarterly* 14.

independently, invoking state or public interests that banish all considerations of equality or dignity.[16]

II. Constitutional Justice at Common Law

A common law judgment offers reasons in support of its conclusions; they are reasons intended to persuade the parties of its correctness, indicating the litigants' moral duties of compliance. Political obligation tracks the political morality on which any interpretation of law depends. The legal requirements judicially identified express the parties' respective moral duties as citizens, obligated to conform their conduct to justice as their community interprets that ideal. It would make little sense for a judge to determine the parties' legal obligations while supposing that they had moral obligations to resist his judgment, even if he thought that the legal rules applicable were in need of reconsideration. While respect for statute and precedent may sometimes preclude a judge from reaching a decision that he would otherwise prefer, he acknowledges the moral force of settled institutional arrangements, which circumscribe his own interpretative freedom. As a loyal participant in a shared practice, the judge must honour the constraints of collegiality: he accepts the authority of higher courts, trusting in their ability to promote a deeper and broader coherence across the law as a whole. The constraints are reasonable because they do not force him to inflict grave injustice – an assertion of state power in breach of basic rights. He would otherwise be compelled to challenge the legitimacy of governmental arrangements, denying any moral obligation of compliance.

While a higher court typically enjoys the freedom to reformulate legal rules in the service of justice – a conception of justice consistent with the legal record, viewed as a whole – lower court judges usually have more limited opportunity to move beyond the immediate context. The judicial power to modify common law rules in the course of adjudication must be exercised with circumspection; judges are charged with ensuring consistent practice across the jurisdiction. While everything is in principle open to reappraisal and revision, progress towards a unified ideal of justice must be measured and incremental. The higher courts are better placed to modify existing rules, when they prove inimical to justice in particular cases, without undermining consistency: their decisions will usually be followed by lower courts, allowing change to be assimilated more evenly across the legal system. A doctrine of stare decisis, then, can be defended as a necessary and legitimate constituent of the legal order, consistent with basic principles of equality and dignity.

The legal positivist may be inclined to object that, however flexible the doctrine of precedent may be, a court is bound by statute; and a statutory rule may impose requirements that conflict with the standards of justice developed by common law reasoning from general principle. In these circumstances, legal and moral obligation may be thought to diverge; a statutory rule, if gravely unjust, may provoke justified disobedience. As a contribution to the larger scheme of public justice, however, a statute cannot contradict that scheme by

[16] See also TRS Allan, 'The Moral Unity of Public Law' (2017) 67 *University of Toronto Law Journal* 1; see further, TRS Allan, 'Principle, Practice, and Precedent: Vindicating Justice, According to Law' (2018) 77 *Cambridge Law Journal* 269.

imposing requirements that undermine it. Being subject to judicial interpretation, a statutory provision has no power to inflict serious injustice; it means what it ought to mean when all the pertinent moral considerations are taken into account. It must be integrated into the larger body of law, reconciling statutory purposes and legal principle as the specific context demands. A judge must interpret the statute on the assumption that its application is intended to respect constitutional rights; public interests must not be advanced by means that flout the equal dignity of persons.[17]

The 'principle of legality' is often invoked to demand that any encroachment on rights be expressly enacted, signalling Parliament's deliberate and informed intention. But any such 'intention' can only be discerned by interpretation, which cannot be divorced from constitutional context. The appropriate reconciliation between statutory purpose and fundamental rights must be a matter of judgement, having regard to all relevant considerations. It cannot be a matter of legislative stipulation, divorced from the circumstances of the particular case in all its moral complexity. However clear the statutory language may be, as regards the general rule it provides, the question of its proper application to particular instances, as they arise in practice, remains. When the rule of law prevails, the citizen enjoys the protection of the law as a whole, mediating between governmental or statutory policy, on the one hand, and its consequences for individual liberty on the other. If it would be a usurpation of the legislative role for a court to override a legitimate statutory policy, reflecting Parliament's judgement of the public good, it would equally be a usurpation of the judicial role for the legislature to determine the particular case. The law applicable to identifiable individuals is always a moral judgement: legal obligation reflects an analysis of the law as a whole, viewed as a unified scheme of justice. That division of power between lawmaker and judicial interpreter is the foundation of the legal protection of human dignity – the means of bringing governance within the rule of law.[18]

In common law adjudication, accordingly, a statutory rule is analogous to its common law equivalent. If we can identify cases falling plainly within its scope, it is because its application in those cases would clearly advance the purposes apparently envisaged, without countervailing injury to important constitutional values or fundamental rights. Moral judgement is inescapable in all cases, whether we are applying a common law or a statutory rule. When the rule is applicable, determining the outcome, the decision is morally justified: we have taken all relevant moral considerations into account. We have deferred to the judgement of elected Parliamentary representatives as far as we think appropriate: we have accepted their right to set the policy agenda, determining the public interest immediately in view. But we have set moral limits to that agenda, or that conception of the public interest, in order to safeguard the law's integrity: we have sought a defensible outcome, reconciling legislative supremacy and the rule of law.[19]

Although Dworkin rightly argued that legal theory must simultaneously address both 'grounds' and 'force' of law – the means of identification of legal propositions and their

[17] Parliament is understood to legislate 'for a European liberal democracy founded on the principles and traditions of the common law': *R v Secretary of State for the Home Department, ex p Pierson* [1998] AC 539 (HL) 587 (Lord Steyn). That understanding places limits on what is commonly, but loosely, treated as an unqualified principle of Parliamentary 'sovereignty': see *R (Jackson) v Attorney General* [2005] UKHL 56, [2006] 1 AC 262 [101]–[102] (Lord Steyn).

[18] See Allan, *Sovereignty of Law* (n 7) Ch 3.

[19] Allan, *Sovereignty of Law* (n 7) Ch 5.

moral bindingness – he failed to see that it is ultimately the same inquiry. While insisting on the moral dimension of interpretation, bringing principle to bear on the facts of legal practice, he thought that those facts might nevertheless be inimical to a morally attractive outcome. If institutional practice were morally defective, afflicted by serious injustice, the best interpretation available might show the law in a poor light. Even if the law as a whole were sufficiently benign to give it legitimacy – people should accept a prima facie obligation to obey – there might be pockets of injustice, against which people could properly rebel. There would in some cases be a conflict between integrity and justice, pitting political obligation against a contrary obligation to resist injustice. If the Fugitive Slave Act, passed by Congress before the American Civil War, were valid, as was widely believed, it created a serious dilemma for judges in the northern states. They were obliged to choose between their legal and extra-legal moral obligations.[20]

We should insist on a stronger connection between integrity and justice than Dworkin allows. The equal status of persons that integrity assumes precludes valid governmental action that, on any plausible view, denies that status. A unified vision of constitutional justice is inconsistent with action that violates its first principles of respect for human dignity: it cannot countenance pockets of grave injustice that flout its moral foundations. While there must be space for argument about the nature and scope of fundamental rights – law as integrity encourages rigorous examination of its own general principles – such debate must respect the parameters that a common public system of justice provides. If there is no agreement even on paradigm cases, marking a shared commitment to certain principles and precedents, the debate is spurious. Legal argument could find no foothold in legal practice, expressing adherence to a common tradition.

The assertion of state power is either legitimate or illegitimate; there is no logical space in between. And law conceived as integrity unites legality and legitimacy. If governmental power were illegitimate, any obligation to obey would be minimal, confined to whatever degree of cooperation were necessary to avoid grave harm to individuals. Legal obligations, in so far as they were acknowledged at all, would not derive from any general theory of public law. When, however, we grant the legitimacy of our political arrangements – we succeed in avoiding scepticism – we must hold government officials to the standards of justice internal to our interpretative standpoint. Political obligation is conditional on the adherence of public authorities to the demands of human dignity; unjustified coercion, in breach of basic rights, is inherently unlawful.

If radical injustice is so endemic or ingrained as to undermine legitimacy, no morally attractive theory of law as a whole is available. Legal practice invites only scepticism: it cannot generate genuine obligations as it purports to do. When, however, we embrace the search for moral coherence – the 'circumstances of integrity' obtain – our theory of public law will rule unconstitutional all assertions of governmental power that violate its requirements.[21] Purported rules that threaten grave injustice are invalid, or must be circumscribed in application to protect basic rights. These are interpretative conclusions implicit

[20] Dworkin, *Law's Empire* (n 5) 219; RM Dworkin, *Justice for Hedgehogs* (Cambridge, Massachusetts, Belknap Press, 2011) 410–11.

[21] For the 'circumstances of integrity', see J Waldron, *Law and Disagreement* (Oxford, Oxford University Press, 1999) Ch 9.

in our constructive account of legal practice, which honours the dignity of persons as a basic premise of legitimate governance. Even if the Fugitive Slave Acts were valid law, as was widely assumed, they could not authorise iniquity. Their literal instructions were subject in practice to the countervailing demands of equality, due process, and federalism – as the most persuasive moral theory of such legal principles defined them.[22]

While a fundamental precept of equality is compatible with a wide discretion to govern in the public interest, as conceived by Parliament or executive government, it remains an important constitutional safeguard. The distinctions drawn between persons must be justifiable not merely by reference to immediate political aims, but also in the light of fundamental duties of impartiality and fairness. An apparently irrational distinction between foreign suspected terrorists, on the one hand, and British nationals under similar suspicion, on the other, was found, accordingly, to indicate an unnecessary and hence unlawful intrusion into liberty.[23] In the absence of apparent need to detain the latter group, it was impossible to defend the detention of the former. Lacking any legitimate justification, the distinction between foreigner and national was no more defensible than one based on race, disability, sex, or sexual preference.[24] Arbitrary distinctions, lacking appropriate justification, are contrary to the rule of law: the assault on legality undermines legitimacy.

The declaration of incompatibility with European Convention rights, issued under the UK *Human Rights Act 1998*, admittedly fell short of a declaration of invalidity.[25] There are grounds, however, for thinking that the Act might have been interpreted, more appropriately, as an immigration measure, upholding the distinction between foreigner and national for as long as deportation proceedings were being lawfully conducted – with appropriate protections of due process for those detained. That course would have avoided leaving the detainees without practical legal remedy against measures of dubious legality. The duty to interpret the law compatibly with Convention rights, under the Human Rights Act (s 3), is supplementary to an analogous duty of interpretation in support of constitutional rights at common law. The Convention in large part echoes the protections for human dignity implicit in the common law – inherent in the moral theory of UK law on which legitimacy depends.[26]

Principles of due process or procedural fairness are fundamental to the rule of law; they supplement principles of equality or rationality by ensuring that the general law is duly applied to particular cases. The law cannot be fairly and consistently applied if those accused of wrongdoing are unable to defend themselves, answering precisely framed charges by calling evidence intended to refute them. Those threatened with the loss of liberty on grounds of suspected terrorist activity are entitled, accordingly, to appropriate procedural safeguards. And such entitlement cannot be cancelled by statute without calling into question the legitimacy, and hence the legality, of the preventative measures in question.

[22] Compare RM Dworkin, 'The Law of the Slave-Catchers' *The Times Literary Supplement* (London, 5 December 1975) 1437.

[23] *A v Secretary of State for the Home Department* [2004] UKHL 56, [2005] 2 AC 68.

[24] ibid [238] (Lady Hale).

[25] Although the offending provisions of the *Anti-Terrorism, Crime and Security Act 2001* were not themselves held invalid, the detention regime was impugned by quashing the Derogation Order, designed to release the British Government from its duties to uphold the right to liberty under Article 5 of the *European Convention on Human Rights*.

[26] For further discussion, see Allan, *Sovereignty of Law* (n 7) 114–19.

A statutory provision that, on its face, forbids disclosure of evidence against the suspect on grounds of national security must be narrowly construed, allowing such disclosure as is necessary to enable the suspect fairly to answer his accusers. In upholding the right to a fair trial in the face of such legislation, the appellate committee of the House of Lords maintained the integrity of the rule of law.[27] The Convention rights served once again to bolster ordinary domestic law: the commitment of the common law to basic procedural fairness was explicitly acknowledged. The doctrine of Parliamentary sovereignty must be understood as a principle of legislative supremacy that operates in harmony with principles of legality that sustain the rule of law. By tolerating breaches of fundamental rights, the courts would undermine the foundations of legality – thereby removing the very ground of the sovereignty doctrine itself.[28]

From an internal, interpretative viewpoint, considerations of legitimacy are always pertinent to legal reasoning. The lawyer attempts to make moral sense of the legal record, showing how statute and precedent can be understood in a manner that justifies state coercion. Respect for the basic rights of persons is a condition of justification. Rules or rulings that, on their face, present a challenge to any plausible moral reading, consistent with basic rights, must be given a more nuanced construction, preserving those rights against unwarranted attack. If no such construction were available – perhaps because the only statutory purpose discernible is the victimisation of despised individuals or groups – the interpreter's allegiance to law would be put in issue. An assault on the moral foundations of law, as the interpreter conceives them, destroys both legal and political obligation.

III. Human Rights and Human Dignity

We determine our legal obligations by interpreting our legal practice, in all its subtle complexity, in light of the moral ideal of legality, or the rule of law. And we may understand the rule of law by reflection on the associated ideal of human dignity, which identifies the conditions under which state coercion has genuine moral authority. The various civil and political rights that we celebrate as natural or human rights – applicable everywhere as limits on, or requirements of, legitimate government – can be understood as expressions of that fundamental idea of dignity. We seek to show what these rights require in the concrete circumstances of our own jurisdiction – here and now.

While dignity is plainly associated with equality – the assumption that the lives of all human beings are of equal value or importance – it is also related to liberty or independence. Each person must have the freedom to lead her life according to her own convictions about what a worthwhile life entails. She can neither be denied the right to think freely about such matters, nor be forced to live against the grain of her own convictions, at least in so far as she does not interfere with the similar freedom of others. Government must not act towards anyone in a manner that denies her equal status as a member of the political community. It cannot deliberately harm her interests, in the absence of any proper

[27] *Secretary of State for the Home Department v AF (No 3)* [2009] UKHL 28, [2010] 2 AC 269.

[28] Compare *Canada (Citizenship and Immigration) v Harkat*, 2014 SCC 37, [2014] 2 SCR 33, adopting an analogous interpretation of the *Immigration and Refugee Protection Act 2001*, preserving compliance with principles of fundamental justice articulated by section 7 of the *Canadian Charter of Rights and Freedoms*.

justification consonant with her equal dignity; and it cannot deny her the ethical independence that respect for that dignity demands.

Dworkin identifies two pertinent principles of ethics, expressing the value of human dignity. The principle of self-respect requires that everyone must treat his own life as a matter of importance: it is objectively important that he should live well in the sense that 'his life be a successful performance rather than a wasted opportunity'.[29] The principle of authenticity, secondly, makes each person responsible for judging what counts as success in his own life: 'he has a personal responsibility to create that life through a coherent narrative or style that he himself endorses'.[30] The latter principle requires ethical independence, which is usurped when anyone is forced to live according to someone else's judgement about the values that his life should display or exemplify. These ethical principles plainly have moral and political implications. The objective value of one's own life is the value of humanity itself, as Kant's philosophy insists: 'You must treat yourself as an end in yourself, and therefore, out of self-respect, you must treat all other people as ends in themselves as well.'[31]

While coercive government is necessary for dignity, providing the conditions that make it possible to live well, as dignity requires, it also threatens dignity by subjecting the many to the power of the few. Political obligation holds, accordingly, only under certain conditions; a government is legitimate only when it meets those conditions. Governments must treat all persons with equal concern and respect. Even when their laws and policies fall short of justice, correctly determined, governments may still be legitimate if they can be interpreted as recognising both the equal importance of each citizen's life and each person's ethical responsibility: 'A government can be legitimate, that is, if it strives for its citizens' full dignity even if it follows a defective conception of what that requires.'[32] Dworkin distinguishes, accordingly, between the basic political right to equal concern and respect, on the one hand, and on the other, a yet more abstract and fundamental right to be treated with the right attitude – the right 'to be treated as a human being whose dignity fundamentally matters'.[33] We must ask whether the laws and policies of any political regime can 'sensibly be interpreted as an attempt, even if finally a failed attempt, to respect the dignity of those in its power'.

In Dworkin's view, legitimacy is a matter of degree because, while a state's laws and policies may in the main show a genuine attempt to protect its citizens' dignity, it may be impossible to reconcile some discrete laws or policies with that attempt. If political processes exist to correct the injustice, the state may preserve its legitimacy and citizens may retain political obligation, at least to a substantial degree.[34] Dworkin suggests that, while certain policies may stain the state's legitimacy without destroying it altogether, it is a matter of the depth or darkness of the stain:

> If it is contained, and political processes of correction are available, then citizens can protect their dignity – avoid becoming tyrants themselves – by refusing so far as possible to be party to the

[29] Dworkin, *Justice for Hedgehogs* (n 20) 203.

[30] Dworkin, *Justice for Hedgehogs* (n 20) 204.

[31] Dworkin, *Justice for Hedgehogs* (n 20) 265. Dworkin invokes what he calls 'Kant's principle', unifying ethics and morality: 'A person can achieve the dignity and self-respect that are indispensable to a successful life only if he shows respect for humanity itself in all its forms': at 19.

[32] Dworkin, *Justice for Hedgehogs* (n 20) 322.

[33] Dworkin, *Justice for Hedgehogs* (n 20) 335.

[34] Dworkin, *Justice for Hedgehogs* (n 20) 322–23.

> injustice, working in politics to erase it, and contesting it through civil disobedience when this is appropriate.[35]

It is not clear, however, that political obligation can really be a matter of degree. If we concede that legal rules do not impose any moral duty of obedience simply in virtue of their status as law, we appear to deny political obligation altogether. There may, of course, be discrete moral obligations arising to cooperate with particular official demands: such cooperation may sometimes serve the public interest, even when we deny any legal duty to comply. And in so far as the law tracks and reinforces the ordinary demands of personal morality, prohibiting such wrongs as killing and assault, it will lend precision to existing moral obligations. But an obligation to obey the law, pursuant to recognition of the legitimacy of political arrangements, must be in its nature all-encompassing. It is the quality of being *law*, correctly determined, that gives governmental requirements their intrinsic moral force.

Admittedly, political obligation is often treated as merely prima facie: the moral obligation to obey may be overridden, at least in exceptional cases, by a contrary moral obligation of resistance to injustice. But that view overlooks or undervalues the role of moral principle in determining the law's content. As I have argued, a gravely unjust provision – so grave as to preclude conscientious compliance – cannot be law in the first place. Its injustice isolates it as fraudulent: it masquerades as law while flouting the standards of justice that legal and constitutional principles impose. An apparently iniquitous measure, violating basic rights, confronts the citizen with a dilemma, which is as much legal as moral in nature. Either that measure, when correctly interpreted, leaves such basic rights intact or else – if treated as valid – it threatens the legitimacy of the legal order. A violation of fundamental rights is an assault on the moral foundations of the polity.[36]

The conscientious citizen must perforce join the interpretative legal debate, invoking constitutional principle, or else turn his back on an illegitimate system that does not deserve his allegiance. The term 'civil disobedience' is inapt, in the first alternative, if it suggests the repudiation of law on moral grounds. The dissentient is instead demanding allegiance to law as it is correctly interpreted, giving appropriate weight to established principle and basic rights. His appeal to legality, as a barrier against arbitrary power, signals his adherence to the integrity of the legal order. He calls on government or the political majority to acknowledge the power of his critique, rescinding its demands as concededly illegitimate and, hence, unlawful.[37]

When we grant the moral nature of law – the critical role of moral judgement in translating official texts and decisions into legal rights, powers and duties – we must recognise the space for moral debate and deliberation within the legal process. No one is required to bow to any prevailing consensus about the law's requirements, which can be determined only by persuasive argument. If the majority is morally bound to defend its own understanding, the dissentient is in the same position: she must argue in support of the rights or interests that she believes to be unfairly and unconstitutionally threatened. If the injustice that she

[35] Dworkin, *Justice for Hedgehogs* (n 20) 323.

[36] By breaching the moral conditions of genuine community, an infringement of basic rights undermines associative obligation. For the conditions of such obligation, see Dworkin, *Law's Empire* (n 5) 199–201. These conditions elaborate the requirement of equal concern, encapsulated in the ideal of integrity: at 213–14.

[37] See further Allan, *Sovereignty of Law* (n 7) 142–43, 157–61.

perceives is grave, and the majority proves unyielding, the dissentient may be forced into scepticism. There is finally no interpretation of legal practice that can render it legitimate: an account that might justify the practice, as she conceives it, turns out to be ineligible on grounds of fit. But the lack of fit is itself a conflict of moral judgement, reflecting deep disagreement about the nature and implications of people's basic rights and, in consequence, the legality of their treatment by officials.[38]

Dworkin's distinction between more abstract and more concrete versions of the basic right to equal concern and respect is designed to distinguish 'human rights', properly so called, from other political rights, which even if possessing legal status depend, in detail, on specific jurisdictional history and practice. The idea is to circumvent moral disagreement by moving to a more abstract level of argument. We may understand the various provisions of the *Universal Declaration of Human Rights*, not as precise definitions of rights, but 'rather as directions pointing to sensitive areas in which a nation's practices might well reveal the unacceptable attitude that violates the basic human right' – showing indifference or contempt toward the human dignity affirmed in the Declaration's preamble.[39] It is largely a matter of good faith and sincerity. While human rights have universal application, the interpretative question is responsive to differences of economic, cultural and political circumstance. Local conditions are relevant to our judgements about good faith and sincerity.

Within our own jurisdiction, however, we must be more robust in our defence of the demands of human dignity, as we perceive them. We cannot rest content with judgements of good faith and sincerity – even if those judgements are likely to depend, to a substantial degree, on the plausibility of the pertinent accounts of human dignity. In the domestic rather than the international context, we must argue about the true requirements of the principle of equal concern and respect. Officials may misunderstand the demands of human dignity, misled by ideological commitments inconsistent with the liberties it supports. There must be democratic debate about the true content of political rights and their counterpart in the legal process – argument over the correct understanding of legal and constitutional rights. We must anticipate disagreement and acknowledge the scope for reasonable differences of view. But we must also insist, individually, on compliance with basic standards of justice, declining to cooperate, if necessary, with official action that infringes them. We seek, each of us, to be governed by rules or rulings that we can accept as morally binding without thereby forfeiting our self-respect.

On the domestic rather than the international plane, accordingly, the distinction between human rights, on the one hand, and other political rights that possess constitutional status, on the other, is no longer salient.[40] All legal rights that curtail the discretion of political authorities, being enforceable in court at the behest of those affected, operate as conditions of legitimacy and legality alike. In a common law legal order, moreover, they have status as common law rights – individual rights that flow from the conception of human dignity implicit in legal tradition and practice, when favourably interpreted. When judges

[38] For discussion of Dworkin's interpretative criteria of fit and appeal, see Allan, 'Interpretation, Injustice, and Integrity' (n 11) 68–74.

[39] Dworkin, *Justice for Hedgehogs* (n 20) 337–38.

[40] Compare with G Letsas, 'Dworkin on Human Rights' (2015) 6 *Jurisprudence* 327, 332–35, arguing that 'human rights' should be taken to refer to '*all* the liberal-egalitarian rights against the government that we have in a constitutional democracy'.

insist on these common law credentials, they are not (or not merely) seeking to entrench judicial power against political change that may sweep away an enacted bill of rights. They recognise their responsibility to fashion a coherent body of fundamental law that, by affirming these basic rights, preserves legitimacy – ties the test of legality to the requirement of respect for human dignity.[41]

IV. Private Conscience and Public Law

The deep integration of law and morality, from an interpretative viewpoint, fosters an attractive vision of liberal democracy. Loyalty to a legitimate regime can readily coexist with the demands of individual conscience – legal integrity, in Dworkin's sense, coinciding with personal integrity, as citizens strive to interpret legal practice in the light of moral principle. Resistance to oppressive rules or rulings can be understood as opposition to illegitimate departures from legal tradition – violations of fundamental rights as defined by that tradition. The question of legitimacy is always central to the issue of legality. Moral claims of right, founded on considerations of justice, have legal counterparts, giving individuals access to independent judicial appraisal of their treatment by a public authority.

A statutory prohibition of assisted suicide, intended as a safeguard for those vulnerable to the influence of unscrupulous advisers, may present an acute moral dilemma in particular cases. When the person seeking help to bring an end to intolerable pain or suffering is physically dependent on others, having no power of independent action, she is deprived of the ordinary freedom to choose the timing of her own death. She is forced to continue a life that she may loathe when other people are normally at liberty, if necessary, to escape a similar fate. Could this restraint nonetheless be *law* – a legitimate restraint that she and her closest advisers must in good conscience observe – despite the manifest inequality entailed? Even if we think that suicide usually demonstrates a tragic failure to appreciate the true value of life – an ethical mistake we deplore – it does not follow that we may properly impose that view on someone who disagrees, especially when we have not ourselves experienced the pain or humiliation that she may be forced daily to endure.[42]

Confronted by a claim of right to assisted suicide, when family members, friends or doctors are available to provide such assistance, the court's legal dilemma reflects the moral one. It is dependent for resolution on a judge's interpretation of constitutional rights – the conception of human dignity expressed in legal practice when correctly understood. While a general rule forbidding assisted suicide may serve as a legitimate protection for the weak and vulnerable, it may require qualification in extraordinary cases. Even when enacted by

[41] See especially *Kennedy v Charity Commission* [2014] UKSC 20, [2015] AC 455 (*Kennedy*) [46] (Lord Mance), envisaging the emergence of a synthesis between Convention and common law; *R (Osborn) v Parole Board* [2013] UKSC 61, [2014] AC 1115 (*Osborn*) [54]–[63] (Lord Reed), affirming that 'the protection of human rights is not a distinct area of the law, based on the case law of the European Court of Human Rights, but permeates our legal system'; and citing *R (Daly) v Secretary of State for the Home Department* [2001] UKHL 26, [2001] 2 AC 532 [30] (Lord Cooke of Thorndon), observing that 'some rights are inherent and fundamental to democratic civilised society', and adding that: 'Conventions, constitutions, bills of rights and the like respond by recognising rather than creating them'.

[42] For helpful discussion, see generally RM Dworkin, *Life's Dominion: An Argument about Abortion, Euthanasia, and Individual Freedom* (London, Harper Collins, 1993) especially Ch 7.

unambiguous legislation, the prohibition need not be construed as an *absolute* rule. It need not be treated as conclusive of every particular case, regardless of all the circumstances. The claimant is arguably entitled to challenge the legitimacy of the rule's application to herself – in her quite exceptional circumstances. And is not the judge, drawing on fundamental principle, empowered to determine the justice of her claim?

The citizen presents a claim of right – an assertion that to deny her the help that she requests is unconscionable and illegitimate. In judging its truth or soundness, the court must determine the limits of the general rule's authority: it must settle its meaning and scope by reflection on its contribution to the larger corpus of constitutional and criminal law. A general principle of legislative supremacy has the consequences that its place in the legal order ordains when we treat the law as a guide to justice. If the court invokes the statutory prohibition to reject the claim – to deny the right alleged – it must do so on the basis of a defensible view of all the pertinent moral considerations. Its theory of legislative authority must reflect a considered view of the conditions of legitimacy. The claimant is entitled to know how, in all the circumstances, the law can properly block her pursuit of her own best interests as she conceives them. The limits of political obligation are put in issue as the claimant challenges the legitimacy, and hence the legality, of her treatment.

Each of the claimants in *Nicklinson* was paralysed as a result of a stroke or accident, and wholly dependent on family and carers.[43] Each regarded his life as undignified, distressing and intolerable, seeking acknowledgment of the right to assistance in ending it. In so far as the *Suicide Act 1961* prohibited assisted suicide in all circumstances, the claimants challenged its compatibility with the *European Convention on Human Rights*, seeking a declaration of incompatibility under the *Human Rights Act 1998*. One of the claimants sought an order requiring the Director of Public Prosecutions (DPP) to clarify her published policy, applicable to assisted suicide, so as to give assurance to those who might help the claimant travel to Dignitas in Zurich that they would not thereby risk prosecution. Section 2(1) of the Suicide Act provided that an offence was committed if a person did an act capable of encouraging or assisting the suicide or attempted suicide of another, and the act was intended to have that effect. The consent of the DPP was required for any prosecution. The Supreme Court was informed that, between 1998 and 2011, over 200 people had travelled to Dignitas to die and that no one providing assistance had been prosecuted.

The focus on European Convention rights, and their mode of enforcement in the United Kingdom, inevitably deflected attention from the legal and constitutional principles applicable in domestic law. Admittedly, the European Court of Human Rights had ruled that it was for Member States to form their own view about the implications for assisted suicide of the right to respect for private life under Article 8.[44] Common law constitutional rights,

[43] *R (Nicklinson) v Ministry of Justice* [2014] UKSC 38, [2015] AC 657 (*Nicklinson*). Between High Court and Court of Appeal hearings, Tony Nicklinson died of pneumonia after a painful course of self-starvation. Paul Lamb was then added as a claimant. 'Martin', the third claimant, had abandoned an attempt to end his life by self-starvation.

[44] While Article 8(1) guarantees everyone 'respect for his private … life', Article 8(2) permits interference with the exercise of the right if such interference is 'in accordance with the law' and 'necessary in a democratic society … for the prevention of disorder or crime, for the protection of health or morals, or for the protection of the rights and freedoms of others'. While affirming that Article 8(1) encompasses the right to decide how and when to die, and to avoid a distressing and undignified death, the Strasbourg Court has also observed that Member States possess a wide 'margin of appreciation' as regards the application of these rights in the national context.

moreover, will usually march in tandem with Convention rights, reflecting similar moral concerns as these have been addressed in previous cases. However, discussion of the appropriateness of a declaration of incompatibility, in all the circumstances, had the effect of excluding serious consideration of the issue of interpretation – the critical issue as regards domestic law, if not also the Convention.[45]

Although the Supreme Court summarily dismissed the argument that the Suicide Act should be read so as to comply with the Convention, it is doubtful whether it was right to do so. Arguably, at least, it was open to the Court to acknowledge an implicit exception to the statutory prohibition. That prohibition did not apply, on correct construction, if in all the circumstances it would penalise conduct necessary to give effect to constitutional rights – specifically, the claimant's right to determine the manner and timing of his own death. In addition to the injunction in the Human Rights Act (s 3) to seek a Convention-compliant interpretation, the appropriate reading was available at common law. It is a general presumption that statutes do not curtail fundamental rights in the absence of explicit enactment to that effect; and section 2 made no mention of the basic rights in question.

The importance of personal autonomy was well established in respect of a hospital patient's ability to decline further treatment, despite contrary medical advice. Provided that she has the necessary capacity to make the decision, understanding its consequences, the patient can refuse the medication on which she depends to remain alive. She is finally responsible for deciding where her own best interests lie.[46] While the intrinsic value of human life is fundamental, underpinning the law in many fields, its relationship with the values of individual autonomy and human dignity is complex and controversial. There is force in the Supreme Court's view that it is only the need to protect the vulnerable that provides a legitimate rationale for a prohibition on assisted suicide.[47] It must otherwise be for individuals to make up their own minds, in exercise of their ethical responsibility, about the permissibility of assisting suicide – the circumstances in which, if ever, it would be right to ask for or lend such assistance.

The Supreme Court was understandably concerned about the difficulties of framing a suitable scheme, permitting assisted suicide in certain cases, while erecting suitable protections for those susceptible to improper pressure. It could not substitute a judicial scheme for a legislative one, enacted by Parliament after full investigation and debate. In affirming the constitutional rights of the claimants, however, the Court would not be usurping the role of the legislature. It would be merely recognising the exceptional circumstances of such claimants and interpreting the law as a whole in an appropriate manner, consonant with their human dignity. Lady Hale rightly denied the legitimacy of an absolute ban on assisting suicide, which unfairly sacrificed the interests of the claimants. No one who had read the claimants' accounts of their lives and feelings could doubt that they experienced the state's interference as a form of cruelty.[48]

[45] A Supreme Court majority declined to determine whether the Act infringed the Convention. Lady Hale and Lord Kerr, however, would have made a declaration of incompatibility. Some of the judges thought that the issues should be left entirely to Parliament to determine (see further below).

[46] *Re B (Consent to Treatment: Capacity)* [2002] EWHC 429 (Fam), [2002] 1 FLR 1090, considered by Lady Hale in *Nicklinson* (n 43) [301]–[304].

[47] See especially Lady Hale in *Nicklinson* (n 43) [311].

[48] See Lady Hale in *Nicklinson* (n 43) [313]. Lord Kerr observed: 'To insist that these unfortunate individuals should continue to endure the misery that is their lot is not to champion the sanctity of life; it is to coerce them to endure unspeakable suffering': at [358].

While in subsequent cases the Court would have to decide how far the exception extended, there is little reason to think that a defensible line could not be drawn between the ordinary case, governed by the general statutory rule, and the truly exceptional case, in which application of the general rule would be intolerably unjust – an infringement of constitutional rights. The extreme physical incapacity of the claimants marks them out as a special class, calling for great compassion. The existence of a statutory rule may qualify, but need not frustrate, the ordinary process of the common law, in which the balance of principles is adjusted in the light of all the circumstances. It is wrong to withhold protection of a person's rights, implicit in the most persuasive interpretation of law, simply because it may encourage others to press less deserving cases.

In summarising the essential requirements to be met before a person should be allowed help to end his life, Lady Hale observed that the Court of Protection and the Family Division regularly applied similar criteria in other types of case.[49] She observed that such an appropriate judicial procedure would be an adequate safeguard for the vulnerable: 'They simply would not meet the qualifications to be allowed help.'[50] She added that it 'would be a more suitably targeted solution than any prosecution policy, however enlightened and humane, could ever be'. A judicial procedure, applying suitable criteria, 'would have the merit of resolving the issue in advance rather than relying on *ex post facto* executive discretion to solve the problem'.[51]

If the universal prohibition were indeed a disproportionate interference with the claimants' rights to choose the time and manner of their deaths, failing to strike a fair balance between such rights and the wider interests of the general community, as Lady Hale concludes, it is hard to accept that jurisdiction did not already exist to vindicate these rights. The Court's assumption that an apparently absolute rule did not allow for implicit exceptions – implicit in the state's commitment to fundamental human rights – and the focus on declarations of incompatibility, as a suitable means of impugning unjust rules, combined to obscure the Court's primary constitutional duty. Preserving the rule of law involves adherence to the individual rights on which legitimacy depends – sustaining citizens' allegiance by acceding to their justified demands for the state to respect their equal dignity. Lady Hale shows that the Court could delineate the pertinent legal criteria, reconciling statute and common law, general rule and specific exception.

Far from usurping a legislative discretion reserved for Parliament, the Court would have been building on legal practice as it already operated. As a matter of policy, the DPP declined to prosecute in cases of assisted suicide involving friends and family members motivated by compassion. Moreover, in *Purdy*, the House of Lords had instructed the DPP to publish his policy guidelines, applicable to cases of assisted suicide, in order to make the risk of prosecution more foreseeable to those who were contemplating lending such assistance.[52] In *Pretty*, the European Court of Human Rights had held that Article 8 of the Convention ensured the right to decide how and when to die, including the right to avoid

[49] A person would need to have the capacity to make the decision for himself. He must have reached the decision freely without undue influence. He must have made the decision in full knowledge of his situation, the options available, and the consequences of the decision. And he must be unable, because of physical incapacity or frailty, to give effect to the decision without assistance. See Lady Hale in *Nicklinson* (n 43) [314].

[50] Lady Hale in *Nicklinson* (n 43) [316].

[51] Compare Lord Neuberger at *Nicklinson* (n 43) [108].

[52] *R (Purdy) v Director of Public Prosecutions* [2009] UKHL 45, [2010] 1 AC 345 (*Purdy*).

a distressing and undignified death.[53] The principle of 'legality' (in the sense invoked by Article 8(2)) demanded, accordingly, a greater foreseeability as regards the administration of the law; and the effect was to strengthen the position of individuals who, out of compassion for a loved one, were prepared to risk prosecution by defying the literal terms of the statutory prohibition.[54] A prosecution conducted in breach of the published guidelines would clearly be questionable: it could be challenged on grounds of irrationality or breach of legitimate expectations.[55]

It was implicit in these arrangements that it would be wrong, notwithstanding the statutory prohibition, to prosecute a person who had acted, in good faith and out of compassion, in circumstances where inaction would have frustrated another's right to choose the time and manner of her death. In substance, if not in form, the absolute prohibition constituted by the literal terms of the statute has been transmuted, humanely, into a general prohibition, respectful of the autonomy of those who may reasonably require assistance in procuring an end to intolerable lives. That autonomy was already an established common law value, protecting a hospital patient's right to refuse unwanted medical treatment even when she is likely to die without it.[56] European Convention rights supplement and overlap with common law rights – rights implicit in the most persuasive account of the 'unwritten' constitution of the United Kingdom.[57]

An interpretation of legal practice, faithful to the moral principles that animate it, must reflect not only the letter of the law, correctly interpreted, but also its regular administration. The Code should accordingly be treated as part of the law in determining the legality of the ban on assisted suicide as a matter of fundamental constitutional law. If it is only in combination with an appropriately framed code of practice, fairly and consistently applied, that the statutory ban is consistent with the basic rights of the claimant – consistent with his human dignity – then executive practice must be treated as an integral part of the law. The prosecution policy translates an apparently blanket ban on assisted suicide into a workable regime, preserving its legitimacy.[58]

[53] *Pretty v United Kingdom* (2002) 35 EHRR 1 [67]; see also *Haas v Switzerland* (2011) 53 EHRR 33 [51]; *Koch v Germany* (2013) 56 EHRR 6 [46], [51]; *Gross v Switzerland* (2014) 58 EHRR 7 [60].

[54] In *Purdy*, the DPP's Code of Practice was regarded, for the purposes of Article 8(2) of the Convention, as forming part of the law in accordance with which an interference with the right to respect for private life may be held to be justified. It could add the precision, and hence the foreseeability, that the principle of legality required: *Purdy* (n 52) [47] (Lord Hope).

[55] The unfairness entailed in such a prosecution would fall within the English doctrine of legitimate expectations, which operates in public law in a manner analogous to estoppel in private law: it is unfair, and hence an abuse of power, to renege on a promise about future action or policy in the absence of countervailing public interest considerations of sufficient strength. It would plainly be hard to establish such a countervailing public interest if it involved arbitrary discrimination between persons similarly situated (comparing the defendant with others who had, in reliance on the official guidance, given assistance to a would-be suicide out of concern and compassion for the person concerned). The doctrines of legitimate expectation and reasonableness are, accordingly, quite closely aligned (see further Allan, *Sovereignty of Law* (n 7) 108–10).

[56] In *Carter v Canada (Attorney General)*, 2015 SCC 5, [2015] 1 SCR 331 [66], the Supreme Court of Canada held that a prohibition on assisted suicide was inconsistent with a person's freedom to request palliative sedation, refuse artificial nutrition and hydration, or require the removal of life-sustaining medical equipment.

[57] Convention rights and common law rights must be understood as an integrated scheme of justice, not treated as wholly separate sources of obligation in the positivist manner (as, for example, in P Sales and R Ekins, 'Rights-Consistent Interpretation and the Human Rights Act 1998' (2011) 127 *Law Quarterly Review* 217). See *Kennedy* (n 41) and *Osborn* (n 41).

[58] See further Allan, *Sovereignty of Law* (n 7) 179–84.

Does this approach contravene the principle, asserted in the *Bill of Rights 1689*, that the executive must not suspend the law or its execution? In *Nicklinson*, Lord Hughes objected to any requirement that the DPP should state in advance when certain conduct will or will not result in prosecution for that reason. She was likely thereby to exempt a group of potential offenders and so modify the law as contained in statute or common law.[59] She was 'in immediate peril of crossing a constitutional Rubicon'.[60] Lord Sumption expressed similar reservations, purporting to identify

> a fine line between, on the one hand, explaining how the discretion is exercised by reference to factors that would tend for or against prosecution; and, on the other hand, writing a charter of exemptions to guide those who are contemplating breaking the law and wish to know how far they can count on impunity in doing so.[61]

There is no unconstitutional suspension of the law, however, when we reject a literal reading of the Suicide Act (s 2(1)), in favour of a more nuanced construction, excluding exceptional cases where an absolute ban would inflict grave injustice. The administrative practice, formalised by the DPP's official Code, affirms and promulgates a lawful and legitimate mode of application, reflecting that construction. It confirms a legal regime on assisted suicide that both honours the statutory ban, as a general rule, and acknowledges the boundaries of that rule – boundaries that recognise the proper autonomy or independence of those who may be wholly reliant on others for help in acting on their own considered and informed decisions. In so far as executive discretion permits many who are technically guilty to escape prosecution, it represents a merciful application of the statutory prohibition. But in so far as it has the effect of exempting those who come to the rescue of people whose suffering is out of all proportion to any legitimate public interest, it acknowledges the constitutional rights that the ideal of legality affirms.

V. Conclusion

In opposition to the standard view of law as a series of discrete instructions for different purposes, which may or may not be just or wise, I have defended a more unified vision of law as justice – justice as embodied in a shared tradition, in which principle and precedent coalesce in a quest to identify and honour the requirements of human dignity. Rules or rulings that violate that tradition, as correctly interpreted, impose no genuine obligations; everyone must accept responsibility, accordingly, for her own interpretative judgement. The requirements of law are dictated by a theory of legal practice – a constructive interpretation, in Dworkin's terms, grounded in moral and political commitment and conviction. The constitutional rights that frame the boundaries of legitimate state action must be ascertained and enforced as guarantees of respect for human dignity. We maintain the rule of law by adherence to these guarantees – by treating them as the essential premises of any legal argument about rights, duties, immunities or powers.

[59] *Nicklinson* (n 43) [272].

[60] See also J Finnis, 'Invoking the Principle of Legality against the Rule of Law' [2010] (4) *New Zealand Law Review* 601, 616, objecting that the 'principle of legality' was invoked 'simply to promote the interest that an admitted prospective law-breaker has in knowing how likely he or his accomplice is to get off scot-free'.

[61] *Nicklinson* (n 43) [241].

When we find the necessary moral resources within our own tradition, we can resist interpretations of law that would, in our best judgement, violate fundamental principles of justice. We can repudiate rules or rulings – or interpretations of rules or rulings – that would infringe human dignity as our practice illuminates that ideal. If necessary, we must read in exceptions or qualifications to general rules, enabling us to further the public good without doing unjustifiable injury to anyone's liberty or well-being. Equality of concern and respect is a demanding standard: it precludes the adoption of absolute rules, impervious to the consequences for those persons whose circumstances may be quite special. *Nicklinson* affords a striking example, forcing us to confront the potential for conflict between legal obligation, as conceived by officials, and the moral independence of persons who are, in substance, forced outside the interpretative community – excluded by the imposition of unreasonable constraints or demands.

Lord Sumption maintained that the question of whether to relax or qualify an absolute prohibition on assisted suicide was 'a classic example of the kind of issue which should be decided by Parliament'.[62] There was no consensus on the choice between two fundamental but mutually inconsistent values: the principle of autonomy competed with the sanctity of life. Any resolution made by judges would amount to the 'imposition of their personal opinions' and therefore 'lack all constitutional legitimacy'. It is doubtful, however, whether we confront a stark choice between inconsistent values. It is more plausible to suppose that we seek a deeper integration of values, ceding a degree of responsibility for judging the implications of life's sanctity, or inviolability, to the person whose life is directly concerned. If, moreover, the relaxation of an absolute prohibition protects the special interests of a limited class of persons – those for whom the prohibition imposes a wholly disproportionate physical and psychological burden – there is no improper invasion of the legislative sphere. There is no imposition of personal opinion, extraneous to legal judgment: there is only a determination of the limits of legitimate coercion, pursuant to the judicial role as bulwark against arbitrary government.

If, as Dworkin claims, political obligation is a more 'protestant' idea than is usually recognised, involving 'fidelity to a scheme of principle each citizen has a responsibility to identify, ultimately for himself, as his community's scheme', we must mark the implications for our grasp of public law.[63] The community's scheme must be articulated by reference to the principles and paradigms on which any plausible interpretation must build. Each interpreter must strive, nevertheless, to articulate its detailed exposition in the light of the political ideals that underpin his allegiance. Legality and legitimacy go hand in hand: that is the promise of liberal democracy, based on principles of freedom and equality. The limits of the powers of public authorities are defined by the overall constitutional scheme, which incorporates the basic rights that equal citizenship demands. There are, accordingly, no legal powers or duties that flout those rights – undermining equality – even if they are asserted in the name of Parliamentary sovereignty. Free citizens live under the rule of law; and the rule of law is a moral ideal, engaging the moral and political convictions of the protestant interpreter. It is to those convictions that any intelligible legal judgment must finally be addressed.

[62] *Nicklinson* (n 43) [230].
[63] Dworkin, *Law's Empire* (n 5) 190.

13

Response to Contributors

JEFFREY GOLDSWORTHY*

I am immensely grateful to the editors and contributors, all of them friends as well as esteemed academic peers, for the great honour they have paid me in creating this book. It will always be one of my favourites! Every chapter deals with issues I have discussed in my work, and I have learnt much from each of them. Here I offer responses that vary considerably in length, depending mainly on the extent to which each chapter engages with my work in ways I disagree with.

I. Intentionalism in Legal Interpretation

A. Larry Alexander

Larry's contribution responds to my recent criticisms of his intentionalist theory of legal meaning in a volume of essays in his honour.[1] Larry is unpersuaded, and argues that while his approach is theoretically superior to mine, the difference is of no practical significance anyway.[2]

I acknowledge that the practical differences are relatively minor. We are both intentionalists, who regard the meaning of a posited law as either identical to or determined heavily by the lawmaker's communicative intentions. That 'or' marks our disagreement. Larry advocates subjective intentionalism (SI), maintaining that interpreters should seek the lawmaker's actual subjective intentions, whereas I defend objective intentionalism (OI), holding that those intentions are relevant only in so far as they were publicly manifested, in the form of textual and contextual evidence reasonably accessible to the public. Larry acknowledges that OI is the majority position among originalists.[3]

As for theoretical superiority, I am not sure what Larry's argument is. He suggests that I trade on a confusion or ambiguity about 'meaning',[4] but I do not understand his argument

* I thank Dale Smith and Kevin Toh for very helpful comments.

[1] J Goldsworthy, 'Subjective versus Objective Intentionalism in Legal Interpretation' in H Hurd (ed), *Moral Puzzles and Legal Perplexities: Essays on the Influence of Larry Alexander* (New York, Cambridge University Press, 2018) 170.

[2] Larry Alexander, 'Goldsworthy on Interpretation of Statutes and Constitutions: Public Meaning, Intended Meaning and the Bogey of Aggregation', chapter 2 of this volume, 5.

[3] ibid 8.

[4] ibid 9.

in the following three paragraphs, which lead to a somewhat different conclusion: that our positions are 'actually two different ways of characterising the same thing'.[5] If so, then surely neither position is theoretically superior to the other, except in so far as one characterisation is more easily understood.

On my view, it is not just a question of which theory provides a better account of textual meaning in general. It is also a question of which theory provides a better account of the conventional legal norms that, in common law systems, ultimately determine the meanings of written laws. I continue to believe that OI fits much better than SI with the interpretive norms traditionally accepted by common law courts. Their long-standing reluctance to consult legislative history as evidence of legislative intent is more consistent with OI than SI.[6] They increasingly draw a distinction between lawmakers' actual subjective intentions, which might be unknowable, and intentions that – through publicly available evidence – have been 'expressed' or 'manifested' in the making of a law.[7] They aim to give effect to the 'objective meaning' of a statute, which is evidenced by both the linguistic conventions that determine literal meanings, and contextual evidence of the legislature's intentions that is readily available to its intended audience, such as common sense understandings of its likely purposes and intentions, the historical circumstances in which the statute was enacted and (to a limited extent) legislative history.[8]

At the conclusion of my contribution to Larry's volume, I deferred consideration of the practical importance of the choice between SI and OI, but suggested that it was likely to be of some significance, because otherwise it would be puzzling that experienced judges so often emphasise the objective nature of the legislative intentions they seek. Furthermore, practical matters such as the admissibility of legislative history are likely to turn partly on that choice.[9] It is also relevant that many (perhaps most) judges and lawyers do not find SI plausible. Consequently, insisting on SI risks discrediting intentionalism in general, and making non-intentionalism appear more attractive than it is. These judges and lawyers are more likely to find OI credible, so even if Larry is right that there is no other significant practical difference between SI and OI, that in itself is a practical reason to prefer OI.

B. Patrick Emerton and Lisa Burton Crawford

Patrick and Lisa reject what they rightly acknowledge to be 'the long-held view' that 'statutes should be interpreted in such a way as to give effect to the intentions of the Parliament that enacted them'.[10] They offer a 'partial defence' of an alternative view recently advocated by some members of the Australian High Court, which they concede remains

[5] ibid.

[6] See A Scalia, *A Matter of Interpretation: Federal Courts and the Law* (Princeton New Jersey, Princeton University Press, 1998) 30–31 on the relatively recent embrace of legislative history by American courts.

[7] R Ekins and J Goldsworthy, 'The Reality and Indispensability of Legislative Intentions' (2014) 36 *Sydney Law Review* 39, 46–47.

[8] Scalia (n 6) 17; see also Ekins and Goldsworthy, ibid.

[9] Goldsworthy, 'Subjective versus Objective Intentionalism' (n 1) 188.

[10] Patrick Emerton and Lisa Burton Crawford, 'Statutory Meaning without Parliamentary Intention: Defending the High Court's "Alternative Approach" to Statutory Interpretation', chapter 4 of this volume, 40.

'uncertain' and 'under-theorised'.[11] This is a form of textualism – although they prefer the term 'legalism'[12] – which holds that the meaning of a statute can be ascertained without resort to legislative intention, except (as I understand it) in the form of a fiction that is 'imputed' to the legislature.[13] As they see it, this meaning is ascertained from two sources:

a) the conventional meaning of the text, which is much richer than its literal meaning by also drawing content from 'established and mutually understood practice[s]' that constitute the contexts in which words are used.[14] Thus, 'our knowledge of the world in general' supplements 'our knowledge of words' to generate the 'purpose and context' from which we derive meaning;[15] and
b) interpretive principles, especially presumptions of fictional legislative intentions, that are 'grounded in' the structure of the *Australian Constitution*.[16] They concede that this aspect of the alternative view is particularly under-developed and requires further explication.

Patrick and Lisa criticise the thesis, propounded by Richard Ekins and me,[17] that legislative intentions are both real and indispensable to statutory interpretation. As to the reality of such intentions, they express no firm opinion; perhaps they are attracted to the alternative view on constitutional rather than metaphysical grounds.[18] Be that as it may, they conclude that Richard and I have failed to provide sufficient detail to show how interpreters can ascertain legislative intentions that actually help to resolve interpretive problems.[19] There is some merit to this complaint, but then, Richard's and my argument was set out in general terms and we made no attempt to apply our theory to any particular statute. We argued, inter alia, that interpretation depends on context and purpose – which Patrick and Lisa accept[20] – and also that this makes sense only if context and purpose help to clarify legislative intention – which they do not accept. If we are right, then to provide the details they seek we need only show how context and purpose can assist in ascertaining the meaning of a particular statute. There are many examples of that.

As to whether legislative intentions are dispensable, Patrick and Lisa provide an alternative account of some examples that Richard and I relied on. They suggest that drafting errors can be detected and corrected without relying on legislative intention, simply by reference to 'an institutionally-mandated requirement that the statute be treated as a coherent whole'.[21] I doubt that every drafting error that has been corrected rendered the statute in which it was situated internally inconsistent – sometimes just very odd, but what authority do judges have to remove oddness from statutes?

They also claim that the meanings of terms or phrases such as 'peace, order and good government' (used in British statutes conferring legislative power on colonial legislatures)

[11] ibid 40–41.
[12] ibid 41.
[13] See text to nn 31 and 39–40, below.
[14] Emerton and Burton Crawford (n 10) 51.
[15] Emerton and Burton Crawford (n 10) 51; see also 49.
[16] Emerton and Burton Crawford (n 10) 41, 47.
[17] See Ekins and Goldsworthy (n 7).
[18] Emerton and Burton Crawford (n 10) 42, 45.
[19] Emerton and Burton Crawford (n 10) 43–44.
[20] Emerton and Burton Crawford (n 10) 46, 48.
[21] Emerton and Burton Crawford (n 10) 45 n 32.

depend not – as I have suggested – on evidence of legislative intention, but merely on established convention.[22] I have two doubts about this. One is that in the very first case that arises in which such a meaning must be determined, there may be no such convention; the court's decision helps to establish the convention. The second doubt is that even later on, it may be uncertain whether the term or phrase bears its conventional everyday meaning or its conventional legal meaning – a possible ambiguity that presumably requires recourse to apparent legislative intention to resolve. Moreover, when there is no real uncertainty, that is surely because there is no real uncertainty about that intention.

Patrick and Lisa also claim that when a statute states that it 'is not intended to do x', this should be understood as a non-literal figure of speech that really means 'is not to be taken as doing x'.[23] But this is far from obvious, and how would we reach that conclusion? The meaning of some figures of speech is virtually fixed by social convention (eg, 'I have butterflies in my stomach'). But otherwise, we understand a word or phrase to be a non-literal figure of speech if there is persuasive contextual evidence of the speaker's intention to use it that way; as Patrick and Lisa observe, 'one can use a figure of speech without being *committed* to a literal understanding of it'.[24] Does Patrick's and Lisa's claim depend on evidence that the legislature was not committed to the literal meaning of the statement – in other words, on evidence of what it intended by uttering it? If not, how do we decide whether the statement should be interpreted literally or not? Perhaps they would reply: 'given that legislative intentions do not exist, the statement should be given a non-literal meaning in order to make sense of it'. But if legislative intentions do not exist, we have only the words with their conventional meanings, and then there would be no basis for understanding them non-literally except through what I call 'rectifying interpretation'.[25] This involves a court changing the meaning of a statute in order to improve it. But if a statutory provision refers to something that does not exist, should it be rectified in order to make some sense of it? Or should it be simply ignored?

Patrick and Lisa say that Richard and I are wrong to assert that inanimate objects do not have purposes; after all, we commonly make and understand statements such as 'a knife has the purpose of cutting'.[26] I concede that this is true, but only in a secondary, derivative or parasitic sense. As I have said more recently elsewhere,

> *strictly speaking* legal norms – like other inanimate objects – do not have purposes. A purpose is a kind of intention: an intention to achieve something. Only intelligent, reasoning beings can have intentions and purposes. It is true that we casually say things such as: 'The purpose of a hammer is to bang in nails'. But a hammer does not have a purpose of its own, which is independent of the purposes of human beings. Its purpose must be the purpose for which it was either designed, or acquired, in order to be used, or for which it is in fact used, and that must be a purpose of the person or people who either designed, acquired or use it. The purpose of a hammer that has not yet been purchased might differ from that of a hammer that has been purchased for some idiosyncratic purpose, such as to form part of a sculpture.[27]

[22] Emerton and Burton Crawford (n 10) 46 n 34.
[23] Emerton and Burton Crawford (n 10) 46 n 35.
[24] Emerton and Burton Crawford (n 10) 46 n 35 (emphasis added).
[25] See text below at nn 71 and 122–32.
[26] Emerton and Burton Crawford (n 10) 48.
[27] J Goldsworthy, 'Functions, Purposes and Values in Constitutional Interpretation' in R Dixon (ed), *Australian Constitutional Values* (Oxford, Hart Publishing 2018) 43, 44–45 (emphasis added).

Dictionary definitions of 'purpose' include many shades of meaning, but they all revolve around concepts such as intention, desire, aim, objective, design and so on. The shade of meaning that applies to inanimate objects is usually something like: 'the object for which anything exists or is done, made, used etc'.[28] That is consistent with my view: an inanimate thing 'exists', or is 'made' or 'used', for some 'object', only if and in so far as some intelligent agent designed, made or uses it to achieve that object.

Patrick and Lisa concede that '[i]t may be that the knife's function [to cut] is itself a consequence of its being built by someone having an appropriate intention'.[29] Yet they go on to assert that 'Texts, too, can have purposes that are independent of the mental states of those who created them.'[30] As an example, they discuss a sign on a hotel door headed 'IN THE EVENT OF FIRE', and argue that although it is uncontentious that this sign has the purpose of telling occupants what to do in the event of a fire, no-one involved in the sequence of actions leading to the placement of the sign need have had the purpose of telling occupants this.[31] I find this possibility extremely unlikely. It is hardly an accident that the sign is prominently displayed; it is the result of a sequence of coordinated intentional actions, which must have been instigated by someone within an organisation that does, or at some stage did, own or manage the hotel. The example may raise the related issue of whether such an organisation can be said to have an intention or purpose. If it were sued for contributing to an occupant's death as a result of a fire, it would plead in its defence that, through its employees and agents, it had taken reasonable steps intended to guide occupants to safety in the event of a fire.

Patrick and Lisa say that the occupant 'is entitled – given the context – to impute certain intentions to the (purely notional) author of its words', as 'part and parcel of recognising the sign's purpose, and is licensed by familiarity not with anyone's mental states, but with the world, and the things in the world the words (so interpreted) refer to …'[32] I respectfully disagree: occupants would impute that purpose to whoever was ultimately responsible for the sign's placement because, given the context, it would seem overwhelmingly more likely than not that they acted with that purpose in mind. On my objective intentionalist theory, that would be sufficient to attribute that purpose to those ultimately responsible for the placement of the sign, even in the extremely unlikely scenario envisaged by Patrick and Lisa. Such a sign would not be taken to have the purpose of guiding anyone if it was evidently not displayed for that purpose: if, for example, it was displayed in a teenager's bedroom, along with other signs apparently stolen for the mischief of it. Nor would the occupants of hotel rooms take such signs seriously if they somehow learnt that they had been placed there by an arsonist seeking to maximise casualties in a planned fire.

Patrick and Lisa discuss Richard's and my example of someone who orders a hamburger without specifying that it be cooked and its ingredients be fresh and edible. We said that 'if [that person] thought about this at all', he 'would expect it to be taken for granted'.[33] They describe the first quotation as a 'tell-tale phrase' revealing that the person's 'individual

[28] *Macquarie Dictionary*, 5th edn (Sydney, Macquarie Dictionary Publishing Pty Ltd, 2009) 1346.
[29] Emerton and Burton Crawford (n 10) 48.
[30] Emerton and Burton Crawford (n 10) 49.
[31] Emerton and Burton Crawford (n 10) 49.
[32] Emerton and Burton Crawford (n 10) 49.
[33] Emerton and Burton Crawford (n 10) 50, quoting Ekins and Goldsworthy (n 7) at 55–56.

subjective intentions' are irrelevant to the meaning of his order.[34] But this misses part of our point. We were relying on John Searle's notion that communication is intentional, and that intentionality depends on a vast 'Background' of unstated assumptions and practical know-how. The full meaning of what we say depends on this Background because our intentions do so. Searle may be wrong, but as I explained more fully elsewhere, his main point is that intentions do not consist solely in what is transparent to consciousness: they are rooted in implicit and even partly unconscious understandings.[35]

In denying that the meaning of the order depends on the speaker's intentions or purposes, Patrick and Lisa consider a case where the speaker actually wanted an uncooked or inedible hamburger. They say that

> the waiter, in virtue of the received practice around the use of the word hamburger in the context of ordering in restaurants, was entitled to have taken the customer (regardless of subjective mental states) to have referred to a cooked and edible hamburger.[36]

I fully agree, except for the words in parentheses. Their point damages Larry Alexander's subjective intentionalism (described above), but not my objective intentionalism. On my view, the waiter was entitled to take the customer to have ordered a cooked and edible hamburger because the available (objective) evidence of the customer's subjective intentions – textual and contextual – suggested that she intended to do so. Her subjective intentions are important, but only in so far as they are objectively manifested and accessible to her intended audience – here, the waiter. If her subjective intentions were made apparent to the waiter, then he would understand the order differently, and the conventional practices that Patrick and Lisa rely on would be outweighed. But if that is so, then how could the speaker's subjective intentions have ever been irrelevant?

Patrick and Lisa have therefore not persuaded me that context and apparent purpose are somehow relevant to meaning intrinsically, in their own right, rather than because they are evidence of intended meaning.

Richard and I expressed concern about the possibility of judges developing common law principles of statutory interpretation in order to expand their ability to control or even limit Parliament's lawmaking authority.[37] Patrick and Lisa suggest two possible solutions. One, which they mention but do not explore, is that 'legislative intention' may be a useful fiction serving as a 'disciplining device' that deters judges from doing this.[38] But I cannot understand how appealing to intentions known to be fictitious could serve that function (why comply with a fiction?), unless the fiction stands for something else that has some disciplinary authority – but what could that be?

The second solution is to abandon the notion that the principles of statutory interpretation are matters of common law. Patrick and Lisa regard their most important contribution to be reinforcing the idea that 'the constitutional structure gives rise to and informs the

[34] Emerton and Burton Crawford (n 10) 50.

[35] J Goldsworthy, 'Implications in Law, Language and the Constitution' in G Lindell (ed), *Future Directions in Australian Constitutional Law: Essays in Honour of Professor Leslie Zines* (Sydney, Federation Press, 1994) 150, 158–61, esp 160.

[36] Emerton and Burton Crawford (n 10) 51.

[37] Ekins and Goldsworthy (n 7) 44–45.

[38] Emerton and Burton Crawford (n 10) 53.

more specific principles … of statutory construction'.[39] But I am sceptical: after all, most of these principles pre-date the Constitution, and they continue to apply to state parliaments whose legislative power is not conferred by the Constitution, and also to parliaments in other common law jurisdictions where the *Australian Constitution* is irrelevant.

According to Patrick and Lisa, constitutionally-based principles of statutory interpretation, and established referential practices, justify intentions being 'imputed' to Parliament, without any need to seek its actual intentions.[40] I am not sure what they mean by 'imputing intentions': do they mean (a) inferring from context and purpose that Parliament actually had these intentions; (b) deeming Parliament to have had these intentions, regardless of whether or not it did or even could have had them; or, if there is a difference, (c) attributing to it fictional intentions? I am therefore not sure how their position differs from my objective intentionalist theory, which also licenses interpreters to impute intentions on the basis of whatever evidence of subjective intentions is publicly accessible (namely, text, context and apparent purpose), which interpreters neither need to nor should look behind.[41]

Almost everything that Patrick and Lisa say in their section II.B. seems consistent with my objective intentionalism.[42] Moreover, I have difficulty understanding what they mean by 'intention' and 'purpose', if it is not Parliament's actual intention and purpose, when they say that the plurality in one case 'drew upon Hansard to confirm that the arbitration regime established by the statute in question … was *intended* to operate summarily and speedily [etc]', and when they approve the further statement that the alternative interpretation 'would frustrate the … evident *purpose* of the statutory scheme'.[43] I am equally puzzled by their apparent approval of a statement that extrinsic materials can be used to establish 'a background understanding of the problems Congress was *trying* to address'.[44] Are the italicised words non-literal figures of speech, which really mean something else, or examples of a phenomenon that Richard and I described: '[j]udges who deny the reality of legislative intentions find it impossible to avoid regular and apparently orthodox reference to them', 'because it is essential to the sensible interpretation of statutes'?[45]

I was not persuaded by the few examples that Patrick and Lisa provide of interpretive principles that could plausibly be regarded as grounded in the structure of the Constitution. One example is the presumption that Parliament legislates prospectively, which they say is based on 'the difficulty and unfairness of binding people to laws that are unknown'.[46] I accept that legislation ought not to be difficult or unfair, but where does the Constitution state or imply this, and that this should inform the interpretation of statutes? Is it in the words conferring legislative power, especially 'peace, order and good government', which Patrick and Lisa rightly describe as 'words of exhortation, reflecting the framers' view that

[39] Emerton and Burton Crawford (n 10) 58.

[40] Emerton and Burton Crawford (n 10) 59 and 56.

[41] See J Goldsworthy, 'Moderate versus Strong Intentionalism: Knapp and Michaels Revisited' (2005) 42 *San Diego Law Review* 669, and Goldsworthy, 'Subjective versus Objective Intentionalism' (n 1).

[42] This includes n 84, and the discussion of *Certain Lloyd's Underwriters v Cross*, in Emerton and Burton Crawford (n 10) 56–58.

[43] Emerton and Burton Crawford (n 10) 57–58 n 88, discussing and quoting from *Probuild Constructions (Aust) Pty Ltd v Shade Systems Pty Ltd* [2018] HCA 4 esp at [48].

[44] Emerton and Burton Crawford (n 10) 57–58 n 88, approving a statement by Jonathan T Molot.

[45] Ekins and Goldsworthy (n 7) 59 and 60.

[46] Emerton and Burton Crawford (n 10) 59–60.

the democratically elected Parliament could be entrusted to act in the best interests of the Commonwealth'?[47] Or are they arguing that the mere fact that a constitution – perhaps any constitution – confers on governmental institutions public power that should be exercised in the public interest entails that a fictional intention to act reasonably and fairly should always be 'imputed' to the legislature? Or, rather than such a general intention, more specific fictional intentions to act according to whatever principles of interpretation existed at the time that constitution came into force? Also, do these imputed intentions only come into play when legislation is textually ambiguous, vague or otherwise unclear – or do they contribute to the meaning of legislation generally? I hope that Patrick and Lisa can supply answers to these questions in a future effort to provide further and better particulars of their alternative view.

C. Dale Smith

Dale provides a characteristically meticulous and illuminating analysis of the nature of statutory purpose. I agree with almost all of it. Although lawyers and judges frequently refer to the purposes of statutes, they have never agreed on anything like a precise understanding of the nature of these purposes. Dale carefully distinguishes three different accounts of legislative purpose, and explains why he prefers the first. Like Dale, I regard a purpose as a kind of intention,[48] and if purpose is to play a useful and distinctive role in statutory interpretation, it must be distinguished from other kinds of intentions. Dale prises apart various kinds of intentions, including communicative intentions, norm intentions and application intentions. He offers good reasons for identifying statutory purposes with application intentions, discusses possible problems with and objections to doing so, and identifies several constraints on which application intentions can count. At present I have nothing useful to add.

II. Originalism in Constitutional Interpretation

A. Larry Solum

Larry provides a careful and sympathetic analysis of my normative defence of originalism in 'The Case for Originalism',[49] and makes many constructive suggestions for elaboration, strengthening and repair. It was impossible for me, in a single chapter covering many other aspects of the originalism debate, to provide a comprehensive discussion of the normative issues. I agree that more needs to be said.

According to Larry, moral and legal claims are both normative claims. 'If an action is legally required, that provides a reason for performing the action'.[50] He recognises that 'there

[47] Emerton and Burton Crawford (n 10) 54.

[48] See above, text to nn 26–28.

[49] J Goldsworthy, 'The Case for Originalism' in G Huscroft and B Miller (eds), *The Challenge of Originalism: Theories of Constitutional Interpretation* (New York, Cambridge University Press, 2011) 42.

[50] Lawrence B Solum, 'Goldsworthy on the Normative Justification for Originalism', chapter 5 of this volume, 70.

are deep questions about the nature of legal normativity'.[51] I can agree that legal claims are normative claims, provided that they can also be regarded as factual claims; provided, in other words, that they are normative in a very weak rather than a robust sense.[52] My view has always been that legal normativity, to have genuine action-guiding force, must be derived from or reinforced by moral or prudential normativity – moral or prudential reasons for applying or obeying the law in question or in general.[53] My normative arguments must therefore have a moral or prudential foundation.

Those arguments are addressed to a broad readership – other constitutional theorists, lawyers, judges, law students and possibly others. When we address our arguments to others, we usually hope that the arguments are both persuasive and capable of being accepted by them. My arguments are aimed at persuading others to share my views, so that moderate originalism is either re-affirmed where it is already established (as in Australia), or adopted where it is not (provided that local conditions are appropriate). Those arguments are therefore implicitly aimed at achieving what Larry calls broad reflective equilibrium.[54] Arguments aimed solely at narrow reflective equilibrium – coherence and mutual support among the constitutional and other judgements of the author, with no realistic hope of persuading anyone else – would be inherently solipsistic and hardly worth publishing, except perhaps to demonstrate the superior consistency of one's views compared with those of others.

Larry is sceptical about my legal argument for originalism, although with respect to the United States rather than Australia.[55] Whether or not originalism is part of the law depends on the legal norms of each particular legal system, and I have pointed out that the United States may differ from Australia in that respect.[56] It may be that during the twentieth century, the US Supreme Court gradually set aside the traditional common law interpretive approach, which was moderately originalist.[57] But it is still possible to maintain the opposite view; as Larry notes, William Baude has recently done so.[58]

Larry observes that 'when nonoriginalist judges [in the United States] justify their decisions, they are not employing originalism as the standard of constitutional fidelity. Instead, they invoke the function, purpose, ideals, principles, or spirit of the constitution.'[59] But this does not by itself prove they are nonoriginalists: it is possible to be a purposive originalist, who thinks that the constitution's original functions, purposes, ideals, principles or spirit should sometimes trump the original meaning of the text.[60] As I see it, to be a genuine nonoriginalist such a judge must not only be a purposivist, but also hold that the

[51] ibid.

[52] D Enoch, 'Reason-Giving and the Law' (2011) 1 *Oxford Studies in Philosophy of Law* 1, esp 16ff.

[53] J Goldsworthy, 'The Self-Destruction of Legal Positivism' (1990) 10 *Oxford Journal of Legal Studies* 449, 453–60. I later retracted some of the claims I made there: see J Goldsworthy, 'Unwritten Constitutional Principles' in G Huscroft (ed), *Expounding the Constitution: Essays in Constitutional Theory* (Cambridge, Cambridge University Press, 2008) 277, section B.

[54] Solum (n 50) 84–87.

[55] Solum (n 50) 72–76.

[56] eg, J Goldsworthy, 'Originalism in Constitutional Interpretation' (1997) 25 *Federal Law Review* 1, section 4 (at 21–24); see also Goldsworthy, 'The Case for Originalism' (n 49) 55–57.

[57] Goldsworthy, 'Originalism in Constitutional Interpretation', ibid 21–24; see also Goldsworthy, 'The Case for Originalism' (n 49) 55–57.

[58] W Baude, 'Is Originalism Our Law?' (2015) 115 *Columbia Law Review* 2349.

[59] Solum (n 50) 75. I develop these ideas in the text to nn 122–32, below.

[60] Solum (n 50).

constitution, without having been amended, may have ceased to serve some of its original purposes, functions, and so on, and acquired new ones. No doubt some Supreme Court judges have taken this view – but how many, and have they openly proclaimed it?

On the latter point, Larry quotes my argument that 'any claim about the lawful scope of judicial authority must pass the test of public candor: If that claim is not and cannot be candidly asserted in public by the judges themselves, it is almost certainly false.'[61] He takes this to make a moral rather than a legal claim, because it is not plausible 'to argue that the test of public candor is a legal principle that renders living constitutionalist opinions invalid if they fail to pass the test'.[62] But my test of public candour was not intended to be either a moral or a legal principle, but rather, an evidentiary test that helps determine what legal authority judges possess. If there is a divergence between how some judges publicly justify their decisions, and how on closer inspection they seem to have actually reached them, the former is usually better evidence of their legal authority than the latter. This is because judges rarely have good reason to conceal or dissemble about their legal authority.[63] In other words, if judges seem to have reached a decision for reasons different from the public justifications they proffered for it, it is usually more likely that they departed from their legal authority, rather than that they exercised a legal authority they attempted to conceal.

I agree with Larry that a thorough normative defence of moderate (or public meaning) originalism would address all the theories of constitutional interpretation that oppose it. He provides a very useful list of them.[64] It includes Dworkin's theory, although Larry Alexander and I regard that as moderately originalist.[65] Many of the others listed are not theories of constitutional interpretation at all, because they maintain that the Constitution should sometimes or often be ignored. This is where my test of public candour should be applied.[66] Surely no court would or could – without immediate drastic repercussions – openly proclaim in a judgment what the anti-interpretivist theories recommend the court should do, such as:

a) act as an ongoing committee of constitutional revision and amend the Constitution if the court sees fit (the Superlegislature Theory);
b) deploy theoretical stances strategically to pursue partisan goals (the Opportunistic Theory);
c) completely ignore the communicative content of the Constitution (the Anticonstitutional Theory);
d) ignore the Constitution and apply, instead, a replacement constitution that the court finds normatively more attractive (the Constitutional Replacement Theory);

[61] Goldsworthy, 'The Case for Originalism' (n 49) 56–57, quoted by Solum (n 50) 74.

[62] Solum (n 50) 75.

[63] Dale Smith has suggested in correspondence to me that judges might have good reason to conceal or dissemble if being candid about the full extent of their legal authority might lead to political controversy about their possessing it, and political initiatives to curtail it. For a possible example, see J Iuliano, 'The Supreme Court's Noble Lie' (2018) 51 *UC Davis Law Review* 911.

[64] Solum (n 50) 79–81.

[65] J Goldsworthy, 'Dworkin as an Originalist' (2000) 17 *Constitutional Commentary* 49; L Alexander, 'Was Dworkin an Originalist?' in W Waluchow and S Sciaraffa (eds), *The Legacy of Ronald Dworkin* (Oxford, Oxford University Press, 2016) 299.

[66] See text to nn 61–63, above.

e) allow the legislature to amend the Constitution by enacting ordinary statutes that are inconsistent with it (in other words, treat the Constitution as if it were an ordinary statute subject to implied repeal by later statutes) (Unconstrained Thayerianism).

Larry acknowledges that, for obvious reasons, no-one openly advocates Opportunism.[67] I suggest that for equally obvious reasons, no judge would openly advocate any of these theories, even if a few individual judges occasionally and surreptitiously put one or another of them into practice. According to my public candour test, that fact is powerful evidence that these theories are all inconsistent with the judges' currently accepted legal obligations. Their proponents must be advocating, instead, surreptitious judicial disobedience of those obligations, to promote justice or good governance. Some other nonoriginalist theories listed by Larry – such as extreme pragmatism – might also collapse into one or another of these more openly anti-interpretivist theories. In the end we would be left with a much smaller number of viable nonoriginalist theories of constitutional interpretation, as distinct from constitutional disobedience. My arguments for moderate originalism are aimed mainly against the former. But taking those arguments further is work for another day.

B. Nick Aroney

Nick is generally sympathetic to my theory of constitutional interpretation, but perceives an 'explanatory gap' between that theory, which he regards as 'geared to the interpretation of particular words, phrases and sentences', and the interpretation of the 'wider linguistic structures of constitutions on the scale of entire paragraphs, divisions and chapters'.[68] Although I have applied my theory to 'structural implications', it 'does not offer a full account of how, in general terms, meaning is generated on this larger scale'.[69] Nick offers a 'mediating theory' aimed at offering 'an account of how we combine considerations of text with considerations of structure, in order to arrive at an interpretation that makes sense of them both'.[70] He apparently regards this as an adaptation of my theory; the former is not only consistent with, but in some ways implied by, the latter.[71]

Nick does not discuss important distinctions I have recently drawn between clarifying, supplementing and rectifying interpretation. The first involves clarifying the pre-existing meaning of a law, the second involves supplementing that meaning when it is insufficiently determinate to resolve a legal dispute, and the third involves altering that meaning when it does not serve the lawmaker's obvious purposes.[72] I assume that Nick is concerned only with clarifying interpretation.[73]

[67] Solum (n 50) 80 n 57.

[68] Nicholas Aroney, 'Originalism and Explanatory Power: Text, Structure and the Interpretation of Constitutions', chapter 6 of this volume, 89.

[69] ibid 90.

[70] ibid.

[71] ibid.

[72] I used to distinguish between 'clarifying' and 'creative' interpretation: eg, J Goldsworthy, *Parliamentary Sovereignty: Contemporary Debates* (Cambridge, Cambridge University Press, 2010) 230. I now subdivide creative interpretation into supplementing interpretation and rectifying interpretation: see J Goldsworthy, 'The Implicit and the Implied in a Written Constitution' in R Dixon and A Stone (eds), *The Invisible Constitution* (Cambridge and New York, Cambridge University Press, 2018) 109, 112ff.

[73] Nick states that he is not concerned with what Larry Solum calls 'construction', as distinct from 'interpretation': Aroney (n 68) 91 n 7. Construction includes what I call supplementing and rectifying interpretation.

I am not sure why Nick perceives a gap between my theory and the interpretation or explanation of large-scale structural features of constitutions. In an article he cites,[74] I provide in relation to clarifying interpretation a theory of what constitutes a genuine structural implication (it must be an obvious implicit assumption), and I provide in relation to rectifying interpretation a theory of when common law interpretive norms permit courts to 'read into' or 'imply into' a law (in other words, fabricate) so-called 'implications' that were not really there before.[75]

On my view, genuine and fabricated implications both depend on evidence of the lawmakers' intentions or purposes. When investigating those intentions and purposes, all of the 'modalities' of constitutional interpretation that Nick discusses (except, possibly, the doctrinal one) could in principle be relevant. Since they must all be taken into account, they will necessarily 'illuminate and discipline' one another, to use Nick's terminology. That is why, as I said, I am not sure where Nick perceives a gap in this account of structural implications.

The mediating theory that Nick proposes to fill this gap is based on the notion of 'explanatory power'. Interpreters should seek the 'best explanation' of the constitution, including both its text and structure.[76] This explanation must draw upon various relevant methods or 'modalities' of argumentation that are mutually illuminating and disciplining. I find many aspects of Nick's approach to be helpful, but others somewhat puzzling.

I may not fully understand how Nick conceives of the relationship between an 'interpretation' of a constitution, in the narrow sense of clarifying its pre-existing meaning, and an 'explanation' of it. He often refers to the 'explanatory power' of an interpretation, and states that 'the goal of interpretation is to arrive at an account that offers the best explanation of the constitution'.[77] All this suggests that a clarifying interpretation and an explanation are one and the same thing: an interpretation of a constitution is also an explanation of it.[78] But what kind of explanation does it offer? Is it an explanation of the constitution's meaning? If so I would be puzzled, because a clarifying interpretation aims to *reveal or clarify* the pre-existing meaning of a law, not to *explain* it.

I am not sure what a full explanation of the meaning of an utterance would consist of, other than a philosophical account of what in general constitutes such meanings and how we ascertain them, together with a causal account of how a particular speaker's intentions and actions brought about an utterance with a particular meaning or meanings. The philosophical account picks out those intentions and actions that are relevant to the ascertainment of meaning. Nick does not provide such a philosophical account, and without it, his discussion of the modalities of interpretation seems entirely prescriptive and epistemological – it prescribes how we ought to enquire into the meaning of a law, without offering any explanation of what it is that constitutes such a meaning. He could build on something like my theory of what constitutes the meaning of a law, and perhaps that is what he is doing.

[74] J Goldsworthy, 'Constitutional Implications Revisited' (2011) 30 *University of Queensland Law Journal* 9, cited in Aroney (n 68) 96 n 25.

[75] See paragraph in which nn 129 and 130 appear, below.

[76] Aroney (n 68) 91.

[77] Aroney (n 68) 91.

[78] Aroney (n 68) 91: 'the most powerful explanation … [is] therefore the best interpretation'.

Without such a theory, an explanation of a law presumably explains why it was designed and enacted as it was – why its text and structures came to be what they are. Since a law is the product of deliberate design, this would seem to require investigating the activities and motivations of everyone involved in the process of design and enactment. Such an explanation would be both more, and less, than an interpretation.

It would be more because, without a philosophical theory of what constitutes meaning, it would be difficult to find any good reason to limit the explanation to intentions and purposes that are relevant to interpretation. Most theorists and practitioners of legal interpretation agree that lawmakers may be motivated partly by purposes – such as to deceive the electorate, or to be re-elected – that are irrelevant to the interpretation of laws they help to make.[79] Yet such objectives would surely belong in a full causal explanation of why a statute was drafted and enacted as it was.[80]

On the other hand, such an explanation would be less than what lawyers regard as a complete interpretation because, as I have mentioned, that may include not only clarification, but also supplementation and (in limited circumstances) rectification.[81] An explanation of the content of a law can provide only limited guidance to judges engaged in supplementing or rectifying that content.

A thorough explanation of the content of a law, as described by Nick, would certainly provide invaluable information to its interpreter, especially one guided by my moderately originalist theory of interpretation. I thoroughly approve of the deft way he harnesses the various modalities of interpretation to the joint task of explaining why the constitution's founders constructed it as they did. I therefore agree that his mediating theory, appropriately understood, and my own, are not only compatible but mutually supportive.

C. Heidi Hurd

Heidi has generously contributed a second insightful critique of my 'moderately originalist' theory of constitutional interpretation,[82] and I welcome this opportunity to offer her a considered response. Her main thesis, on both occasions, has been that my theory fails to securely occupy middle ground between strong originalism and nonoriginalism, and that my best chance of preventing it collapsing into one or other of those extremes is to adopt a Burkean version of political and social conservatism.

In section I. of her chapter, Heidi questions both strong originalists' and my reliance on lawmakers' intentions, but eschews the most common challenge, which is to the very existence of collective or group intentions.[83] Instead, she asks what kind of intentions determine what referring terms in constitutions refer to. She canvasses six possibilities – intentions

[79] See Dale Smith's contribution, 'What is Statutory Purpose?' in chapter 3 of this volume, 25 at text to n 50.

[80] Nick says that lawmakers' intentions are relevant to a law's meaning 'only if they have a demonstrable influence on some feature or features of its text and structure, its ethical principles and its prudential compromises': see Aroney (n 68) 101. But that does not rule out ulterior purposes.

[81] See text to above n 71, and below nn 122–32.

[82] The first was H Hurd, 'Living in the Past: Burkean Conservatism and Originalist Interpretation' in J Goldsworthy and T Campbell (eds), *Legal Interpretation in Democratic States* (Aldershot, Ashgate, 2002) 173.

[83] HM Hurd, 'The Moral Motivations for Moderate Originalism' in chapter 7 of this volume, 117 n 10.

about exemplars, conventional word meanings, hypothetical applications, denotations, larger purposes and unconscious intentions – but concludes that none of them either work or are acceptable to originalists.[84]

I do not see why, once the reality of group intentions is conceded (even if only for the sake of argument), referential intentions are any more problematic in the case of laws and lawmakers than they are in the case of ordinary utterances and speakers. If in talking to me you apparently refer to something, I might have some difficulty in determining exactly what you are referring to. But I would not have any great theoretical difficulty in taking you to intend to refer to something, or agonise over exactly what kind of intention is involved. We attempt to determine people's referential intentions in the same way that we attempt to determine their other intentions – we use whatever evidence is available to us. In the case of reference, and meaning in general, we take into account both the conventional meanings of the words they uttered, general principles or norms of communication that we assume they complied with, and contextual evidence of what they intended to communicate. That contextual evidence may include many of Heidi's candidate intentions: intentions about exemplars, conventional word meanings, hypothetical applications, denotations, larger purposes and apparent unconscious intentions. In the case of reference, the question is what, in the light of all this evidence, the speaker appears to have intended to refer to.

As I have demonstrated at length elsewhere,[85] the conventional meanings of words (or intentions about such meanings) will often be insufficient because there are various inexplicit components of meaning.

For example, some words – such as citizen, alien, foreign, native, queen, mayor – function somewhat like indexicals. It is part of their meaning that they involve a relation between a person and a place, and when the place is not explicitly specified (as in 'I am a citizen') it must be fixed by context. Section 51(xix) of the *Australian Constitution* gives the Commonwealth Parliament power to make laws with respect to 'aliens', but it does not explicitly specify the relevant place. In its context, it is obviously intended to refer to people who are aliens – non-subjects or non-citizens – in relation to the Australian community. It is not intended to refer to aliens in relation to other countries, since that would include everyone, or to aliens in the science-fiction sense (aliens to Planet Earth). Although the reference is obvious, it is not determined solely by the conventional meanings of the words that constitute the text; dictionary definitions of 'alien' are consistent with the alternatives just dismissed, whose absurdity is made obvious by contextual evidence of authorial intention.

The conventional meanings of some words and phrases are ambiguous, and can be disambiguated only by resort to contextual evidence of intention. Section 119 of the *Australian Constitution* provides: 'The Commonwealth shall protect every State against invasion and, on the application of the Executive Government of the State, against domestic violence.' Today, the conventional meaning of 'domestic violence' is (something like) 'violence within the home, especially spousal and partner violence'. According to one nonoriginalist theory that Heidi mentions, 'judges must interpret legal texts according to their

[84] ibid 5–8, 117–20.

[85] Goldsworthy, 'The Implicit and the Implied in a Written Constitution' (n 72) 109. I borrow freely from this in what follows.

plain (ie, conventional) meaning *at the time of their decisions*'.[86] But that would be deeply counter-intuitive in this instance. The context – textual and historical – establishes that these words were intended to mean (something like) 'local rioting or rebellion'.

A constitutional provision like any utterance can include an ellipsis, a term I use in a non-technical sense to refer to an omission of a word or words in an uttered sentence due to the reasonable expectation that it will be taken for granted by the intended audience, who will 'fill in' the meaning of the sentence through contextual enrichment.[87]

Some sentences are inherently elliptical, requiring pragmatic enrichment to express complete propositions: for example, 'She is ready' [for what?]. Section 92 of the *Australian Constitution* is a legal example: it provides that 'trade, commerce, and intercourse among the States … shall be absolutely free' but fails to specify what it is to be absolutely free from. This gave rise to more litigation than any other interpretive issue concerning the Constitution, and was only finally resolved in 1988 when the High Court filled in the ellipsis by inferring the intended meaning from historical contextual evidence.[88]

Other uttered sentences need completion to avoid absurdity: for example, 'Everyone has gone to Paris' would usually be understood non-literally to mean that everyone in some contextually salient group, rather than everyone in the universe, has gone to Paris. Section 51 (ii) of the *Australian Constitution* gives the Commonwealth Parliament power to makes laws 'with respect to taxation'. This surely does not refer to all taxation, including state taxation; otherwise, the Commonwealth Parliament could amend and repeal state tax laws. Lawyers naturally understand the section to mean 'with respect to [Commonwealth] taxation', because of their knowledge of the founders' broader purposes, evidenced by other parts of the Constitution.

All these examples concern express meanings, which often depend on contextual as well as textual evidence of communicative, including referential, intentions. I have not even mentioned implied meanings, which are even more difficult for non-intentionalists to accommodate, since by definition they are not conveyed by conventional word meanings alone.[89] The main point, though, is that there can be many different kinds of evidence of referential and other communicative intentions, including Heidi's five candidates.

Heidi sometimes suggests that my moderate version of originalism is the result of 'concessions' to the more extreme positions on either side of it – strong originalism and nonoriginalism – concessions whose 'most obvious rationales' make it vulnerable to collapsing into one or the other of those positions.[90] But it is not the result of concessions. Instead, it is the position that is most consistent with all the complexities of: conventional legal understandings and norms (in Australia, if not the United States); common-sense distinctions between interpretation and amendment; philosophical accounts of meaning, both express and implied; and normative considerations such as the rule of law and democracy. Moderate originalism sits at the intersection of all these relevant considerations. If it happily combines some of the supposed benefits of both strong originalism,

[86] Hurd, 'Moral Motivations' (n 83) 131.
[87] Kent Bach calls ellipses 'implicitures', from the adjective 'implicit': see K Bach, 'Conversational Impliciture' (1994) 9 *Mind and Language* 124.
[88] *Cole v Whitfield* (1988) 163 CLR 360.
[89] See Goldsworthy, 'The Implicit and the Implied in a Written Constitution' (n 72).
[90] Hurd, 'Moral Motivations' (n 83) 127.

and nonoriginalism – such as some degree of both stability and flexibility[91] – that is a collateral benefit rather than a justification. It would be more accurate to think of those other positions as acquiring partial plausibility by emphasising some aspects of the correct position (moderate originalism) while ignoring others. The real danger is not my position collapsing into theirs, but vice versa.

For example, when Heidi refers to 'how much Goldsworthy concedes to the non-originalist natural law theory of interpretation defended by Michael Moore',[92] she mischaracterises as concessions what are really straightforward aspects of my position. Moore argues that constitutional terms should be interpreted in light of our best moral and scientific theories concerning the nature of whatever those terms refer to. For example, a term that refers to water should be interpreted as referring to the substance that modern science has proved to consist of H_2O, and a term that refers to equality should be interpreted as referring to whatever social relationships are shown by the best moral philosophy to warrant that label.[93] I agree with this, provided that all the admissible evidence suggests that the lawmakers intended to use relevant terms to refer to whatever objects possess objective properties revealed by the best scientific or moral theories. But we cannot assume, without some enquiry, that the lawmakers have done so. As Heidi notes, they might have used ostensibly scientific terminology in a non-scientific, lay-persons' sense; for example, in an old statutory interpretation case, it was concluded that 'vegetable' had been used in an ordinary, everyday sense rather than in a scientific, botanical sense, and therefore that tomatoes should be classified as vegetables rather than as fruit.[94] Determining the lawmakers' referential intention is crucial to establishing what kind of terminology they used: whether is it ordinary, or specialised, technical terminology.

So instead of my position being at risk of collapsing into Moore's, his position is in danger of collapsing into mine. This is revealed by Heidi herself, when she observes that Moore 'would certainly allow the context and purpose of the law to inform the interpretive question … but … would not allow objectively-evidenced authorial intentions to settle the question of how words ought to be interpreted'.[95] Moore's position is at risk of collapsing into mine because context and purpose are best understood *as* objective evidence of authorial intentions; it is very difficult to see what they could be, or why they would be relevant to interpretation, otherwise.[96]

Heidi also warns that my position might collapse into either a historical plain meaning theory, or a public meaning originalist theory.[97] This does not alarm me, because again, it would be a question of which theory is collapsing into the other. She observes that plain meaning and public meaning theorists can accommodate '[t]hose things that Goldsworthy thinks of as sources of implied meaning', because '[w]hat makes the meaning of legal language plain – what fixes its conventional content – can surely be things other than semantics – eg,

[91] Hurd, 'Moral Motivations' (n 83) 127.

[92] Hurd, 'Moral Motivations' (n 83) 129.

[93] See Hurd, 'Moral Motivations' (n 83) 129–30.

[94] Hurd, 'Moral Motivations' (n 83) 129 n 54, referring to *Nix v Hedden*, 149 US 304 (1893).

[95] Hurd, 'Moral Motivations' (n 83) 129 n 54.

[96] For a previous discussion of Moore's interpretive theory, see Goldsworthy, *Contemporary Debates* (n 72) 256–63.

[97] Hurd, 'Moral Motivations' (n 83) 128–29.

the context which provides the pragmatics of utterance'.[98] But what I think of as sources of implied meaning generally do not fix 'conventional meanings'. Some implications are fixed by conventions, but other implications, ellipses and implicit assumptions are revealed by contextual evidence of authorial intentions that is particularistic and probabilistic, rather than embodied in specific pre-existing conventions. If 'plain meaning' is understood in a capacious sense, so that it depends on publicly available evidence of authorial intentions in addition to social conventions, then a plain meaning theory may well be tantamount to my own theory. Larry Solum's version of public meaning originalism is also very close to my theory, as he observes in this volume.[99]

Heidi suggests that lawmakers usually care more about how their laws will be applied than about how they will be understood, and therefore would prefer that priority be given to their application intentions rather than what I call their enactment intentions, which concern what laws they intended to enact. She asks why, if I am prepared to override their application intentions, I am not also prepared to override their enactment intentions.[100] Perhaps in some cases their enactment could be regarded as including a drafting error, and corrected. But courts are justifiably very reluctant to do this; such errors must be obvious and easy to correct without substantive redrafting. Otherwise, the law is what the lawmakers enacted, not what they should have enacted to achieve their application intentions, and they are stuck with it.

Heidi also claims that my normative arguments – such as my appeal to the rule of law – and (what she regards as) my conceptual arguments are insufficient to establish moderate originalism rather than a rival theory.[101] I agree. As I said earlier, moderate originalism rests on diverse grounds that are, or can be lightly revised so as to be, coherent: legal interpretive conventions (at least in Australia), common sense understandings of 'interpretation' and 'meaning', philosophy of language dealing with the nature of meaning, express and implied and norms of political morality (the rule of law, democracy and so on). It is unlikely that any single argument, by itself, can refute rival theories.

I will not say much about section III. of Heidi's paper, partly because for the reasons already given I do not need to rely on Burke's conservative political philosophy, but also because I doubt that doing so would greatly assist me. I suspect that Burkean conservatism would not vindicate moderate originalism, but instead, a constrained, cautious and incremental progressivism – perhaps something like David Strauss's 'common law constitutionalism'.[102]

I would add that, in response to Heidi's contrary assumption, I do not regard originalism as inherently politically conservative. It is the traditional common law approach to the interpretation of legal instruments, and especially statutes. The consequences of preserving the original meaning of those instruments are politically conservative if their content is politically conservative. If their content is politically liberal or progressive, then so are the consequences of preserving their meaning; a 'living tree' approach that sought to change that meaning in a politically conservative direction would then be politically

[98] Hurd, 'Moral Motivations' (n 83) 128 n 51.
[99] Solum (n 50) 68.
[100] Hurd, 'Moral Motivations' (n 83) 129–30.
[101] Hurd, 'Moral Motivations' (n 83) 130–32.
[102] DA Strauss, *The Living Constitution* (New York and Oxford, Oxford University Press, 2010); for Burke, see 41–42, 44, 47–48 and 62.

conservative. In Malaysia, for example, it is Islamists who should favour a nonoriginalist approach to the interpretation of the national constitution, and liberal pluralists who should favour originalism.[103]

Heidi repeats the old objection that originalists insist 'that the dead continue to have power over the living'.[104] But in addition to pointing out that the very enterprise of law inherently involves past decisions governing the present to some extent, I have consistently denied this:

> [If a constitution] includes an amendment procedure that is reasonably democratic and practicable, today's generation is not restricted by the dead hand of the past in any invidious sense. Those who are restricted … are government officials, legislative, executive and judicial, who might otherwise have had power to alter the constitution themselves. The strongest normative argument for originalism therefore appeals, not to the authority of the dead hand of the past, but to that of the living hand of the present: 'the people' today, or their representatives, who have exclusive legal authority to change their own constitution. The most powerful objection to non-originalism is that it usurps their power to change their own constitution.[105]

D. Kevin Toh

Kevin seeks to raise doubts about originalism in constitutional interpretation by drawing analogies with musical interpretation, informed by the modern philosophy of music. He hopes that, as well as illuminating common issues, this might help sideline political controversies that distract attention from fundamental philosophical questions.[106] I found his chapter fascinating. I think I agree with him up to a point – although this may depend on what we both mean by 'originalism' – but I am not sure whether or how far he would go beyond that point. This is no doubt because his chapter is an admittedly preliminary consideration of the issues, leaving much to be developed in future work.

Kevin's analogy has forced me to ponder questions, about music, that I have not seriously considered before. Although I am ignorant of the philosophy of music, I feel bound to venture some response to his intriguing suggestions. I will confine myself to western classical music written in scores according to notational conventions developed by the end of the eighteenth century. It is that kind of music that provides Kevin with his most promising analogy.

Kevin suggests that what constitutes an authentic (or faithful) interpretation of a written constitution, or written musical work, depends largely on the ontological question of what constitutes that constitution, or musical work.[107] His core proposition is that the musical work is not the same as the meaning of the score, even if the score is supplemented by unwritten, conventional norms of performance and/or unwritten instructions

[103] See Y Tew, 'Comparative Originalism in Constitutional Interpretation in Asia' (2017) 29 *Singapore Academy of Law Journal* 719, 726–29, and 'Malaysia's Invisible Constitution' in Dixon and Stone (n 72) 376, esp 396.

[104] Hurd, 'Moral Motivations' (n 83) 132.

[105] Goldsworthy, 'The Case for Originalism' (n 49) 57.

[106] Kevin Toh, 'Authenticity, Ontology and Natural History: Some Reflections on Musical and Legal Interpretations' in chapter 8 of this volume, 146.

[107] ibid.

passed on by the composer.[108] This enables him to defend the possibility of an authentic interpretation of the musical work that departs from the meaning of the score, even when understood in that capacious way. Indeed, an interpretation that 'takes some liberties with the score' – even 'an electrifyingly new … [and] revolutionary interpretation' – might be 'truer or more faithful to the relevant musical work, more authentic, than any that would adhere strictly to such a score'.[109] This might be so even if the new interpretation, which need not adhere 'strictly' to the score, was not intended or even envisaged by the composer.[110]

Opinions of professional musicians no doubt differ, as do opinions among lawyers about constitutional interpretation. I note, in passing, the opinion of Sviatoslav Richter, one of the most acclaimed classical pianists of the twentieth century:

> The interpreter is really an executant, carrying out the composer's intentions to the letter. He doesn't add anything that isn't already in the work. If he is talented, he allows us to glimpse the truth of the work that is in itself a thing of genius and that is reflected in him. He shouldn't dominate the music, but should dissolve into it.[111]

Kevin's different opinion is based on:

a) claims by musicologists that musical works can have an inner 'logic', 'nature' or 'potential' that their composers might not have fully appreciated, which a subsequent interpreter may bring out.[112] This is supported by anecdotes, such as Rachmaninoff supposedly applauding a revolutionary interpretation of his third piano concerto by Horowitz for being 'how it should have been performed all along';[113]
b) the observation that an authentic interpretation of a musical work must realise a number of incommensurable values, in addition to considerable fidelity to the score, such as vibrancy, creativity and emotional expressiveness. An interpretation that is strictly faithful to the score but otherwise deficient (perhaps plodding and dull) might be less authentic than an alternative that takes liberties with the score but better conveys the work's emotional content.[114]

I am not sure how far Kevin would want to take his argument. No doubt any attempt by a composer to set out a musical work in written form, and to prescribe how it should be performed, is necessarily under-determinate in many respects and leaves much to the discretion of the performer even if the score is supplemented by unwritten instructions or conventional norms of performance. The same is true of written laws, but I suspect not to the same extent. It would generally be undesirable for a composer of music to attempt to remove all scope for creativity on the part of the performer. As Kevin observes, if such an attempt succeeded, 'frequenting of concert halls to listen to performances of the same work, or buying multiple recordings of the same work, would make little sense'.[115]

[108] ibid sections II. and III.
[109] ibid 150–51.
[110] ibid 150–51, 153–55.
[111] B Monsaingeon, *Sviatoslav Richter, Notebooks and Conversations* (Princeton, Princeton University Press, 2002) 153.
[112] Toh, 'Authenticity, Ontology and Natural History' (n 106) 150–51 and 153–55.
[113] Toh, 'Authenticity, Ontology and Natural History' (n 106) 151 n 18.
[114] Toh, 'Authenticity, Ontology and Natural History' (n 106) 152.
[115] Toh, 'Authenticity, Ontology and Natural History' (n 106) 153.

A consequence is that any musical work can be interpreted and performed in many different ways: at different speeds and volumes, with different phrasing and emphases, and so on. If it is, in fact, the same musical work being interpreted, then the work in itself must surely consist of something that is common (or largely common) to all the various interpretations of it. This might suggest that the musical work is, in fact, the meaning of the score, perhaps supplemented by some unwritten conventional norms. But Kevin apparently believes that an authentic interpretation might depart not only from such conventions, but also from the score itself.

It is not clear to me what Kevin thinks the musical work consists of; we must await the future development of ideas that he sketches in the last third of his chapter. Here he argues against various candidates, including the meaning of the score (even when supplemented by unwritten conventions and instructions), and the understanding of, or the meaning intended by, the composer. But he does not yet offer a positive account of what a musical work is, other than that it is an abstract object whose content may 'depend' on aesthetic value judgements.[116] I find this mysterious: is the musical work some kind of aesthetically ideal Platonic form, which even the best score merely approximates? But if so, no-one would ever actually perform the musical work; every performer would inevitably get it wrong.

At this stage of Kevin's thinking, it is also unclear how far an interpretation can depart from the score, or the composer's intentions, and still be considered as an interpretation of the work. He says that '[t]he creative decisions that performers of written compositions make in their performances are not all that different from the decisions that composers make in composing variations on a given theme (as Beethoven did on Diabelli's waltz)'.[117] But in his *Diabelli Variations*, Beethoven clearly created a new work, even if it was inspired by Diabelli's theme. The question arises: when does a very creative interpretation of a musical work become the creation of a new work? Can the interpreter ignore not only directions in the score as to tempo and volume, but also some of the notes that are inscribed? Kevin refers to performers taking 'some minor liberties with the score'.[118] But why not major liberties? How much rewriting of the score is consistent with the work remaining the same?

It may be that this is a question of degree, and that the concept 'musical work' is inherently vague. If so, the answer in any particular case must depend on highly contestable aesthetic judgements, but that would rarely matter much for practical purposes. What is important is that a creative performance is deemed valuable, at least by some listeners, whether or not it really amounts to the performance of a new work. With respect to music there is no pressing practical imperative requiring authenticity or fidelity as Kevin uses those terms. Purists who frown on any departure from musical works as originally written or intended by their composers can refuse to listen, and no harm is done. That other music lovers enjoy the new interpretation (or work) need have no negative impact on the purists. There is no good reason for Beethoven purists to fret about other people enjoying Walter Murphy's disco-inspired *A Fifth of Beethoven*, or even claiming (absurdly, I admit) that it is an authentic interpretation of the *Fifth Symphony* in Kevin's sense of term.

[116] Toh, 'Authenticity, Ontology and Natural History' (n 106) 162 and 163–64.
[117] Toh, 'Authenticity, Ontology and Natural History' (n 106) 153.
[118] Toh, 'Authenticity, Ontology and Natural History' (n 106) 154.

This is where constitutional interpretation surely differs. The very idea of a written constitution was invented by the American founders in order to achieve much more clarity and precision than earlier unwritten, customary constitutions possessed.[119] They sought this partly because written constitutions amount to settlements – even if only temporary ones – of extremely important practical questions that affect every citizen, directly or indirectly. These questions, if not effectively settled, are prone to generate conflict and even violence. One of them concerns how the settlement itself is to be changed in the future: constitutions usually prescribe formal procedures for their own future amendment. What would happen if judges interpreting constitutions were to indulge in the radical creativity that some musicians use in performing other people's compositions, inspired by the judges' own moral and political value judgments (or creative 'imagination'),[120] thereby apparently evading that amendment procedure? Citizens who disapprove of the change and rightly perceive their interest in the status quo to have been overridden, would justly complain that their interest had been harmed in ways they cannot avoid by simply refusing to listen. They would not be mollified by the claim that what they perceive as change is merely apparent, and really amounts to an inspired revelation of the constitution's unexpressed inner logic or true nature. They are likely to angrily reject that as fraudulent.

This is subject to some qualifications. First, I have always acknowledged that sometimes written constitutions contain genuine, unexpressed implications. For example, they may include implicit assumptions, which are so obvious that the constitution's makers took them for granted or expected subsequent interpreters to do so.[121] The existence of such implications depends on the intentions and purposes of the makers: to say that something has been taken for granted is to say that some person or persons took it for granted. These implications may be part of the inner 'logic' of a constitution, but I take it that this is not Kevin's point; he seems to envisage creative but nevertheless authentic interpretations that go further than revealing genuine implications.

Second and more importantly, I too envisage this. In recent work I have acknowledged that courts sometimes properly change or rectify, rather than just supplement, the meanings of provisions in statutes and constitutions. This is nevertheless classified as a kind of interpretation, which I call 'rectifying interpretation'.[122] There are arguably at least four situations in common law jurisdictions in which rectification of legal instruments by courts is tacitly accepted as legitimate, even if this is rarely explicitly acknowledged. It is notable that in all four situations, the lawmakers' purposes are crucial both in justifying and limiting the changes that judges are arguably entitled to make. The judges act as the lawmakers' 'faithful agents' by adjusting the meanings of provisions in order to give better effect to their purposes.

Judges may sometimes correct obvious drafting errors, including inconsistencies, although these are very rare in constitutions. A drafting error is obvious when there is an obvious discrepancy between what a provision expressly provides, and what the lawmaker

[119] J Goldsworthy, *The Sovereignty of Parliament, History and Philosophy* (Oxford, Clarendon Press, 1999) 209.

[120] Toh, 'Authenticity, Ontology and Natural History' (n 106) 173.

[121] Goldsworthy, 'Constitutional Implications Revisited' (n 74) 13–15 and 18–22.

[122] Goldsworthy, 'Constitutional Implications Revisited' (n 74) 12; J Goldsworthy, 'Clarifying, Creating and Changing Meaning in Constitutional Interpretation' (2013) 14 *German Law Journal* 1279, 1280–82 and 1292; Ekins and Goldsworthy (n 7) 61–62; Goldsworthy, 'The Implicit and the Implied in a Written Constitution' (n 72) 110–12.

clearly intended it to provide, given the law's subject matter and purpose. The error is corrected by adjusting the law's meaning to give better effect to its purpose.[123]

What used to be called 'equitable interpretation' of provisions has sometimes been used to add qualifications to laws to avoid unintended and undesirable consequences in unusual and unanticipated circumstances.[124] The interpretation of s 117 of the *Australian Constitution* might provide an example (although alternatively, it might be regarded as an example of an implicit assumption). This prohibits the imposition within any State of a 'disability or discrimination' on anyone who is a resident of some other State. This would not be interpreted as requiring that temporary visitors from other States be able to vote in elections for the State Parliament, despite there being no express qualification to that effect.[125] The need for this qualification, and possibly others, was probably not realised when the provision was drafted and adopted. Once again the lawmaker's apparent purpose is crucial, in determining whether a consequence was probably both unintended and unwanted.

The textual meanings of provisions may sometimes be adjusted incrementally to enable them to achieve their intended purposes, if unanticipated social or technological developments would otherwise have made that impossible.[126] For example, the *United States Constitution* vests exclusive power in Congress to raise and maintain 'armies' and 'a navy' and to regulate 'the land and naval forces'.[127] When military aircraft were developed, it would have defeated the provision's obvious purpose if Congress had been denied the power to raise and maintain an air force. It is widely accepted that in such cases, courts may adopt a purposive rather than a strictly textual interpretation, by stretching the provision's textual meaning to give effect to its original purpose in contemporary circumstances. Elsewhere, I have argued that this justifies the High Court adopting an expansive interpretation of the word 'marriage' in the *Australian Constitution*, so that it includes same-sex marriage. Even though the word was not used in that sense in 1900, this would better serve the founders' intended constitutional design in giving power over marriage to the Commonwealth Parliament rather than leaving it to the diversity of state laws.[128]

A so-called 'implied term' can – as common lawyers oddly say – be 'read into' or 'implied into' (in other words, inserted into) a law on the ground that it is practically necessary for the law to achieve one of its intended purposes. Here, too, purpose is crucial, both to justify and to limit the change that is made. I call these 'fabricated implications', because they are really inserted by an act of rectification, as distinct from genuine implications that are revealed by clarifying the pre-existing meaning of the text.[129] If the framers erroneously believed that the inserted term was not practically necessary to achieve their purposes, it is

[123] DC Pearce and RS Geddes, *Statutory Interpretation in Australia*, 7th edn (Sydney, LexisNexis Butterworths, 2011) 50–52; A Scalia and B Garner, *Reading Law: The Interpretation of Legal Texts* (Thomson/West, 2012) 234–39.

[124] See, eg, J Evans, 'A Brief History of Equitable Interpretation in the Common Law System' in Goldsworthy and Campbell (n 82) 67; J Evans, 'Reading Down Statutes' in R Bigwood (ed), *The Statute: Making and Meaning* (Wellington, LexisNexis, 2004) 123; R Ekins, *The Nature of Legislative Intent* (Oxford, Oxford University Press, 2012) 275–84.

[125] *Street v Queensland Bar Association* (1989) 168 CLR 461, 491–93 (Mason CJ), 512–14 (Brennan J), 546–48 (Dawson J), 559–60 (Toohey J), 583–84 (McHugh J).

[126] Goldsworthy, 'The Case for Originalism' (n 49) 62–63.

[127] *United States Constitution* art I § 8.

[128] J Goldsworthy, 'Interpreting the *Constitution* in Its Second Century' (2000) 24 *Melbourne University Law Review* 677, 699–701.

[129] Goldsworthy, 'Constitutional Implications Revisited' (n 74) 18–22, where I referred to 'spurious' instead of 'fabricated' implications.

hardly plausible to regard it as an implicit assumption or any other kind of genuine implication. When what we say or write turns out to be deficient, genuine implications do not magically spring up to protect us from our mistakes.[130]

The danger of courts doing this is obvious. Constitutional provisions are enacted to serve chains of purposes of increasing abstraction, ending in very abstract purposes such as advancing democracy, justice, liberty, equality and human dignity. Consider the possible consequences if judges could legitimately start with such an abstract purpose, and then reason that – although the constitution-makers took a different view – some provision not included in the text is in fact necessary to achieve that purpose, and therefore should be 'implied into' the text. Nothing could then stop the judges using such purposive reasoning to rewrite the Constitution. Nevertheless, as the great American jurist Learned Hand observed, 'In construing written documents it has always been thought proper to engraft upon the text such provisions as are necessary to prevent the failure of the undertaking'.[131]

These four ways by which common law courts are arguably entitled to rectify a law, might all be regarded as departing from the law's original textual meaning in order to give effect to its inner 'logic' and real 'nature'. All are examples of 'purposive' as opposed to 'textual' interpretation, the relevant purposes being those of the lawmakers. Perhaps Kevin would regard this as inconsistent with originalism. I do not: I have only ever defended what I call 'moderate originalism', which permits some incremental departures from original textual meaning in the service of clear original purposes.[132]

I wonder how much further Kevin thinks that a radically creative interpretation can go, without losing its authenticity by, in effect, unlawfully changing the constitution. Could it override the text so as to give better effect, in the opinion of the judges, to the constitution-makers' most abstract purposes? Could it do so in order to give effect to supposedly contemporary purposes that the constitution-makers would never have endorsed? Underlying these questions is the ontological question that Kevin has not yet attempted to answer: if the constitution is not the meaning of its text, contextually enriched by publicly available evidence of the constitution-makers' intentions and purposes,[133] what is it? I await with great interest the answers that Kevin will provide as he further develops his analogy with music.

III. Legislative Supremacy

A. Alison Young

Alison has contributed a profound reflection on the role of referendums within the British constitution, which at least since AV Dicey's classical account of it, has been generally

[130] Goldsworthy, 'Implications in Language, Law and the Constitution' (n 35) 150, 168–70.

[131] Learned Hand, *The Bill of Rights* (Harvard, Harvard University Press, 1958) 29; see also at 14 where he uses the term 'interpolate'.

[132] See also text to n 60, above.

[133] I ignore here the status of judicial interpretations of the Constitution that are erroneous but binding due to the doctrine of stare decisis. They are part of constitutional law, which is built on the foundation of the written Constitution without being part of it, albeit part of the nation's constitution in a broader sense of the term.

thought to vest legal sovereignty in Parliament but political sovereignty in the electors ('the people').[134] It is a system of representative democracy punctuated by occasional exercises of direct democracy through referendums. Looming large in Alison's discussion is the perceived recent rise of populism throughout the world. She poses various questions, including: when – as a matter of both political morality and law – should a representative democratic institution such as Parliament, possessing legal sovereignty, defer to the outcomes of direct democracy, expressing political sovereignty through referendums? Furthermore, what constitutional arrangements would strike the best balance between representative and direct democracy, in accommodating the legitimate demands, while also suppressing the dangers, of populism?

To help us answer these questions in the British context, Alison reflects on the referendum held in 2016 to decide whether or not Britain should leave the European Union, which exposed a divergence of opinion between a majority of the electors, who voted to leave, and a majority of the members of Parliament, who wanted to remain. In the much discussed case of *Miller*,[135] the UK Supreme Court had to decide whether or not the outcome of the referendum had altered the power of the executive government to formally commence the process of withdrawal.

Alison compares how Dicey, Michael Gordon and I, who have expressed different opinions about parliamentary sovereignty, would answer her questions. Our differences concern the extent to which the British Parliament can use its sovereign lawmaking power to control its future use of that power, by requiring that it comply with special lawmaking procedures or forms. Dicey denied that it could do so at all;[136] Gordon favours an ample power to do so, including power to require that future legislation on specified issues be approved in a referendum;[137] while I adopt a middle position, accepting that Parliament can enact purely procedural or formal requirements, as opposed to requirements that would effectively abdicate or substantially diminish its sovereign power to legislate as it chooses.[138] On my view, it follows that Parliament by itself cannot require that the approval of the electorate be obtained by referendum before it may legislate: that would be to abdicate or substantially diminish part of its sovereign power to legislate as it chooses. Parliament could effectively enact such a requirement only if the legal foundation of its own authority – the general consensus among senior legal officials that HLA Hart called the 'rule of recognition' – were changed. I was gratified to learn that Alison believes that my theory generally answers her questions better than the others.[139]

Alison poses two legal questions, one broader than the other, and a normative question. The narrower legal question is whether Dicey and I would agree with the conclusion of the Supreme Court that, as a matter of law, the 2016 referendum made no difference to the powers of the executive government. Although Dicey is known as the high priest

[134] Alison L Young, 'Populism and Parliamentary Sovereignty: The Goldsworthy Solution' in chapter 9 of this volume; AV Dicey, *Introduction to the Study of the Law of the Constitution*, 8th edn (London, Macmillan, 1915).

[135] *R (Miller) v Secretary of State for Exiting the European Union* [2017] UKSC 5, [2018] AC 61.

[136] Dicey (n 134) 65–66.

[137] M Gordon, *Parliamentary Sovereignty in the UK Constitution: Process, Politics and Democracy* (Oxford, Hart Publishing, 2015), esp chs 7 and 8.

[138] Goldsworthy, *Contemporary Debates* (n 72) Ch 7.

[139] Young (n 134) 176–77.

of parliamentary sovereignty, Alison provides an interesting survey of how he increasingly advocated referendums as a remedy for perceived flaws in parliamentary democracy. I believe she is right that Dicey would nevertheless have agreed with the Supreme Court in *Miller*. As she acknowledges, parliamentary sovereignty was not really at stake in that case;[140] even if the Court had concluded that the executive government could commence withdrawal without prior parliamentary authorisation, Parliament's power to override or regulate executive action was never in doubt. She is also right about my own position; unless the statute mandating the referendum dealt with the issue, expressly or impliedly, the referendum would not have altered executive power or its exercise.

The broader legal question is a hypothetical that reduces to the much-discussed conundrum already mentioned: can Parliament effectively bind itself to comply with the result of a referendum by enacting what is called a 'self-entrenched' provision, which requires a referendum not only to legislate on a specified topic, but also to repeal the referendum requirement itself (thus preventing its repeal by the ordinary legislative process)? That possible device never occurred to Dicey; it seems to have been invented and enacted in 1929 in New South Wales, where it was held by the courts to be legally binding.[141] It is therefore unclear what Dicey would have thought, although I believe he would have denied that such a device would be binding in Britain. Gordon approves of the device, because it would enhance the power of the political sovereign – the electorate. Alison rightly attributes to me the 'more subtle'[142] opinion that the device would not succeed unless it could plausibly be regarded as having helped to change the ultimate rule of recognition of the British constitution, a conclusion that should not be reached unless certain additional conditions are satisfied. So as she acknowledges, my answer would depend on what further facts are hypothesised.

Alison's normative question is whether parliamentary sovereignty is best justified as an expression of popular sovereignty, and if so, whether parliament should always defer to the will of the people.[143] She uses this question to explore what constitutional arrangements would best accommodate the legitimate demands, while also minimising the dangers, of populism – or in other words, provide useful correctives to parliamentary democracy while avoiding threats to liberal principles and pluralism.

I may sometimes have used the terms 'popular sovereignty' or 'the sovereignty of the people'. But in 'The Case for Originalism' I explained why I do not believe that anyone – not even 'the people' – can possess political sovereignty, if that means a legally and morally unlimited power to make political decisions. I believe that legal sovereignty can (and does) exist, because it is subject to moral limits, but that moral sovereignty cannot exist, because it would not be subject to such limits. Moral authority to egregiously violate morality cannot exist.[144] It may be true that the will of the people should usually prevail, but it must always be subject to moral limits. Perhaps that is all that is meant by those who advocate popular sovereignty. But it surely follows that Parliament should not always defer to the will of the

[140] Young (n 134) 175.
[141] *Attorney-General (NSW) v Trethowan* (1931) 44 CLR 394 and 47 CLR 97; for full discussion, see Goldsworthy, *Contemporary Debates* (n 72) Ch 6.
[142] Young (n 134) 189.
[143] Young (n 134) 176.
[144] Goldsworthy, 'The Case for Originalism' (n 49) 58–59.

people. One of the advantages of representative democracy is that public affairs can be given more careful and well informed scrutiny than the vast majority of individual members of the general public can undertake.

I am pleased that Alison regards my middle position as striking a better balance between direct and indirect democracy, and therefore a better means of accommodating the potential benefits and dangers of populism, compared with the positions of Dicey and Gordon.

B. Richard Kay

Rick's chapter is an intriguing modern update of a venerable critique of populist democracy, namely, that the general populace is often too ignorant and prejudiced to be entrusted with uncontrolled political power.[145] He also discusses a modern version of the traditional solution to the problem, which I along with others have toyed with: that empowering judges to enforce constitutional rights may be the equivalent of including an 'aristocratic' element in a balanced system of 'mixed government' that moderates the democratic element.[146]

Through the centuries, suspicion of majority rule has been rife among the better educated classes, who have feared the ignorance, stupidity and vulgarity of the masses.[147] John Stuart Mill admitted that his commitment to democracy cooled in the 1840s because he 'dreaded the ignorance and especially the selfishness and brutality of the mass'. He proposed that educated people should have more votes, in proportion to the level of their education, than the mass, to ensure more enlightened and rational decision-making.[148]

A similar idea has recently been advocated by Jason Brennan, whose book *Against Democracy* defends 'epistocracy', meaning rule by citizens with sufficient relevant knowledge to participate competently in public decision-making.[149] Rick cites Brennan's book, and another recent work by political scientists CH Achen and LM Bartels, *Democracy for Realists: Why Elections Do Not Produce Responsive Government*.[150] Their arguments rely mainly on information about the behaviour of American voters. I am unable to assess that information, or how similar the behaviour of voters in other Western countries is. I suspect that in some countries with smaller populations and superior public education (as in Scandinavia), and/or with compulsory voting (as in Australia), the average voter might be better educated, more engaged and more conscientious than in the United States. But I must leave such questions to another occasion.

I myself have expressed the suspicion that in modern Western democracies

> a substantial number of influential members of the highly educated, professional, upper-middle class have lost faith in the ability of their fellow citizens to form opinions about important matters of public policy in a sufficiently intelligent, well-informed, dispassionate, impartial, and carefully

[145] Richard S Kay, 'Democracy, Mixed Government and Judicial Review' in chapter 10 of this volume.

[146] ibid section II.B.; Goldsworthy, *The Sovereignty of Parliament* (n 119) 200–201; Goldsworthy, *Contemporary Debates* (n 72) 10–11.

[147] A Arblaster, *Democracy* (Milton Keynes, Open University Press, 1987) 6 and see generally chs 3 and 4.

[148] Quoted in ibid 48.

[149] J Brennan, *Against Democracy* (Princeton, Princeton University Press, 2016), cited by Kay (n 145) 208 n 58.

[150] CH Achen and LM Bartels, *Democracy for Realists: Why Elections Do Not Produce Responsive Government* (Princeton, Princeton University Press, 2016), cited by Kay (n 145) 200 n 5.

> reasoned manner. … If I am right, the main attraction of judicial enforcement of constitutional rights in these countries is that it shifts power to people (judges) who are representative members of the highly educated, professional, upper-middle class, and whose superior education, intelligence, habits of thought, and professional ethos are thought more likely to produce enlightened decisions.[151]

As a member of the highly educated, professional, upper-middle class, I have sometimes shared this distrust of the competence of many of my fellow citizens. But even if this is justified, and some remedy is desirable, it need not take the form of an American-style Bill of Rights.

The American model of entrenched constitutional rights is no longer the only alternative to untrammelled legislative sovereignty. New 'hybrid' models pioneered in Canada, New Zealand and Britain allocate much greater responsibility for protecting rights to courts, without completely abandoning the principle of legislative supremacy. Judges there have not been given ultimate authority on all questions of rights. Section 33 of Canada's *Charter of Rights*, which famously enables legislatures to legislate 'notwithstanding' most Charter rights, 'was included … for the very purpose of preserving parliamentary sovereignty on rights issues'.[152] (I have argued that the wording of this override clause is problematic, but could be substantially improved.)[153] Parliaments in New Zealand and Britain were deliberately left with discretion as to whether or not to defer to judicial decisions concerning the compatibility of their statutes with rights. If an 'aristocratic' element has been added to the political process, its primary function is arguably 'to improve the quality of the debate over human rights, not to impose its will on the legislature by force of law'.[154]

These models purport to embody a compromise combining the best features of the British model of legislative sovereignty, and the American model of rights protection, by authorising courts to pronounce on the compatibility of legislation with protected rights while preserving the legislature's authority to have the final word.[155] This arguably adds a further check or balance to the lawmaking process without diminishing its fundamentally democratic character.

I am not an implacable opponent of judicial involvement in rights protection. In *The Sovereignty of Parliament, History and Philosophy*, I expressly disavowed any intention of arguing against the adoption of a bill of rights.[156] That book was aimed at refuting what is now called 'common law constitutionalism', which holds that the common law either already protects fundamental rights from legislative violation, or could legitimately be developed by the judiciary so as to do so.[157] I regard the new hybrid models as important experiments in constitutionalism. Universal adoption of the American model of constitutionally entrenched rights would, in my opinion, be premature and dangerously complacent, ruling out possibly superior alternatives.

[151] Goldsworthy, *Contemporary Debates* (n 72) 10–11.

[152] PW Hogg, AA Bushell Thornton and WK Wright, 'A Reply on "*Charter* Dialogue Revisited"' (2007) 45 *Osgoode Hall Law Journal* 193, 201.

[153] See Goldsworthy, *Contemporary Debates* (n 72) 219.

[154] Goldsworthy, *Contemporary Debates* (n 72) 11–12.

[155] Goldsworthy, *Contemporary Debates* (n 72) 11–12, 201, see generally Ch 8.

[156] Goldsworthy, *The Sovereignty of Parliament* (n 119) 8 and 279.

[157] Goldsworthy, *The Sovereignty of Parliament* (n 119) 8 and 279.

C. Richard Ekins

I thank Richard for his enthusiastic and laudatory agreement with my defence of the British doctrine of parliamentary sovereignty against its many recent critics.[158] Both Richard and I disapprove of America-style constitutionally entrenched and judicially enforceable bills of rights in established western democracies. Richard maintains that I understate several of my arguments against such bills of rights, which are or can be made more powerful. I accept that he may be right, and welcome the reinforcements he helpfully provides. We also reject the theory known throughout the British Commonwealth as 'common law constitutionalism', which holds that where it operates the common law is the ultimate constitutional foundation, even where there is a written Constitution. Its proponents claim that this common law constitution limits legislative power, and therefore no parliament in a common law system can be truly sovereign.[159] Richard and I agree that this claim is based on historical and philosophical errors, which he helpfully summarises.

But Richard dissents from my more open-minded attitude to the 'hybrid models' of rights protection, including the *Canadian Charter* with its notwithstanding clause, and statutory bills of rights that authorise creative interpretations but not invalidation of other statutes. As explained in my response to Rick Kay, I regard these as experiments in constitutionalism whose consequences are worth monitoring. It is possible that some of them will improve the protection of rights without sacrificing the fundamental principle of legislative supremacy. I have taken that view partly because I sometimes share doubts about the capacity of many of my fellow citizens to vote in a sufficiently intelligent and informed manner. Richard is right to say that I 'largely … avoid the question' of whether these models should be adopted.[160] If we treat them as experiments, we need to give them more time before drawing firm conclusions about their merits and demerits. In so staunchly opposing all these models, Richard proves to be a more stalwart defender of legislative supremacy than me. He makes very telling criticisms of my position, and in due course, he may be proved right.

Richard devotes most of his discussion of the hybrid models to Canada's, and we agree on its flaws. I have previously argued that the wording of the notwithstanding clause has contributed to its virtual desuetude, because it suggests that any legislature that employed it has overridden the Charter of Rights itself, rather than a reasonably debatable judicial interpretation of the Charter.[161] Richard agrees.[162] But I have speculated that a differently worded notwithstanding clause might have different consequences,[163] a possibility that has not yet been put to the test. Nevertheless, I agree with Richard that the New Zealand and British hybrid models are much less damaging to legislative supremacy and democratic decision-making than the Canadian one.[164]

[158] Richard Ekins, 'Models of (and Myths about) Rights Protection' in chapter 11 of this volume.

[159] Trevor Allan, whose contribution to this volume is discussed next, is the leading academic proponent of this view.

[160] Ekins (n 158) 240.

[161] See Goldsworthy, *Contemporary Debates* (n 72) Ch 8 at 219; see Ekins (n 158) 244 n 79.

[162] Ekins (n 158) 244.

[163] Goldsworthy, *Contemporary Debates* (n 72) 219–20 and 222.

[164] Richard suggests that I have lumped all of them together in one 'hybrid model', which he rightly says does not exist: Ekins (n 158) 240 and 246. But I have generally, if not always, referred to a variety of hybrid models: see, eg, Goldsworthy, *Contemporary Debates* (n 72) 79–80.

D. Trevor Allan

I am glad that Trevor has contributed to this volume.[165] In constitutional theory he has been my most enduring protagonist; for many years we have debated whether or not the doctrine of parliamentary sovereignty is part of the British constitution.[166] Our many exchanges have been mutually respectful, fair and helpful in clarifying the issues between us.

Trevor has been heavily influenced by the jurisprudential theory of Ronald Dworkin, but now chides Dworkin for failing to take his own insights to their logical conclusions. Commenting on Dworkin's acknowledgement that law can conflict with justice, Trevor says that '[i]t is doubtful … whether Dworkin's analysis can be sustained'.[167] He takes Dworkin's interpretive theory of law to entail conclusions similar to those of strong natural law. Government action inconsistent with fundamental rights 'lacks legal force or validity',[168] so 'a gravely unjust provision … cannot be law',[169] 'even if [it is] asserted in the name of Parliamentary sovereignty'.[170]

But before holding that a statute is invalid, judges should strive to give it a meaning consistent with justice. '[A] statutory provision has no power to inflict serious injustice; it means what it ought to mean when all the pertinent moral considerations are taken into account.'[171] Moral judgement plays 'a critical role … in translating official texts and decisions into legal rights, powers and duties'.[172] For example, a provision apparently inflicting serious injustice might be held to be impliedly qualified so as not to do so.[173] It follows that the *Human Rights Act 1998* (UK) ('HRA') is almost superfluous: the duty it imposes, of interpreting statutes so as to be compatible with protected rights, is 'supplementary' to a pre-existing and independent duty to interpret statutes so as to be compatible with 'constitutional rights at common law'.[174] Therefore, were the HRA repealed, presumably nothing much would change.[175]

I regard all these claims as diverging radically from constitutional orthodoxy in Britain. Significantly, Trevor acknowledges that the legal positivist view is more commonly held than his: 'Discussions of political obligation usually proceed on the assumption that the law's requirements can be identified independently of questions about their moral bindingness … as a matter of social fact.'[176] He later refers to this as 'the standard view'.[177]

Trevor's chapter does not pursue his debate with me, but instead, assumes the correctness of his position and develops its consequences for the concepts of legality, legitimacy

[165] TRS Allan, 'Political Obligation and Public Law' in chapter 12 of this volume.

[166] See the partial list of our exchanges in ibid, 245 n 1, and TRS Allan, *The Sovereignty of Law: Freedom, Constitution and Common Law* (Oxford, Oxford University Press, 2013).

[167] Allan, 'Political Obligation and Public Law' (n 165) 252; see also 256.

[168] Allan, 'Political Obligation and Public Law' (n 165) 252; see also 256.

[169] Allan, 'Political Obligation and Public Law' (n 165) 260.

[170] Allan, 'Political Obligation and Public Law' (n 165) 268.

[171] Allan, 'Political Obligation and Public Law' (n 165) 255.

[172] Allan, 'Political Obligation and Public Law' (n 165) 260.

[173] Allan, 'Political Obligation and Public Law' (n 165) 262–65 and 268.

[174] Allan, 'Political Obligation and Public Law' (n 165) 257; see also 266 esp n 57.

[175] Allan, 'Political Obligation and Public Law' (n 165) 262, on entrenching judicial power against 'political change that may sweep away an enacted bill of rights'.

[176] Allan, 'Political Obligation and Public Law' (n 165) 249.

[177] Allan, 'Political Obligation and Public Law' (n 165) 253 and 267.

and obligation (both legal and political). I have no quarrel with the way he explores the implications of his position, and applaud the clarity of its exposition. But it might be useful for me to comment once again on the questionable philosophical premises that underpin it.

Our debate has gone through many rounds, in both journals and the books we have written: argument, counter-argument, rejoinder, counter-rejoinder and so on.[178] Yet neither of us has altered the other's views in any important respect, although we can hope to have persuaded some others. This raises the question: why has our debate been so unproductive in terms of shifting one another's views? Could the reason be that our disagreements extend deep into philosophical foundations? I thought of this when I read these words in Liam Murphy's '*What Makes Law?*'[179] Murphy says that the two main rival camps, positivism and non-positivism,

> represent two fundamentally opposed visions of the kind of thing law is, and … nothing so much as an argument is likely to move either side closer to the other. … [N]o argument for either side is likely to carry more conviction than the foundational initial stance that each brings to the table. … I am unaware of any argument that makes use of premises that don't, in effect, require either side to give up its foundational commitment.[180]

While I suspect this is true, a full explanation for our impasse must go further. The problem is not only that Trevor is an ultra-Dworkinian and I am a legal positivist. My defence of parliamentary sovereignty can be – indeed, has been – reworked into an interpretive argument along Dworkinian lines.[181] But competing Dworkinian arguments are very hard to refute because they ultimately rest on contentious moral judgements, which are almost impossible either to prove or disprove.

Brian Leiter claims that if Dworkin's theory were right, it would be possible that no-one could truly know what the law is, making it a 'Theory of Esoteric Law'.[182] For Dworkin, and also Trevor, the truth of a proposition of law is a function of the best theory of the law as a whole, the one that best satisfies the dimensions of fit and of moral justification, where the balance between fit and justification itself depends on moral judgement. Leiter's point is that, given these criteria, we can never be sure that we have established which theory is the best, and so we can never truly know (although we can believe) that a legal proposition is true. The legal positivists' theory makes truth about the law more attainable, because it is ultimately a matter of fact.[183]

The relative imperviousness of Dworkinian interpretations to effective counter-argument is likely to be a massive problem at a practical as well as theoretical level, given the risk of officials and citizens subscribing to different and incompatible interpretations of their legal arrangements due to divergent moral judgements. I once assumed that Trevor regarded the interpretation of the highest court as having special, binding authority, but he has often denied this. As he reiterates in this contribution, each individual is responsible for

[178] See n 166, above.

[179] L Murphy, *What Makes Law*? (New York and Cambridge, Cambridge University Press, 2014).

[180] ibid 3.

[181] See, eg, the final chapter of Goldsworthy, *The Sovereignty of Parliament* (n 119), esp 254 and 271.

[182] See B Leiter, 'Book Review' (2006) 56 *Journal of Legal Education* 675, 675; B Leiter, 'Explaining Theoretical Disagreement' (2009) 76 *The University of Chicago Law Review* 1215, 1248.

[183] See, eg, A Marmor, *The Language of Law* (Oxford, Oxford University Press, 2014) Ch 3 ('Truth in Law').

his or her own interpretive judgement about the law,[184] even though their reasoning and conclusions may be controversial.[185] An observation of Jeremy Bentham seems apposite: 'from a set of data … law is to be extracted by every man who can fancy that he is able: by each man, perhaps a different law: and these then are the *monades* [basic metaphysical entities] which meeting together constitute the rules' of law.[186] As Gerald Postema commented, this 'transforms a matter of public rules into a matter of essentially and unavoidably private conjecture'.[187]

The practical consequences of interpretive disagreement about constitutional fundamentals could be disastrous. As I have argued at length elsewhere,[188] if Parliament and the judiciary were to adopt conflicting interpretations of Britain's unwritten constitution (such as mine and Trevor's), the authority of both interpreters might itself be in dispute. It is hard to see how that dispute could, in practice, be resolved by Dworkinian interpretation. To suggest that the legally correct interpretation would be whichever of the contenders (Parliament's or the judges') was truly the best would hardly be helpful. Both could plausibly claim that their interpretation was the best, in terms of either 'fit', or moral justification, or both. As Jeremy Waldron has put it, 'the prescription most commonly advanced by the [moral] realist, "*Choose the objectively right answer*", is, though metaphysically admirable, politically impotent'.[189] His point is corroborated by the fact that when judges disagree among themselves about the best interpretation of ordinary law, for practical purposes their disagreement is not, and could not be, resolved by the criterion of objective rightness or truth. That is precisely what is in dispute. Their disagreement is settled, instead, by an accepted decision procedure whereby the interpretation of the majority prevails. Unfortunately, there would be no accepted decision procedure should Parliament and the judiciary disagree about parliamentary sovereignty: the disagreement would extend to decision procedures, and therefore might have to be settled by brute force.

It follows that even if one of these two conflicting interpretations of the constitution were 'correct' according to Dworkinian criteria, this could not be proved. Appeal to moral truth cannot provide the stable foundation that any legal system needs to function effectively or even to persist. What is needed is widespread official consensus either as to the location and scope of lawmaking authority, or as to the location of authority to resolve disagreements about such matters – which would sooner or later amount to the same thing. Any assumption that judges necessarily possess superior authority of the second kind would beg the question.

The possibility of dangerous disputes between branches of government about their constitutional authority can never be prevented. But such disputes would be more likely to

[184] Allan, 'Political Obligation and Public Law' (n 165) 260–61 and 267–68.

[185] Allan, 'Political Obligation and Public Law' (n 165) 252.

[186] J Bentham, *Of Laws in General* (edited by HLA Hart) (London, Athlone Press, 1970) 192, quoted by G Postema, *Legal Philosophy in the Twentieth Century: The Common Law World* (Dordrecht NL, Springer, 2011) 541.

[187] Postema (n 186) quoting himself in 'The Normativity of Law' in Ruth Gavison (ed), *Issues In Contemporary Legal Philosophy: The Influence of H.L.A. Hart* (Oxford, Clarendon Press, 1987) 81, 103.

[188] J Goldsworthy, 'Parliamentary Sovereignty and Constitutional Change in the United Kingdom' in R Rawlings, P Leyland and AL Young (eds), *Sovereignty and the Law: Domestic, European and International Perspectives* (Oxford, Oxford University Press, 2013) 50.

[189] J Waldron, 'Moral Truth and Judicial Review' (1998) 43 *American Journal of Jurisprudence* 75, 81.

arise and less likely to be resolvable without resort to force if a theory of law were widely accepted that holds moral truth to be the ultimate criterion of legal truth.[190] Legal systems are more likely to be stable and effective if people accept either some version of legal positivism, which holds that law ultimately rests partly on a widespread consensus among senior officials about fundamental constitutional norms, or some form of consensus-seeking interpretivism that does not require moral judgement.[191] Whether this is a reason for adopting a particular concept of law, or for understanding our concept of law as already incorporating one of these views, is a question for another occasion.

[190] *cf* D Smith, 'Agreement and Disagreement in Law' (2015) 28(1) *Canadian Journal of Law and Jurisprudence* 183, 190–94.

[191] See, eg, K Toh, 'Jurisprudential Theories and First-Order Legal Judgments' (2013) 8(5) *Philosophy Compass* 457, 465–66, for a non-Dworkinian interpretive method.

LIST OF PROFESSOR JEFFREY GOLDSWORTHY'S PUBLICATIONS

Books (Authored)

1. *Parliamentary Sovereignty: Contemporary Debates* (Cambridge, Cambridge University Press, 2010) i–xii, 1–326.
2. *The Sovereignty of Parliament: History and Philosophy* (Oxford, Clarendon Press, 1999) i–x, 1–319.

Books (Edited)

1. *Interpreting Constitutions: A Comparative Study* (Oxford, Oxford University Press, 2006) i–xvi, 1–353.
2. *Protecting Rights without a Bill of Rights: Institutional Performance and Reform in Australia* (with T Campbell and A Stone) (Aldershot, Ashgate, 2006) i–x, 1-348.
3. *Protecting Human Rights: Instruments and Institutions* (with T Campbell and A Stone) (Oxford, Oxford University Press, 2003) i–xxii, 1–344.
4. *Legal Interpretation in Democratic States* (with T Campbell) (Aldershot, Ashgate/Dartmouth, 2002) i–xiv, 1–266.
5. *Judicial Power, Democracy, and Legal Positivism* (with T Campbell) (Aldershot, Ashgate/Dartmouth, 1999) i–xvi, 1–435.

Book Chapters

1. 'The Case Against a Constitutional Bill of Rights in Australia' in M Groves, D Meagher and J Boughey (eds), *The Legal Protection of Rights in Australia* (Oxford, Hart Publishing, forthcoming 2019).
2. 'The Implicit and the Implied in a Written Constitution' in R Dixon and A Stone (eds), *The Invisible Constitution* (Cambridge and New York, Cambridge University Press, 2018) 109–45.
3. 'Subjective versus Objective Intentionalism in Legal Interpretation' in H Hurd (ed), *Moral Puzzles and Legal Perplexities: Essays on the Influence of Larry Alexander* (Cambridge and New York, Cambridge University Press, 2018) 170–88.
4. 'Functions, Purposes and Values in Constitutional Interpretation' in R Dixon (ed), *Australian Constitutional Values* (Oxford, Hart Publishing, 2018) 43–60.
5. 'Originalism in Canada and Australia: Why the Divergence?' (with Justice G Huscroft) in R Albert and D Cameron (eds), *Canada in the World: Comparative Perspectives on the Canadian Constitution* (New York, Cambridge University Press, New York, 2018) 183–208.
6. 'Constitutionalism' (with L Burton Crawford) in C Saunders and A Stone (eds), *The Oxford Handbook of the Australian Constitution* (Oxford, Oxford University Press, 2018) 357–78.
7. 'The Principle of Legality and Legislative Intention' in D Meagher and M Groves (eds), *The Principle of Legality in Australia and New Zealand* (Sydney, Federation Press, 2017) 46–71.
8. 'Is Legislative Supremacy Under Threat? Statutory Interpretation, Legislative Intention, and Common Law Principles' in *Upholding the Australian Constitution* (The Samuel Griffith Society, 2016) Vol 28, 36–45 [also published in (November 2016) 60 (11) *Quadrant* 56–61].
9. 'The Brennan Court' (with P Emerton) in R Dixon and G Williams (eds), *The High Court, the Constitution and Australian Politics* (Sydney, Cambridge University Press, 2015) 261–83.
10. 'Parliamentary Sovereignty and Constitutional Change in the United Kingdom' in P Leyland, R Rawlings and A Young (eds), *Sovereignty and the Law: Domestic, European and International Perspectives* (Oxford, Oxford University Press, 2013) 50–67.

11. 'Constitutional Interpretation' in M Rosenfeld and A Sajo (eds), *The Oxford Handbook of Comparative Constitutional Law* (Oxford, Oxford University Press, 2012) 689–717.
12. 'The Case for Originalism' in G Huscroft and B Miller (eds), *The Challenge of Originalism: Theories of Constitutional Interpretation* (New York, Cambridge University Press, 2011) 42–69.
13. 'Original Meanings and Contemporary Understandings in Constitutional Interpretation' in HP Lee and P Gerangelos (eds), *Constitutional Advancement in a Frozen Continent: Essays in Honour of George Winterton* (Sydney, Federation Press, 2009) 245–68.
14. 'Unwritten Constitutional Principles' in G Huscroft (ed), *Expounding the Constitution: Essays in Constitutional Theory* (Cambridge, Cambridge University Press, 2008) 277–312.
15. 'The Myth of the Common Law Constitution' in D Edlin (ed), *Common Law Theory* (Cambridge, Cambridge University Press, 2007) 204–36.
16. 'Australia: Devotion to Legalism' in J Goldsworthy (ed), *Interpreting Constitutions: A Comparative Study* (Oxford, Oxford University Press, 2006) 106–60.
17. 'Conclusions' in J Goldsworthy (ed), *Interpreting Constitutions: A Comparative Study* (Oxford, Oxford University Press, 2006) 321–45.
18. 'Questioning the Migration of Constitutional Ideas: Rights, Constitutionalism and the Limits of Convergence' in S Choudhry (ed), *The Migration of Constitutional Ideas* (Cambridge, Cambridge University Press, 2006) 115–41.
19. '*Trethowan's* Case' in G Winterton (ed), *State Constitutional Landmarks* (Sydney, Federation Press, 2006) 98–128.
20. 'Manner and Form Revisited: Reflections on *Marquet's* Case' in M Groves (ed), *Law and Government in Australia* (Sydney, Federation Press, 2005) 18–43.
21. 'Parliamentary Sovereignty and Statutory Interpretation' in R Bigwood (ed), *The Statute: Making and Meaning* (Wellington, LexisNexis, 2004) 187–210.
22. 'Judicial Review, Legislative Override, and Democracy' in T Campbell, J Goldsworthy and A Stone (eds), *Protecting Human Rights: Instruments and Institutions* (Oxford, Oxford University Press, 2003) 263–79.
23. 'The Debate About Sovereignty in the United States: A Comparative and Historical Perspective' in N Walker (ed), *Sovereignty in Transition* (Oxford, Hart Publishing, 2003) 423–46.
24. 'Legislative Intentions, Legislative Supremacy, and Legal Positivism' in J Goldsworthy and T Campbell (eds), *Legal Interpretation in Democratic States* (Aldershot, Ashgate, 2002) 45–65.
25. 'Legislative Sovereignty and the Rule of Law' in T Campbell, K Ewing and A Tomkins (eds), *Sceptical Essays on Human Rights* (Oxford, Oxford University Press, 2001) 61–78.
26. 'The Development of Parliamentary Sovereignty' in HT Dickinson and M Lynch (eds), *The Challenge to Westminster: Sovereignty, Devolution and Independence* (Edinburgh, Tuckwell Press, 2000) 12–21.
27. 'The Philosophical Foundations of Parliamentary Sovereignty' in J Goldsworthy and T Campbell (eds), *Judicial Power, Democracy and Legal Positivism* (Aldershot, Ashgate/Dartmouth, 1999) 229–50.
28. 'A Role For the States in Initiating Referendums' in *Upholding the Australian Constitution* (The Samuel Griffith Society, 1997) Vol 8, 39–58.
29. 'Commentary [Lionel Murphy and Judicial Method]' in M Coper and G Williams (eds), *Justice Lionel Murphy: Influential or Merely Prescient*? (Sydney, Federation Press, 1997) 259–74.
30. 'Implications in Language, Law and the Constitution' in G Lindell (ed), *Future Directions in Australian Constitutional Law: Essays in Honour of Professor Leslie Zines* (Sydney, Federation Press, 1994) 150–84.
31. 'Constitutional Law (with P Hanks) in R Baxt and AP Moore (eds), *An Annual Survey of Australian Law 1992* (Adelaide Law Review Association, 1993) 67–101.
32. 'The Constitutional Protection of Rights in Australia' in GJ Craven (ed), *Australian Federation: Towards the Second Century* (Melbourne, Melbourne University Press, 1992) 151–76.
33. 'Constitutional Law' (with P Hanks) in R Baxt and AP Moore (eds), *An Annual Survey of Australian Law 1991* (Adelaide Law Review Association, 1992) 109–146.
34. 'Constitutional Law' (with P Hanks) in R Baxt and G Kewley (eds), *An Annual Survey of Australian Law 1989* (Sydney, Law Book Co, 1990) 164–89.
35. 'Constitutional Law' (with HP Lee) in R Baxt and G Kewley (eds), *An Annual Survey of Australian Law 1988* (Sydney, Law Book Co, 1989) 1–15.
36. 'Constitutional Law' (with HP Lee) in R Baxt and G Kewley (eds), *An Annual Survey of Australian Law 1987* (Sydney, Law Book Co, 1988) 140–64.

37. 'Constitutional Law' (with HP Lee) in R Baxt and G Kewley (eds), *An Annual Survey of Australian Law 1986* (Sydney, Law Book Co, 1987) 187–206.
38. 'Constitutional Law' (with HP Lee) in R Baxt and G Kewley (eds), *An Annual Survey of Australian Law 1985* (Sydney, Law Book Co, 1986) 130–56.

Articles in Scholarly Journals

1. 'Tom Campbell on Judicial Activism' (2017) 42 *Australian Journal of Philosophy* 247–55.
2. 'Originalism in Australia' (2017) *DPCE Online* 607–15, at www.dpceonline.it/index.php/dpceonline/article/view/432/421.
3. 'Kable, Kirk and Judicial Statesmanship' (2014) 40 *Monash University Law Review* 75–114.
4. 'The Constitution and Its Common Law Background' (2014) 25 *Public Law Review* 265–83.
5. 'The Reality and Indispensability of Legislative Intentions' (with R Ekins) (2014) 36 *Sydney Law Review* 39–68.
6. 'Clarifying, Creating and Changing Meaning in Constitutional Interpretation' (2013) 14 *German Law Journal* 1279–95.
7. 'Legislative Intention Vindicated?' (2013) 33 *Oxford Journal of Legal Studies* 821–42.
8. 'Constitutional Cultures, Democracy, and Unwritten Principles' [2012] *University of Illinois Law Review* 683–710.
9. 'Interpreting the Australian Constitution: Express Provisions and Unexpressed General Principles' (2012) 24 *Giornale di Storia Constituzionale* ('*Journal of Constitutional History*') 119–33.
10. 'Symmetric Entrenchment of Manner and Form Requirements' (with T Roszkowski) (2012) 23 *Public Law Review* 216–22.
11. 'Constitutional Implications Revisited' (2011) 30 *University of Queensland Law Journal* 9–34.
12. 'The Limits of Judicial Fidelity to Law: *The Coxford Lecture*' (2011) 24 *Canadian Journal of Law and Jurisprudence* 305–25.
13. 'Structural Judicial Review and the Objection from Democracy' (2010) 60 *University of Toronto Law Journal* 137–54.
14. 'Constitutional Interpretation: Originalism' (2009) 4 *Philosophy Compass* 682–702 (online journal) (www3.interscience.wiley.com.ezproxy.lib.monash.edu.au/cgi-bin/fulltext/122439499/PDFSTART).
15. 'Justice Windeyer on the Engineers' Case' (2009) 37 *Federal Law Review* 363–74.
16. 'Research Grant Mania' (2008) 50 *Australian Universities' Review* 17–24.
17. 'Abdicating and Limiting Parliament's Sovereignty' (2006) 17 *King's College Law Journal* 255–80.
18. 'Is Parliament Sovereign? Recent Challenges to the Doctrine of Parliamentary Sovereignty' (2005) 3 *New Zealand Journal of Public and International Law* 7–37.
19. 'Legislative Intentions, Legislative Supremacy, and Legal Positivism' (2005) 42 *San Diego Law Review* 493–518.
20. 'Moderate versus Strong Intentionalism: Knapp and Michaels Revisited' (2005) 42 *San Diego Law Review* 669–83.
21. 'Homogenizing Constitutions' (2003) 23 *Oxford Journal of Legal Studies* 483–505.
22. 'Judicial Review, Legislative Override, and Democracy' (2003) 38 *Wake Forest Law Journal* 451–72.
23. 'Raz on Constitutional Interpretation' (2003) 22 *Law and Philosophy* 167–93.
24. 'Author's Introduction' and 'Author's Reply' (2002) 27 *Australian Journal of Legal Philosophy* 137–41 and 191–204 (in Book Symposium on *The Sovereignty of Parliament, History and Philosophy*).
25. 'Dworkin as an Originalist' (2000) 17 *Constitutional Commentary* 49–78.
26. 'Interpreting the *Constitution* in Its Second Century' (2000) 24 *Melbourne University Law Review* 677–710.
27. 'Constitutional Implications and Freedom of Political Speech: A Reply to Stephen Donaghue' (1997) 32 *Monash University Law Review* 362–74.
28. 'Originalism in Constitutional Interpretation' (1997) 1 *Federal Law Review* 1–50 [republished in T Campbell and A Stone (eds), *Law and Democracy* (Aldershot, Ashgate/Dartmouth, 2002) 401–50].
29. 'Fact and Value in the New Natural Law Theory' (1996) 41 *The American Journal of Jurisprudence* 21–46 [republished in RP George (ed), *Natural Law* (Aldershot, Ashgate/Dartmouth, 2003) 3–28].
30. 'Marmor on Meaning and Interpretation' (1995) 1 *Legal Theory* 431–56.
31. 'Some Scepticism About Moral Realism' (1995) 14 *Law and Philosophy* 357–74.
32. 'Is Jurisprudence Liberal Ideology?' (1993) 12 *Oxford Journal of Legal Studies* 548–70.
33. 'Internalism, Externalism and Moral Scepticism' (1992) 70 *Australasian Journal of Philosophy* 40–60.

34. 'The "Principle in *Ranasinghe*": A Reply to HP Lee' (1992) 15 *University of New South Wales Law Journal* 540–45.
35. 'Well-being and Value' (1992) 4 *Utilitas* 1–26.
36. 'The Self-Destruction of Legal Positivism' (1990) 10 *Oxford Journal of Legal Studies* 449–86.
37. 'Realism about the High Court' and 'Reply to Galligan' (1989) 18 *Federal Law Review* 27–39 and 50–54.
38. 'Manner and Form in the Australian States' (1987) 16 *Melbourne University Law Review* 403–29.
39. 'Nozick's Libertarianism and the Justification of the State' (1987) 29 *Ratio* 180–89 [republished in A Levine (ed), *The State and Its Critics* (Edward Elgar, 1992) Vol 1, 219–28].
40. 'Detmold's "The Unity of Law and Morality"' (1986) 12 *Monash University Law Review* 8–26.
41. 'Hayek's Political and Legal Philosophy: An Introduction' (1986) 11 *Sydney Law Review* 44–63.
42. 'God or Mackie? The Dilemma of Secular Moral Philosophy' (1985) 30 *The American Journal of Jurisprudence* 45–78.
43. 'Legal Rights, Subject Matters and Inconsistency' (1981) 7 *Adelaide Law Review* 487–505.

Articles in Non-Refereed Journals

1. 'Losing Faith in Democracy: Why Judicial Supremacy is Rising and What to Do About It' (May 2015) 59 (5) *Quadrant* 9–17 also published on Policy Exchange Website at: www.policyexchange.org.uk/events/item/losing-faith-in-democracy-why-judicial-supremacy-is-rising-and-what-to-do-about-it?category_id=37].
2. 'The Preamble, Judicial Independence and Judicial Integrity' (2000) 11 *Constitutional Forum* 60–64 (Centre for Constitutional Studies, University of Alberta, Canada).
3. 'The High Court, Implied Rights and Constitutional Change' (March 1995) 39(3) *Quadrant* 46–54.

Review Essays

1. 'Redemptive Originalism' (2012) *Ethics* 785–90.
2. 'Should Judges Covertly Disobey the Law to Prevent Injustice?' (2011) 47 *Tulsa Law Review* 133–40.
3. 'Legislation, Interpretation, and Judicial Review' (2001) 51 *University of Toronto Law Journal* 75–86.

Blog and Web Posts

1. 'The Real Standard Picture, and How Facts Make It Law; a Response to Mark Greenberg', SSRN, posted 4 November 2018 at: https://papers.ssrn.com/sol3/papers.cfm?abstract_id=3262448.
2. 'Parliamentary Sovereignty's Premature Obituary', *UK Constitutional Law Group Blog*, posted 9 March 2012 (http://ukconstitutionallaw.org/blog/).

Reports

1. 'Good Practice Guide to Teaching Statutory Interpretation' (with J Barnes, J Dharmananda and A Steel) (Council of Australian Law Deans, July 2015) 1–50.

Encyclopaedia Entries

1. 'Constitutionalism' in G Claeys (ed), *Encyclopedia of Modern Political Thought* (New York, Sage/CQ Press, 2013) Vol 1, 186–90.
2. 'Separation of Powers' in G Claeys (ed), *Encyclopedia of Modern Political Thought* (New York, Sage/CQ Press, 2013) Vol 2, 744–45.
3. 'Legal Philosophy' in G Oppy and N Trakakis, *A Companion to Philosophy in Australasia* (Clayton Vic, Monash University Publishing, 2010) 398–402.
4. 'Australia Acts' in B Galligan and W Roberts (eds), *The Oxford Companion to Australian Politics* (Melbourne, Oxford University Press, 2007) 53.
5. 'Constitutional Law' in B Galligan and W Roberts (eds), *The Oxford Companion to Australian Politics* (Melbourne, Oxford University Press, 2007) 134–35.
6. 'Implied Rights' in B Galligan and W Roberts (eds), *The Oxford Companion to Australian Politics* (Melbourne, Oxford University Press, 2007) 265–66.
7. 'Originalism' in B Galligan and W Roberts (eds), *The Oxford Companion to Australian Politics* (Melbourne, Oxford University Press, 2007) 380.

8. 'Legal Positivism' in T Blackshield, M Coper and G Williams (eds), *The Oxford Companion to the High Court of Australia* (Sydney, Oxford University Press, 2001) 547–48.
9. 'Hayek, Friedrich von (1899-1992)' in CB Gray (ed), *The Philosophy of Law: An Encyclopedia* (New York and London, Garland, 1999) Vol I, 350–51.

Minor Publications: Prefaces, Book Reviews, etc

1. 'Foreword' to L Burton Crawford, *The Rule of Law and the Australian Constitution* (Sydney, Federation Press, 2017) v–vi.
2. *Review of Se-shauna Wheatle's 'Principled Reasoning in Human Rights Adjudication', International Journal of Constitutional Law Blog*, 24 October 2017 at: www.iconnectblog.com/2017/09/goldsworthy-on-wheatle.
3. 'The Law and the Profits' (review of M Thornton, 'Privatising the Public University; The Case of Law') (2013) 55 *Australian Universities' Review* 92–95.
4. 'A Life Beyond the Court of Public Opinion' (review of AJ Brown, 'Michael Kirby: Paradoxes/Principles') *The Age*, 11 June 2011, Life & Style section, 33.
5. 'Introduction' in J Goldsworthy, *Interpreting Constitutions: A Comparative Study* (Oxford, Oxford University Press, 2006) 1–6.
6. 'Introduction' in T Campbell, J Goldsworthy and A Stone (eds), *Protecting Rights Without a Bill of Rights: Institutional Performance and Reform in Australia* (Aldershot, Ashgate, 2006) 1–13.
7. 'Preface' in J Goldsworthy and T Campbell (eds), *Legal Interpretation in Democratic States* (Aldershot, Ashgate/Dartmouth, 2002) xi–xiv.
8. 'Preface' in T Campbell and J Goldsworthy (eds), *Judicial Power, Democracy and Legal Positivism* (Aldershot, Ashgate/Dartmouth, 2000) xiii–xvi.
9. Book Review: S Ratnapala and GA Moens (eds), *Jurisprudence of Liberty* (1996) 18 *Adelaide Law Review* 337–40.
10. Book Review: F Schauer, *Playing By the Rules* and A Marmor, *Interpretation and Legal Theory* (1995) 21 *Monash University Law Review* 142–44.

INDEX